Phenomenology and Marxism

The International Library of Phenomenology and Moral Sciences

Editor: John O'Neill, ***York University, Toronto***

The Library will publish original and translated works guided by an analytical interest in the foundations of human culture and the moral sciences. It is intended to foster phenomenological, hermeneutical and ethnomethodological studies in the social sciences, art and literature.

Phenomenology and Marxism

Edited by Bernhard Waldenfels,
Jan M. Broekman, and Ante Pažanin

Translated from the German by
J. Claude Evans, Jr

Routledge & Kegan Paul

London, Boston, Melbourne and Henley

Translated from Phänomenologie und Marxismus
Bd 1 Konzepte und Methoden; *Bd 2* Praktische Philosophie

This translation first published in 1984
by Routledge & Kegan Paul plc

14 Leicester Square, London
WC2H 7PH, England

9 Park Street, Boston, Mass. 02108, USA

464 St Kilda Road, Melbourne,
Victoria 3004, Australia and

Broadway House, Newtown Road,
Henley-on-Thames, Oxon RG9 1EN, England

Set in Press Roman
by Hope Services, Abingdon, Oxon
and printed in Great Britain
by The Thetford Press Limited,
Thetford, Norfolk

Library of Congress Cataloging in Publication Data

Phänomenologie und Marxismus. English.
Phenomenology and Marxism.
(International library of phenomenology and moral sciences)
Papers originally presented at an annual workshop held 1975–1978 at the Inter-University Centre in Dubrovnik, Yugoslavia.
Translation of: Phänomenologie und Marxismus.
Includes index.
1. Phenomenology – Addresses, essays, lectures.
2. Philosophy, Marxist – Addresses, essays, lectures.
I. Waldenfels, Bernhard, 1934– . II. Broekman, Jan M.
III. Pažanin, Ante. IV. Title. V. Series.
B829.5.P442613 1984 142'.7 83-27246

British Library CIP data available

ISBN 0-7100-9854-5

CONTENTS

II Practical philosophy

PREFACE

The essays collected here under the title *Phenomenology and Marxism* were originally presented at a workshop which took place annually between 1975 and 1978 at the Inter-University Centre in Dubrovnik, Yugoslavia. The course was organized by a Belgian, a Yugoslav and a German, and participants were teachers, assistants and students from a whole series of countries. The setting of the workshop in an old sea-faring and merchant city on the Dalmatian coast is indicative of the interest in phenomenology which one encounters in Eastern European countries, which are now very much under the influence of Marxism. We set ourselves the task of making this interest fruitful.

The title 'Phenomenology and Marxism' should serve the function of marking out a field within which there is room for various attempts at entering into a dialogue. Of course, such dialogues are nothing new; indeed, there is already a very colourful and chequered history with its privileged points of encounter and major protagonists. Let us begin with *Germany*, the country which gave birth to both phenomenology and Marxism. Aside from the early Marcuse, the Marxist-inspired critical theory of the Frankfurt School tended to take a very negative stance toward phenomenology. On the other hand, repeated references to phenomenology by Adorno, Horkheimer and today by Habermas demonstrate a critical interest in this new manner of viewing and thinking about the world.[1] In *France*, debates between Marxism and phenomenology have played a central role. Concerning the post-war period, it suffices to mention names such as Sartre, Merleau-Ponty, Hyppolite or the Vietnamese Tran-Duc-Thao. Under the influence of Kojève's famous lectures, Husserl, Heidegger, Hegel and Marx entered the French philosophical consciousness together. A great deal of this influence continues in the political thought of C. Lefort and C. Castoriadis, both of whom were stimulated by Merleau-Ponty's *Adventures of the Dialectic*. The same holds true of the thought of P. Ricoeur and M. Henry. Even the work of Lacan, Lévi-Strauss, Foucault, Althusser or Desanti would have been impossible in the absence of a continual critical reference to phenomenology and Marxism.[2] In *Italy*, the group centred around E. Paci and the journal *Aut-Aut* has been pursuing a synthesis of Husserlian and Marxist ideas since the 1950s. Here, in addition to the specifically Italian phenomenological tradition, Gramsci's philosophy of praxis plays a central role. Traces of these Continental attempts can also be found in Anglo-Saxon countries. Here one can mention the authors in the journal *Telos*. But also ethnomethodologists such as Garfinkel can count on generating a certain amount of interest within Marxist circles when they methodically put social rules out to play in order to make visible the all-too-obvious and engrained, yet unspoken, structures of everyday life.

Turning to the Eastern European scene, phenomenology has been able to partially retain and partially recover a certain role in the discussions of an intellectual public deeply impregnated by Marxism. This is especially the case in *Poland*, where Ingarden's work still influences younger philosophers, and where, especially in recent years, in the course of attempts at social renewal, one could observe an increasing interest in phenomenological ideas and methods. The journal *Dialectics and Humanism* (Warsaw) became the major source of information for Western readers. One can only hope that these new beginnings will not be pulverized in the wheels of politics. In *Czechoslovakia*, Prague at one time had a close contact with Husserl via its philosophical and linguistic circle. This contact was continued by Patočka, a student of Husserl's, and by Kosík, a phenomenologically inspired Marxist. With regard to *Hungary*, there have been intensive discussions with phenomenology in the Lukács-inspired 'Budapest School', for example in the work of M. Vajda. Here the participants are no longer quite so quick to speak of a 'destruction of reason' (Lukács). Aside from many other developments which must remain unmentioned here, or which have escaped our attention, we must mention *Yugoslavia*, the setting for our own discussions. Both within and outside of the 'Praxis' group we find the influence of Husserl and Heidegger, Sartre and Merleau-Ponty giving Marxism a very special tone. From the German perspective, it is perhaps not too immodest to recall the efforts of Landgrebe, Fink and Volkmann-Schluck in opening up a dialogue. Finally, in recent years we find a new, more than merely historically oriented interest in Husserl in the *Soviet Union*. Here too there were individuals who prepared the way, such as the philosopher G. Špet, who introduced phenomenology in Russia at a very early date, and there are very early connections in R. Jakobson's linguistics and in Bachtin's dialogical theory of literature, which offers a variety of perspectives for a phenomenology of language and dialogue. In light of this renewed interest in phenomenological, ethnomethodological and interactionist approaches in the social sciences,[3] we might recall the 1920s and scientists such as L.S. Vygotski and A.R. Luria, in whose work phenomenology and Gestalt theory played a central role in a psychology oriented toward social and cultural phenomena.

This survey of the contemporary state of the discussion[4] is not meant to give rise to euphoria, which would be even more out of place today than during the period of our meetings in Dubrovnik. But it cannot be denied that the various attempts which have been mentioned here are evidence of the fact that unbiased motives and interests are at work here, and that they are successful in creating a common ground which is not totally dependent on specific political developments. In the work of the late Husserl and increasingly in the work of the post-Husserlians, phenomenology has become more and more aware of its social, historical and linguistic implications, thus tending to anchor the subject in the life-world. On the other hand, a Marxism which did not take up the aspirations of everyday praxis, and which failed to continually take seriously the critique of the fetishism of categories and institutions, would remain piecework even in the eyes of its founder and of many of his disciples. This is reason enough to think that the one has something to say to the other, even if it cannot be expected to be the last word.

There is a whole series of points of contact, be it the relation of history and life-world, of the interpretation and critique of everyday life, of corporeal behaviour and praxis, of the constitution of meaning in communication and co-operation, of tradition and ideology or of teleology and dialectics. The field of discussion which is opened up here provides room for the investigation of historical contexts, for common research programmes and methodological reflections. On the assumption that neither phenomenology nor Marxism takes the stage as completed doctrines, we are no longer confronted with a fenced-off realm, nor with a defined field of battle, but rather with historically developed points of departure, points of emphasis and points of view for a continuing reflection and investigation. In this sense, the contributions to this volume are a mirror of the variety of perspectives, of intellectual attempts which are deserving of attention even when their limitations are apparent. The contemporary state of the discussion is such that related questions from recent hermeneutics, critical theory, so-called structuralism or analytic philosophy make their appearance. The fact that, as this volume demonstrates, we do not find closed ranks of phenomenologists squaring off against closed ranks of Marxists can only serve the project of turning to 'the things themselves'.

The liveliness and fruitfulness of an intellectual tradition is essentially dependent upon the degree to which it is ready and able to expose itself to questions, even when they are posed from other points of view. Where this is not the case, we find the danger of petrification into a scholasticism in which the phenomenological reduction or the dialectic are reduced to methodological tricks or verbal exercises. Were I to be asked about the point at which the genuine impulses of phenomenology and Marxism might encounter one another, I would mention, for example, *a vision which transforms the seen*. Such a vision would not be a mere mirroring, but rather a kind of activity, and this activity would be anything but a mere routine, since it would allow for a continual shift of vision. The good and the bad look, the correct and the false word – ethics and logic do not begin with the tablet of commandments, but already with the fascination and snares of everyday life.

I would like to thank Claude Evans for making these texts available to a non-German-speaking audience. It is to be hoped that Anglo-Saxon phenomenologists and Marxists, and their followers and heretics, will pick up the possibilities which are offered here and carry on the discussion in their own fashion and in their own direction.

Bochum, October 1983 Bernhard Waldenfels

Notes

1 Cf. Ulf Matthiesen, *Das Dickicht der Lebenswelt und die Theorie des kommunikativen Handelns*, Munich, Fink Verlag, 1983.
2 Cf. Bernhard Waldenfels, *Phänomenologie in Frankreich*, Frankfurt am Main, Suhrkamp Verlag, 1983.
3 Cf. I. Lonin, 'Sozialphänomenologische Themen in der sowjetischen Soziologie und Sozialpsychologie', in R. Grathoff and B. Waldenfels (eds), *Sozialität und Intersubjektivität*, Munich, Fink Verlag, 1983.

4 For a more complete survey, cf. B. Waldenfels, 'Sozialphilosophie im Spannungsfeld von Phänomenologie und Marxismus', in *Contemporary Philosophy: A New Survey*, ed. G. Fløistad, Vol. 3, The Hague, Martinus Nijhoff, 1982.

PART I

Concepts and methods

CHAPTER 1

Phenomenology and Marxism in historical perspective

Fred Dallmayr (Notre Dame, Indiana)

The topic of phenomenology and Marxism immediately confronts us with a whole series of problems. To begin with, there are terminological problems. Both 'phenomenology' and 'Marxism' are very broad and ambiguous concepts, and there is no general consensus concerning their precise usage. In order to guard against the charge of a rash orthodoxy, I shall tend to draw the lines very broadly. With reference to 'phenomenology', the following discussion exhibits at most a temporal restriction in that the accent lies on fairly recent lines of thought which flow from Brentano and Husserl. Aside from this restriction, the term is understood in a very general manner according to which it includes (to mention only a few high points) Husserl's 'pure' theory of knowledge, Heidegger's ontology of *Dasein*, French existential phenomenology as well as the hermeneutics which has developed largely under Heidegger's influence. When viewed in this very broad manner, phenomenology includes a variation (and occasionally a dramatic controversy) on the theme of human self-consciousness: whereas in Husserl knowledge is grounded in the constitutive power of a purified ego-consciousness, and whereas the French school, at least initially, merged intentionality with the Hegelian dialectic of consciousness and nature, Heidegger transformed *Existenz* into a permeable structure open to Being – with the result that hermeneutics can decipher subjective intentions and ego-consciousness only via tortuous detours through the interpretation of historical texts and communicative experiences.[1] I use the term 'Marxism' in an equally tolerant, non-restrictive sense; without regard to the terminological rules proposed by one ideological party or the other, I shall grant the term to all of those who join the struggle against existing forms of economic and political exploitation, working to bring about a free and less conflict-laden ('classless') society.

In addition to such terminological questions, the topic also presents us with difficult theoretical problems. What about the relationship between the two concepts? Doesn't the effortless conjunction attempt to cover over a deep and perhaps unbridgeable chasm between the two in all too simple a manner? At first glance there does indeed seem to be a sharp opposition between the two concepts. Phenomenology is generally understood to be concerned with the analysis of consciousness and with the investigation of subjectively intended sense; Marxism, on the other hand, is generally identified with economic determinism or with a materialism which reduces the striving for sense to an epiphenomenon according to the maxim that (economic) being determines human consciousness. At this point I would like to briefly indicate my own standpoint. It seems to me that there is indeed a tension between the two concepts of our topic, a tension which should not be played down. But if the concepts are forced into the dichotomy of idealism and materialism, of material being and consciousness, there is no room for further discussion; in this case the conjunction would be at most the sign of a cheap compromise or of an opportunistic attempt to make room for a 'third way'. The terminological decisions above were partially the result of a concern to moderate the abrupt nature of the confrontation. But even when we adopt such liberal conventions, the relation between the terms remains complex and full of tension; even if we succeed in avoiding the dangers of a rigid orthodoxy, the historical development shows that the scale of relations ranges from reciprocal hostility through an uneasy cease-fire to a (cautious) fraternization. A genuine reconciliation seems to me to depend upon this presupposition: that both phenomenology and Marxism be interpreted in a critical sense, where a 'critical' attitude indicates not merely the readiness to lecture to the opponent, but also the capacity of self-criticism and continued learning in the interest of truth. When viewed in this critical-Socratic manner, phenomenology and Marxism are not merely superficially compatible, they complement one another in important ways: as a result of its engagement in a contradictory reality, Marxism can protect phenomenology against a superficial descriptivism and a superficial transfiguration of reality, whereas phenomenology can warn Marxism against both a narrow objectivism and a Young Hegelian know-it-all attitude – as well as against the ecstasy of apparently unlimited material progress and technological domination.

The following discussion attempts to follow the reciprocal relations between the two positions in historical perspective. It by no means aims at producing an exhaustive treatment. In this context I would like to concentrate on only two conspicuous and (I think) especially instructive episodes in the philosophical struggle: the early writings of Georg Lukács and some of the works of leading representatives of existential and radical phenomenology in France and Italy. In a sense, the two episodes can be viewed as stages on the path of political disillusionment. Whereas the high point of Lukács's early work coincides with the triumph of the Russian Revolution, the movement of existential and radical phenomenology arose in the context of the rise of Fascist expansion and later under the auspices of the political-economic restoration in Western Europe. Of course, from a philosophical point of view a political disillusionment need not be a bad thing; the dampening of eschatological expectations might encourage self-criticism and dialogue between antagonistic positions – in our case between phenomenology and Marxism.

1 The intuition of essences and dialectics: Georg Lukács

Embryonic forms of contacts or at least affinities between the two positions can be traced back to the period prior to the First World War. This was the period in which Husserl published his *Logical Investigations* and the first volume of the *Ideas*. These were also the years in which Marxism – after a period of philosophical shallowness and lethargy – began to win new impulses, especially in connection with the renewal of its Hegelian heritage. The historical point of departure for both positions was the same or at least roughly comparable. Both arose against the background of a rather common positivism which set out to reduce individual and social life to physical or biological elements. Both lines of thought fought against the cynicism which resulted from positivism and against the relativistic disintegration of philosophical categories which impregnated the intellectual life of the *fin-de-siècle* and the ebbing liberal-bourgeois epoch. Both Husserl as well as Neo-Hegelianism and neo-Hegelian Marxism were influenced to some extent by Dilthey's 'life-philosophy' (*Lebensphilosophie*), although both schools considered the concept of 'life' to be too vague for purposes of philosophical or social theory. Both positions had roots in contemporary Neo-Kantianism, especially in the 'Southwest German School' founded by Windelband and Rickert; but both lines of thought attempted to overcome the harsh neo-Kantian antinomies (between inner and outer, knowledge and action) or at least to moderate them – phenomenology by emphasizing the intuition of essences and Hegelian Marxism by attempting to produce a view of the totality of social tendencies.

This very complex intertwining of intellectual relations appears most clearly and forcefully in Lukács's early writings. Lukács grew up and studied in Budapest, Berlin and Heidelberg, where he came into contact with the most important streams of thought and with leading thinkers of the age. His relation to Marxism goes back to his school days.

> My first acquaintance with Marx (with the *Communist Manifesto*) [writes Lukács in an autobiographical note (from 1933)] came at the end of my studies at the *Gymnasium*. The impression was extraordinarily great, and as a university student I read a number of works by Marx and Engels (such as *The 18th Brumaire* and *The Origin of the Family*) and studied especially the first volume of *Capital*.

Although his reading convinced him of the 'correctness of some of the basic points of Marxism', he by no means considered himself to be a Marxist at that time. He held the materialist point of departure to be 'completely antiquated epistemologically' (he drew 'no distinction between dialectical and non-dialectical materialism'). With regard to epistemological, aesthetic and moral-practical questions he was much more strongly indebted to the philosophy of consciousness in the form of Dilthey's *Lebensphilosophie* and in more rigorous form in Neo-Kantianism with its various derivative forms. As he himself admits, 'the neo-Kantian theory of the "immanence of consciousness"' fitted his 'class position and world view', perfectly.[2] In Berlin he was intimately connected with Georg Simmel and attempted to integrate his partial knowledge of Marx as well as possible into Simmel's neo-Kantian sociology. In Heidelberg he came under the influence of Windelband and Rickert, and met Emil Lask and Max Weber.

The most important philosophical contribution of the Heidelberg or Southwest German variety of Neo-Kantianism was the sharp distinction between the scientific 'explanation' of empirical processes and the interpretative 'understanding' of significant contents – a distinction which Dilthey's attention to concrete historical processes moderated to some extent. The interpretative access to significant contents is, according to Windelband and Rickert, by no means a matter of empirical-psychological empathy; sense and culture belong to a realm of hyper-empirical values to which only a hyper-empirical or transcendental consciousness has access. In the rejection of 'psychologism', Windelband and Rickert were obviously sympathetic to Husserl's attempts to provide a non-empirical foundation of logical structures and to uncover the 'pure' forms of consciousness with the aid of the *epoché* or 'bracketing' of empirical reality. At this point it should be noted that Emil Lask was engaged in an at least partial reconciliation between phenomenology and Neo-Kantianism at a very early date, and his writings provide a connection not only between Rickert and Husserl, but also between Rickert and the early Heidegger. And with regard to this last bridge, one should note that from the neo-Kantian point of view the relation between the realm of sense and reality – or, in the language of phenomenology, between essence and appearance – does not imply some sort of theory of strata or a pre-established harmony, but potentially exhibits a very tension- and conflict-laden character; when transferred to the practical-moral level, the epistemological distinction could easily lead to a tragic view of life. At this point the work of Kierkegaard, up to that time largely neglected, would become increasingly important, especially the conflict between a longed-for purity and absoluteness of experience and a meaningless reality which Kierkegaard's work documents. As Lukács himself reports, Kierkegaard played an 'important role' during his youth.[3]

Lukács's position during his student years can be clearly seen in *The Soul and the Forms* which appeared in 1911. The 'forms' of the title are hyper-empirical, literary-aesthetic senses and essences, which are available to the human 'soul' via a non-psychological, intuitive understanding. Lucien Goldmann has interpreted this work in its historical context in a very pregnant and instructive manner. Goldmann points out that Lukács 'performed the service – or had the luck – of finding himself at the meeting point of three major streams of German university philosophy: Heidelberg Neo-Kantianism, Dilthey's elaboration of the concepts of "sense" and "understanding", and Husserlian phenomenology'; this meeting point was a great moment which 'perhaps partially allowed [Lukács] to rediscover the tradition of classical idealism by defining *sense* in terms of the relation between the *soul and the absolute*'. According to Goldmann, Lukács's book was by no means a 'sudden new creation' without predecessors; 'the encounter between phenomenology and the Heidelberg neo-Kantian school' had already announced itself in a number of attempts before finding its 'theoretical expression' in Lukács. Goldmann refers especially to Husserl's essay 'Philosophy as Strict Science' which appeared in *Logos* (1910), the house organ of the Heidelberg neo-Kantians – the same journal in which *The Soul and the Forms* was originally published. With reference to the theory of forms, Goldmann finds in Lukács's book a 'synthesis between two essential ideas of phenomenology and the Dilthey school', the 'a-temporal essence' and 'understanding' – a synthesis which allowed Lukács 'to develop the concept of the *essence as significant structure*, which he was to modify and make more precise later, but which always remained in the center of his thought'. Goldmann sees a certain emphasis on the Husserlian intuition of essences over against the theory of understanding in this synthesis. He writes:

> In confronting Dilthey's vague and blurred concepts of sense and understanding with the characteristic phenomenological demand for precision . . . he simultaneously took one step forward and one back. His replacement of Dilthey's vague concept of understanding by the idea of a strict and precise description, which phenomenology demanded and had shown to be possible, a description which alone makes it possible to fashion an operative scientific instrument out of the concept of significant structure – all that was progressive. The reactionary step was his abandonment of Dilthey's *historical* approach under the influence of the same phenomenology . . . in order to reintegrate the Husserlian idea of an *atemporal essence*.[4]

According to Goldmann, Lukács's early work was characterized not only by the affinity to Husserl's intuition of essences, but also by the anticipation of central existentialist themes. In the confrontation between an atemporal, pure essence and the everyday world, Lukács proclaimed an insoluble-discordant or 'tragic' world-view which at that time seemed to him to be the 'only true' and possible world-view. According to Goldmann, the basic moral-practical problems posed in this work were: 'Under what conditions can human life be authentic? By means of what circumstances, attitudes and modes of action does it lose its authenticity?' In posing these questions Lukács swims against the current of the shallow faith in progress of the bourgeoisie and rediscovered the radical 'problematic of Pascal and Kant'; he is probably the first person in our century 'to pose the questions concerning the relations between the *individual*, *authenticity* and *death* in their full pregnancy and urgency'. In this sense – as Goldmann writes in a somewhat exaggerated formulation – 'the rebirth of European philosophy which follows the First World War and later came to be called existentialism seems to begin with the book *The Soul and the Forms*'. In Goldmann's usage, the concept 'existentialism' obviously is the name of a direction of thought which, under the influence of Kierkegaard, is impregnated by the experience of anxiety and the proximity of death. He also interprets Heidegger's *Being and Time* in a similar light (which would seem to be an overemphasis on the anthropological, 'existential' elements in the book). Goldmann expressly aims at the comparison with Heidegger, although he attributes greater consistency to Lukács:

> Since man is mortal, the only authenticity which is available to him lies in a univocal and decisive consciousness of his limits and the resulting worthlessness of the world and the necessity of its radical rejection. The distinction between *that* life which is aware of the limits, loneliness and rejection, and *that* life which in contrast consists in illusion and weakness and acceptance of everyday reality, corresponds completely to Heidegger's later distinction between authentic and inauthentic *Dasein*.[5]

At the beginning of the First World War Lukács wrote another work on the theory of literature which brings a similar attitude – although with deviations – to expression: *Theory of the Novel* (first published in book form in 1920). This work held on to the conception of the forms as pure essences; but Lukács now deals with types of literature in which the relation between protagonist and world is less hopeless and insoluble than is the case in tragedy, for example. Briefly, *Theory of the Novel* moderated the sharp antinomy of essence and reality by taking account of transitions – and especially Hegel's concept of mediation – but at the same time the prospect of reconciliation is either bypassed or located in a utopian distance. According to Lukács himself, the study manifests a cautious transition from subjective to 'objective idealism', in which Hegel won 'increasing significance'. The work dealt with epic forms of literature in a broad sense – forms which (according to Goldmann) are 'realistic' in contrast to the forms Lukács had previously dealt with, and which, although they did not 'affirm the existing reality', still rested upon 'at least a positive attitude toward a *possible* reality whose possibility is grounded in the existing world'. The emphasis of the work lay upon the epic category of the novel, which Lukács considered to be the most important form of literature of the bourgeois epoch, an epoch in which the individual, while living in society, also lived against it. Whereas the traditional epic was based on an unbroken social community, 'a radical opposition between man and world, individual and society is required for the existence of the novel'.[6]

The following stages of Lukács's biographical development are well known; I shall therefore restrict myself to a few brief sketches. The spread of world war brought Lukács closer and closer to Marx and the contemporary communist movement. The reports of the October Revolution in Russia were good news for him, since he held it to be a ray of light for mankind and a signpost pointing to the way out of capitalism and bourgeois decadence. When, one year later, Hungary offered the chance to imitate the Russian Revolution, Lukács joined the Communist Party (whose leader at that time was Béla Kun). He threw himself into practical-revolutionary activity, simultaneously devoting himself to a renewed and more intensive study of Marx's economic writings, as well as economic history and the history of the workers' movement. In the following years he served as minister in the short-lived Hungarian Soviet Republic. The collapse of this republic and the emigration to Vienna did not lead to a decline of revolutionary engagement. Vienna – at that time a centre of the international revolutionary movement – offered a great deal of support for the expectation of a rapid change in the world situation. As editor of the journal *Communism*, Lukács became the spokesman for a political line which he himself later called 'ultra-left subjectivism' and which was based on the 'very passionate belief' 'that the great revolutionary wave which would lead the whole world, or at least all of Europe, to socialism in a very short time, had by no means ebbed as a result of the defeats in Finland, Hungary and Munich'.[7] In 1923 Lukács published a collection of essays which is surely the high-point of his early work, some of the essays going back to the period of the Soviet Republic: *History and Class Consciousness.*

We cannot attempt an extended presentation of this collection here. At this point I would merely like to give a brief sketch of some of the central lines of thought, if only because the work has had such a strong influence on the subsequent intellectual development of Marxism; following this sketch I shall point out some aspects which are directly relevant for our theme. The central achievement of *History and Class Consciousness* was surely to be found in the attempt to reconciliate the theory of the political–economic class struggle with the Hegelian legacy of the dialectic (whereby it should be noted that Hegel's dialectic is abridged in a rather audacious manner and the idealistic aspects sharply underlined). Rejecting the positivist levelling as well as the pure contradictions of the neo-Kantian antinomies, Lukács attempted to regain a coherent philosophical basis for Marxism.[8] The book follows Hegel in presenting modern history as a process of self-externalization and the recovery of consciousness, a process which moves from the loss of meaning to a broader historical understanding. According to Lukács, the modern period is characterized by the attempt to grasp the entire world on the basis of human self-consciousness and the clear categories of reason; a one-sidedly theoretical reason is, however, helpless *vis à vis* the causal order of empirical reality. With the development of the capitalist social order the individual consciousness became increasingly a mere function of economic production and of the exchange of commodities. As presented in the major chapter dealing with 'Reification and the Consciousness of the Proletariat', the capitalist commodity structure has the effect of transforming all contacts between individuals into commodity relations, thus giving the relations between persons 'the character of things' and, as it were, a 'ghostly objectivity'. The reifying influence of economic structure affects all realms of intellectual and practical life; all aspects of experience appear as mere facts or complexes of facts which are the objects of scientific research, thereby producing scientism.[9] As Lukács adds, bourgeois thought recognizes only one counter-pole to reification: individual morality, which is, however, helpless in the face of the lawfulness of nature and condemned to tragic failure. Only a historical–dialectical approach is capable of overcoming the conflict. Capitalism flourishes on the basis of the exploitation of that social class to which it owes its own productivity: the exploitation of the proletariat. Should the proletariat become conscious of its role, it is capable of transcending the contemporary calamity in the direction of a new synthesis; this occurs by means of dialectical praxis in which the proletariat transforms the objective class situation and thus does away with itself as a class.

Does this line of thought have anything to offer for our topic? It seems to me that there is a series of relevant points. To begin with, Lukács by no means abandons the concept of the forms in this work; he merely gives it a historical–dialectical twist. As we have seen, this concept is closely related to the phenomenological intuition of essences. *History and Class Consciousness* repeatedly speaks of essences and forms. Thus, one reads of the 'essence' of pre-capitalist and capitalist society, of the 'essence' of class consciousness and the 'essence of the commodity structure'; in certain cases the circulation of commodities is presented as the 'universal' or 'constitutive form' of a society. To be sure, essence and forms are not static essences which are hidden behind the individual objects, but rather can be determined only on the basis of a total view or by means of an integration of partial moments in a concrete whole. This is related to the fact that Lukács calls the concept of the 'concrete totality' the core of the Marxist method, the 'authentic category of reality'.[10] Another closely related point of contact between phenomenology and Lukács's dialectic lies in the emphasis on 'consciousness'. According to Lukács's argument, the grasp of the essence or concrete totality is not possible in just any arbitrary situation, but rather presupposes a developed society and in addition a privileged class consciousness which makes possible insight into the situation as a whole. 'First with the appearance of the proletariat,' he writes, 'is the knowledge of social reality completed' and 'it is completed when the class standpoint of the proletariat is found, from which the whole of society becomes visible'. In this context Lukács understands class consciousness to be not merely an empirical-psychological state, but rather as the potential capacity for insight into the structure of society – a capacity whose awakening and activation presupposes a kind of shock or shaking-up (comparable to the phenomenological *epoché*). Once awakened, class consciousness constitutes reality, just as it recognizes itself in this reality. It should be noted that the constitutive role of consciousness in this dialectic bears not only a contemplative but also a practical character: the proletariat's knowledge of reality is coextensive with its transformation.[11]

A few years after its appearance Lukács repudiated *History and Class Consciousness* – indeed, his entire early work. This episode is too well known to require a detailed discussion here. The fading away of the hope for a world revolution, the increasing strength of the Soviet Union, the beginnings of the rise of Fascism – all of these developments were surely important political-strategic reasons for the repudiation. It is clear that *History and Class Consciousness* was indebted to the traditional philosophy of consciousness in many respects. This was obvious in the emphasis (the *over*emphasis) on the role of consciousness as opposed to nature and in the one-sided praise of the dialectical perspective on history as opposed to scientific research. And the discussion of class consciousness also exhibited in many respects abstract utopian-visionary aspects. But above all the emphasis on the proletariat as the identical 'subject-object' of history was an idealistic exaggeration by no means free of apocalyptic or 'messianic' trimmings (to use Lukács's own expression).[12] Against this background, Lukács's search for greater matter-of-factness and his attempt to put the dialectic closer to the ground of epistemological realism is thoroughly understandable. But, even if one shares the reservations concerning idealism and subjectivism, the vehemence with which Lukács attacks his own early writings is curious. During the following years, and especially during his stay in Moscow, Lukács became the spokesman of a rigorous Marxist–Leninist materialism and the bitter enemy of all 'bourgeois' lines of thought – including those lines of thought which had enjoyed great sympathy in his early writings (such as phenomenology and existentialism).[13] The intensity of his hostility begins to moderate slowly only in the post-war years following his return to Hungary and finally made way for a more conciliatory attitude after the Budapest uprising. In his final years Lukács worked on a comprehensive theory of society or social ontology – a work in which traditional materialism yields to a sense-critical, dialectical realism (partially indebted to Nicolai Hartmann) and which gives a central role to the phenomenological investigation of human everyday life within the theory of social reality.[14]

2 Existential and radical phenomenology

Lukács's life work, at least after *History and Class Consciousness*, stood under the banner of the victorious Russian Revolution and the slow consolidation of the Soviet Union – and later under the influence of the spread of socialism in Eastern Europe. In the light of these decisive experiences it is not entirely surprising that the tragic-eschatological tendency of his early years later made way for a (to be sure, not blind) trust in reality and in the reasonableness of history. The situation of the generation of left-wing thinkers who came of age in the 1920s and 1930s in the shadow of Hitler and Mussolini was completely different. Social reality and history had to appear to them less as the unfolding of a wise plan than as the product of an evil arbitrariness or senseless caprice. Above all, the French intellectuals had to sense the brutality and capriciousness of history when their country was overrun by Hitler's tanks. But the situation was similar in other continental European countries where Fascism was either (as in Italy) home grown or established by means of outside force.

The practical result of these experiences was not – at least in the case of left-wing intellectuals – simple resignation or a retreat into the private sphere, but a more powerful will to rebellion and confrontation. Against this background, some of the characteristic aspects of French existentialism – and radical humanism in general – of those years become comprehensible: the link between despair and revolutionary verve, activism and the absence of any faith in progress. The situation was eased by the fall of Hitler and Mussolini, but not completely transformed; in the light of the resurgence of conservative and reactionary tendencies in Western Europe, existentialism and radicalism had to continue to play an important role in cultural life.

Lukács's intellectual world is radically divorced from that of the existentialist generation not only because of the experience of the Soviet revolution, but also because of a fact that is central for our topic: his relation to the connection between phenomenology and Marxism. Whereas in Lukács's work the two perspectives continued to stand in a tense struggle – sometimes moderated by cease-fires – an almost effortless (and perhaps superficial) symbiosis began to develop during the Second World War. This symbiosis was of course strongly influenced by the practical experience of the time and aided by a specific interpretation of the two perspectives. In partial dependence on Husserl, phenomenology was understood by French existentialism (and radical humanists in other countries) above all as a rigorous philosophy of consciousness – with emphasis on the constitutive role of consciousness. This reception, in turn, was no accident: its way was prepared in France by the strong influence of the Cartesian heritage and in the rest of Western Europe by the dominance of idealistic schools in the first years of our century. To the extent that phenomenology and *Daseins*-analysis were mixed up with one another, one generally finds an acceptance of the voluntaristic-anthropological elements in Heidegger's *Being and Time*. On the other hand, Marxism was generally understood as a synonym for revolutionary praxis in these years; especially in the French Resistance, it became the main pillar and rallying point for the rebellion against purely external oppression. The premises of the symbiosis become visible in this manner: both perspectives stand under the sign of 'alienation'; both articulate the demand for an overcoming of external coercion. Conceived against this background, the symbiosis naturally demands a price: in phenomenology the reference to the object (the relation of consciousness to the 'intentional object'), in Marxism the concrete-historical content of the theory is forced to the back of the stage.[15]

It goes without saying that the symbiosis does not always take on exactly the same form in the work of the various thinkers – and in the work of the same thinker at different times. The following discussion concentrates on two of the main representatives of existential and radical phenomenology in France and Italy, and I shall concentrate on especially illustrative phases of their life work (again in the interest of a brief profile). I shall begin with the working out of a pure existential phenomenology in Sartre's early work – a perspective in which 'in-itself' and 'for-itself', external objects and human freedom clash directly. The discussion follows Sartre's development up to his first attempts to unify phenomenology and Marxism – attempts in which the capacity for absolute freedom on the part of particular individuals is carried over somewhat abruptly to the praxis of the proletariat. I shall then turn to the leading representative of left-wing or radical phenomenology in Italy, Enzo Paci, whose works, while not dismissing the themes of alienation and reification, project the possibility of a synthesis or overcoming of the reified external world by means of subjective praxis. The discussion is rounded off by references to Merleau-Ponty, especially to his attempt to reconceptualize the antinomies of subject and object, consciousness and objectness and to render them harmless by means of an integration into a more interactive-participatory *Daseins*-perspective. In a sense, the development of left-wing phenomenology repeats the stages of classical German philosophy. Whereas Sartre's early work aims roughly at a quasi-Kantian dualism of phenomenal lawfulness and noumenal freedom, Paci attempts to get rid of the opposition by means of a rather Fichtean incorporation of the external world into self-positing consciousness. Merleau-Ponty's work tends towards a more objective-integrating dialectic – and finally in the direction of a position in which the priority of being to consciousness is thematized anew.

French existentialism – indeed existentialism in general – is usually identified with Sartre's philosophy, and his thought is often identified with his early work, especially *Being and Nothingness*. This is certainly a distortion. There is no question but that Sartre – more than any other existentialist – had a decisive effect on the generation of the immediate post-war period. But it should not be forgotten that important details of his position have changed since the end of the war, even if the main thrust has remained constant. In addition, even if the early work is taken as the point of orientation, his thought exhibits very idiosyncratic aspects which are by no means characteristic or binding for existentialism in general. Sartre took over from Husserl typical ingredients of the phenomenological method, above all the postulate of the reference of all objects of experience to intentional acts of consciousness; in doing so he radicalized Husserl's method of transcendental reduction. Whereas Husserl still identified pure consciousness with a (be it transcendentally cleansed) ego-consciousness, in his early writings Sartre defended the thesis that the ego belongs among the objects in the world and is thus at intentional disposal. With this bracketing of the ego – which, of course, was not thought to detract from personal responsibility – Sartre developed the conception of an absolute antinomy: that between the world of objects and a consciousness which is completely emptied of objects and thus free. The abruptness of the antimony was sharpened by elements borrowed from Heidegger's *Being and Time*, above all by the acceptance or variation of categories such as 'thrownness', '*Angst*' and 'decisiveness' to action. The theoretical structure was crowned by additions from Hegel's conceptual arsenal – the dialectic taking on the form of an atemporal antithesis between consciousness and external nature.[16]

The structure of Sartre's early thought is most clearly visible in *Being and Nothingness*. The book begins by contrasting subject and object, or – in Hegelian terminology – the two modes of being of the 'in-itself' (*en-soi*) and the 'for-itself' (*pour-soi*). The category of the 'for-itself' signifies pure consciousness and free subjectivity, the concept of the 'in-itself' an atemporal objectness and self-contained objectivity. The two modes of being are not completely separate from one another, since they are held together in human experience – if only in a precarious manner. The human situation (*la réalité humaine*) is characterized as 'being-in-the-world' – an expression which indicates that man participates both of the world of objects as well as consciousness. In contrast to the positivity of the world of things or phenomena, the realm of the 'for-itself' is characterized by lack, negativity or transcendence; the relation between things and consciousness thus basically coincides with that between being and nothingness. From the perspective of consciousness (especially the questioning consciousness), the objective world appears as a world of pure possibilities and boundless variability. Although man is not pure spirit, since he is always intentionally integrated in the world of things, his existence is no more than the fertile soil of dynamic restlessness in the world. According to Sartre, it is man's fate to continually transcend his surrounding world in the direction of its and his own possibilities; he only exists 'in that he continually tears himself away from that which is'.

Defined as the soil of negation and transcendence, human existence necessarily coincides with free self-assertion. In Sartre's presentation, freedom is not an accidental aspect but rather the essence of existence. 'Freedom arises out of the negation of the call of the world,' writes Sartre, 'it appears as soon as I detach myself from the world in which I had engaged myself in order to experience myself as consciousness.' And freedom is by no means a synonym for free-floating intellectuals. Along with Heidegger, Sartre assumes that man is always 'thrown' into a pregiven 'situation' or environment. But this situation is by no means hopeless or completely determining; the context becomes one's own human situation only when it is consciously accepted, modified or rejected. Man's 'thrownness' thus by no means restricts the individual's complete and unlimited responsibility for his position and actions; every attempt to shove this responsibility off on to the world of things or external circumstances is a sign of 'bad faith' (*mauvaise foi*). In spite of all difficulties and hindrances, man must continually invent and realize himself and his future. In another Heideggerian twist Sartre describes human existence as a continual 'project' of self-realization – a project which must be freely planned and carried out by the individual. 'Man is what he does,' asserts Sartre emphatically, and goes so far as to add that everything that is is a 'human undertaking'. 'Man is free,' one reads elsewhere, 'because he exists not in-himself but for-himself. Freedom is precisely the nothingness which was in the hearts of men and which forces human reality to *make* itself rather than simply be.' With regard to the final success of the undertaking, however, Sartre is anything but romantic: his discussion of the realization of the 'fundamental project' (*projet fondamental*) of existence has a deep tragic note. Since consciousness experiences itself as lack and is oriented towards fulfilment and wholeness, the 'for-itself' continually strives to turn itself into a permanent 'in-itself'. Human existence thus appears as a 'naturally unhappy consciousness'.

In view of this emphasis on self-creation (and in spite of the transformation of the category of the ego), it is not surprising that Sartre's thought – along with the traditional philosophy of consciousness and Husserl – is threatened by solipsism. He faces this threat directly and even attempts to sharpen the dilemma by rejecting all compromises. Just as he had reckoned the concrete ego to the world of things, he refuses to follow Husserl in viewing other human beings as being constituted in ego-consciousness, preferring to view the existence of the other (at least in the first instance) as a contingent 'fact'. The other is, however, immediately taken up into the mill wheel of consciousness and external world. Sartre treats interpersonal relations under the rubric of the look or of being seen (*le regard d'autrui*). The look of the other transforms one's own existence into an object, a barrier or a means for the freedom of the other; from this point on 'it is a matter of my being as it presents itself in and through the freedom of the other'. As the 'hidden death of my possibilities', the look of the other transforms my existence into a natural phenomenon and 'steals' or usurps my own world. But the process of reification and alienation is not one-sided; in the reciprocity of the look, the world of interpersonal relations appears fundamentally as a world of competition and conflict. According to Sartre, the individual has two central alternatives for reacting to the existence of the other: he can either accept his own reification and adapt himself to the others in the hope of participating in their freedom; or he can mount a counterattack and attempt to reify the other and absorb his freedom and consciousness. Both courses of action – that of masochism and that of sadism – are in the last resort unsuccessful; both alternatives fail to institute a genuine interpersonal relation, since they result in extinguishing a 'for-itself' or consciousness. To this extent, we do not find a dialectic between subjects in Sartre, but at most a back and forth or a 'circle' of reification in which 'every attempt enriches itself from the failure of the other'.[17]

Sartre's intellectual world as it comes to expression in *Being and Nothingness* is obviously separated from Marxism by a chasm. The lack of a genuine interpersonal dialectic puts his thought in close relationship to the Kantian antinomies or to a Kierkegaardian tragic view of life; the emphasis on the individual and the problematic of individual existence blocks the way to a treatment of concrete social structures. In addition, Sartre's radical concept of freedom poses the question how the concept of existence as conscious 'project' and the thesis of the practical production of the world can be integrated into a perspective which gives being a priority over against consciousness. Just how difficult these questions and barriers are can be seen clearly in Sartre's early attempts to harmonize existentialism with Marxism and the proletarian workers' movement; the essay 'Materialism and Revolution' from 1946 is most instructive in this context. The essay attempts to interpret the proletarian revolution as a transcendental project of the workers' movement – a project whose opposition to the capitalist system of exploitation and reification opens the way for human self-determination. Against this background it is clear that the identification of Marxism and dialectical materialsm is absurd – since 'materialism' involves, according to Sartre, the assumption of a self-contained world of things. As he tries to show, the materialistic doctrine is nothing other than mystical positivism and disguised metaphysics. He says that the doctrine initially takes up the positivist strategy of successive unmaskings, but then leaves this path in a leap of faith: with positivism it begins by denying all transcendence, traces spirit back to matter and finally eliminates every trace of subjectivity 'by the reduction of the world and human existence to a system of objects related to one another by natural laws'. But whereas positivism refuses to give any answer to ultimate questions, materialism responds to them with speculations in which matter is declared to be the 'essence of things' and consciousness the product of matter. According to Sartre, materialism thus adopts 'an *a priori* position with reference to a problem which infinitely transcends our experience', and it is hard to avoid the conclusion that what we are dealing with here is a 'metaphysical doctrine, and that the materialists are metaphysicians'.

This disguised metaphysics, which is only partially concealed by positivism, is in Sartre's view the reason for the unending confusion among Marxists and in the Marxist theory. This is proven by materialist epistemology. In holding fast to the picture theory and the attack on subjectivity, writes Sartre, materialism acts as if it has taken care of the problematic of consciousness. But this is a transparent diversionary tactic:

> In order to eliminate subjectivity, the materialist declares himself to be an object, i.e. an object of scientific research. But as soon as subjectivity is reduced to the world of objects, the materialist plays a trick: instead of viewing himself as an object among objects and under the control of natural causality, he turns himself into the *objective observer* and claims to have nature in itself, as it really is, in grip.[18]

The substitution of objectivity for subjectivity is merely sleight-of-hand and puts the famous 'scientific rationality' of the doctrine in question. To the extent that consciousness is really a by-product of matter, a mere playtoy of natural laws, one can understand how the thought as effect might mirror the world as pure cause, but not at all how it can go on to comprehend complex contexts and to the development of theories: 'How can a reason in chains, which is completely governed from without and guided by blind causes, still be called reason?' But once reason begins to totter, materialism itself is robbed of its own foundation as a rational theory with a claim to be true. Thus, Sartre claims that the materialist doctrine contains an internal contradiction and thus refutes itself. After getting rid of metaphysics with the aid of positivism, and then getting rid of positivism with the aid of a leap of faith, the doctrine finally contradicts itself in the assertion that man is nothing more than matter: 'In the final analysis the whole complex collapses'.

In Sartre's view, the collapse of materialism does not involve negative consequences for Marxism itself. The rest of the essay is devoted to working out a defensible theoretical foundation which is genuinely appropriate to Marxism. In Sartre's presentation the core of Marxist epistemology is not the picture theory – the demand for a correct mirroring of external objects in thought – but rather the conjunction of knowledge with praxis and above all with human labour (where 'labour' is understood as dealing with and transforming the world of objects). A pure passive-receptive mirroring of the external world, he writes, is at most appropriate to the theoretical or political understanding of the given ruling class or elite, for example, the bourgeoisie in the contemporary world. A class which is interested in preserving the *status quo* must be delighted to find an epistemology which claims 'to grasp the world as it is, i.e. from the point of view of pure contemplation' and which insists that 'one can only know the world but not change it'. But for a suppressed class – such as the proletariat – the thesis of the 'primacy of pure knowledge' is completely intolerable, since it turns its repression into a permanent state of affairs. If the proletariat is to free itself from repression and reification, it cannot be satisfied with a passive-receptive mirroring of the contemporary situation; it must engage itself practically. As the theory of proletarian rebellion, Marxism must thus be understood fundamentally as a philosophy of revolutionary praxis. The emphasis on praxis is not, however, a turn to blind activism or to a superficial pragmatism; praxis requires an epistemological foundation, and this foundation can only be found in the concept of 'labour' as dealing with objects – a concept in which knowledge of reality and practical activity converge. Marxism, says Sartre, requires an epistemology 'which demonstrates that human reality is activity and that the active cultivation of the world is identical with knowledge of this world as it is – i.e. that praxis is a demasking of reality and simultaneously a modification of this reality'.

If this epistemological thesis is valid, then the proletariat (and along with it, Marxism) has a privileged access to the grasp of reality – without any debt to materialism.

In view of the brutality of its exploitation, the proletariat is, as it were, forced to rebel against the social order, and it can only do this effectively by negating the given objective world with its reification in the name of a radically new 'project' and a new concept of human society. In this context, the proletariat as worker is superbly prepared for the concrete realization of its project, since at work the proletarian continually deals with negation and reorganization. In working over the materials at hand he attains a 'domination over the world of things' and discovers himself as the 'source of unlimited possibilities of dealing with and transforming material'. The exploitation of this practical knowledge in the service of the proletarian class struggle presupposes merely a clear definition of the social context: as soon as the worker understands himself as a member of a working class it is possible to integrate his individual consciousness into proletarian class consciousness. Working with material objects thus turns out to be the paradigm for revolutionary praxis; just as in the case of labour, the class struggle is a matter of an act of negation and transcendence – now in a collective frame of reference. As opposed to 'orthodox' distortions, Marxism must thus be understood to be a 'philosophy of transcendence' and as a philosophy of radical freedom. 'The possibility of rising above a situation in order to win a perspective', the essay closes, 'is precisely what we call freedom. No materialism, regardless of what variety, can come to terms with this situation.'[19]

As we see, even in the post-war period Sartre remains true to the radical concept of freedom from his early writings, although the emphasis on labour involves a stronger mediation with reality. But the incorporation of this concept of freedom into Marxism has serious consequences for Marxism – consequences which Sartre neglects to mention. Just as the early phenomenological work bore the stamp of the opposition between consciousness and the objective world, now revolutionary praxis is only meaningful against the background of continual exploitation; just as in *Being and Nothingness* consciousness as the 'for-itself' could never merge with the 'in-itself', no matter how hard it tried, in 'Materialism and Revolution' the class struggle can never come to an end. Sartre's historical perspective thus projects less a classless society than a continual alternation of various varieties of social sadism and masochism. His later writings have perhaps moderated this dilemma, but it remains present; I shall have to restrict myself to a few brief remarks here. It seems to me that Sartre's late work moves farther and farther away from a philosophical elaboration of phenomenology and existentialism, moving in the direction of historical-sociological and literature-critical analyses. In the *Question of Method*, existentialism as 'ideology' is contrasted with genuine 'philosophy' – the former thus becoming a temporary 'Band-aid' for Marxism. The 'progressive-regressive' method, which Sartre sketches following Henri Lefèbre, restricts phenomenology to a diachronic understanding of history in contrast to synchronic science, whereby the relation to Dilthey's theory of *Verstehen* remains unclear. The discussions of the dialectic in the *Critique of Dialectical Reason* do not, as far as I can see, go beyond *History and Class Consciousness*, indeed, in many points – such as the individualistic accent and in the conceptual scheme – they fall back below the level of Lukács's work.[20]

The antinomical character of Sartre's intellectual world has been criticized from various points of view, among others also by phenomenologists and Marxists. Enzo Paci, the leading representative of the left-wing Husserlians in Italy, has distanced himself from Sartre's position for phenomenological as well as Marxist reasons. According to Paci, Sartre's thought suffers from an inadequate phenomenological foundation and especially from insufficient use of the phenomenological method of the 'reduction'; in other words, the tracing back of all experiences to the 'concrete subject and its intentionality'; only by means of a rigorous application of the *epoché* and the recognition of the constitutive role of subjectivity, claims Paci, can one bridge the rupture from without and within, and merge the objective world with consciousness. From a Marxist point of view, the performance of the *epoché* has the effect that in the long run the class struggle is absorbed into radical-intentional praxis. Paci's ideas on these matters have gone through various turns over the years, and I cannot go into them individually here. Whereas in the first years after the war he was closely allied with French existentialism, he later turned more and more to a radically interpreted Husserlian perspective, emphasizing the egological components. In more recent work he seems to have moved away from a strict egology in the direction of a position which tries to embed the functioning of ego-consciousness in social structures. In our context I shall restrict myself to a work from his Husserlian phase which contains the critique of Sartre mentioned above: *The Function of the Sciences and the Meaning of Man.*[21]

Large portions of this work are a commentary on Husserl's *The Crisis of European Science* and an attempt to unify Husserl's arguments with Marxism. Paci tries to demonstrate that Western civilization is in the grip of a profound crisis, a crisis which is by and large the result of capitalism and technology. The core of the crisis is the progressive alienation and reification of human relations and the reduction of man to an object among other objects, a process which is propelled by the pressure of the capitalist methods of production and the scientific idolizing of the objective world. The only possibility of effectively responding to this crisis is to be found in a radical reflection and reorientation as is attempted in phenomenology and a phenomenologically rejuvenated Marxism; Husserl's *Crisis* and Marx's *Capital* are the beacons for this renewal. The deep fermentation in our epoch, Paci writes, is 'an expression of man's struggle for his own self-understanding and for his own meaning'. In our century it is above all Husserl's phenomenology which has put the question of meaning at the centre of attention: 'Phenomenology is concerned to give man back his "subjectivity". It attempts to return man to himself – freed from every fetish, from every mask which conceals or distorts his humanity.' In the attempt to penetrate the barrier of reified or fetishistic appearances, Husserl's philosophy wins an immediate practical significance: 'Within every human being – and here we interpret Husserl in a radical sense – there is a latent humanity, a humanity which is as yet embryonic, but which can be born should man wish, should he accept the responsibility for the realization of his possibilities.' In the rigorous distinction between essence and appearance Paci sees Husserl going far beyond other philosophers; the reason for this lies in the phenomenological method of the *epoché*, i.e. in the uncovering of 'authentic-intentional' life below the surface of facticity. Phenomenology 'attempts to lead man to self-consciousness, to self-realization, to self-constitution and transcendental foundation'. Since the human world of appearances is reified and concealed, the method of *epoché* or bracketing is necessary: 'Transcendental foundation presupposes transcendental reduction to pure, i.e. transcendental subjectivity.'

In defining his position Paci appeals to the Husserlian concept of the 'life-world', understood as the prepredicative, preconscious or 'precategorial' context or background of experience. But in contrast to some existentially oriented phenomenologists, he refuses to sever this context from transcendental consciousness or transcendental subjectivity. In spite of a series of opposing statements in Husserl's works, Paci holds that such a separation simply cannot be defended. Phenomenological 'epoché', Paci writes, is always simultaneously 'a reduction to transcendental subjectivity and to the life-world'; the transcendental reduction, he adds, is the most comprehensive phenomenological method and leads to a subjectivity 'which is not merely mythological' and includes both transcendental consciousness and the concrete 'subject of flesh and blood'. Regardless of whether the emphasis is placed on the concrete or the transcendental aspect, subjectivity has a central importance for Paci: it is the origin of intentional sense in the world, a sense which is, as it were, latently present in the concrete life-world and merely awaits conscious articulation. Indeed, the significance of subjectivity goes even further: in constituting sense, it simultaneously constitutes the world. As the study puts it, phenomenology teaches 'that the world *is* to the extent that it is significant, to the extent that the truth which lives within it is discovered and made the goal and intentional purpose of human life'. In view of the conjunction of reality and intentionality, Paci holds that one can say that 'the being of the world is constituted by subjectivity', indeed that 'subjectivity – understood as subjective-intentional activity – includes the entire world within itself'. From this perspective, intentionality has a radical, practical task – that of constantly protecting sense and reality from objectivation and reification: 'Transcendental consciousness, as the being of the world constituted in consciousness, can never be satisfied with accepting a pre-given (false) reality. It is rather an active production of sense: a forming subjectivity.' Phenomenology thus possesses the key to revolutionary renewal: 'The transcendental *epoché* is a *total* transformation.'

Once Marxism is interpreted as revolutionary praxis, Paci thinks that the bridge from Husserl to Marx is no real problem. He does admit that Husserl did not pay enough attention to the realm of the forces of production and the relations of production, but once economic needs are seen to be an integrating element of everyday experience in the life-world, intentionality and class struggle form a unity. But the bridge – and Paci is very clear about this – is confronted by an important barrier: the usual identification of Marxism with materialism (whereby the latter refers to a world of things 'in themselves'); but he does not consider the barrier to be insurmountable; indeed, he thinks that it basically rests upon a misunderstanding. Matter and nature are in his opinion only apparently opposed to consciousness. Although it presents itself only in the form of 'impenetrable, opaque, external resistance', matter can be 'reduced to a mode of experience' or to the experience of the 'hardness of the world of things'; from the perspective of the life-world 'it turns out that even external or material nature is internal to the extent that it is a question of an experiential modality of transcendental subjectivity'. 'Lifeless matter', as he puts it in another context, is living and '*subjective* in its own manner'. In view of this conception of matter and materialism it is understandable that Paci interprets Marxism above all as critique of bourgeois objectivism and capitalist reification, and that he sees its main goal in the renewal of radical-intentional praxis:

> By means of the return to the subject and its activity I discover that the world of appearances is an abstraction invested with merely apparent reality, which also transforms the worker into an abstraction. This is precisely what Marx elaborated in *Capital* by uncovering the real human being behind every form of appearance which has gained a false reality as a result of exchange, wage labor and capital. The original concreteness which is Marx's genuine point of departure is the subject.[22]

In spite of a temporary slip into naturalistic terminology, this was also Engel's opinion: 'With regard to phenomenological analysis, the dialectical modalities – such as those which Engels presented as natural laws – must necessarily begin with subjectivity, a subjectivity understood both in the sense of a point of departure and in the sense of a living, operative presence.' Paci thus sees the core of dialectical materialism to lie 'in the insertion of the dialectic into subjectivity and the penetration of subjectivity as the causal element into every dialectical modality'.

The works of Paci and Sartre which we have discussed by no means exhaust the possibilities for building bridges between existential or radical phenomenology and Marxism. In closing, I would like to mention briefly some lines of thought in Merleau-Ponty, a thinker who as a phenomenologist opened up important new continents for contemporary philosophy and who simultaneously was close to Marxism throughout his life (although his distaste for Marxist orthodoxy grew from year to year). Along with Sartre, Merleau-Ponty expanded the range of the phenomenological method from the pure theory of knowledge to the concrete 'life-world' and the realm of practical-social questions, but without identifying phenomenology with subjective-intentional praxis (and without ever losing sight of Husserl's emphasis on the necessity of careful description and analysis). In spite of the danger of oversimplification, one might characterize his approach as being dialectical-participatory: a perspective according to which knowledge is only possible in terms of a detour through nature and one's fellow men, and that the experience of sense is not so much an act of constitution or taking possession than participation in the world. From his earliest writings on, Merleau-Ponty directed his energies critically against the project of an egological-solipsistic intuition of essences – with the argument that such a project ignores human 'being-in-the world' and thus the embeddedness of thought in intersubjective language and transindividual frameworks. 'The idea that we can penetrate directly to the essence of things turns out on closer inspection to be incoherent. What we find is at most a path, an experience which slowly refines and corrects itself with the help of dialogues with oneself and with others.' This emphasis on the concrete context of experience by no means indicates an identification of phenomenological knowledge with widespread opinions or prejudices. Perception, in Merleau-Ponty's account, not only participates in the human surrounding world but also in the world of intentional objects. Precisely because experience is not a pure act of consciousness, 'reality' does not signify simply a 'thing-in-itself' transcendent to consciousness, but rather the horizon of possible experience (and possible knowledge):

> I cannot even imagine a place at which I am not simultaneously present. But even that place where I am is never completely mine; the things I see are objects of experience for me only under the condition that they always refer beyond their immediately given aspects. There is thus a paradox of immanence and transcendence in perception: immanence, since the object of experience is never totally foreign to the experiencer; transcendence, since it always contains more than it immediately reveals.[23]

When interpreted from Merleau-Ponty's point of view, phenomenology can be seen to have a great deal to offer the Marxist self-understanding at a variety of points. For example, his thought can stimulate a renewal and reformulation of materialist epistemology. In his work on perception and above all in his late works on the genealogy of knowledge, Merleau-Ponty increasingly turned towards a sense-critical realism or 'hyper-realism' which is in many respects perhaps comparable to the position of the late Lukács and which makes it possible to pose anew the question concerning the priority of being to consciousness and the question of the sense of this priority. Equally noteworthy is the relevance of the analyses of the life-world for the practical-political problems of our time. In historical perspective it is perhaps not an exaggeration to characterize the phenomenological movement as the swan song of modern individualism. In the work of Husserl and that of his immediate disciples, the modern, egological philosophy of consciousness experienced a late, impressive flowering. But with the turn to the life-world, the dominate role of reflection was put in question, and this went hand in hand with the increasing 'decentrizing' of the individual. Merleau-Ponty's life work does remain true to Husserl's basic intentions, but it follows out the implications of the turn to the life-world in detail. Without offering a political programme, his social-philosophical works circumscribe the contours of a self-critical, 'liberal' Marxism – a position which puts 'possessive individualism' in its place without defending a blind collectivism. The motto for such a position appears already in an early essay; *'un Marxisme sans illusions, tout expérimental'*.[24]

Notes

1 In my own opinion, the positions listed here are not quite so disparate as it may seem at first glance. If one takes Husserl's 'noesis-noema' relation – the assertion that consciousness is always 'consciousness of something' – seriously, one can no longer straightforwardly include Husserl's phenomenology with traditional philosophy of consciousness. At any rate, self-consciousness' self-possession no longer seems quite so clear-cut as it once did, finding its way to itself only over the world. The liberal linguistic conventions adopted here can appeal to the testimony of experts; e.g. Herbert Spiegelberg's *The Phenomenological Movement: A Historical Introduction*, 2 volumes, The Hague, Martinus Nijhoff, 1969. In a more recent study, Don Ihde has emphasized the relations between Husserl and Heidegger. (Cf. 'Phenomenology and the Later Heidegger', *Philosophy Today*, vol. 18, 1974, pp. 19-31.)

2 Georg Lukács, 'Mein Weg zu Marx' (1933) in *Schriften zur Ideologie und Politik*, Neuwied and Berlin, Luchterhand, 1967, pp. 323–4.

3 Georg Lukács, 'Vorwort' (1967) to *Geschichte und Klassenbewußtsein*, Neuwied and Berlin, Luchterhand, 1968, p. 11.

4 Lucien Goldmann, 'Zu Georg Lukács: Die Theorie des Romans', in *Dialektische Untersuchungen*, Neuwied and Berlin, Luchterhand, 1966, pp. 286–92.

5 Ibid.

6 Lukács, 'Mein Weg zu Marx', op. cit., p. 325; Goldmann, 'Zu Georg Lukács', op. cit., pp. 292–6.

7 Lukács, 'Mein Weg zu Marx', op. cit., p. 327; 'Vorwort' (1967) op. cit., p. 15.

8 As Goldmann writes: 'This position of Lukács gave the Marxist work its coherence again and allowed all so-called "dualities", "incoherencies", "confusions", "philosophical absurdities", etc. to disappear with one blow. Thus, it seems to us that Lukács's position is the only possible point of departure for a genuine regeneration of dialectical thought in its full power and fruitfulness.' (Cf. 'Gibt es eine marxistische Soziologie?', in *Dialektische Untersuchungen*, op. cit., p. 229.)

9 Lukács writes:

> The fetishistic character of the economic order, the reification of all human relations, the continual expansion of a division of labor which dissects the process of production in an abstract-rational manner without regard for the human possibilities and abilities of the immediate producers, etc. transform the phenomenon of society and simultaneously its apperception. 'Isolated' facts arise, isolated complexes of facts, autonomous partial realms (economy, law, etc.), whose immediate form of appearance seems to be already prepared for a scientific investigation. Thus, it must count as being especially 'scientific' to think this tendency – which is immanent to the facts themselves – to the end and to raise it to science. Whereas the dialectic, which emphasized the concrete unity of the whole in contrast to all of these isolated and isolating facts and partial systems, a unity which unmasks this appearance as a mere appearance – although an appearance which capitalism necessarily produces – this dialectic seems to be a mere construction. (Cf. *Geschichte und Klassenbewußtsein*, op. cit., pp. 177, 257.)

10 Ibid., pp. 191, 228, 257.

11 Ibid., p. 193. One might also ask whether the dialectical–idealistic conception of the proletariat as a subject and object of knowledge does not have a subterranean connection to the 'noesis-noema' relation. Goldmann summarizes the situation in the following manner:

> The methodological significance of *History and Class Consciousness* consists in the fact that Lukács replaces the phenomenological idea of the a-temporal significant structure characteristic of the two earlier works by the dialectical–Marxist concept of the temporal, dynamic, significant structure, a concept which is based on the idea of the totality. On this basis he developed

> the other two fundamental Marxist concepts of the *attributed consciousness* and the *objective possibility*, with whose aid the human sciences at long last attain the status of a positive and operative discipline. (Cf. 'Zu Georg Lukács', op. cit., p. 309.)

12 Lukács speaks of the 'messianic–utopian goals' of the sects of the 1920s and notes: 'The proletariat as the identical subject–object of real human history is thus not a material realization which overcomes the idealistic thought construction, but rather an over-Hegeling of Hegel, a construction which in a daring intellectual elevation over any and every reality aims at objectively outdoing the master.' (Cf. 'Vorwort' (1967), op. cit., pp. 15, 25.)

13 Cf. Lukács, *Existentialismus oder Marxismus?* (With the appendix 'Heidegger Redivivus'), Berlin, Aufbau Verlag, 1951; 'Die Zerstörung der Vernunft' (1954), in *Georg Lukács Werke*, vol. 9, Neuwied, Luchterhand, 1960.

14 The first three chapters of the announced *Ontologie des gesellschaftlichen Seins* have been published to date: *Zur Ontologie des gesellschaftlichen Seins: Hegels falsche und echte Ontologie*, Neuwied, Luchterhand, 1971; *Die ontologischen Grundprinzipien nach Marx*, Neuwied, Luchterhand, 1972; *Ontologie-Arbeit*, Neuwied, Luchterhand, 1973.

15 With reference to French existential phenomenology, Lukács notes that it developed at a point

> at which the perspectives of the liberation from Fascism were already visible, thus at which – precisely as a result of the long domination of Fascism – the longing for freedom was the fundamental experience of the intelligentsia in all of Europe, above all in those lands with a democratic tradition. This experience was – and this is especially true for the Western countries – freedom in general, abstract, without any analysis, without differentiation; in short, freedom as a myth, which precisely because of this lack of contours could unite everyone who had been an enemy of Fascism under its flags. (Cf. *Existentialismus oder Marxismus?*, op. cit., p. 50.)

16 Herbert Marcuse sketched Sartre's perspective in this way: 'Sartre's concept of the free subject is in the first place a reinterpretation of the cartesian *cogito*; but his development follows rather the tradition of German than French rationalism. Indeed Sartre's book is by and large a recourse to Hegel's *Phenomenology of Spirit* and Heidegger's *Being and Time*. French existentialism reanimated many of the intellectual tendencies which were alive in the Germany of the 1920s and fell victim to the Nazi system.' (Cf. 'Existentialismus' (1948), in Marcuse, *Kultur und Gesellschaft* 2, Frankfurt am Main, Suhrkamp, 1965, p. 52.)

17 Jean-Paul Sartre, *L'Etre et le Néant, Essai d'ontologie phénoménologique*, Paris, Gallimard, 1943; English translation: *Being and Nothingness*, trans. Hazel Barnes, London, Methuen, 1969.

18 Sartre, 'Matérialisme et Révolution', *Les Temps Modernes*, June 1946.
19 Ibid.
20 Sartre, *Critique de la Raison Dialectique, précédé de Question de Méthode*, vol. I, Paris, Gallimard, 1960; English translation: *Critique of Dialectical Reason*, New York, Schocken, 1976.
21 Enzo Paci, *Funzione delle Scienze e Significato dell'Uomo*, Milan, Il Saggiatore, 1963; English translation: *The Function of the Sciences and the Meaning of Man*, trans. Paul Piccone and James E. Hansen, Evanston, Northwestern University Press, 1972.
22 Ibid.
23 Maurice Merleau-Ponty, 'The Primacy of Perception and Its Philosophical Consequences', in *The Primacy of Perception*, ed. and trans. James M. Edie, Evanston, Northwestern University Press, pp. 12–42.
24 Maurice Merleau-Ponty, 'Concerning Marxism', in *Sense and Nonsense*, trans. Hubert L. Dreyfus and Patricia Allan Dreyfus, Evanston, Northwestern University Press, 1964, pp. 94–124.

CHAPTER 2

Marxism and the hermeneutic tradition

Marek J. Siemek (Warsaw)

There can be no doubt that hermeneutics or hermeneutic philosophy plays a central role within the theoretical reality of contemporary thought, i.e. in the thought of the second half of our century. The 'philosophers of sense' are among those who are most responsible for the profound transformations which the form and structure of basic philosophical problems have experienced since 1960. Every direction of thought which hopes to keep pace with and actively participate in this process of transformation will have to accept the hermeneutic school as an important partner. This is especially true for Marxism, which clearly has more in common with hermeneutics than with any other philosophy and finds a greater chance for a fruitful dialogue here than anywhere else. Partnership, however, requires a genuine and global confrontation of the two points of view, a confrontation which has yet to take place and which is becoming an increasingly urgent task for Marxists. The theses which I shall defend do not pretend to be this confrontation; they rather have the task of pointing out the necessity of such a confrontation and of sketching some of the points at which the confrontation might begin.

If one understands 'hermeneutics' in the broadest sense as a certain kind of intellectual activity and a certain ability which results from this activity, namely the activity and ability of criticism and interpretation, then there can be no doubt that Marxism is and always has been a hermeneutics. The essence of historical materialism or Marxist dialectical philosophy (I use the two terms interchangeably) is to be found in that endeavour which lies at the heart of every other form of interpretation, namely the endeavour to understand the 'hidden sense' of directly visible phenomena. This endeavour passes through the same doubt as every other form of critique, doubt in the apparent evidence of this direct 'seeing'. In this sense the Marxist dialectic is a kind of hermeneutic 'reading'. But the specific 'text' which dialectics 'reads' and attempts to reconstruct is not written in semantic objects (words, signs or meanings), but rather in units which are broader and more fundamental: in sense-constituting relations where the direct semantics of meanings is always 'inscribed' in the ontology of its contemporary historicity. Here one does not 'read' the word, the meaning or the logos, but rather the prior, pre-logical and pre-semantical conditions for the unity of words and things, meanings and their objects, of logos and praxis. Reading a 'text' is always the uncovering of a 'counter-text', of the historical form of objectivity which is the point of departure of a given text but which as such is overlooked and ignored, or literally disguised by its discourse. This is the manner in which Marx read the English national economists and Hegel's philosophical writings; this is the way Lenin read the *narodniki* and Plekhanov, the way Gramsci read Croce, the way Lukács read the revisionist theoreticians of the 2nd International, and the way Brecht read the propaganda of the Fascist ideologists. In all of these examples, interpretation and critique are inseparable; together, and only together, they constitute the indivisible act of 'understanding' in which the demystification of meanings is identical with the penetration of the fetishized structure of all forms of objectivity which hide behind these meanings. The foundation of this act is always a certain 'hermeneutic' activity. In this sense, hermeneutics can be considered to be an integral element in dialectical thought.

But the fact is that in the intellectual history of the last century the convergence of hermeneutics and Marxism has been persistently obscured by two interrelated circumstances: the theological origin of hermeneutics and the naturalist self-interpretation of Marxism. It must be remembered that hermeneutics discovered the whole philosophical problem of 'word' and 'sense' as the fundamental structures of historicity in the course of reflection on the problem of word and sense as it appears in divine revelation. This original perspective of transcendence, this deliberate orientation of the 'reader' towards the personal concept of an author who stands behind the great book of our world, appears again and again in the most prominent representatives of hermeneutic philosophy. Hermeneutics has a predilection for a quasi-religious language; and even when it is not theology or philosophy of religion in a straightforward sense (as in Schleiermacher, Bultmann or Eliade), it is still ruled by the tendency to treat all forms of intelligent communication according to the model of that direct dialogue which human subjectivity carries on with the Supreme Interlocutor. It goes without saying that this is and was a tendency which is anything but conducive to a fruitful dialogue with Marxism, especially since Marxism has by and large developed under the strong influence of a world-view which is diametrically opposed to all theological religious world-views, namely philosophical naturalism. Around the turn of the century, the Marxist dialectic – this philosophical theory of historicity, this ontology of sociality – was rather violently forced into a 'naturalistic costume' which did not fit at all. Historical materialism became a variety of the evolutionary metaphysics of 'matter'; Marxist critique was replaced by the formula of causal 'explanation'. Marxism began to speak a quasi-scientific language.

In this situation the two traditions simply had no access to one another. Within the theoretical field defined by the scientism of the nineteenth century, dialectics and hermeneutics were to be found at the extreme ends of the *episteme* of the period. The Marxists, oriented towards the contemporary models of scientificity, uncritically transferred the cognitive perspective of the natural sciences to the realm of history and social life. In this perspective, which was especially popular among the theoreticians of the 2nd International (Lafargue, Plekhanov, Kautsky, Bebel and Mehring), there was no place for the question concerning the specific character of the 'phenomena of signification' such as meanings and ideas, values and goals. The social world of human relations and actions remained embedded in the uniform structure of objectivity which is peculiar to 'natural' processes; the simple genetic-causal analysis became the only acceptable method for reflecting on historical and cultural phenomena. The Marxist slogan of the functional dependence of the superstructure, i.e. all forms of social consciousness, on the economic base, became, in spite of repeated objections by Marx and Engels, a handy and exhaustive schema for explanation which claims a universal applicability and validity. The Marxist dialectic of historicity was suppressed by a vulgar economism, by the mechanistic theory of the 'factors', by various forms of social Darwinism, by the inadequate determinism which trumpeted the 'unshakeable laws of history'. It is clear that this kind of Marxism, reduced to a pre-dialectical naturalism, could only view hermeneutic reflection as its own contradiction.

The hermeneutic tradition, in turn, tended to aggravate rather than weaken this antagonism. The reason is not hard to find: in the epistemic field of theory as it was formed by the naturalism of the nineteenth century, hermeneutics could find a place only as the counterpole of the accepted model of knowledge and cognitive rationality – as its antithesis, mere opposite, its negative form. In this manner, hermeneutics ended up in the orbit of a philosophical and methodological anti-naturalism even after it had undertaken to free itself from the burden of theology. The famous 'anti-naturalist breakthrough' in the philosophy of the early twentieth century, which is usually linked to Dilthey and the general direction of thought known as *Lebensphilosophie*, was actually nothing other than the search for a new place for hermeneutics, a place in addition to the accepted forms of knowledge and thus in opposition to them. The specific character of the 'phenomena of meaning' was defended by clearly distinguishing them from and opposing them to the natural forms of objectivity. Historicity was defined as non-nature, 'understanding' as the antithesis of scientific 'explanation'. But no one questioned the very conditions of validity of the traditional model of knowledge as elaborated by naturalism and positivism; no one subjected it to a fundamental philosophical analysis and critique. All that was demanded was merely a 'spatial' limitation of its scope to the domain of nature and the natural sciences such that space remained for the separate and autonomous sciences of 'spirit', culture, history and society. The problem of hermeneutics became the problem of the methodology of these new 'human sciences' (*Geisteswissenschaften*), which had to come to terms with the traditional natural sciences – and did so by opposing them. This status of the hermeneutic sciences signified in reality their integration into the theoretical field which was determined by the naturalism and scientism of the nineteenth century. In the final analysis it was a matter of establishing the 'sciences of understanding' (or, as Dilthey called them, the 'descriptive sciences') as sciences, i.e. of allowing them to participate in the presupposed division of the world and knowledge into the particular spheres of *episteme*, which were strictly separate from one another, purged of all interpenetration. At precisely this point arose the inevitable conflict with naturalistic Marxism. The claims of hermeneutics were directly aimed at the world of social-historical objectivity and thus at that region which historical materialism had always considered to be its classic field of investigation, and which in the newly developing human sciences was at all costs to be shielded from the jurisdiction of naturalistic scientism.

But this conflict was inevitable only against the background of the structure of a common theoretical field which was tacitly accepted by both sides: the epistemic field, i.e. the field within which hermeneutics and historical materialism appeared as two different – and thus in fact contradictory – forms of direct *episteme*, as two forms of 'objective' knowledge of the reality of the human world, especially with reference to the unquestioned facticity and evidence of the world of 'nature'. This theoretical structure, a product of the nineteenth century, has been subjected to radical changes in the twentieth century. The basic direction of these changes consists in the fact that philosophical thought has tended to withdraw from the immediate epistemic field of theory in order to bring forth a new field in various manners: the epistemological field. This is true above all for hermeneutics and Marxism. These two traditions, – which have developed independently, generally without even paying attention to one another – have brought about a final disintegration within the inner structure of the total *episteme* of the nineteenth century. They have dissolved this structure in similar manners: by stepping out of it and describing it in its totality from outside, i.e. by uncovering its conditions of possibility, which are not directly visible, and its limits, which cannot be seen from within; by drawing attention to the fundamental historicity of its origins and functional laws; in short, by 'criticizing' and 'interpreting' it. In so doing the two traditions have satisfied some of the concrete conditions for a mutual understanding. In freeing themselves in the same manner first from the whole network of traditional oppositions as they appear on the epistemic level – namely from the oppositions between naturalism and anti-naturalism, natural science and human science, science and philosophy, fact and value, explanation and understanding, nature and historicity – dialectics and hermeneutics confront one another for the first time within the same theoretical field, facing the same problems. They attack these problems from different sides, but in converging directions; they embody two points of departure for contemporary epistemological reflection.

In the case of Marxism, the new theoretical level and the new theoretical field were not achieved by means of a revision or modernization of the traditional Marxist problematic, but rather by means of a complete and consequent return to it, namely by the return to Marx himself, to the author of *Capital*, the *Communist Manifesto* and the *Eighteenth Brumaire*. In any case, this return to the sources is characteristic of the mainstream of Marxist philosophical research in the twentieth century, to the extent that names such as Lenin and Rosa Luxemburg, Labriola and Gramsci, Lukács and Brecht are representative.

In removing the all too tight 'naturalistic costume' of Marxist theory which originated in the period of the 2nd International, these developments gave the *dialectic* its proper place again, understanding it in a genuinely Marxist manner: as the 'revolutionary–critical' method of reflecting on the totality of social life, as the epistemology of historicity, as 'the ontology of social being' (Lukács). The materialist dialectic, which had been pressed into the non-dialectical structure of epistemic thought by the materialism of the nineteenth century and turned into the 'science of the most general laws of the movement of matter', barren in its abstractness, became once again that which it had been for Marx: the movement which recognizes the whole of the epistemic level in all of its constitutive oppositions and divisions and which thus becomes epistemological thought, a 'philosophy of praxis' (Gramsci) which is simultaneously the 'theory of theory' (Lukács).

The renaissance of a genuine Marxist dialectic of historicity has brought something to light which had remained completely invisible on the basis of the earlier naturalistic slogans, namely the presence of the hermeneutic problem at the centre of the Marxist philosophical problematic. It has turned out that historical materialism, once it is freed from its 'naturalistic costume' and its quasi-scientific style – and that means, once it is raised to its proper level of theory – is also a specific mode of hermeneutic 'reading'. It considers genuinely 'significant' phenomena to be genuine reality, i.e. social–historical objectivity and not 'natural' objectivity (the latter is, on the contrary, always merely secondary with respect to the former: 'nature', with its characteristic forms of objectivity, is a kind of social fact). In investigating these phenomena, it considers the 'meaning' to be their essential element; it sees in that consciousness which lives in its world and provides this world with its meanings not an epiphenomenon, a product or a reflection of some kind of substance (including a 'material' substance), but rather an inalienable element of the real ontological structure of the world; within this world there is no extra-historical objectivity, i.e. an objectivity which does not bear an internal reference to that subjectivity whose engagement occurs within the world itself, and by the same token no subjectivity whose locus lies outside of its own objectivations. Historical materialism is a kind of hermeneutics for the additional reason that, as a mode of activity and as a form of intellectual labour, it essentially involves an 'understanding' reflection on its object and on itself.

In 'reading' the phenomena it investigates, Marxist historical materialism makes use of a typically hermeneutic perspective of totality – an originally sense-constituting structure that provides meaning to all of its elements and their mutual relations. In addition, historical materialism constitutes this totality in its articulated mediations and thus as a complex and interwoven system of significant structures in which signs and meaning, words and things, the consciousness of the persons who experience history and their unconscious, history-laden social praxis refer to one another. Finally, neither this totality nor its mediations are something which is directly and 'objectively' given, i.e. by their very nature they cannot be subjected to an objective epistemic analysis in the traditional 'scientific' manner; it is rather a question of epistemological categories *par excellence*, i.e. of categories of an 'object' which does not exist independently from the use of these categories. Capital, commodity, social formations, class struggle, class interests, ideology – all are such epistemological objects. Historical materialism, which is constituted by the question of their objectivity, produces them by means of its own cognitive act (this is the reason why this specific act of knowledge is simultaneously 'directly practical'). Such objects can only be 'seen' from this cognitive point of view. The question is not neutral with respect to its objects; on the contrary, it determines their own objectivity and is the source of their significance. But for precisely this reason, the question itself is a sense-constituting intentional movement, a project within the realm of significance it constitutes, a project in which the questioner takes a step beyond his own historicity and simultaneously reveals it. To this extent historical materialism is not merely a *theory of history*, but also a *self-knowledge of the historicity* of its own thought and action. Moreover, the validity of the theory is in this case inseparable from the adequacy of the self-knowledge, the correctness of the interpretation cannot be separated from the discernment of the critique and self-critique. Thus, Marxism as dialectical philosophy of historicity is involved in the same 'hermeneutic circle' as all other attempts at an understanding reading of our world. The difference is perhaps that it, in contrast to the majority of the others, sees the possible ways out of this entanglement, for it sees them in the conscious stepping beyond the magic circle of interpretation and in the reference to the real historicity of human action, to material praxis which not only 'reads' the significance of the world but also creates and changes it.

One point must be emphasized: in order to reach the epistemological level of theory, Marxism did not need some new inspiration from outside. It merely had to put an end to the long forgetfulness of its own sources, reject the naturalistic self-mystification, this 'false consciousness' of itself which it took on in the context of the culture of the nineteenth century, and rediscover the original intention of the Marxist revolutionary-critical dialectic. The hermeneutic tradition, on the other hand, had to take a longer and more tortuous road in developing the contemporary form of its theoretical field.

To begin with, Freud and Freudianism have made a substantial contribution here. Psychoanalysis has not merely enriched traditional hermeneutics with new techniques of understanding interpretation by opening up and investigating new regions of significant reality, it not merely contributed to the more exact investigation of the nature of symbols and symbolic relations, but also, and perhaps for the first time with this degree of clarity, perceived the need for a new ontology of the hermeneutic problem. It was precisely in the work of Freud and his followers that the logos of pure meaning at long last forfeited its immanence; at this point the problem of sense was removed from the quiet circle of self-transparent consciousness. For analysis, reading sense always means pushing the sense beyond this circle, thereby breaking through the closed 'noosphere' of the contents of consciousness to reveal its 'other side'; it means uncovering the unconscious – the pre-reflexive, truly existential foundation of all consciousness, the region of a complete inconsistency and contingency, the absolute limits of any and every discourse. Freud thus gave hermeneutics a new direction: towards the *sources* of significance, towards the understanding of understanding. In continually oscillating between the two extremes of human discourse – the significant openness of the word and the silence of Being – psychoanalytical reflection sketched for hermeneutics the first outlines of a new field of thought in which the hermeneutic problem appears as the question of the 'archaeology of sense': as the question of the original level of pre-semantical presuppositions of all significance, of the originary character of a truth which is prior to all consciousness and is always 'signified' by consciousness itself and thus 'uncovered'. Of course, one can actually attribute to psychoanalysis only the constant search for this truth and not its actual discovery. Psychoanalysis searched for it first in the impulsive sphere of the purely biological instincts of the 'It (or Id)'; later, in Jung and in the philosophy of culture of the late Freud, it searches for it in the archetypical structures of a collective imagination and a collective memory. Fromm and the culturalists specified these questions and shifted them to the field of the primal form of sociality by interpreting the symbolism of significant reality as the 'forgotten language' of reciprocal human relations and interaction. But only with the work of the Frankfurt School – with Adorno, Habermas and to some extent Marcuse – was the psychoanalytical tradition and Freud's earlier radicality revived, this time, however, with direct reference to the historical (i.e. social, economic and political) presuppositions of sense and 'non-sense'. Interpretation once again became above all a critique; word and meaning were discovered to be instruments and simultaneously objects in a battle between the real socio-political forces. As in Freud, the hermeneutics of truth is complemented by a hermeneutic of falsehood and violence. The problem of 'understanding' was in the final analysis identified with the problem of the impossibility of understanding, with the dramatic discovery that the means of human communication in the contemporary world are at the same time (and perhaps above all) tools of social and class repression.

Secondly, contemporary research into language and communication provided the hermeneutic tradition with new material. Of special importance was the development of so-called structural linguistics, which originated in the work of de Saussure and the Prague Circle. Structural linguistics has produced a long series of highly interesting theoretical innovations in the last twenty years, whose significance extends far beyond the realm of linguistics in the narrow sense, aiming rather at laying the foundations for a general philosophical theory of signs and meaning. I am thinking above all of the lines of research represented by Roland Barthes and Umberto Eco, who call their work 'semiology' in contrast to Anglo-Saxon 'semiotics', which was developed in a positivist spirit. Semiotics, which deals above all with formal logical problems of meaning and has a special interest in the logical semantics of various languages, can be viewed as an immediate epistemic form of the theory of signs. Sign, meaning and language are taken as something given in semiotics, an isolated facticity which need only be described and analysed formally. The semiological direction shifts these problems into a completely different theoretical field in the attempt to produce an epistemology of the sign. Meaning is understood above all as the constitutive form of discourse and communication, and thus as an original mode of existence of every cultural reality. From this point of view the strictly semantic problematic loses its autonomy and becomes in a sense the 'sign' of a more encompassing whole in which it is always involved, it becomes a moment in a relation which always transcends it. Here too the question is directed not at meaning itself but rather at the 'meaning of meaning'. Semiology searches for comprehensive structures in which all meaning is constituted. It is a reflection on the structural conditions of possible significance. It discovers that these conditions are congruent with the original conditions of socialization. The purely social nature of language and communication is revealed here for the first time. The 'sociology' of the sign is no longer secondary to its formal 'semantics', something which is added to the latter from outside, but is identical with it. 'Meaning' does not exist outside of this thoroughly social, subjective-objective relation between 'meaning' (*Meinung*) and 'meant' (*Gemeinten*), just as the content of individual speech – *parole* – is the mere realization of the social rules of the language – *langue*. Neither the first nor the second moment can be legitimately made into an autonomous theoretical object. Semiological analysis always finds both of them simultaneously in the unity of their common structure and, at the same time, in extreme opposition: it is a theory of the *totality* which is constituted in such an opposition. This totality can be called 'culture' or 'socialization'. But it is no longer a matter of culture in opposition to nature as was the case in Dilthey's human sciences; it is not a matter of this pure historical world of subjective significance and values, separate from the objectively given world of nature and its external objectivity. The new theoretical reality which semiology discovers and investigates is rather the fundamental realm of a meaningful historicity, in which the distinctions between 'object' and 'subject', externality and internality, history and nature – always within their proper limits – first take shape.

But as significant as these impulses from psychoanalysis and semiology may have been for contemporary hermeneutics, the decisive role in the transformation of the traditional theoretical realm in which the whole problematic of Dilthey's 'understanding' moved was played by Husserl and the phenomenological movement. This describes perhaps best of all the complete philosophical autonomy of the hermeneutics of the twentieth century; it is – as Ricoeur has correctly noted – a 'hermeneutics which is grafted onto a phenomenological tree'. It must be added, however, that this is not an unnatural graft; phenomenology shifts the problem of sense and understanding from the very beginning into the centre of attention, although from a new theoretical perspective. It was Husserl who in his critique of psychologism and a Diltheyian historism led the hermeneutic problematic out of the epistemic field of theory once and for all. Husserl is the first to make these problems the object of a 'transcendental' reflection – a reflection which reproduces the original, pre-epistemic level of understanding experience in which all secondary, factual forms of our subjective-objective *episteme* find their sources and their theoretical foundations. Only at this point does hermeneutics cease to be the 'logic' or 'methodology' of a certain kind of knowledge, namely of the human sciences, which must defend their autonomy over against the natural sciences; only at this point did it abandon its 'anti-naturalist' self-understanding, a self-understanding which was itself a result of naturalism. In the new, epistemological domain of theory which is opened up by the transcendental reduction, hermeneutics is simply identical with philosophy in general, with the understanding description of the primordial sources and necessary structures of all cognition and all 'known' objectivity. This original understanding not merely precedes, problematizes and renders comprehensible everyday consciousness but also the sciences themselves – namely science in general, the 'human sciences' as well as the 'natural sciences', science as a comprehensive type of *episteme*, as a specific kind of theoretical attitude which is intimately bound up with the corresponding structure of its objectivity. All scientific knowledge is included in the phenomenological *epoché*, along with the natural attitude; the field for hermeneutic investigation begins on the far side of these boundaries. To this extent, Husserl's question as to the 'sense' lies *beyond* the whole opposition between naturalism and anti-naturalism, natural science and human science, explanation and understanding. It thematizes this opposition, the indispensable structural conditions for the internal organization of the entire epistemic level of knowledge. This is the essence of the Husserlian attempt to 'ground' science philosophically, to investigate its foundations. This is a hermeneutic undertaking *par excellence*.

Phenomenology not only gave hermeneutics this new cognitive status by defining its transcendental position with reference to science and everyday consciousness. Something more important took place here: Husserl also noted and pointed out the original significance of the ontological function of hermeneutics. It was above all Husserl who brought contemporary thought to accept a fact which every genuine philosophy today must recognize: every question concerning 'being' is a question concerning the understanding of 'being'. This is thus a perspective from which the problem of objectivity cannot even be formulated without reference to the transcendental acts of consciousness which provide every object with its particular 'objective sense'; on the other hand, it is a perspective from which consciousness itself is always a 'consciousness of something' – and thus in turn only appears in a structural intertwining with the 'understood' object. Questions concerning meaning and understanding thus appear precisely at the point at which phenomenological reflection concerning 'being' and 'consciousness' have their foundation: for Husserl hermeneutics is the central point for both the entire problematic of 'constitution' and for the theory of 'intentionality'. The hermeneutic perspective is responsible for the fact that the significance of the two important concepts of classical metaphysics – being and consciousness – are here subject to a radical transformation. But this also signifies a transformation of their position within the whole of the philosophical problematic. If being is always understood as being, i.e. if it is always referred to the subjectivity which experiences it, and if consciousness always signifies *understanding a being*, i.e. an intentional movement which aims at something other than consciousness itself, then hermeneutics becomes 'fundamental ontology'. The entire traditional, 'ontic' opposition between being and consciousness, an opposition which is equally typical for the old metaphysics and for the new anti-metaphysics of the positivists and naturalists, is overcome and replaced by the hermeneutic concept of sense which on this basis becomes a genuinely ontological concept.

Thus, phenomenological ontology is an ontology of sense. This is the reason why Husserl's philosophical undertaking turns out to be so significant for contemporary hermeneutics. But the decisive step in this direction of 'grafting the hermeneutic flower onto the phenomenological tree' is ascribed to Heidegger – and that not without reason. One can at most say that in the classical Husserlian texts these problems are present at the immediate operational level of the 'labour of thought', but not that they contain a fully elaborated theoretical framework. What we find here is more a hermeneutics in practice than a hermeneutic philosophy. Husserl's late texts from the 1930s, which concentrate on the problems of the crisis of the European Sciences, contain attempts at consciously elaborating the conceptual foundations of a new hermeneutic ontology. These attempts concentrate on the concept of historicity as the highest ontological category; the perspective of phenomenology as a transcendental philosophy of culture, as it appears in these texts, is oriented in terms of this category. By rooting all sense and all understanding in the original, pre-reflexive stratum of the life-world – and thus in the historical and social realm of action and word, language and labour, needs and meanings, where 'objectivity' is always a world which is already experienced by conscious subjects and the consciousness of these subjects is given in a *cogito* which is always already objectively embodied – the late Husserl himself discovered this new philosophical perspective, which is in principle contained in his earlier work (the discovery of this perspective is incorrectly attributed to his followers alone).

Contemporary hermeneutics did of course attain its mature form in Heidegger's thought. It was the author of *Being and Time* who uncovered the novel presence of the hermeneutic problem in the new intellectual dimension which phenomenological philosophy had developed. One can say – again citing Ricoeur – that in Heidegger's work the hermeneutic problems openly and directly became ontological problems, and vice versa. 'Understanding' is understood as the unsurpassable horizon and simultaneously as the fundamental structure of the being of human *Dasein*. On the other hand, being turns out in the final resort to be identical with the movement of the meaningful 'revealing' (*Enthüllung*) of truth, with the 'presence' (*Anwesen*) of an original sense. The word, the *logos* and the *hermeneia*, is not merely a sign in this new ontology, an indifferent medium, a neutral instrument by means of which we can come into contact with an extra-linguistic reality. It is rather the fundamental structure of being: the place in which the 'openness of being' reveals itself immediately and at the same time the only form in which this revealing takes place. Thus, the word is the bearer of the historicity of being; the hermeneutic time of the 'speaking' and 'spoken' subjectivity is the dimension of the word and determines its fundamental ontological characteristic: finitude. These three themes are central for Heidegger's philosophy of historicity. This philosophy is, first, a philosophy of language: if one takes language in its ontological character as origin, it loses the apparent transparency which it would receive as a purely conventional medium; it is, as it were, robbed of its ontological innocence. Language itself becomes a problem for the philosopher who speaks; thus the well-known peculiarities of this discourse in which one attempts through speech to reach the origins and limits of speech. This is the reason why Heidegger so persistently works on the words, as if he wanted to overcome their resistance and penetrate to the secret elementary stratum of a primordial sense. At this point the historicity of meaning becomes the genealogy of reality itself. Philosophy is the art of reading the roots of the words, the art of discovering the truth anew as it once revealed itself in the linguistic archetypes. But, second, this is the reason why such a philosophy must actively place itself at the disposal of this 'history', becoming a co-creator of history by means of an 'axiogenic' intention, a dialogue with it – in short, a word in time and through time. Temporality is here the peculiar dimension of meanings and simultaneously the unsurpassable form of its understanding. It determines the structure of 'being-in-the-world' – the fundamental mode of existence of historical subjectivity, the sole absolute existential definition of that which constitutes precisely its non-absoluteness. Thus, such a philosophy is, third, a philosophy of the ontological finitude of all historical being, i.e. of the entire subjective-objective modality of 'being-in-the-world'. By leading the way to an ontology, hermeneutics uncovers the absolute limit of all 'understanding'. It discovers that sense is always at the mercy of the pure facticity of events and that the 'openness of being' is nothing more than a narrow 'clearing' of word and understanding which illuminates the dark shadows of the silent opacity.

It would be hard to overestimate the extent of Heidegger's influence on contemporary hermeneutics. Various elements of his thought can be found in the most prominent contemporary representatives of this tradition: in Ricoeur and Gadamer. Both – although each in his own manner – continue Heidegger's fundamental philosophical perspective, according to which hermeneutics is the fundamental ontology of historicity. Both centre this new hermeneutic ontology around the same central themes: word, time and finitude as the three basic existential determinations of every discourse and all historical being. To be sure, their road – to quote Ricoeur once again – is 'the longer road'; they do not try to realize the ontological significance of hermeneutics 'directly', as did Heidegger, who pursued it solely in the immanence of philosophical discourse, but rather circuitously and, as it were, in stages, in the course of a detailed, almost 'empirical' survey of the whole complexity and fullness of meaningful concretion. Here hermeneutic reflection is much more modest in the plotting out of great intellectual projects, but it discovers in this problematic a greater multiplicity of forms and investigates each of them with more patience. Both, Ricoeur and Gadamer, are thoroughly familiar with the various levels of meaningful reality and the many types of understanding experience. The field of hermeneutic problems is once again very broad: it extends from detailed practical-methodological questions of the 'art of interpretation', through a theory of signs and symbols, the problems of cultural expression and communication, the philosophy of language, the analysis of human interaction in society and culture, the description and theory of the realm of ethical, aesthetic and religious values, to the general philosophy and epistemology of the historicity of human being.

As an investigation of consciousness and its intentional acts (perception, feeling, imagination, the symbolic creations of a collective unconscious) hermeneutics comes into close contact with psychological and socio-psychological experience: here hermeneutics is primarily a descriptive analysis of the conscious experiences of the subject and of the various forms of its intentional 'expression' in the intersubjective world of cultural communication. This is precisely what primarily interests Ricoeur. The author of *Finitude et culpabilité* puts great emphasis on the expressive functions of the forms of meaning. He is concerned with meaningful forms, above all as symbolic articulations of specific attitudes, strivings and values which are concealed behind them (and which are first revealed by hermeneutic analysis); hermeneutics 'explains' these forms of meaning and with their help 'reads' the text which has always already begun and never comes to an end, which is coded in word, image and concept, in myth and ritual, in the social prestige of tradition and the moral certainty of an individual conscience, in the public claim to scientific truth and in the intimacy of religious experience. One can diminish a more 'theoretical' hermeneutics of structure from this 'interpretive' hermeneutics of expression, the theoretical interest coming perhaps more clearly to expression in Gadamer. The primary theme here is above all the genuine 'substance' of the phenomena of meaning, the form and structure of objectivity proper to them, with attention concentrated on language as the source and unrestricted measure of all sense. Here hermeneutic reflection is more of a theory of the word and meaning than a direct 'reading' of specific contents; it has a stronger contact to linguistics, semiology or to the theory of communication than to psychology or semantics. It investigates various 'languages' as comprehensive systems of signs rather than individual 'utterances'. It takes up the more general theoretical problems of the methodology and epistemology of hermeneutic knowledge. But these differences are not of the essence. Both authors pursue an open reflection, and in their research they are often very close to one another, in posing similar questions and offering converging answers. This convergence is easy to account for, since both authors move in the same basic region of theoretical reality and in the same intellectual perspective. Both take the problematic of sense and understanding to be located in the new epistemological field of theory, in which hermeneutics lays claim to the universal dignity of a philosophy of historicity. Heidegger's reflections pursued above all the elaboration of this new theoretical region as a whole. But it was Husserl who first plotted out its boundaries. To this extent, contemporary hermeneutics as a whole is a post-Husserlian movement: it not merely takes the 'longer road' to a phenomenological ontology of sense but also accepts this ontology as its most important philosophical presupposition – a presupposition which it continually develops and concretizes, but only to return to it from the other side.

This fact also explains another convergence, the convergence between the hermeneutic direction of contemporary post-phenomenological thought and its existential versions. In closing, I would like to say a few words about the latter. I am thinking above all of the philosophy of Sartre and Merleau-Ponty. With respect to these authors, it seems to me that it is long since time to drop the misleading, though widely accepted, label 'existentialism' and to read their works in a manner which is appropriate to their titles and contents, i.e. as texts which move in the field of phenomenology and, more precisely, phenomenological ontology, psychology and epistemology. *Being and Nothingness*, *The Phenomenology of Perception*, *The Structure of Behavior* and even *The Critique of Dialectical Reason* are above all works which continue the authentic Husserlian problematic, and they can only be understood against this background. This, and not the 'existential' problematic, is the source of their fundamental convergence with Heidegger's thought. But just for that reason it is not surprising when their basic cognitive perspective comes so close to that of hermeneutic philosophy. Here too, ontology passes directly over into hermeneutics, and philosophical reflection is above all a theory of sense-constituting historicity. In retaining the initial phenomenological perspective of 'understanding' as the fundamental mode of being of all historical existence, Sartre and Merleau-Ponty attempt to describe this 'being' in its general structure, and that means also in its particular forms and concrete mediations. The meaningful and meaning-constituting historicity of the subject which experiences the world of objectivity is located here at the original ontological level of intersubjectivity – where the *cogito* cannot be separated from its bodily and material articulation, where the logos of all meaning arises out of a pre-linguistic and pre-predicative praxis, where the consciousness of the subjects is essentially engaged in the structures and mechanisms of their social interaction.

One can, of course, wonder about the degree to which Sartre's and Merleau-Ponty's thought can be integrated into the hermeneutic streams of contemporary philosophy. I have merely attempted to demonstrate the basic convergence of these two lines of thought – a convergence which doubtlessly has its origin in the common Husserlian background and in the search for a new ontology of historicity which Husserl initiated. If we include Sartre and Merleau-Ponty in the panorama of contemporary hermeneutic philosophy as continuations of phenomenological ontology, this is especially instructive with regard to our central question, the question as to the relation between the hermeneutic tradition and Marxism, the question concerning the prospects for a theoretical confrontation between them. In the work of these two philosophers, more than anywhere else, we find the possibility and the need for such a confrontation, and the first presuppositions for its realization are already satisfied. Sartre and Merleau-Ponty (regardless of their differences) have produced the most far-reaching attempts to date at formulating the hermeneutic problem in such a manner that, losing nothing of the philosophical universalism of the Husserlian perspective, it is shifted into the immediate vicinity of the traditional Marxist problematic. In these authors we find the historicity of Husserl, Heidegger and the post-Heideggerian hermeneutics most intimately linked to the typically Marxist dimension of material concreteness, which is determined by such seemingly not very hermeneutic modes of existence as needs, labour and struggle. In their work the problem of sense is transformed into the problem of a sense-constituting praxis of the historical 'subject–object', a praxis which articulates meaning in the resistant substance of 'non-sense': the freedom of acts and the contingency of events, sheer violence or a violence which clothes itself in the costume of ideological mystifications. Finally, here the word and every significant expression is understood as an ontological modality of social being, and hermeneutics becomes a dialectic which encompasses the totality of being and all of its subjective-objective mediations.

Thus, Sartre's and Merleau-Ponty's phenomenology of historicity amounts to a concrete proposal for the 'translation' of the hermeneutic problematic into the language of Marxist philosophy. This is of course not to say that we find a fully satisfactory translation here, or that this proposal is the only one possible. But one can surely hope that the tendency which is at work in this attempt will be taken up and developed in the theoretical reality of contemporary philosophy. Contemporary hermeneutics is more and more aware of the need for a confrontation with Marxism and increasingly seeks it. It may well be that the inner logic of the hermeneutic problem itself – especially when this problem is shifted into the post-Husserlian and thus epistemological field of theory – leads inevitably in one way or the other to an encounter with the Marxist dialectic, i.e. with the second great epistemology of our time.

This inner need for a dialogue with Marxism is thus obvious – and not merely in the case of Merleau-Ponty and Sartre, and of a group of younger philosophers influenced by them, who are the clear links between the first two and post-Heideggerian hermeneutics (e.g. François Chatelet or Kostas Axelos). One sees this need at work in thinkers who are more directly and unambiguously to be included in the hermeneutic movement. This is, for example, the case with hermeneuticians of the post-Freudian movement (with Fromm and Marcuse, and even more so with the 'Frankfurt School': Adorno, Horkheimer and Habermas), where we can observe a process in which the differences between psychoanalytical 'interpretation' and Marxist critique of the ideological deformations of consciousness slowly disappear and the entire problem of communication is shifted to the level of a 'critical theory of society' (Habermas). One can also observe this need in the case of the 'philosophers of sense', representatives of structuralism and semiology who – like Barthes or Eco – tie the formal analysis of signs and their various systems to the historical-ideological analysis of the social and political functions of this 'sense'. (This is the essence of Barthes's demythologizing 'structural activity', which is so similar to the Marxist critique of the fetishism of commodities or to the 'German Ideology', especially when it serves the analysis of the concrete 'myths' of contemporary bourgeois society.) Finally, we can observe the openness to an encounter with Marx in the most prominent representatives of contemporary hermeneutics. Ricoeur has devoted his research more and more to the realm of social-historical praxis, to the *par excellence* dialectical relation between language and labour, to the hermeneutics of social interactions, including their productive, technological and political varieties. Among the various 'dimensions of historical consciousness', Gadamer recognizes one which is determined by the history-making activities of larger groups of human beings, of social classes, and by the interplay of class conflict and class interests, and his logic of historical knowledge often draws upon the dialectics of Marx, Lenin, Lukács and Gramsci. It goes without saying that this never amounts to a complete agreement with the Marxist perspective, not even with respect to the historicity of the macro-structures of social life and culture. Here too (and above all in Ricoeur and Gadamer) the hermeneutic tradition remains true to its theological origin and its basic ethical-religious intentions. Thus, in the final analysis there always remains a residuum of 'ultimate matters' about which hermeneutics is silent and where it contents itself with attentively listening to the well-known Word. Marxism knows nothing of the sound of this inner voice of a religious transcendence, but it does not refuse anyone the right to listen to it. But with respect to all that is capable of being given expression, which is audible and available in the public space of discourse, the voices of hermeneutics and Marxism, which up to now have all too often talked past one another, can and should carry on a genuine dialogue.

It is not an exaggeration to summarize this by saying that hermeneutics is necessarily referred to a confrontation with Marxism. Is Marxism with equal necessity referred to such a confrontation? To put it bluntly: more than to anything else. Genuinely Marxist dialectical thought currently finds its most serious philosophical partner in hermeneutics – especially in that hermeneutics which derives from Husserl and phenomenology. The hermeneutic tradition seems to have begun to appreciate this state of affairs and thus, at least for the time being, to have realized what it might learn from dialectical materialism. It is time for Marxists to become equally aware of the possibilities for a fruitful dialogue with hermeneutics. I do not intend to offer a complete survey of these possibilities, but I would like to point out at least the most important of them.

Marxism needs hermeneutics, i.e. it can and should learn something of great philosophical importance from it, something that could broaden its traditional philosophical horizon. This is the case in at least three areas of problems, which correspond to three different levels of theoretical thought. The first concerns the immediately epistemic level of method and methodology in the knowledge of social-historical reality. The decisive point lies in the conscious and comprehensive utilization of hermeneutic techniques of 'reading' and 'understanding description' in the investigation of all kinds of phenomena of social life and culture. To repeat: historical materialism always was a genuine application of these techniques – it was 'critique' and 'interpretation'; from this point of view the classical Marxist literature can be taken as a storehouse of model cases for a hermeneutics of various phenomena. But Marxism did not always have a sufficiently well-developed theoretical and methodological awareness of the techniques which it itself applied. In addition, it all too often restricted their application to the identification of macro-structural regularities and thus unnecessarily renounced the fruitful possibilities which these techniques offer for the investigation of superstructure phenomena, of forms of social consciousness, of cultural phenomena in the broad sense. The investigations of Gramsci and Lukács, the experience of the new aesthetics of Brecht, Piscator or the Soviet avant-garde of the 1920s, many attempts of the Frankfurt School (e.g. the works of Walter Benjamin or Adorno's *Philosophy of New Music*) and, finally, the attempts of Goldmann and his school with their Marxist studies of literature, all demonstrate the degree to which such a genuinely Marxist 'hermeneutics of culture' can open up new perspectives.

Secondly, Marxism has fruitful points of contact with hermeneutics on the epistemological level, i.e. on the genuine level of its philosophical theory. Here it is important that the 'hermeneutic nucleus' which was always an element of the genuinely Marxist dialectic – this ontology of historicity, this philosophical theory of social being – be brought to light. The hermeneutic tradition – at least at those points at which its quasi-theological style can easily be reduced to a minimum – is today capable of pointing out to Marxism some fundamental problems of this new ontology, problems which in existing historical materialism either remained unrecognized or were not elaborated. As an example I would like to mention only the central problem of language – above all with respect to its 'ontological' functions, which delimit the absolute horizon for every historical intersubjectivity and in this manner lays the very foundation for 'social being', probably to the same extent as does material production. Marxist reflection on language, meaning and communication to date has stood almost without exception under the methodological or logical-semantical perspective which was taken over from positivism. The elaboration of the foundations of a genuinely Marxist dialectical philosophy of language is one of the most urgent tasks for the future – and here one can learn a great deal from post-Husserlian hermeneutics. Another example: philosophical questions concerning science, concerning an appropriate model for its cognitive rationality, its socio-cultural sources, functions and boundaries – in short, concerning the historicity of the theoretical and practical reality which is built up by science. And again: Marxist reflections on these questions to date have been almost exclusively monopolized by positivist thought. One often hears the slogan of a Marxist 'methodology of science' or of a 'science of science', but even when such a reflection opposes positivism, it continues to move within the theoretical field opened up by positivism – a field in which the philosophical problem of the sciences always takes on an immediately epistemic form. To this extent Marxism still lacks a genuine philosophy of this special social and historical phenomenon constituted by the modern sciences; it still lacks the corresponding critique (in the Marxist sense of the word) and a corresponding dialectical theory. Here too, a confrontation with the questions of contemporary hermeneutics, which has long since begun to explore these problems, can prove to be extremely fruitful for Marxism.

Thirdly, this dialogue is also of such central importance for Marxism because it concerns its own philosophical identity, its self-knowledge. The hermeneutic tradition is a serious and demanding partner. It goes without saying that a discussion with it is harder to lead than a discussion with philosophically insignificant opponents, e.g. with traditional Neo-positivism, Neo-Thomism or so-called existentialism. But only a serious discussion of this kind can stimulate authentically Marxist thought and reanimate its best tradition. It is just not true that the truly dialectical tradition has always been alive in Marxism; quite the contrary, history shows that it all too often has sunk into dogmatic self-forgetfulness. The dialogue with hermeneutics promotes most especially that which is most important in the struggle against this self-forgetfulness: Marxism's memory of its own sources, its own historicity, its own errors. Perhaps more than any other philosophy, contemporary hermeneutics directs the Marxist's attention – if only indirectly, via critique and calls for clear positions – to the point at which the real problematic of Marxist philosophy lies, to the level on which its theoretical thought moves, to the nature of the theoretical and practical reality it investigates. This is no small thing, especially when one considers that not all contemporary Marxists are clearly aware of this identity of their philosophizing, and there is no agreement among them as to what Marxist philosophy is and what it is not. It is clear that these answers will not come from hermeneutics; these are questions for which Marxists themselves must find the answers in the course of a fundamental critical and self-critical reflection, an 'auto-hermeneutics' of historical materialism and dialectics. The dialogue with hermeneutics is so useful because it continually provokes this reflection. A good dialogue partner is one who has something interesting to say to us; but a partner who continually forces us to think about what we are really saying and thinking is even better.

CHAPTER 3

The problem of teleology and corporeality in phenomenology and Marxism

Ludwig Landgrebe (Cologne)

This chapter bears a double title, and this requires a word of explanation. It is not a matter of two separate problems which can be discussed one after the other. On the contrary, it is not possible even to approach the problem of teleology in an adequate manner if the approach is not based on an analysis of corporeality, i.e. of man as a corporeal being. The thesis which is to be elaborated and defended here is that this intimate connection between the two problems exists both in phenomenology and in Marxism, and opens up the possibility of a fruitful dialogue. 'Phenomenology' and 'Marxism' are global titles and we must therefore sketch the sense in which they are to be understood here.

The phenomenology in which this intimate connection of the two problems becomes visible is Husserl's phenomenology, especially that of Husserl's late work *The Crisis of the European Sciences*, along with the reflections, especially from the 1930s, which belong in this context. Husserl's reflections on the problem of teleology are to be found above all here. The problem of corporeality is to be found already in the second volume of his *Ideas*, in the third chapter of part two, 'The Constitution of Psychic Reality Through the Body', and in the third volume of the *Ideas* (especially Beilage I), in the *Analyses of Passive Synthesis*, the *Lectures on Phenomenological Psychology* and the final portions of the third volume of the *Phenomenology of Intersubjectivity*. These references serve merely the function of orientation and do not mean that we are concerned with Husserl's interpretation. Husserl did not leave behind a finished systematic 'theory'. The great influence of his phenomenology is based on precisely this unfinished character: in his analyses Husserl posed many more problems and questions than he himself was able to investigate systematically.

Between what appears to be a systematic commitment to a specific position in his earlier writings and the investigations of his late work lies a long development whose results called for a revision of many of his basic concepts, a revision he was only partially able to carry out. He thus confronts us with the task of continuing his work where he left off and working out on this basis the systematic connections between his various lines of thought, connections he was often only able to hint at. This is especially true for the context of the problems of teleology and corporeality. Here too, we cannot simply refer to Husserl's texts; what is required is a *reconstruction*. Reconstruction does not mean construction in the sense of free invention. It must rather be oriented in terms of the *aporias* which his analyses produce and which he to some extent explicitly recognized as such. There is hardly a single objection to Husserl's work which one cannot find Husserl raising against himself. Some hints concerning the direction which such a reconstruction must take can be found in my essays 'The Phenomenology of Corporeality and the Problem of Matter' and 'The Philosophical Problem of the End of History' (in *Phenomenology and History*).

A similar initial orientation is required with regard to Marxism. Here too we must go back to the point at which the relations between the two problems of teleology and corporeality become visible in a manner which allows us to see how they relate to phenomenological questions and analyses. For this task the early texts of Karl Marx himself are decisive. We shall be concerned above all with the early writings up to the *Communist Manifesto* and the *Critique of Political Economy* of 1857, the preparatory work for *Capital*. Here Marx worked out the methodological principles and terminology which were decisive not only for his entire subsequent work, but also for the entire subsequent development of Marxism. The theoretical and, above all, practical political dispute between the various schools of Western and Eastern Marxism turns on the question of the correct understanding and correct application of these tools which Marx forged. Many of his own formulations, which for him had a rather experimental or polemical meaning, have been turned into fixed stereotypes. Here, as in our discussion of Husserl, we shall not be concerned with Marx-interpretation. All of the questions which concern Marx-interpretation, whether he repudiated the humanistic programme of his youth (as Althusser would have it), whether his ideas were vulgarized by Engels – all of these theses, for which there are as many arguments for as against, will be put aside here.

Marx did not set out to develop a philosophical theory of society, although the entire modern theory of society is inconceivable without his work, and elements of such a theory can certainly be found in his analyses. But he himself viewed his analyses as a tool for understanding the historical situation of his age and for working out answers to the question what could and must be done in this situation. The important thing here is that we be clear about the problems of modern society which he was the first to see, and which have remained the same unsolved problems in spite of all historical change, both for the Western world as well as for the parts of the world in which Marxism has become the official doctrine. Only because they have remained fundamentally the same problems was it possible that Husserl, working from a very different perspective, could be led to them; only against this background is it possible to bring the phenomenological approach in dialogue with the Marxist approach.

In formulating these problems, Marx was dependent on the terminology which had been developed in the tradition of modern philosophy. He could not have even formulated his problems in a comprehensible manner without this language; it offered him alternatives which have the appearance of being absolute, which cannot themselves be put into question, such that specific lines of inquiry and questioning are, as it were, prescribed. Examples would be 'spirit' and 'matter', 'idealism' and 'materialism', 'subject' and 'object' along with their derivatives, to mention only a few of the most important. Thus, in trying to understand Marx's theses we must be aware of the fact that his formulations may well obscure that which he saw rather than exposing it, since it cannot be expressed in these alternatives. This is an important maxim, important not only with respect to Marx but also to Husserl. His terminology too is still that of the classical tradition of philosophy. He too attempts to analyse states of affairs which spring from the alternatives suggested by this terminology. This is true both for the analysis of corporeality and for the analysis of teleology. The meaning of Husserl's technical terminology changes in the course of his investigations, but in such a manner that he was often unaware of this change, such that he was often trapped by his own terminology. Heidegger attempted to avoid this danger by shaping a new terminology in *Being and Time*. But in doing so he put us in the uncomfortable position of having to translate his insights into our familiar and traditional language. Thus, no matter how familiar and trustworthy the terminology may appear to be, we must be very careful not to mistake the preliminary meaning of a name for the intended states of affairs themselves. This holds for Marx as well as Husserl. Only in this manner can we understand the limited, though within this limitation legitimate, justification of calling the Marxist investigations 'materialist', and the extent to which one can say, for example, 'history is the genuine natural history of man'. This presupposes an adequate explication of the concepts of nature and matter, which is possible only in terms of an analysis of corporeality. And only against the background of this analysis of corporeality can we understand the sense in which we can speak of teleology.

The following section offers, in the form of theses, a sketch of the questions which are to be discussed. In view of the preparatory function of these themes, they will be explicated in a very elementary descriptive manner which takes off from states of affairs which are quite familiar and self-evident prior to all philosophical reflection, states of affairs that may well appear banal.

1 Introduction

(a) We shall not discuss the *problem of teleology* and the possibility of forming teleological concepts as a general problem, but only to the extent that we can speak of a *teleology of history* as that process in which we are unavoidably always already involved – unavoidably not only in the sense that we are always already affected by it, but also in the sense that we are also forced to engage ourselves actively in this process. In this context we normally make the distinction between nature and history. The quotation from Marx above shows that he puts this distinction in question, and in Husserl's work too history is finally understood such that it includes the process of nature. What that might mean we shall see later. One normally understands 'nature' and natural processes as a causal nexus in which events occur in accordance with their own laws, whereas history is understood as that process which takes place by means of human activity (*res gestae*).

The question whether this human efficacy is teleological is not a peculiarly philosophical question. It is a question which men have always had to ask because they are themselves active in the process of history, and all being-active presupposes the idea of a goal of this activity. Man lives in the world in accordance with the notions he has concerning that which his action can bring about and what the means of this action are, and what he can hope and expect from this action. This is not only true of individual actions but for this process as a whole when man is threatened by crisis: 'Where will it all end, what can I expect from it and how, in the light of this, can I act in a *meaningful* manner?' 'Meaningful' here means: taking account of that which is to be expected. Thus, in terms of its origin, action is never a mere causal efficacy; it is teleological to the extent that it is guided by the projection of a goal towards which the process is oriented. What we call the meaning of the process is determined with regard to its goal or purpose. The question of the meaning of the historical process is not, as Karl Löwith tried to show (in *Weltgeschichte und Heilsgeschehen*), a question which makes sense only against the background of Jewish-Christian eschatological faith and thus ceases to make sense when this tradition falters. It is, as Kant says, 'in a marvellous manner bound up with general human reason' (in the essay 'The End of All Things'). As we have already mentioned, for Marx it was the experience of a radical historical crisis which forced him to pose the question concerning the meaning of this process in order to then answer the question what is to be done. His point of departure was that history must be understood to be teleologically directed towards the realization of a meaning if our being-active is to find its proper direction. But this goal-directedness should not be philosophically or religiously explained by means of the assumption of a higher power which determines the goal. On the basis of the analysis of concrete historical events it could be understood as their tendency. Marx sketches his programme as early as September 1843 in a letter to Ruge: 'Reason has always existed, but not always in reasonable form. The critic can thus take up every form of theoretical and practical consciousness and develop the true reality out of the *inherent* forms of existing reality as its ought and goal.' This is a statement which Husserl could have made. For Husserl too the goal of human development is the realization of reason – whereby this word cannot be understood in the strict sense of the rationalist tradition – a path along which the development first comes to itself in an 'intentional' striving which becomes clear about itself and its goal only in the course of its own development. The most elementary form of this process is an obscure striving which is not clearly aware of its own goal. Husserl speaks of a 'primal striving' (*Urstreben*) which guides the most elementary forms of being-active. In view of this kinship, the attempt to bring the phenomenological and the Marxist approaches to the problem of teleology into dialogue with one another is demanded by the things themselves.

(b) *The concept of transcendental phenomenology*. Husserl calls his mode of investigation transcendental-phenomenological. At this point we shall only say enough to provide an initial understanding of what Husserl means. This concept of the transcendental is not identical with the Kantian concept. It has taken up Locke's question concerning the origin of our representations. Formally, the Husserlian and Kantian concepts of the transcendental share the fact that both signify 'critique': critique of our use of traditional philosophical concepts, the question of the *quid juris* of their use in the explication of our experience. In this sense 'transcendental' means nothing other than the absolute opposite of every kind of dogmatism. Here too Husserl's concept agrees with Kant's. But Husserl's concept goes further. It not only means critique of dogmatism in metaphysics, which was Kant's target, but also critique of the hidden metaphysical implications in anti-metaphysical positions, especially in positivism and naturalism, thus critique of the naïve use of *all* traditional philosophical concepts with whose aid we attempt to come to terms with ourselves and our world. For Kant, transcendental critique is primarily critique of our knowledge of the 'external' world, of 'nature', i.e. examination of the legitimate range of the concepts of the functions of thought by means of which experienced nature is scientifically known. We can ignore the fact that this is a one-sided aspect of Kant's philosophy, since this is the aspect which has been historically important. For Husserl, on the other hand, transcendental critique includes the examination and critique of the concepts which we form on the basis of our experience of ourselves, with which we attempt to come to terms with our life in our social world. The sciences of man, his society and history also thematize this experience, and their results function as givens for transcendental phenomenology in much the same manner in which Kant took the natural science of his time as his point of departure. But this does not mean that phenomenological investigations are simply compiled out of the accepted results of these sciences which, in the form of psychology, sociology, etc., deal with man from various points of view. Here too, transcendental critique deals with the specific legitimacy and limits of these specific points of view. It is the *question concerning their origin in the experience of pre-scientific life*. This life itself is to be investigated, this experience is to be interrogated as to the sense it bears prior to all scientific explication; the concepts of the sciences of man are to be examined as to the extent to which they do justice to this experience. Thus, the first step of transcendental critique concerns the analysis of pre-scientific life. The theme of this analysis is the 'life-world' and the question as to how all of the concepts which man forms of himself are based on the structures of the life-world. In our context it is above all the question of the origin and thus the legitimacy within the life-world of the notion of a teleological efficacy, and the question of the justification for understanding the process in which man finds himself entwined as a teleological efficacy. Thus, we must now turn to the question of:

2 The origin of the idea of teleological efficacy in the corporeal constitution of man

(a) *Motility as the most elementary structure of human activity.* Husserl's notion of a 'primal striving' points in the direction of that dimension of our experience of ourselves in which we become acquainted in an original manner with teleological efficacy, on the basis of which we can form a concept of history as a teleologically determined process. The first question is thus: where is this 'primal striving' to be found? It is found in the human body with its sense organs, which man sets in motion. It is set in motion in a manner which can be expressed as an 'I move myself' (*Ich bewege mich*) when a reflection on the execution of this movement occurs. But it can also occur without reflection and this is generally the case. The striving which sets it in motion works, as Husserl puts it, 'anonymously' in this case. Movement as moving-oneself (*Selbstbewegung*) ('*I* move *myself*') is more than mere change of spatial position. Modern philosophy restricted the question of movement to the *motus localis*, understanding movement only in this sense. This was an abstraction, an abstraction which is the foundation of the possibility of modern natural science in the form of 'classical' mechanics. We are not interested in giving a definition of movement in the *broad* sense which is relevant in our context. When we speak of movement and moving-oneself, these terms are to be understood in their 'deictic' sense, so that they reflect the various levels of meaning which the word has in everyday speech. This phenomenological approach could be understood as a kind of *ordinary language approach*. The use of these terms serves only to indicate that which every person is already familiar with from his own experience – a familiarity which need not necessarily be given explicit formulation. That which is moved by the 'primal striving' in such a manner that it moves *itself* is the body, or, more precisely, the sense organs with which it is equipped. But it is only a body which moves *itself* in that it is *my* body, your body, the body of someone who 'has' it in controlling its movements within certain limits. Husserl speaks in this context of 'governing (*walten*) in the body'. We shall pass by the question *who* or *what* it is that governs in the body for the moment, since it includes a whole bundle of questions which must be 'unpacked' phenomenologically step by step. With reference to this moving-*oneself* – an expression which in its deictic function means *more* than can be *comprehended* in its predicative universality – we can see the sense in which this talk of body and the senses, 'sensuousness', is to be understood in phenomenological analysis.

(b) *Sensuousness is 'sensuous activity'.* The expression 'sensuous activity' refers to Marx's 'Theses on Feuerbach'. Before we can discuss the legitimacy and significance of this reference, we must introduce the basic elements of the phenomenological analysis of sensibility and the body.

The most elementary mode of activity, which founds all other activities, is the goal-directed activity of the sense organs. Husserl introduced the word *kinaesthesia* for this; literally: a movement which is aware of itself in the process of its own execution. Husserl demonstrated the significance of the senses as a mode of being active for securing any knowledge of perceivable material objects as early as 1913 in the second volume of his *Ideas*. In his anthropology, Gehlen later speaks of a 'retro-sensation' (*Rückempfindung*) of motor movements on the basis of which we gain impressions of optical, acoustic, tactual things. Here we are aware of the receptive sense organs as that which we have to set in motion. In order to have a tactual impression, I must grasp with my hands, push against things, etc. In order to see a thing correctly, I must turn my head, change the position of my body, etc. This is bound up with oculomotoric movements which we are generally not even aware of, which are only accessible to us by means of external observation. But they do not occur arbitrarily, they are brought into play by the impulse to see more clearly. In these movements man learns at a very early point in his development what he is capable of doing. Only in the activation of his so-called faculties of sense does he learn this in a manner which cannot be improved upon. In this sense Husserl says that 'the "I move myself" precedes the "I can"'. This is even true at the early stage of the child's pre-linguistic development at which the goal-directed movement of the members of the body are exercised and imitated. This is the first discovery of the baby, prior to all formation of a consciousness of an I, that it is capable of being and learns to be the master of the motoric of its own body in order to approach and appropriate that which it wants and needs. This is a becoming aware of the link between the motor movements of the body which can be steered at will and the sense impressions which result from such movement. This brings to expression a certain understanding of oneself as a centre of spontaneous movement which has its origin in oneself, movement which is goal directed and controllable, such that it can be corrected if it does not yield the expected results.

This very early discovery, which every human individual must make in the course of his or her development, is, as it were, the *hour of the birth of man's humanity*. It is the unavoidable presupposition for all higher-level achievements of spontaneity which are not exhausted in sensuous activity and which allow us to understand man as an active creature whose activity is guided by foresight and intent. The linguistic articulation of the anticipatory representation of the goal which is to be reached by the activity also belongs here. But it too is sensuous activity which produces the sound as an articulation which comes back to the ear as an event in the sensuously present surrounding world and thus makes possible the control of the appropriateness of the articulated sound to that which is to be said and thus to the correction of the linguistic utterance. These are the most fundamental, and in this sense transcendental conditions under which alone man not only becomes acquainted with his surrounding world, but learns to move in it in such a way that this acquaintance is at all possible. This recognition and understanding of the world in which we live is not exhausted by the faculty for having representations; its roots lie deeper. Every theory of understanding which reduces it to recognition in the sense of insight, to the insightful representation of a state of affairs, is fundamentally inadequate. Human understanding is primarily a *self-understanding of one's own abilities*, a point on which Heidegger has insisted. The 'I can' or the 'possible' as that of which one is capable, is thus a fundamental category in Husserl's analysis of the way in which we become conscious of our world; and the most elementary of human capacities is the capacity for motility among the things which surround us. Man dwells among them by conducting himself with regard to them. Conduct is thus self-steered movement among the things, in the first instance, understood literally as approaching, distancing oneself, touching, etc.

The concept of conduct or behaviour can be made more precise in this manner. When behaviourism and the behavioural sciences hold that behaviour and the distinctions relevant to it can be scientifically investigated only by means of the external perception of processes of movement, it has suppressed the question and forgotten how it came by the concept of behaviour in the first place, and what distinguishes behaviour from any other observable processes of movement. It has forgotten the scientist's experience of his own self-steered movement, which is what makes such a distinction and with it the demarcation of his field of research possible in the first place. This is only one example of the manner in which transcendental phenomenological analysis not merely takes up the results of empirical research but at the same time criticizes it for forgetting its own presuppositions.

To be sure, one also speaks of animals and their behaviour, and here it is true that only external observation is possible. The animal can tell us nothing and we can say nothing about the manner in which an animal 'experiences' its behaviour. One does, of course, also say that the animal moves *itself* in its surrounding world, i.e. it is not merely moved by external causes as is a lifeless object (movement understood here in the many-sided Aristotelian sense, as change of place and position, as qualitative change and as growth and decay). Biological research also encounters the limits of a possible causal explanation when it encounters the phenomena of the self-control and self-complementation of the living organism. It must assume a principle which makes this possible, even if the mode of its teleological efficacy eludes all empirical research and its necessarily quantifying tools. Cybernetics too has its absolute limit here. If the organism were to be explained as a cybernetic apparatus, it would have to be conceived in such a manner that it would have the ability to invent itself and to produce a new organism in line with this invention.

In contrast to the modes of behaviour of animals, which we can only observe from outside, human movement is reflexive in a pregnant sense. It is only here that the reflexive 'oneself' receives its authentic meaning. Movement is that movement of the body which I can become aware of as a movement which *I* have set into motion; it is equally an awareness of the impulse guided by striving and awareness of the movement that results and is simultaneously perceivable. The ground of the movement is itself experienced in this awareness, and as soon as linguistic abilities are developed it is given a loud expression in the child's 'I want!' It is this becoming-aware-of-one's-own-power which must be brought into play if a desired goal is to be reached, for example, the grasping movement of the hand or the movement of crawling or walking in order to approach the thing desired. Thus, kinaesthetic movement cannot be understood simply as motion in space. In this case, space would be simply presupposed as given, and the question how we develop our representation of space and spatial relations is forgotten. Kinaesthetic movement is always experienced as a teleological efficacy; it is always goal directed; the goal must somehow be in view as that which is not yet attained, as that which is to be attained by means of one's own activity. Failure to realize the goal is the occasion of a primitive experimentation as a kind of elementary learning process in which the movement is practised until it realizes its goal.

With the demonstration of this relation we have thus found the *transcendental ground of the legitimacy of speaking of active forces* (*wirkende Kräfte*). This ground lies in the manner in which we become immediately perceptually aware of powers in our experience of ourselves as setting ourselves in motion and bringing about changes in our environment; for example, we experience the hardness or softness of a thing in the *resistance* which our impulse of grasping or shoving encounters: we have experienced this and received this sensuous impression *because* we move in those ways. What is originally given is not a mere sequence of sense data which are simply there, but rather a 'because – thus'. Hume could not do justice to the origin of our representations of causality in the widest sense because he simply presupposed the concept of sensibility as suffering – a concept which has dominated discussions of perception since Aristotle. This is also present as something self-evident in Kant's definition of sensibility as receptivity, and he was thus forced to look for the origin of these representations in the categories of the understanding, thus overlooking their elementary foundation in sensory kinaesthesia. This is a critical restriction of the transcendental philosophical approach, one which has broad implications.

This insight into the origin of all of our representations of efficacy and active forces shows that our representations of an effect can only be given intuitive content when it is a matter of teleological efficacy which is determined in terms of a goal. Indeed, causality in the *narrow*

(Humean) sense, according to which a *post hoc* is understood as a *propter hoc*, does not correspond to any intuition. This is the reason why all mythology conceives of causal agency on the model of ourselves as causal agents, i.e. as personal causal forces. *The world picture which is oriented in terms of our immediate experience of forces is thus a teleological world picture*. There is a very obvious reason for this: a methodological process of abstraction is required in order to view the processes surrounding us without regard to the correlation to our own movements in which we originally experience them. It is this 'self-forgetfulness' (Husserl) which makes possible natural science in the modern sense as a tool for the domination of nature. It had to exclude the teleological reference to the observer and thus all intuitive talk about causality and movement, such that all relations between observable processes in an experiment could be represented in the language of mathematical formulae.

We must now discuss the consequences which this has for the phenomenological concept of the body and corporeality.

(c) *The concepts of the functions of corporeality are transcendental concepts*. This thesis may appear a bit curious at first glance. One might object that the body is one material thing among others and thus an object of external experience, and thus to be distinguished from the transcendental functions on the basis of which it becomes experienceable for us. The word 'material' is used here in the very general and vague sense in which Husserl as well as Marx initially adopted it from the philosophical tradition, the sense which is also a part of everyday language. Natural processes are called 'material' – in Husserl 'material reality' – in this sense, and one speaks of 'natural matter' and of nature as the 'external world' as opposed to an 'inner world' as 'spiritual' or as 'consciousness', a region of the 'objective' on the one hand and the 'subjective' on the other. We shall ignore for the moment the fact that this is only *one* of the possible meanings of the ambiguous word 'nature': it is of course possible and at times necessary to consider the body as just another thing in space. Its movements are subject to the same physical laws. When the child begins to exercise its powers in kinaesthetic movement, it obeys these laws without 'knowing' the first thing about them. But in doing so it comes to know them in a very primitive and elementary manner. As we have seen, it has already become practically acquainted with the distinction between movement which occurs without its involvement and movement which it itself sets into motion. We can presuppose all of this as being obvious. But it is the task of phenomenological analysis to show how and as what our respective bodies are there for us in the elementary kinaesthetic movements. The body is there for us in the presence of the functioning of its limbs in such a manner that we have an immediate control over their movement within certain limits. A person can only move his *own* limbs by means of his *own* impulse, all other things around us only via the movement of the body, and if they do not approach us by means of their own movement we can approach them or distance ourselves from them by means of our kinaesthetic movements.

All of this appears to be banal. But we have already seen that the *origin of all our representations of space and spatial relations* lies in these movements. That is, in this movement we experience the fact that the things that surround us are *oriented in terms of our body*, to the right and left, front and rear, above and below as the most primitive specifications of spatial position which can be pointed out and understood by deictic movements prior to all linguistic development. This capacity to understand a pointing gesture is a specifically human ability. Even the higher animals cannot understand pointing. Kant was quite aware of these facts in his works 'On the First Ground of the Distinction of Regions of Space' and 'What Does It Mean: To Orient Oneself in Thought?' But for reasons mentioned above, he was unable to take them into account in his transcendental aesthetic. In our most elementary experience, the body is there for us as the 'zero-point of all orientation' (Husserl, *Ideen III*, *Husserliana* V, p. 158) in our world. We are inescapably 'there' (*da*) in the world as this specific human individual here and now; with reference to this 'There' (*Da*) everything else around us is 'over there' (*dort*). This 'There' is always presupposed if we are to experience being affected by the things around us, for example, in the 'stimuli' of our senses. This does not merely mean that man as a thinking creature can only exist if he is a corporeal creature which appears somewhere in the world. That is nothing new. What is meant here concerns rather the specific mode of existing. The philosophical tradition distinguishes existence from essence – in the German scholastic tradition *Dasein* and *Wesen* – and puts them into relation with one another. The existing individual exemplifies a universal, is the contingent realization of a universal essence or species in an individual specimen. This is also the logic of the concept of the individual. In contrast, the 'There' which is experienced in the zero-point function of the body is, as it were, an *absolute determination*. Of course, if we speak of *our* 'There', this demonstrative always also signifies *a* There at a given point in time and with its specific position in space, which is preceded by and followed by other Theres. But this mode of speech is the result of a reflection in which the There is already objectivated as one among others, which can be taken up one after the other by a, to use Kantian terminology, 'fixed and abiding self'. This is precisely the reflection by means of which Hegel's dialectic of sense certainty is brought into motion. It is supposed to show that this supposed immediacy of the 'this – now – here' which explicates the There of the individual subject is in truth mediated – mediated by the identity of the 'I' which remains a constant in these determinations. In spite of the legitimacy of these considerations as a critique of sense data theories, it shifts the ground of the identity in the multiplicity of the 'There' into the thinking ego and thus overlooks the fact that man has a much more elementary experience of himself as an active creature in the execution of the active kinaesthetic becoming acquainted with the world, and this at a point at which it is impossible to speak of an ego-consciousness or of thought. Thus, it is not in the *ego cogito* but at a much deeper level that the acquaintance with one's own There is an apodictic and incorrigible certainty. It has the character of fundamental facticity, and is in this sense immediate and absolute. As an *absolute fact* it is the *most fundamental transcendental condition of possibility of all activity and functioning* in which the experienced world is available for us.

It must be noted that this amounts to a revision of the Husserlian account of fact and essence in the form it takes especially in the *Ideas*. Husserl was not able to carry out this revision himself, although suggestions in this direction can be found in his latest fragmentary sketches. According to this revision it would be false to say that this 'There' as absolute fact signifies contingency in the sense of merely fortuitous existence:

> It is nonsense to say 'accidental', since the accidental presupposes a horizon of possibilities within which the accidental signifies one of the possibilities, the one which in fact occurs . . . 'absolute fact (*Faktum*)!' – in the normal sense of the word 'fact' this is nonsense, the same holds for *Tatsache*, since there is no *Täter* here. It is precisely the absolute (which cannot be called 'necessary' either), that which is the ground of all possibilities, all relativities, all conditions, that which gives them sense and being.

> The absolute contains within itself its ground and its absolute necessity as the one 'absolute substance'. Its necessity is not essential necessity, which would leave open a realm of contingency. All essential necessities are moments of its fact, are modes in which it functions with respect to itself – its modes of understanding or being able to understand itself (*Husserliana* XV, p. 386).

It is clear that this absoluteness cannot be understood in the sense of the 'absolute' of modern metaphysics, though many of Husserl's formulations are misleading in this respect. What is at issue here is the *marking out of the limits which transcendental reflection encounters* and which remain insurmountable for it.

(d) *The functions of corporeality cannot be grasped by the alternative 'material-spiritual' or 'psychic'.* How are body and corporeality to be conceived phenomenologically? Here we can take some of Husserl's formulations in the *Ideas* as our point of departure. On the one hand, one can say that man 'is in nature only because the body is in the first instance a material thing in spatial nature' (*Ideen II*, *Husserliana* IV, p. 138). But this statement is not based on external observation. Rather, 'what we call the body already has a stratum which belongs to the psychic (*seelischen*). . . . We must thus first abstract from this stratum in order to reach the merely material body' (*Ideen III*, p. 118). This means that our existence 'in nature' is always already experienced as such in the execution of kinaesthetic movement. In it we already have an elementary experience of 'nature' as the experience of the entanglement of our corporeal action with the causal nexus of nature. Thus, the corporeal is, on the one hand, 'given as tied up in the causal nexus of physical nature' (*Ideen II*, p. 138); on the other hand, the body belongs to 'psychic reality'. Its modes of movement are not determined by the laws of physical causality alone. The expressions 'psyche' (*Seele*) and 'psychic' are used by Husserl in the general, Aristotelian sense in which 'soul' is the name for the principle on the basis of which the living organism steers itself in its movement and realizes itself (*Entelechie*). But the 'curious thing [is] that *material things* are conditioned exclusively from without and not by their own past; they are realities without a history'. Material reality essentially involves:

> the ideal possibility that in cyclical processes it [can] return under identically the same external circumstances under which it existed

> in the past. Though this may be totally improbable. But material reality is such that in such a cyclical return it would have to have the same total state. In contrast, it belongs to the essence of psychic reality that it *cannot* in principle return to the same total state: psychic realities have a *history*. Two neighboring cycles of external circumstances would affect the same soul in the same manner, but within the soul itself the psychic processes could not be the same, because the earlier state conditions the later state (ibid., p. 137).

We need not here deal with the question whether and to which degree Husserl's thesis that nature has no history might be put in question in the light of the second law of thermodynamics, the law of entropy. It turns out that there are irreversible processes in nature; in this sense one could speak of a history of nature. But one cannot say that nature *has* a history in the same sense in which we say 'psychic realities *have* a history'. They have a history in that earlier states functionally determine later states. This can be demonstrated in terms of the elementary processes of practising successful kinaesthetic movements. In this sense one can say that animals are capable of 'learning'. In this context the word means only that an earlier movement is not simply past, but that its success or failure influences the manner in which the later movement is carried out. Of course, in the case of animals one cannot say that this influence is a matter of the earlier movement's being retained in memory, since memory in the only normal sense of the term presupposes the possibility of the linguistic articulation of that which is remembered. This is not to say that memory without language is impossible. There are surely borderline cases which are illustrated by the way in which dream images can appear.

The sense of the expression 'having a history' is best illustrated by the way in which the memory of the success or failure of an earlier, identical or similar activity can decisively influence current goal-directed activity. This need not always be the case; there are habitual activities which take place, as it were, automatically. To say that 'psychic reality', i.e. man in his respective 'There', *has* a history thus means that in the respective 'There' of his conduct this history is explicitly (as in memory) or implicitly co-present in the form of what Husserl calls a 'sedimented' history. It is co-present in the 'There' as its respective life history 'between birth and death'. This reference to the limits of this history indicates that this life history is not exhausted by the history of its formation, by the influences through which it was formed, but that it is at the same time its natural history in that it is dependent on the functioning of its corporeality, its power and its weaknesses. This life history, which cannot be exchanged for that of another, irrevocably separates the individual in its 'There' from the life history of every other. It is teleological in that its course is dependent upon its goals and interests, and its attempts to take them into account.

Before moving on to the question of the significance of this teleology for the teleology of history, we shall summarize the implications of this discussion for the phenomenological concept of life.

Our starting point here is our earlier remarks on Husserl's use of the expression 'soul'. He uses this term in the Aristotelian sense as a title for the principle of the unity of the living organism. But this is a purely formal definition which does not determine *what* the body really is. The body teleologically unites its vital functions in which it maintains and supports itself. We can only 'get control of' some of them, such as the kinaesthetic functions, within certain limits, govern them and become aware of them. Others occur without our doing and independent of our awareness of them. We are at most aware of their normal functioning in a general feeling of well-being, of their dysfunctioning in listlessness and pain. But this does not tell us anything about who or what it is which maintains their functioning in this manner. If it is a phenomenological principle that no concept is to be admitted which does not allow for a corresponding intuitive experience, then we have no concept of the body in this sense. It is of course easy to see that it is more than a material thing. It may be unavoidable to say that it is the place at which the material and the 'psychic' or 'spiritual' or consciousness come together. But no one has been able to show how this coming together actually takes place. One can of course investigate the dependence of conscious functions on brain functions, just as one can investigate the reciprocal dependence of physiological functions among themselves and with respect to that which results from them. But it has hitherto proven impossible to show how consciousness arises on the basis of physiological functions, feelings and sensations. All of the philosophical theories which have been developed, psychophysical parallelism, *influxus physicus*, etc. always presuppose two functions of different kinds which must then be brought into some sort of relation to one another, and without this distinction there could be no medicine and no natural science. But in the manner in which we become aware of our body and its kinaesthetic functions in the 'There' of their execution, at the point at which it is there for us in the first place, we know nothing of two sorts of forces whose sources we could name. We only know of that force which is let loose by our impulse, and of the resistence and limits which it encounters.

And these limits cannot be called simply 'outer' or 'inner' without further ado, since they are there for us as limits, e.g. in the pain of over-exertion or of a dysfunction in a bodily process we are unaware of. We experience our existence as a 'corporeal' being only in the unity of its execution in the respective 'There'. This 'There' is an absolute determination, since we cannot pursue our inquiry on to a ground of unity at a still more fundamental level which would be accessible to our experience and thus available for a conceptual determination. In this sense, the 'There' is also a transcendental determination, since it poses a limit of our possible knowledge. This is not to say that it would not be perfectly legitimate, e.g. to ask where a certain pain comes from, whether it comes from an external cause or, in the absence of such a cause, whether it may not come from one's own inner organs. In this case 'internal' means that which comes from my own body, and 'external' signifies that which does not come from here but rather from there, from the thing which exercises its causality from over there, against which I have, for example, stumbled. On the other hand, if I, for example, consider my intention according to which I move my hand, I am inclined to call the intention 'internal' and distinguish it from the movement which is 'out there', saying 'the inner has become outer'. Unavoidable as these distinctions may be in everyday circumstances, they do not make it possible to say what the 'inner' and the 'outer' really are. One should not forget that we are dealing with 'determinations of reflection', as Kant demonstrated in the 'Amphiboly of the Concepts of Reflection' in the *Critique of Pure Reason*. This is the root of the 'transcendental appearance' of the existence of two different regions of substantial causality. That which we immediately experience as our 'There' in the unity of our action is divided by such reflection into a multiplicity of elements which are given different names in isolation from one another. This is unavoidable, since only in this manner can we come to an understanding with ourselves and with others concerning that which takes place around and with us. But the transcendental phenomenological investigation of the origin and the limits of the legitimacy of such distinctions points out the fact that the names involved in these distinctions may not be hypostatized as the names of independent substances or forces such as 'matter' or 'spirit', since the question of their relations to one another would remain unanswered and indeed unanswerable. The history of modern philosophy has made this clear enough. This difficulty appeared in its beginnings in Descartes in the fact that he on the one hand reckoned *sentire* to the *modis cogitanda*, but on the other hand could not avoid recognizing that sensations are distributed within the body and are thus to be reckoned to the extended substance. This is the result of the hypostatization of the distinction between 'inner' and 'outer' to absolute determinations, whereby he overlooks the fact that the way we make these distinctions depends on the direction of our current interest: whether we call the body our inner in order to distinguish it from the way it is affected by external things, or whether we distinguish the intention and the impulse as our inner from the kinaesthetic movements which they set into play and which are visible to us ourselves as something outside.

We encounter similar ambiguities in the word 'nature'. If we understand nature as the sum total of processes available to outer perception, and thus hypostatize it to a 'nature-in-itself', we forget the sources out of which we came to know something like 'nature' in an original manner in the first place, namely in the intertwining of our self-steered kinaesthetic processes with the causal nexus of so-called 'external' nature. As we have seen, this 'forgetfulness' is methodologically necessary for the constitution of the exact sciences of nature. But transcendental philosophy has the task of understanding this forgetfulness *as* forgetfulness, and thus of reminding us of the fact that *the nature which we come to know in the course of our own practical activity is more than the nature which is available to exact scientific research and experimentation.* As we have seen, this practical acquaintance is the motive for distinguishing that which we can bring about ourselves from that which sets a limit to this ability. Such distinctions and such names can never have the sense of inquiry into something more basic than the absolutely experienced factual 'There', but can only be an explication of that which is given on the basis of this 'There'.

In what follows we shall investigate the significance of these phenomenological analyses of the body and corporeality for the problem of the teleology of history.

3 The teleological continuity and unity of history is not predetermined, but must be produced in the particular 'There'. Thus, the idea of a teleology of history does not have its origin in 'theoretical' considerations, but in practical human interests

In arguing for this thesis we must first answer a preliminary question. We have seen how all notions of a teleological efficacy have their origin in the self-experience of the zero-point function of the body, in which every individual discovers his own absolute 'There'. The individual's history is co-present in the 'There' of his most basic activity of the senses, co-present as his life history between the poles of birth and death. Corporeality is the reason why all 'behaviour' is based in an intentional 'primal striving' (Husserl). His intentionality is characterized by the relations of fulfilment and disappointment. Every individual is faced with the question of whether he experiences his existence in his life history to be successful, 'happy' or a failure. Failure signifies disruption of the teleological continuity, loss of personal identity; success signifies maintenance of teleological unity. It is thus clear in which sense we can speak of teleology here; it must always be achieved anew. In this sense Husserl says: 'Being a subject means being teleological.' But the given individual in the 'There' of his life history and its teleology is irrevocably separated from the 'There' of every other by the perspectivity of this 'There'. Each individual has his life history *as his own* history which cannot be exchanged for the history of another. To be sure, one can speak of teleology in this context. But if the origin of all our ideas of teleological efficacy is to be found in this teleology of the given individual and in the absolute isolation of his 'There', how can we legitimately speak of a teleology of *history* pure and simple? History is, after all, something quite different from the life history of the given human individual. History is the history of 'humanity' or the 'human species'. Is this not a kind of analogy between that teleology which we experience in ourselves and a process which we cannot experience in the same reflexive manner? If that were the case, the analogy would be highly suspect, since this would mean that reason, which belongs to one's own teleology as the *possibility* of choosing a successful path in life, would be projected, in the form of 'reason in history', into a process in which experience cannot find any such reason.

This becomes clear when we take a closer look at what it means to say that the life history of the given individual is co-present in the individual's 'There', not merely when we expressly recall it, but rather in the form of what Husserl calls 'sedimented' history. This is true at the most elementary level of corporeal motility. An element of life history is present in every movement we have learned to carry out successfully. It is also co-present as a product of activity, product not only of one's own activity but above all of the other's productive activity. These products are 'there' for sense perception as objects which refer implicitly to their producer. Thus, history is that which has occurred in the past, is present in its remnants, monuments and written texts, but which is also 'there' as that which its producer left incomplete and which calls for completion by us. All of this is 'sedimented activity', as is language with its grammar and vocabulary. Every activity which refers back to a sedimentation is such in an 'absolute' 'There' which is not mine and not ours but that of others whose life histories belong to the past. But if every individual is, as it were, enclosed in his own absolute 'There', how can such references to the 'There' of others be experienced and understood as such? Would this not presuppose an '*a priori*' acquaintance with the Thou, the We, the 'other'? This is certainly true, but the origin of this acquaintance should not be looked for at too high a level. The given absolute 'There' in its living execution is not the 'There' of an individualized 'I think', since becoming self-aware of oneself as I is a mode of self-consciousness which must be individually developed in the life history of every individual in his own 'There'. Thus, the roots of the original acquaintance with the 'There' of the other cannot be found in the functions of the I-think and its linguistic articulation; it is to be found in the execution of the elementary functions which are guided by the 'primal striving' of the given 'There'. Communication occurs here prior to all ability to speak and think.

Thus, the concept of human society as a 'communication society' is too narrow if communication is only understood as linguistic communication. Habermas neglects this fact in his discussion of the *a priori* of language (in *Knowledge and Human Interests*). But this neglect is very widespread. Lorenzen-Kamlah's *Logical Propaedeutic* also presupposes a concept of everyday language in which the original deictic and thus 'prepredicative' reference of linguistic articulation to the particular lived 'There' is not taken into account. Waldenfels, in contrast, refers to this 'underground' of dialogue in his book *The Middle Realm of Dialogue* (*Das Zwischenreich des Dialogs*).

From the perspective of phenomenology, this problem is nothing other than the problem of the *transcendental conditions of possibility of intersubjectivity* – the Husserlian title for human society. This problem is not the creation of a philosophy of consciousness and the ego. It does not suffice to say that we must take the fact that man is a social animal as our point of departure, that what really exists thereby demonstrates its own possibility. The problem is to understand how this very obvious fact is a fact *for man himself*. If one simply takes this fact as point of departure, it is impossible to show how individualization is possible; if one takes the self-certainty of the individual 'I' as point of departure, it is impossible to show how sociality is possible. In this sense the question concerning the transcendental conditions of possibility of intersubjectivity is unavoidable. If it makes sense to talk about such conditions, then this must correspond to something which can be shown to be a moment in our most elementary experiences: in the most elementary, that is, in the corporeal experiences which are guided by 'primal striving'. 'Primal striving' always belongs to the individual, individualized human being which is 'There' in its own activities. How is it possible that this striving, in the individualization which necessarily exists in the form of the 'There' in its corporeality, refers to the Other?

Following a series of unsatisfying attempts to elaborate a theory of intersubjectivity, Husserl's latest manuscripts give some hints at the direction in which the answer to this question can be found. He asks: 'May we not, must we not presuppose a universal instinctive intentionality which unitarily constitutes every primal present and which presses on from present to present in such a way that all content is content of the fulfilment of these drives and is intended prior to its achievement?' (*Husserliana* XV, p. 595). Primal presence is that which we have called the 'absolute There'. Its reflective analysis leads to the 'I-structure' which indicates the absolute individualization, but also to 'the more primitive founding stratum of egoless striving, which in the course of a consequent interrogation leads back to that which is presupposed by and makes possible sedimented activity, to the radically pre-egological sphere' (ibid., p. 598). It should be noted that this assertion would have no transcendental significance if it were only the result of inferring from that which is given in original experience to that which is not so given. This concept of an egoless striving must rather be referred to an experiential content which allows us to speak of a universal instinctive intentionality in such a manner that the individualization of the 'absolute There' is not cancelled in this instinctive intentionality, but rather from the very beginning refers to the other and thus to a common 'There'. Husserl finds this primal drive in the sexual drive as 'instinctive intentionality of communalization' (quoted by Waldenfels, *The Middle Realm of Dialogue*, op. cit., p. 298). As a primal drive it is from the very beginning referred to the other and finds its fulfilment and disappointment in the other: 'the reference to the other *as* other and to his correlative drive lies in the drive itself'. In its 'fulfilment we do not have two separate fulfilments of the one and the other primordiality respectively, but a unity of the two primordialities which arises in the intertwining of fulfilment' (*Husserliana* XV, p. 593f.). Primordiality is the realm of that which is available to every individual in consequent (transcendental) reflection on the experiential content which is included in his 'There'. The result of the fulfilment of this 'primal drive' can be the birth of a new human being with its own inexchangeable 'There' and its own history, whose possibilities are co-determined by the inheritance from its ancestors which is 'sedimented' in it.

Thus, procreation and birth are not only themes for biology, but have a transcendental significance as condition of possibility of history. This is not a banality, since this is the ground of the possibility of forming concepts with which we can understand the structure of history. This is the ground of the distinction between generations in which that which we have in common – many generations always live together in the same epoch – appears in different perspectives on the basis of the different stages on life's way. In this manner the common history of a family, a people, an epoch is formed. Every individual which is born into it has *his* time, the time which is allotted to him. Thus, the fact that there is *one* history *as* history for us *presupposes on the one hand the generativity of the 'life of the species' and on the other hand the absolute individualization of the particular 'There' of its members*. Society as the 'life of the species' is only possible in that this life of the species becomes history through absolute individualization, i.e. becomes a history which humanity *has* as the life of the species. Animal communities have no history, the living and dying of its members is a succession. 'The bees of which Ovid sang built their hives according to the same laws as do the bees today.' Only by means of the clarification of this situation can Marx's enigmatic words 'Man is a creature for himself, *and thus* a species being', be understood and the hypostatization of the species – the word *itself* signifies an abstraction – become the title of the active force, i.e. of the 'transcendental subject' of history. It is not sufficient to say that this situation is an expression of the dialectic of the universal and the particular, individual, and thus to formalize it. A phenomenological-transcendental investigation must inquire into those contents of experience which provide the ground of possibility of such a dialectic. We have already seen that this ground is not to be found at the level of reflection, but in circumstances of life which lie deeper.

Here we can only sketch on this basis the implications of Husserl's late work, understood in the light of the clarifications we have attempted here, for the problem of teleology, implications which Husserl was not able to elaborate in detail.

The 'There' of the individual member of human history is its 'There' as the corporeally motile subject. In its corporeal motility it is acquainted with 'nature' from the very beginning because it, with its corporeally founded 'primal drives', 'belongs to' this nature. It is a 'There' at its 'place' in nature, and for us this place is the 'earth'. It 'inserts itself into a universal "natural history" which extends to man as a living organism' (quoted by Waldenfels, *The Middle Realm of Dialogue*, op. cit., p. 336 fn.). Human history is not merely natural history, but the natural processes are its ground in that the 'earth' is the name for the totality of conditions which set the boundaries for all human activity and thus for human history in the sense of *res gestae* – a limitation which we become more and more clearly aware of as the process of 'dominating' the earth proceeds. *The absoluteness of the 'earth', as the limit of every possible 'There', belongs to the absoluteness of the 'There'.* We need not discuss space flight here, since it can only take place 'with reference to earth'. 'Earth' in this sense is thus a transcendental limiting concept.

Here we can see that in talking about history, whose teleology is in question here, we mean *our own* history in which we find ourselves today. It is the history of the European nations and culture which have produced a style of science and scientificity which is the ground of the claim to domination of all events on the earth and the idea of planning the fate of human society by means of 'technologizing' and thus by means of science itself. With every step towards realizing this claim, all other world cultures, the high civilizations and the archaic cultures, were taken up into a unitary process in which the idea of a *world* history of humanity became a reality. This entire history is thus unavoidably co-present in our experienced 'There', and this presence is the presence of a 'crisis' which encompasses the entire world. In this sense, Husserl investigates in his late work the 'crisis of European science', searching out the origins and possibilities of overcoming this crisis. In the reflection of the individual on his own life crises, the first question is: 'Why did things turn out this way, why doesn't that which I have achieved correspond to that which I was striving for?' Similarly, in this crisis the first step of reflection concerns the question of its origin. Husserl thus poses the question of the 'primal institution' (*Urstiftung*) of this style of science, an institution which is one of the great achievements of the Greeks, and the question whether this development in fact corresponded to what this primal institution intended. If this can be shown, then the will of this primal institution must be taken up into our own willing if this process is to be a meaningful one for humanity and not fall short of this rational sense. Thus, teleology is not a predetermined element of this process, but is a matter of our own readiness and ability to produce it. In this sense, teleology must first be produced in every 'There' of history. Whether or not humanity will continue to have *a* history depends upon the degree to which this succeeds. The question whether history *has* a meaning is thus not a question which can be answered by means of observation. It can only be answered by means of our own practical action.

4 In conclusion, we must inquire into the significance of these phenomenological investigations into the connection between corporeality and teleology for a proper understanding of the philosophical implications of the work of Karl Marx

When we inquire into the philosophical implications of Marx's approach, this should not be mistaken for the attempt to reconstruct his 'philosophy' on the basis of his analyses and demands. He never intended to work out such a philosophy. But he did make use of the conceptual instruments of philosophy which his age provided as a tool for the analysis of the historical-social situation, for answering the question of what was to be done in its 'There'. All of his work thus amounts to *investigations with a practical intent*, and he pursued them only as far as seemed to be necessary for the realization of this intent. But the conceptual language of this traditional philosophy sketched out for him a range of possibilities and limits, within which his questions could be formulated in the first place.

This can be seen in the demand that sensibility be understood as 'sensuous activity'. The polemical introduction of this title was sufficient for his goal of distinguishing his position from that of Feuerbach, and he did not intend to develop a theory of sensibility which would give philosophical precision to this talk of 'sensuous activity'. But even if he had wanted to do so, the presuppositions for the success of such an enterprise were not satisfied at that time. The basic concepts of the psychology of his time, and indeed up to the end of the nineteenth century, were dominated by attempts to classify 'psychic phenomena' which were rooted in the old scholastic tradition of faculty psychology. It thus lacked a concept of activity which was appropriate to dealing with sensibility. The first impulses towards a fundamental revision appear only in our own century, more or less simultaneously in Husserl's analyses of kinaesthesia and in the experimental investigations of Gestalt psychology, which opposed the 'atomism' of traditional psychology. Only against this background was it possible to produce a decisive refutation of Pavlov's theory of the 'conditioned reflex' (cf. E. Straus, *Vom Sinn der Sinne*, 1936), which had dominated Soviet psychology up to then.

It is only against this background that the ambiguities in those basic Marxist concepts which determined the linguistic-terminological limits of the development of his central problems can be clarified.

Thesis: *The concept of nature is not univocal in Marx. Its ambiguity is the cause of the debates concerning the correct Marxism.*

This is not the place to discuss the literature which is devoted to this concept (cf. A. Schmidt, *The Concept of Nature in Marx*, 1978). Our task is rather to develop the problem within the context of our discussion.

Marx understands 'nature' on the one hand in contrast to 'spirit' on the other hand in the sense of 'essence' (*Wesen*). *Wesen* has come down to us as the translation of the *essentia* of the scholastic tradition of German philosophy – *essentia* in contrast to *existentia*, translated by *Dasein*, *Wesen* and *Natur*. (The origin and role of this distinction in the history of ideas is presented in the articles 'Essenz' and 'Existenz' in the *Historisches Wörterbuch der Philosophie*.) In this sense the expression 'human nature' is ambiguous. Marx generally uses this expression in the sense of essence. We cannot discuss this ambiguity of 'nature', which runs through the entire scholastic tradition of philosophy. This is not the essential ambiguity which is behind the debates concerning 'Marxism'. Only against the background of the phenomenological analysis of the 'senses' is it possible to see this ambiguity as such. This analysis has demonstrated that in this elementary activity nature is broader than that which becomes the theme of the exact and biological sciences in their investigation of nature. Overlooking this distinction is what Husserl criticizes in the *Crisis* as the 'objectivism' of modern science: the sciences are characterized by a 'forgetting' of the 'life-world', i.e. of the life-worldly reference to 'nature' in which human beings stand and have always stood *prior* to all scientific research. And it is not only the crisis of the modern sciences which lies in this forgetting, but also the crisis of the 'pre-scientific' world. A remedy for this crisis can only take the form of a 'science' of a different style as a 'science of the life-world', whose point of departure and mode of investigation can only be worked out by transcendental philosophy.

This ambiguity in the concept of nature and in the sciences of nature runs through all attempts to interpret the Marxist texts and through the dispute concerning the true significance of the Marxist approach. The ambiguity in the concept of 'nature' thus produces the ambiguity in the concept of science. It is also decisive for the understanding of the relation between the 'material basis' and the 'superstructure', and for the dogmatizing of this relation. Talk about a 'self-movement of matter' can only be meaningful if it is not understood as a process which has taken place 'in-itself' and can only be pictured in our conceptual thought and scientific research; it is only comprehensible when it is understood that we can only speak of such movement because we ourselves, each of us in his absolute 'There', experiences him or herself as caught up in this movement. Thus, talk about 'matter' and its motion only has a legitimate sense when it is referred to that which we come to understand in correlation to our sensuous activity, thus in this life-worldly reference which cannot be clarified by the objective sciences of nature, but only by the philosophically grounded science of the life-world. Many empirical sciences will have to contribute to the development of this science, but the task of co-ordinating these contributions and bringing them together in an appropriate manner is a philosophical task. Marx was certainly aware of this correlation of human activity to nature when he, in his Paris manuscripts, refused to say what nature really is in abstraction from this correlation. Thus, in Marx's own work the meaning of the ambiguity of the concepts of nature and science remains undecided.

Only when we have seen through this ambiguity can we understand that the science of the basis which Marx projected is not a science in the sense of the natural sciences, but a science of the structures of the life-world in which alone nature is originally there for us as a 'basis'. Against this background we can read the genealogy of labour out of the appropriation of nature as property and thus the genealogy and transformation of the forms of property, which Marx sketched in the *Critique of Political Economy*, as a life-world correction to the limitations of classical political economy, which absolutized the existing circumstances and worked on the basis of static relations without taking into account their historical origin and the role of their own problematic in human history.

The development of the 'means of production' and the 'powers of production' as the basis of human history must also be understood in the sense of a genealogy in the realm of the life-world. Once this is done, the idea of a basis which provides for its own overthrow (cf. *Capital*, vol. II) must be corrected or made more precise. It is surely true that this overthrow depends on relations which are independent of men, but that does not mean that such an overthrow can occur with the necessity of natural law, but only that social action *as* action has to obey its own structural laws which are not of a natural scientific kind. Thus, one can legitimately speak of a 'material basis', but only if this is not understood in the sense of a 'pure' nature, of which we can know nothing, but only with reference to the corporeally active and in this activity teleologically directed human beings. For this reason, the laws of the 'appropriation' of nature are not laws in the sense of the exact natural sciences, but deal with typical regularities in the behaviour of groups of human beings under specific economic conditions. Man never acts in terms of natural conditions which can be determined as what they are in abstraction from his behaviour; he conducts himself with respect to them by means of the *ideas* of them which he in one way or another always has, and one must be familiar with these ideas if one is to understand the behaviour of the given group.

Only in this relation and within this limitation can the concepts of nature and matter and of natural history as the true history of man be given an experiential sense. Only against this background can one say with precision in what sense and with what right we can speak of history as the natural history of the human species and what the meaning of talk about man as species-being is. Here we can only point to the significance of the phenomenological clarification of the relation between absolute individuality and specific generality.

Such phenomenological clarifications do not have the task of instructing Marx as to what he really saw and wanted. But they can help us understand the reasons for the incredible influence of the Marxist tradition. These are to be found precisely in the very different formulations he gave his problems, something which should make it impossible to dogmatize his teachings, which he violently resisted. If phenomenological transcendental philosophy also means critique of dogmatism and openness to the problems which are posed in our 'There', it must also take up the problems Marx posed *as* problems in its theory of crisis, for they deal with the same crisis, though in an *earlier* form than *ours*.

CHAPTER 4

Overcoming the opposition between idealism and materialism in Husserl and Marx

Ante Pažanin (Zagreb)

Let us begin with a simple question: What do idealism and materialism mean in the metaphysical tradition of Western philosophy?

Materialism and idealism are of course two basic ontological options in metaphysical philosophy. These options attempt to answer the question of Being as the fundamental philosophical question by explaining that Being is a material or spiritual substance. In so doing, they introduce matter or the idea as metaphysical entities which exist in themselves.

But original experience knows nothing of such a separation of the real into a material and a spiritual region. This is confirmed by early Greek philosophy, as well as by all genuinely philosophical experience. In the philosophy of the pre-Socratics we find no trace of a distinction, to say nothing of a separation or isolation of the material from the spiritual. Thus, it is false to understand the primal elements of the Milesians such as water, earth, fire and air, or Anaximander's *apeiron* as matter in the sense of metaphysical materialism. They are rather underdetermined in this respect and serve the function, as the word *apeiron* itself clearly shows, of expressing infinite, unlimited Being. By the same token, it would be a mistake to take 'Being' in Parmenides, '*logos*' in Heraclitus or '*nous*' in Anaxagoras as spirit in the sense of metaphysical idealism.

The fact that philosophy did not begin with the opposition between metaphysical materialism and idealism has implications for the fate of philosophy today and in the future: one can suspect that philosophy and human thought will by no means remain tied to the alternative of metaphysical idealism and materialism. The two traditional lines of thought must be overcome in the light of their shortcomings, inadequacies and onesidedness. We shall attempt to demonstrate this in this chapter, using as our examples the supposed materialist Karl Marx and the supposed idealist Edmund Husserl.

With reference to the critique of dogmatism, these two thinkers play the same role today that Kant and Hegel played in the last two centuries. In both Husserl and Marx we find an overcoming of both idealism and materialism and their dogmatic opposition. In this sense we can speak of phenomenology and Marxism as two of the most important movements in contemporary philosophical thought. I wish to place the emphasis on movements of historical philosophical thought and not on finished systems of philosophy, although in our own century – appealing to Karl Marx – attempts have been made to establish dialectical materialism in opposition to idealism. For this reason we shall contrast the original historical materialism of Karl Marx with all other forms of materialism, including the dialectical materialism of our century. This is the sense in which we understand Marx's demand for an overcoming of idealism as well as materialism, for 'spiritualism disappears along with the opposing materialism'.[1]

In opposition to various tendencies of a 'resurrection of metaphysics' and a 'restitution of idealism' in our century, Husserl demands not merely the overcoming of the ontological opposition between idealism and materialism, but rather 'the phenomenological dissolution of all philosophical oppositions'.[2] We shall discuss this Husserlian demand in the second half of this essay, after having thematized Marx's relation to traditional materialism and his demand for an overcoming of the alternative of materialism versus idealism.

1 Marx and materialism[3]

As we have already noted, Western philosophy begins neither with materialism nor with idealism; this opposition is not a characteristic of the entire history of human thought, not even of the entire history of philosophy. Rather, it is restricted to those epochs in which a separation of matter and spirit and the priority of the one or the other prevailed. To be sure, matter and spirit were not always determined and conceived in the same manner in these epochs. For this reason we must be careful to distinguish not merely between these two basic options themselves, but also between their specific types and forms, taking into account the concrete forms they take on in the history of Western metaphysics. This is of decisive significance for our understanding of materialism in the work of Karl Marx and for its relationship to other forms of materialism.

In the effort of understanding his own post-Hegelian situation, but also with the goal of establishing communism as the 'new Athens', Marx devoted himself to a detailed study of Western metaphysics, especially ancient Greek philosophy, with a view to drawing a world-historical parallel between the specific periods and representatives of Greek and modern philosophy. As we know, he published a portion of these investigations in his dissertation *On the Difference Between the Philosophies of Nature of Democritus and the Epicureans*, which was influenced by the general sympathy of the Young Hegelians for classical antiquity and especially for late Greek philosophy. In the footnotes to the dissertation one can see that Marx pursued these historical analyses and reflections in order to become clear about the possibilities for life and thought in general in the post-Hegelian situation.

The 'new Athens' later becomes communism for Marx, i.e. the new '*polis*' in which all will be free and equal, such that there are neither slaves nor masters. The 'new Athens' also represents the new mode of thought which is to surpass metaphysical philosophy as historical thought. In developing both the idea of the new world and of this new mode of thought, Marx's knowledge of ancient Greek philosophy was certainly of great assistance. For this reason, we wish to direct our attention to it a bit longer, for the difference between Democritus and Epicurus also accounts for a number of contemporary differences.

The assumption of a complete identity between Democritus' and Epicurus' physics dominated, according to Marx, for a long time. This prejudice is unfortunately still widespread, a prejudice which completely neglects the peculiarities of Epicurus' philosophy of nature. In opposition to the 'old, established prejudice of identifying Democritean and Epicurean physics' Marx is concerned to demonstrate a 'difference between Democritean and Epicurean physics in spite of their similarities'.[4] Epicurus' 'physics' is indeed by no means a sensualistic continuation of Democritus' atomism, and the declination of the atoms is not an inappropriate and 'unfortunate' idea, as even Dilthey and the traditional history of philosophy would have it. What we find here in Epicurus is actually the idea of freedom, which has tremendous significance not only for the understanding of the peculiarities of the Epicurean philosophy of nature, but also as an explanation of happy human life in general and of the world as a whole.

Democritus taught that there are atoms surrounded by an empty space which makes rectilinear motion possible. As a consequence of the fact that the atoms have different weights, they move at different speeds. The atoms collide with one another, whereby it is possible that things disappear and arise according to the necessity of a rectilinear movement which is made possible by the empty space and the collisions of the atoms, the collision being conditioned by the quantitative properties of the atoms. Epicurus accepts the Democritean idea of the necessity of a 'movement in straight lines' as well as that of the collision or, as Marx says, the 'repulsion of the atoms', but he does not stop there, going on to introduce the 'declination of the atoms from a straight line' as a new kind of movement of the atom through which, according to Marx, the 'actual soul of the atom. . .is represented'. The declination or deviation of the atom is the law which 'rather permeates the entire Epicurean philosophy in such a way that, needless to say, the manner in which it manifests itself is dependent on the sphere in which it is applied'.[5] Just as the declination of the atom, which signifies contingency or freedom, is only possible on the basis of the necessity of a rectilinear movement of the atoms, the 'repulsion of the many atoms' is itself only possible in connection with the declination of the individual atoms. The repulsion of many atoms is an immediate consequence of the declination of the atom. In this sense, as Marx correctly notes, the 'repulsion of the many atoms [is] the necessary realization of the *lex atome*, as Lucretius calls the declination'. Thus, repulsion must be added to the other forms of movement, the rectilinear and the deviation, as a third movement, since in it 'every determination is posited as a special existent'. In addition, 'Thus, in the repulsion of the atoms their materiality, which was assumed as given in the declination, is synthetically unified.'[6]

On this basis it is clear why Marx's sympathies as a dialectician and philosopher of history and freedom are on Epicurus' side: Epicurus, in his essential idea of the declination of the atom, i.e. of the contingency or freedom of the individual, recognized the authentic 'essence of repulsion' as the 'first form of self-consciousness, which grasps itself as immediate-existent, abstract-individual', whereas Democritus, Marx goes on to say, 'knows only their material existence'. In this sense, Democritus, in contrast to Epicurus, turns 'what for the latter was a realization of the concept of the atom into a violent movement, a deed of blind necessity'.[7] The declination of the atom is of universal significance. Marx concludes: 'Just as the atom frees itself from its relative existence, the straight line, by abstracting from it, deviating from it: in the same manner, the entire Epicurean philosophy deviates from the restrictive existence at which at every point the concept of abstract particularity, the independence and negation of all relations to others is to be presented in its existence.'[8]

The universal significance of the declination of the atom as the difference between the philosophies of nature of Democritus and Epicurus is expressed in the fact that it indicates a *deviation from the 'straight line' 'everywhere where the concept of abstract particularity is to be presented . . . in its existence' and freedom,*[9] regardless of whether it is a matter of 'meteors' and heavenly bodies, pain and delight or of the human world or the gods. The declination makes possible the appearance of the individual in its totality. And 'there, where the abstract particular appears in its highest freedom and independence, in its totality, there the existent, before which the particular deviates, is all of existence'.[10] Man and his world are thus 'all of existence', in other words, the single actual world.

In accordance with his theory of the declination of the atom and according to the model of the gods in Greek art, Epicurus' gods 'deviate from the world' and settle in the 'interstices of the real world',[11] unconcerned with human existence. In view of the general narrowness and religious prejudices of his age, Epicurus attempted to use the declination of the atoms to account for man in his 'highest freedom and independence', in his totality as 'the whole of existence' and single true 'reality', in which there is no place for gods; this reality is, as the human world, indeed the 'whole of existence', so that the gods deviate into extra-worldly and inter-worldly or interstitial regions.

The Epicurean understanding of the repulsion of the atoms is not restricted to the realm of physics; it has a *universal significance for the explanation of the human world*, but in such a way that it can do justice to the peculiarities and special qualities of the specific spheres. Thus, the concrete form of repulsion 'in the realm of the political [is] the *contract*, in the social realm *friendship*'.[12]

That which we have demonstrated on the basis of the difference between Democritus and Epicurus could also be demonstrated with respect to Holbach and Helvetius within French materialism. Since he stands on Epicurus' side, Marx favours Helvetius' materialism as opposed to the materialism of the rest of the French Enlightenment as the second significant form of traditional materialism. The third form of traditional materialism is, of course, Feuerbach's. We cannot go into this here, although we would find that ontological, epistemological and other philosophical problems are handled much more clearly in traditional materialism than in the texts of many contemporary 'dialectical' materialists.

The conception of nature which appears as early as Marx's dissertation reappears in all of his later writings. Indeed, it is one of the basic elements in his conception of nature. The otherwise very solid work of A. Schmidt[13] does not discuss the philosophy of nature of the dissertation. But especially the last chapter of the dissertation is of fundamental significance. Here Marx compares the 'natural science of self-consciousness' as developed by Epicurus with Democritus' 'empirical investigation of nature'. Marx stresses that:

> in Epicurus atomism with all its contradictions is carried out and completed as the natural science of self-consciousness, which is its own principle under the form of abstract particularity. . . .
> In Democritus, in contrast, the atom is merely the universally objective expression of empirical research pure and simple. Thus, the atom remains for him a pure and abstract category, a hypothesis which is the result of experience, not its energetic principle, which thus remains without realization, just as real research into nature is not determined by it in any further manner.[14]

It is well known that, and why, Marx preferred the natural philosophy of Epicurus. But instead of drawing the consequences from this reference, Marxism has tended to remain rooted in the empirical investigation of nature as founded by Democritus and continued by the positivism of the nineteenth and twentieth centuries, be it in the sense of the individual sciences, or in the sense of dialectical materailism, from which each expected an affirmation of his own *a priori* metaphysical theses. In his conception and explanation of the world Marx takes neither 'abstract categories, hypotheses', which are taken over as the mere result of experience, nor dialectical-materialist metaphysical principles as his point of departure, but rather the historical reality which bears within itself the principle of its own occurrence.

For this reason, we shall now attempt to sketch the sense of Marx's original historical materialism. Just as we have emphasized his sympathy for Epicurus and Helvetius, we shall underline the historical character of his thought. But the following must be noted if misunderstandings are to be avoided: although Marx's sympathies belong to Epicurus, especially to his theory of the 'declination of the atom from the straight line' as the freedom of individual existence and the understanding of 'repulsion' as the 'first form of self-consciousness', it would be false to try to restrict his original historical materialism and his idea of the totality of the historical structure to some form of traditional materialism. In addition, that means that it would be equally false to reduce Marx's materialism to the subjective line of contemporary, so-called 'creative Marxism', as well as to the so-called objective line of the Democritean-Holbachian or dialectical-materialistic school of thought. Marx's original historical-materialistic thought transcends this opposition too in transcending traditional idealism and materialism as well as their varieties. This can be shown more clearly by taking a closer look at Marx's concept of nature.

'Nature', as Marx writes in his *Political and Philosophic Manuscripts*, 'taken abstractly, for itself, and fixedly isolated from man, is *nothing* for man'.[15] On the other hand, man has 'actual, sensuous objects for his nature as objects of his life-expressions' only because he himself 'is a corporeal, actual, sentient objective being'.[16]

In *Capital* too Marx emphasizes again and again the historical-social character of the concept of nature and the natural origin of man. 'Man himself, viewed as the impersonation of labour power' is nothing other than 'a natural object, a thing, although a living conscious thing'.[17] The relation between man and nature appears most clearly in labour. Labour is the 'urgent manifestation' of labour-power, and as 'the creator of use-value. . .it is an eternal nature-imposed necessity, without which there can be no material exchanges between man and Nature, and therefore no life'.[18] In his analysis of the commodity, Marx emphasizes again and again that labour is referred to something which can be neither dissected into subjective and social determinations nor elevated to an objective metaphysical reality. 'If we take away the useful labour' which is to be found in the dress, screen, etc. (i.e. in the use-values), 'a material substratum is always left which is furnished by Nature without the help of man'.[19] This natural material substratum is, as we have already seen, taken purely for itself absolutely nothing. Marx determines this substratum neither as a spiritual nor as a material entity. By no means does he determine it as something 'objective' – and to this extent Marx is not committed to a metaphysical objectivism – nor does he dissect it into something purely subjective – to this extent Marx avoids modern subjectivism. Rather he sees it as a presupposition which asserts itself as a moment in the dialectical process of production in history, i.e. in the production of life itself.

This conception of the unity of nature and history, of the objective and the subjective, the thing and man, recalls Aristotle's conception of matter and form as well as the Hegelian conception of being and movement. The Aristotelian and Hegelian moment comes to expression not only in the early writings, but just as clearly in *Capital* and especially in the *Grundrisse*:

> This *form-giving* activity consumes the object and consumes itself, but it consumes the given form of the object only in order to posit it in a new objective form, and it consumes itself only in its subjective form as activity. . . . But as *product*, the result of the production process is *use-value*.[20]

The unity of natural and social, material and formal, objective and subjective moments of the production process manifests itself in use-value as product. In spite of all transformations and refinements of the form, this process never yields the so-called 'pure form'. This distinguishes Marx from Aristotle as well as from Hegel. Matter separated from form is nothing, just as nature is nothing when it is separated from man and his forming activity. The use-value demonstrates most clearly that the natural, material element in everything is preserved in spite of all transformation. There is no existence without it, just as there is no life without the formal, subjective moment. Marx's original conception of the unity of nature and history is thus preserved in his later work. It protects him from the objectivism as well as the subjectivism of modern philosophy.

Marx's original conception of the human understanding of the world is well known under the title of historical materialism. The expression materialism and its derivatives are freed from their metaphysical meaning in Marx, but not in Engels and in dialectical materialism. Here we find the decisive differences between Marx and Engels with respect to the basic philosophical problems and the problematic of nature. Whereas Engels and the entire dialectical materialism, whose dialectic grounds a nature in itself, remain caught in the metaphysical tradition and its battle between 'the idealistic and materialistic camps in philosophy', as Engels puts it in *Ludwig Feuerbach and the End of Classical German Philosophy*, Marx is concerned with a transcendence of idealism as well as materialism – indeed, with transcending the entire metaphysical tradition and its alienated forms of human existence. Admittedly, Marx too often calls his conception 'materialistic' and 'materialism', but never dialectical materialism, for by materialism he understands not one of the two opposed lines of philosophical thought, thus by no means an extension and improvement of traditional materialism, but rather his own originally historical materialism and that of Engels as presented in their common efforts such as the *German Ideology*. Thus, this historical materialism is for Marx not an application of the later so-called dialectical materialism to history and society, but rather the original and unitary grasp of nature and history, i.e. a real humanism as completed naturalism, which as a unitary grasp of matter and idea represents the transcending of materialism as well as idealism: it is the truth of the old opposition. The term materialism and its derivatives belong with most other similar terms to the metaphysical tradition from which Marx emerged. Thus it is understandable that he uses such expressions even when he is thinking of something fundamentally new, for the simple reason that no other expressions were available with which he could express his critique of and transcendence of the tradition to which he belongs. In this context it is clear that the proper understanding of the matters with which he is concerned has to be of first priority, and not the terminology itself, for the experience of truth and the coming to terms with the things themselves makes possible not only a new and original use of the traditional expressions but also the creation of new concepts which would be adequate to contemporary historical existence and the historical process. Thus, Marx remains the radical critic of the traditional and the founder of the new, originally historical thinking, although he makes use of the terminology of the metaphysical tradition, even up to the point of calling his own basic position 'historical materialism' and 'real humanism'.

But whereas one can recognize in Marx the clear intention to give expression to the historical world of man in an adequate manner – and this is by no means pure matter or pure reality, neither naked thing (*res*) nor naked nature in itself, but rather matter, thing, nature in historical formations – this is not the case in Engels. For him materialism means precisely what it had meant in the entire philosophical tradition, namely a line of philosophical thought opposed to idealism, a line of thought which gives a traditional answer to questions concerning the relation between being and thought, matter and idea, object and subject, namely that matter is primary and consciousness secondary. This materialism is not even capable of grasping a correlation between subject and object, consciousness and matter, to say nothing of their truth in the unity of the opposites. Even when Engels writes in *Ludwig Feuerbach* that 'materialism signifies nothing other than the study of the real world', he does not transcend the boundaries of the metaphysical tradition but remains – as his comments here and in other texts show – within the spell of this tradition. By materialism he does not understand the study of the concrete historical world in the sense of original historical materialism, but in the sense of the dialectically developed materialism of the Holbachian tradition. Engels was, of course, the first Marxist to extend the dialectic to nature in itself. On the basis of this extension as a metaphysical Holbachian-Hegelian addition to the original historical materialism, the formalism and schematism of the dialectic was able to develop within Marxism as a new kind of metaphysics in the form of dialectical materialism. And this is just the logical consequence of turning away from the ground of history – in the first place a consequence of the retreat from the horizon of historical praxis, just as the 'dialectical-materialist' verbalism and a scholasticism of this sort are the fruit of an 'elaboration' of the dialectic of nature as a new metaphysics with 'universally valid features' and 'necessary laws' which – like the diamond – are to be scientifically discovered and applied in all areas: from the inorganic matter which exists 'in itself' to the matter which thinks and exists 'in itself and for itself'.

It is well known that Marx did not reject every conception and interpretation of nature, not even every dialectic of nature. Indeed, he developed implicitly and explicitly a specific dialectic of nature, the only one about which we can meaningfully speak, within his conception of human labour and praxis as the medium of natural history and historical nature. To be sure, Engels never gave up the conception of history as the horizon of human life, but he was concerned, 'following Hegel's false example',[21] to extend the dialectic to nature in itself, i.e. to complement his own (and Marx's) dialectic of labour and praxis (i.e. the dialectic of historical nature and natural history) by a dialectic of nature in itself. Engels was apparently never aware that he actually undermined the original conception of historical materialism in doing this. In giving metaphysics a priority over against the dialectic, he made the dialectic dependent on precisely this metaphysics. Materialism and idealism are the two sides and the two essential possibilities of this metaphysical tradition. In this sense, Marx's naturalism-humanism is a demand for the transcendence of both metaphysical options. From the standpoint of historical materialism, the idea of a rivalry with idealism is meaningless. Dialectical materialists, on the other hand, are proud to have their own philosophical system with which they can confront idealism and other metaphysical schools. They are generally unaware of the fact that they do worse in this rivalry than even the idealists, as the example of Engels and Hegel makes clear. That which was possible for the idealist Hegel in the elaboration of his system of absolute knowledge against the background of metaphysical idealist presuppositions is fundamentally impossible for the historical materialist if he does not want to become a pure idealist or idealist in its otherness, i.e. a metaphysical materialist. But precisely this is what the dialectics of nature and Engels's dialectical materialism produced in their imitation or – as one might say – in their materialist reading of Hegel. It seems to be forgotten that for Hegel nature is actually the idea of nature and that he can thus legitimately speak of a dialectic of nature as the presentation of the idea in its otherness. But precisely this is illegitimate for the materialist. Thus Marx was doing nothing other than drawing the consequences of his historical materialism in rejecting speculations about an unhistorical nature. The question of nature in itself, i.e. a – as Marx puts it – nature 'isolated from praxis', is a 'purely scholastic question'.[22]

The Marxian conception of the unity of nature and man is grounded in the fact that one can meaningfully speak of nature only to the extent that it is somehow a historically mediated nature, i.e. only to the extent that it has become a humanized or even a historical nature.

In the *German Ideology* Marx elaborates this idea in the following manner:

> We know only a single science, the science of history. One can look at history from two sides and divide it into the history of nature and the history of men. The two sides are, however, inseparable; the history of nature and the history of men are dependent on each other so long as men exist.[23]

To be sure, these sentences along with the entire paragraph they belong to were crossed out by Marx himself. This has prompted some editors not only to leave this passage out of published editions; they sometimes do not even mention its existence. This crossed-out passage has also served as an excuse to declare the basic idea of a unity of nature and history to be unmarxist and unacceptable.

What is Marx talking about in this text? As the text itself makes clear, there is not a single idea there which could not be found in other texts by Marx. And why then did Marx cross out this paragraph?

It seems to me that there is no other, no deeper reason than the simple fact that Marx decided to begin the section dealing with 'ideology in general, specifically the German philosophy' with the next paragraph, and not with the passage we are dealing with. The new, i.e. the following paragraph, begins with the words:

> The premises from which we begin are not arbitrary ones, not dogmas, but real premises from which abstraction can only be made in the imagination. They are the real individuals, their activity and the material conditions under which they live, both those which they find already existing and those produced by their activity.[24]

This text is indeed more appropriate than that of the first passage for beginning a chapter which will deal with German philosophy as ideology which does not inquire into 'the connection between German philosophy and German reality' or into the 'actual presuppositions' of life itself. In placing these sentences at the beginning of the section, Marx emphasizes the antidogmatic character of his approach, for nature cannot be simply posited as a dogma but must be understood as the self-realizing actual presupposition which exists for us at all only in history. The crossed-out passage might, in line with its significance for the composition of the work, have been placed in the preface or in the introduction to the entire work – and not in a special chapter – for it actually gives a synthesis of Marx's thoughts concerning nature and man up to 1845-6. It makes it easier to understand the work itself in its basic intention and in its connection with the preceding theoretical development.

The general significance of the *German Ideology* is that of a testimony of the maturity of Marx's and Engels's conception of the world and human life. In its chapters the work offers discussions of concrete problems of the 'ideology' of specific 'philosophical recipes and schemata' and a settling of accounts with their representatives. It is important to emphasize that Marx and Engels present their common conception of nature and history in this joint effort and that above all they had definitively worked out their materialist conception prior to 1845-6 – the materialist dialectic or historical materialism, which is by no means to be identified with the later dialectical materialism. They worked out their historical-materialist conception of the world together, and completed and affirmed it in their later works – Engels even in his *Dialectics of Nature*, independently of his attempts to supplement this conception in a dialectical-materialist direction. Engels was not clear about the fact that in so doing he actually undermined this common product, and that this original historical-materialist conception as a 'philosophy' of historical life makes Marxism superior to all other philosophical positions.

That Marx's only reason for crossing out the passage in question really was the one suggested is shown by a comparison of this text with the immediately following pages, especially where Marx criticizes Bruno Bauer for his separation of nature and history as if 'man did not always have before him an historical nature and a natural history',[25] or when he criticizes Ludwig Feuerbach for his failure to understand the relation between 'industry' and the 'sensuous world (*Umwelt*)' and for his influence on science and even on the 'pure natural sciences'. 'He [Feuerbach] does not see how the sensuous world around him is, not a thing given direct from all eternity, remaining ever the same, but the product of industry and the state of society.'[26] The separation of nature and history has the consequence that Feuerbach

> gives no criticism of the present conditions of life. Thus he never manages to conceive the sensuous world as the total living sensuous *activity* of the individuals composing it; and therefore. . .he is compelled to take refuge in the 'higher perception' and in the ideal 'compensation of the species', and thus to relapse into idealism at the very point where the communist materialist sees the necessity, and at the same time the condition, of a transformation both of industry and of the social structure.[27]

Thus, 'As far as Feuerbach is a materialist he does not deal with history, and as far as he considers history he is not a materialist. With him materialism and history diverge completely'.[28] Marx's charge against Feuerbach here holds in general for contemporary dialectical materialism and its separation of nature and history, of natural and social science. Marx is concerned here to demonstrate their unity, for even the so-called 'pure' natural sciences, just like the entire human world, is the 'product' of those human activities and relations which make men what they are, just as men make the relations what they are.

This dialectical or historical-materialist conception of the human world is typical not only of Marx's early writings but of his entire corpus. The presuppositions which constitute a thinker's point of departure should not be taken as dogmas, but must rather be accounted for as presuppositions of real human existence – which fulfil and confirm themselves in the production and reproduction of life itself as well as in the understanding and scientific investigation of this life and this historical development. As early as in the *Holy Family* (1844–5), Marx charges 'critical criticism' with 'excluding man's theoretical and political conduct toward nature [i.e.] natural science and industry, from the historical movement'.[29] Precisely because it separates history from nature, the 'spiritualistic, the theological critical criticism does not see the birthplace of history in the coarse-material production on earth but rather in the hazy cloud-formation in the heavens'.[30] Already the young Marx sees not only the two extremes: unhistorical nature and unnatural history, but transcends them in the horizon of praxis as the real world of active human beings. Just as history cannot be dissected into a misty cloud-structure-in-the-sky in the sense of the 'critical critique' and its contemporary idealistic spokesmen, nature cannot be understood as a dogma in the sense of pre-Feuerbachian materialism and its later descendants.

The deep connection between Marx's early writings and his later works are often kept carefully concealed even today. The passage from the famous 'Preface' to the *Critique of Political Economy* of 1859 in which Marx writes that he and Engels settled accounts with their 'one-time philosophical conscience' (1845) is often quoted without mention of the fact that the *German Ideology* is that work in which Marx and Engels not only settled accounts 'with our former philosophical conscience' but that they 'worked out' their 'views... *jointly*'.[31] Marx writes that they have come to a 'self-understanding'. There is a particular interest in concealing the sense in which Marx and Engels 'have explained' things at that time and just what kind of 'views' and 'self-understanding' they are talking about. It is, as we know, the original materialist conception of history.

Thus, if Marx and Engels worked out their materialist conception of history in the *German Ideology* and in so doing came to terms with their 'former philosophical conscience', it can only be the 'philosophical conscience' of the metaphysical tradition which Engels later was the first to re-establish within Marxism when he replaced the original historical materialism by the dialectic of nature as a curious mixture of pre-Feuerbachian metaphysical materialism and Hegelian philosophy of nature. Engels's 'supplementation' of historical materialism produced the dialectical materialism of the twentieth century, a philosophical system which dialectically understands and explains the world as a material substance in its development from inorganic up to thinking matter. Instead of historical materialism as a critical science which attempts to grasp the concrete historical, i.e. the human–historical world as a whole, dialectical materialism appears in the twentieth century with its division of the human world and knowledge into the realm of nature in itself and that of human society, in '*Diamat*' and '*Histomat*', in ontology–epistemology–logic and philosophy of society, in natural and social science, which are all to follow the same procedures.

Of course, Engels could hardly suspect that the dialectic of nature which he prepared as early as the 1850s and later inaugurated would have such consequences, both for his and Marx's original conception and interpretation of the human world and for the fate of Marxism in the first half of the twentieth century. Engels could not know that his endeavours in the area of the philosophy and dialectics of nature would, to paraphrase Engels himself, lead to a 'new natural-scientific materialism' and a 'pre-Kantian' metaphysics. For instead of solving the problem historically, dialectical materialism re-establishes the French Lamettrie–Holbach version of pre-Kantian, 'dialectically' interpreted metaphysics. Marxian materialism must be distinguished from idealism as well as from traditional materialism and naturalism. As we have seen, Marx takes nature as his point of departure, not a nature separated from man, but rather historical nature and human life, for man himself is not a pure spirit but rather a spiritual–bodily being. In this sense, Marx succumbs neither to the objectivism and naturalism nor to the subjectivism and anthropocentrism of modern and contemporary philosophy in his conception of nature and history, but transcends idealism and materialism as well as their contemporary descendents in his original historical thought.

2 Husserl and idealism

What we have said in Section 1 about Marx, his relation to materialism and his transcendence of the alternative between materialism and idealism can be demonstrated in a similar manner concerning Husserl's relationship to idealism and his call for a 'phenomenological dissolution of all philosophical oppositions'.

In the final part of the third version of the *Encyclopaedia Britannica* article of autumn 1927, Husserl writes the following about phenomenology, 'its proper function' and its relationship to metaphysics:

> The universal self-reflection of humanity takes place in [phenomenology] as absolutely universal science; its results, continually expanding in breadth and completeness, the theories and disciplines are in the final analysis called to regulate via insight a genuine human life. With regard to metaphysics, phenomenological philosophy is anti-metaphysical only in the sense that it rejects every metaphysics which draws sustenance from extra-scientific sources and every metaphysics which moves in empty substructions. But the old metaphysical tradition and its genuine problems must be posed on the transcendental ground and find their pure formulation here, the phenomenological method producing their solution. The complete formation of the idea of a universal phenomenology leads back to precisely the old concept of philosophy, that of the universal and absolute, i.e. the completely justified, science.[32]

I have discussed Husserl's most important attempts at a 'complete development of the ideal of a universal phenomenology' in my dissertation.[33] In so doing I was able to show, on the basis of the lectures now entitled *First Philosophy*, that Husserl was on the point of going beyond 'the old tradition of metaphysics' as early as 1923. This is given an even clearer expression in the title to the sixteenth chapter of the final version of the *Encyclopaedia Britannica* article: 'The Phenomenological Dissolution of all Philosophical Oppositions'. It is a question of the phenomenological dissolution of the 'traditional ambiguous oppositions of philosophical points of view'.[34] There are various kinds of such oppositions. In the first version of the article they are called the oppositions between 'rationalism (Platonism) and empiricism, subjectivism and objectivism, idealism and realism, ontologism and transcendentalism, psychologism and anti-psychologism, positivism and metaphysics'.[35] As Husserl himself says, one finds here 'at every point justified motives' at work, but 'everywhere half-measures and impermissible absolutizing of merely relative and abstractly justified one-sidednesses'[36] rule the day.

How are these 'half-measures' and 'impermissible absolutizing' of the metaphysical oppositions dissolved or overcome? According to Husserl their overcoming takes place fundamentally by means of 'the originally giving intuition'. What this signifies can be shown most simply in terms of the opposition between empiricism and rationalism:

> Empiricism can only [be overcome] by the most universal and consequent empiricism, which substitutes for the restricted 'experience' of the empiricists the necessarily broadened concept of experience, the originarily giving intuition, which in all of its forms (intuition of eidos, apodictic evidence, phenomenological intuition of essences, etc.) establishes the type and form of its justificatory power (*Rechtgebung*) by means of phenomenological clarification. As eidetics, on the other hand, phenomenology is rationalistic, but it overcomes restricted dogmatic rationalism by means of the most universal investigation of essences with unitary reference to transcendental subjectivity, I-consciousness and the objectivities of which we are conscious.[37]

Husserl explains the overcoming of the opposition between subjectivism and objectivism even more clearly:

> Subjectivism can only be overcome by the most universal and consequent subjectivism (transcendental subjectivism). In this form it is simultaneously objectivism to the extent that it represents the legitimacy (*Recht*) of every objectivity which is sustained by harmonious experience, underlining its full and genuine sense, against which the supposedly realistic objectivism sins in its lack of understanding of transcendental constitution.[38]

The overcoming of the metaphysical alternatives of idealism and materialism or realism are of the greatest importance for our current interest. For although, as Husserl says, 'tracing back all of being to transcendental subjectivity and its constitutive intentional achievements [allows] only a *teleological* view of the world..., phenomenology also accords a core of truth to *naturalism*'.[39]

Thus, Husserlian phenomenology and its 'idealism' bears naturalism, or as Husserl puts it 'natural realism completely within itself'[40] —just as Marxian materialism bears idealism within itself. Indeed, just as Marxian historical materialism as the 'completed naturalism of man and the completed humanism of nature'[41] represents the real humanism, and as such can represent the truth of idealism and materialism only in the form of their overcoming, Husserlian phenomenology as 'investigation into the essences of ego-consciousness and conscious objectivities' represents the 'justified motives', i.e. the overcoming and truth of those 'merely relative and abstractedly justified one-sidednesses'. One can even go so far as to say that just as Marx's historical materialism as the unitary 'science of history' allows for the distinction but in no sense the separation of nature and history, Husserl's phenomenology calls for the overcoming of the alternative of objectivism and subjectivism and 'the other oppositions which play a role here'.[42]

Although Husserl talks about the 'living intentions' of ancient as well as modern philosophy, and is very open to 'stimulation from the great figures of the past', his phenomenology rejects 'all philosophical Renaissances'.[43] In this sense, phenomenology as 'philosophy of the most original and universal self-reflection'[44] is a new mode of original human thought and universal historical self-reflection.

This overcoming of the traditional metaphysical oppositions is the real intention not only of the work of Marx and Husserl, but also of contemporary historical thought in general. We, however, have deliberately restricted our attention to these two thinkers. Marx demands the development of 'a single science, science of history', which is to develop historically 'the actual logic of its actual object' and in so doing make the 'realization of philosophy' possible, and Husserl calls for 'the complete development of the idea of a universal phenomenology', which is to develop 'the originally giving intuition' everywhere and in so doing make possible 'a truly human life'.

This entire problematic need not be discussed here all over again, it is enough to recall it.[45] But it seemed to us important that we at least suggest that the basic ontological problematic in Marx and Husserl is a necessary preliminary for all further philosophical work. For, as Landgrebe has put it:

> if we today, on the basis above all of Heidegger's work, speak of the 'end of metaphysics' as if it were simply obvious, we understand the sense of these words only when we follow the manner in which leave is taken from metaphysics in this work [Husserl's *First Philosophy*], as it were, behind Husserl's back. One might say that this work *is* the end of metaphysics in the sense that continuing under the cast of its thought and its concepts. . .is no longer possible after this.[46]

And Heidegger understands phenomenology itself as:

> the possibility of thought which transforms itself and which only in this transformation remains a possibility in which thought can satisfy the claim of that which is to be thought. If phenomenology is experienced and maintained in this manner, then it can disappear

as a title in favour of the matter of thought, whose openness remains a secret.[47]

What Heidegger says here is true not only of phenomenology but also of Marxism – indeed, it is true of every philosophy which does not take finished philosophical systems, standpoints and world-views as point of departure, but rather the things themselves and real problems. For only in thinking about what matters does the 'matter of thinking' show itself. In this sense, Husserl calls us back to 'the things themselves', and Marx calls not for the matter of logic, but for the 'logic of the matters', which must be seen, 'experienced and maintained'.

Notes

1 Karl Marx, 'Kritik des Hegelschen Staatsrechts', in *Frühe Schriften*, vol. I, Stuttgart, Cotta Verlag, 1962, p. 315.
2 Edmund Husserl, 'Der Encyclopaedia Britannica Artikel', in *Husserliana*, vol. IX, The Hague, Martinus Nijhoff, 1968, p. 299.
3 The first part of the present essay is a shortened version of my essay 'Marx i dijalekticki materijalizam', which originally appeared in *Praxis*, vol. 3, 1965, pp. 115–30, and was reprinted in my book *Marx i materijalizam*, Split, 1972.
4 Marx, 'Kritik des Hegelschen Staatsrechts', op. cit., p. 25.
5 Ibid., p. 42.
6 Ibid., pp. 43–44.
7 Ibid., p. 45.
8 Ibid., p. 42.
9 Ibid., p. 43.
10 Ibid.
11 Ibid.
12 Ibid., p. 45.
13 A. Schmidt, *The Concept of Nature in Marx*, New York, Schocken Books, 1978.
14 Marx, 'Kritik des Hegelschen Staatsrechts', op. cit., p. 69.
15 Karl Marx, *Writings of the Young Marx on Philosophy and Society*, ed. and trans. Lloyd D. Easton and Kurt H. Guddat, Garden City, NY, Doubleday, 1967, p. 335.
16 Ibid., p. 325.
17 Karl Marx, *Capital. A Critique of Political Economy*, vol. I, New York, International Publishers, 1967, p. 202.
18 Ibid., pp. 42–3.
19 Ibid.
20 Karl Marx, *Grundrisse*, trans. Martin Nicolaus, New York, Vintage Books, 1973, p. 301.

21 George Lukács, *Geschichte und Klassenbewußtsein*, Berlin, 1923, p. 17.
22 Karl Marx, 'Second Thesis on Feuerbach', in *Writings of the Young Marx on Philosophy and Society*, p. 401.
23 Karl Marx and Friedrich Engels, *Feuerbach: The First Part of 'The German Ideology'*, London, Lawrence & Wishart, 1973, p. 15.
24 Ibid., p. 18.
25 Ibid., p. 29.
26 Ibid., p. 28.
27 Ibid., pp. 30–1.
28 Ibid., p. 31.
29 Karl Marx, *Die Frühschriften*, Stuttgart, Cotta, 1953, p. 338.
30 Ibid.
31 Karl Marx, 'Zur Kritik der politischen Ökonomie', in *Marx-Engels Werke*, vol. 13, Berlin, Dietz Verlag, 1961, p. 10.
32 Husserl, 'Der Encyclopaedia Britannica Artikel', op. cit., p. 526.
33 A. Pažanin, *Das Problem der Philosophie als strenger Wissenschaft in der Phänomenologie Edmund Husserls*, Cologne, 1962; reprinted in *Wissenschaft und Geschichte in der Phänomenologie Edmund Husserls*, The Hague, Martinus Nijhoff, 1972. Cf. especially the third part: 'Die Wege zur Verwirklichung der Philosophie als Wissenschaft in der Sicht der transzendentalen Phänomenologie'.
34 Husserl, 'Der Encyclopaedia Britannica Artikel', op. cit., p. 253.
35 Ibid.
36 Ibid.
37 Ibid., p. 254.
38 Ibid., pp. 253–4.
39 Ibid., p. 301.
40 Ibid., p. 254.
41 Marx, *Die Frühschriften*, op. cit., p. 237.
42 Husserl, 'Der Encyclopaedia Britannica Artikel', op. cit., p. 254.
43 Ibid.
44 Ibid.
45 Cf. 'Vom transzendentalen Subjektivismus zur Geschichte' and 'Das Problem der Geschichte bei Hegel, Husserl und Marx', in Pažanin, *Wissenschaft und Geschichte in der Phänomenologie Edmund Husserls*, pp. 112–85, as well as my studies 'Wahrheit und Lebenswelt beim späten Husserl', in *Phaenomenologica*, vol. 61, pp. 71–117, and 'Über die Möglichkeit einer phänomenologischen Philosophie der Politik', in *Phänomenologische Forschung*, vol. 3, 1976.
46 Ludwig Landgrebe, *Der Weg der Phänomenologie*, Gütersloh, Mohn, 1963, p. 165. Concerning the problem of the 'conceptuality' (*Begrifflichkeit*) of metaphysics, phenomenology and Marxism, cf. Landgrebe's essay on teleology and corporeality in this volume (Chapter 3).
47 Martin Heidegger, *Zur Sache des Denkens*, Tübingen, Klostermann, 1969, p. 90.

CHAPTER 5

Towards an open dialectic

Bernhard Waldenfels (Bochum)

The choice of this theme represents an attempt to find a level of inquiry and discourse on which phenomenologists and Marxists can seriously encounter one another. The theme seems to me to cut in both directions, so both sides should feel challenged. In view of the fact that the representatives of the two lines of thought take different problems as their points of departure, it would already be progress if we could discover points of common concern which would guarantee that we do not simply talk past one another. This dialogue is threatened both by the danger of a defensive polemic which hardens one's own standpoint and by a superficial eclecticism which brushes over the genuine differences. These dangers can be countered by a willingness to open up one's own field of vision with reference to a common object of discussion. In this sense, I shall take phenomenology as it has developed from and beyond Husserl as my point of departure, and I shall assume that neither phenomenology nor Marxism exist in a finished form and that, among others, so-called structuralism can stimulate both sides in important ways. It goes without saying that I am joining a discussion which is already in progress.

1

I shall begin with some preparatory remarks concerning the concept of dialectics and its qualification as an open dialectic.

Anyone who speaks of dialectics exposes himself to the multifarious and problematic 'adventures of the dialectic'. In addition, as successors to Hegel, Marxists lay immediate claim to the pursuit of dialectical thought, whereas nothing of the sort is true of phenomenology.

If we are to do more than merely adapt our word usage to one another, we must demonstrate that something like dialectics manifests itself in the course of the investigation itself. But what kind of dialectics would this be?

I shall begin by emphasizing three points which must be taken into account if we are to stay in contact with the dialectics which Hegel inaugurated and which lives on in Marxism.

(a) The dialectic deals with the *links between and position of individual moments in a whole*; it is thus to be sharply distinguished from an *isolating thought* which dissolves reality into a collection of facts which are merely externally related to one another or buries the facts beneath a foreign cloak of essential determinations.

(b) The dialectic deals with the *transition between the phases of an overarching process and its direction*; it is thus opposed to a '*fixating*' thought which reduces the process to isolated individual phases or degrades them to mere variations of unchangeable essential structures.

(c) The dialectic deals with the *reciprocity between subject and object, subject and co-subject in a process of constitution* in which each simultaneously forms and transforms itself; it thus resists a *separative* thought which separates outer from inner in a dualistic manner or reduces the one to the other.

In short, the dialectic mediates synchronically between the individual moments and the whole, diachronically between the individual phases and the process as a whole, and thereby mediates between subject and object or co-subject.

What can be meant by an openness of the dialectic in this context? One can define openness as *indeterminacy* in the sense of a threefold 'not yet': the whole is not yet completely determined; the process has not yet reached its goal; subject and object or subject and co-subject are not yet completely reconciled with one another and perfectly realized (*zu sich gekommen*). Viewed in this manner, the openness appears as a *provisional*, transient moment comparable to a movement which has not yet rounded itself into a circle. Contradictions between the mediating individual moments drive the development on in the direction of its immanent goal; the unambiguous teleology is by and large maintained, in spite of the factual limitations of the given stage of development.

I would like to maintain that this conception does not do justice to human praxis and its historical development. But what might openness signify, if not this? It can signify that *indeterminacy is intrinsic to determinacy as its back side.*

This points in the first place in the direction of a *logic of the gaze* which cannot be taken up into a logic of the concept. Husserl says in this connection that every perception of a thing 'leaves open a great variety of things pertaining to the unseen faces' and that the course of experience always involves 'new horizons of openness' (*Cartesian Meditations*, §19). Merleau-Ponty appeals to the invisible, which is not merely 'a *de facto* invisible, like an object hidden behind another, and not an absolute invisible, which would have nothing to do with the visible. Rather it is the invisible *of* this world, that which inhabits this world, sustains it, and renders it visible.' The visible and the invisible are related to one another as 'the obverse and the reverse of one another'.[1] And Althusser refers to a 'necessary invisible connexion between the field of the visible and the field of the invisible, a connexion which defines the necessity of the obscure field of the invisible, as a necessary effect of the structure of the visible field'; 'the oversight is an oversight that concerns *vision*: non-vision is therefore inside vision, it is a form of vision and hence has a necessary relationship with vision'.[2] These various hints could also be made fruitful for a theory of action and a logic of emotion.

We are also referred to a *logic of question and answer*[3] which cannot be reduced to a logic of contradiction, a dialogic in which statement and rejoinder are registered as moments of a forthcoming synthesis. A question initiates something, it gives the discussion a direction by excluding others, and opens up the framework in which a possible answer can move. An answer cannot contradict the question, but it can suit the question or not, and this requires its own rules of composition.

Openness in the sense of an essential indeterminacy in determinacy leads to a unique form of dialectic. With reference to the three points mentioned above, we have the following results:

(a) The whole to which the individual moments refer is a *variable horizon* (in contrast to a total determination).
(b) The overarching process within which the individual phases are ordered is an *ambiguous process* (in contrast to a univocal orientation).
(c) The reciprocity between subject and object, between subject and co-subject, takes the form of a *continual process of coming to terms*

with one another (*Auseinandersetzung*) (in contrast to a final reconciliation).

What we are left with is an internal nexus of the individual moments and phases; but this nexus makes room for ruptures, collapses, reversals and new beginnings, whose contingency cannot be caught up by a pre-given or pre-planned rationality. It seems to me that it is only in this manner that human experience and praxis allow for the development of the novel and original instead of merely unfolding that which is already present in reality.

2

As a field for the application and critical examination of these general theses I have chosen the theory of meaning, which has played a decisive role in phenomenology from its beginnings in Husserl's *Logical Investigations*. The constitution of experiential reality manifests itself here in a manner which stubbornly resists an intuitionistic understanding of phenomenology. This constitutional problematic is also unavoidable for a fully developed Marxism.[4] In the following step-by-step characterization I shall give the theory of meaning a relatively neutral form which allows for further specification and differentiation. It also allows us to draw on Gestalt and structuralist theories for a dialectic of experience and behaviour.

(a) *The difference between reality and meaning*. For a phenomenology which wants to be more than the art of careful observation and description, a phenomenology which rather thematizes the modes of appearance of the things in contrast to their self-existence (*Selbstsein*), the basic formula is not 'something is' but rather '*something appears as something*', i.e. it appears in a specific meaning. And if we take the corresponding behaviour as our point of departure, the formula is not: 'we mean something', but rather, '*we mean* (see, hear, judge, treat, effect) *something as something*'. This significational difference is the fundamental difference which cannot be undercut and cannot be derived from anything else, since any such attempt presupposes it. The 'as' is the point on which human behaviour and worldly reality turn. It is a matter of a *unity in difference* which resists the dualistic conception of external reality and internal consciousness. But it is also a matter of a *difference in unity* which excludes a reductionist approach. Meaning cannot be reduced to a part of reality; the experienced is not a pure given, as certain forms of realism or positivism would have it (the model of the mirror). This speaks against, for example, a behaviourist theory which reduces sense to physical stimulus.[5] By the same token, reality cannot be reduced to a moment of meaning; that which we experience is not a pure creation, as certain forms of idealism would have it (the model of creation). This speaks against theories of consciousness which take the object to be a pure *X* of possible determinations. Rather, reality is constituted *in* theoretical and practical experience. What we are confronted with here is a horizontal mediation of inner and outer, of the subjective and the objective. Correctly understood, the phenomenological reduction is nothing other than the conscious return to this difference; it serves simultaneously the 'liberation of the "subject"' and the 'liberation of the "object"'.[6]

The irreducibility of the significational difference thus implies that experience is always interpreted and digested experience. The facts, that which is given in our cognition and is the result of our action, are always *significant facts*. There is no 'direct' cognition and no 'direct' action. 'Direct contact with the thing itself is a dream.'[7]

When Marx refers to a social situation in which 'subjectivism and objectivism, spiritualism and materialism, action and passion' cease to be oppositions,[8] this practical solution too points to a constitutional problematic: the processing and assimilation of the given are not a mirroring in consciousness, are something other than mere physical change. It is always a simultaneous 'change' and 'self-change' (cf. the 'Third Thesis of Feuerbach'). The ideological distortion of reality and practical alienation also imply that something appears as something other than that which it is, or that the works take on another meaning than was intended. Obfuscation and alienation move within the significative difference.

K. Kosík can thus write: 'Human consciousness is at once a "reflection" and a "project", it registers as well as constructs . . . is both receptive and active' (op. cit., p. 12). And when he calls social reality a 'unity of being and meanings, of reality and sense', he rejects an idealism which separates meaning from material reality, turning it into an independent reality, as well as a naturalistic positivism which robs reality of all meaning and thus mystifies it (ibid., p. 148).

The neglect of meaning leads to an inarticulate mass, the neglect of reality to an incomprehensible emptiness. Pure facts without significance and pure meaning without reference to facts are only conceivable as limiting cases which we can approach by means of abstractive procedures and lived abstractions. If we attempt to escape fully the dialectic of meaning and reality, the human world in which we make ourselves understood disappears, and along with it the foundation for such abstractions.

(b) *Meaning and the field of meaning.* If something is not simply in itself, nor simply there for us, but rather appears and is intended as something, this something in its signification is never fully determinate. The given signification allows for further determinations, internal and external determinations which are co-present as inner and outer horizons. In other words, the meaning sketches out a general framework that is more or less determinate. The further course of experience is thus traced out in advance, but not unambiguously. In this context Husserl speaks of a 'determinate structure', of 'structural types', of a 'rule structure' (*Cartesian Meditations*, §§19–22). The meaning thus opens up a field of meaning which extends to the world as the universal horizon of actual experience.

The additional, potential determinations are referential contexts (*Verweisungszusammenhänge*) which spring from the meant itself; that which is intended refers beyond itself, and it is only in so doing that it is itself. 'Grasping is a grasping-out, each perceived object has an experiential background' (*Ideas I*, §35 [my translation – JCE]). The result is a dialectic of the individual and the whole. The *totality* is not something really at hand (totality as the sum total of individual facts); it is also not something which is ideally added by thought (totality as idea, as abstract universal), but is co-present, co-experienced, co-intended (totality as horizon). Since the whole is never itself an object, it is an *open* whole, a 'field' in which the individual is determined. What we are confronted with here is a vertical mediation of particular and universal.

This dialectic is expressed in the fact 'that generalization is the internal connection of facts and that a fact itself mirrors a certain complex' (Kosík, op. cit., p. 25). If the facts are absolutized, the world disintegrates into isolated particulars; if the whole is hypostatized and privileged, the concrete totality yields to a 'false totality' in the course of a 'subjectivism' which neglects the facts or does violence to them in the name of a 'higher reality' (ibid., p. 27).

The difference between reality and signification along with the field of signification is not a static structure, but is the result of a continuous process of differentation. In order to explain this, I shall take the reciprocal variability of meaning and reality as point of departure. We find a different accentuation, depending on whether we take the one or the other as invariant.

(c) *Relative constancy of meaning.* To begin with: *different* things can appear as the *same.* Meaning embodies a general aspect, a general scheme, and thus extends beyond the individual fact; every act of meaning is a 'meaning more', as Husserl puts it (*Cartesian Meditations*, § 20); it involves an excess of meaning. Thus, the meaning is relatively *constant* with respect to the variability of the individual examples and circumstances; it appears as invariant to the extent that specific variables are excluded as irrelevant. This makes a *transposition* of meaning possible. The same things maintain a constant size and colour in spite of changing distance, perspective and lighting; different things are taken to be examples of a single type of object (*a* tree, house, etc.); learning skills also refers to typical instruments and situations; finally, the constancy of meaning mediates intersubjectively between different individual experiences and actions.

This constancy gives experience directives and contexts; it is the basis of the relative reliability of the things and the familiarity of the world. As long as this identity of meaning is maintained, experience moves within a fixed framework which only allows for *further determinations.* What we are confronted with here is an openness *within* specific rule structures. The following considerations show that this constancy is not absolute.

(d) *Potential change of meaning.* The *same* thing can also appear as *something different.* The given meaning does not exhaust the possible significations of reality; every fulfilment of our intentions is confronted with a superabundance of the given, with an excess of reality. On this basis a *redetermination* is possible. Old and new meaning can complement one another (Napoleon as victor of Jena and as defeated of Waterloo) or be disjunctive. In the latter case there is a conflict or correction: that which is intended is not merely *more* than we intend, but *other.* To the extent that the revisability of our assumptions presupposes the incompleteness of our experience, this is of fundamental importance.

The possibility of a change of meaning and of redetermination throws light on the significative difference. Every concrete meaning embodies a perspective, i.e. it is based on a *selection*: a '*so* instead of *so*', 'this way rather than that way'. The choice of the point of view in a given thematization determines what counts as relevant and what not; to this extent meaning and significance are intimately connected with one another. Thus, for example, for an impressionist like Monet, the cathedral in the morning light is not the same as in the evening light, since he is precisely interested in the light in which the cathedral presents itself; the subject is taken up into a frame of reference which is different from the established styles of painting. Cubism, which is interested in the simultaneity of modes of appearance, exchanges this frame of reference for still another.

In this manner, not only is it possible for something *new* to appear in our experience and our praxis within a fixed framework; it is also possible that something *novel* appears, which breaks out of the existing framework and leads to its transformation. Change of meaning implies the surprising, unfamiliar, foreign and strange, which constitute the backside of the domesticated world – a factor of threat, but also a stimulus for innovation in which an openness with respect to existing rule structures manifests itself. The ambivalence of the strange, which simultaneously attracts and repels, an ambivalence which appears in the experience of the child as well as in situations of crisis, is an affective index for this duality. This dialectic of the old and the new, in which the productivity of experience and praxis is concentrated, eludes a rationalism which intercepts the stimulus of the novel by means of *a priori* forms which are fixed once and for all, and thus degrades cognition to recognition.[9] But this dialectic also eludes an empiricism which registers the unusual as mere factual irregularity and is condemned to eternally running after the facts.

3

As preparation for my concluding reflections, I would like to indicate briefly how the theory of meaning sketched above can be translated into the language of Gestalt theory and structuralist thought. With regard to the attempt to integrate the relevant results of research in the human sciences into a phenomenological theory, I refer here especially to the work of A. Gurwitsch and M. Merleau-Ponty.

Let us begin with Gestalt theory.[10] I shall introduce some of the basic assumptions which are relevant to the preceding discussion.

(a) The beginning is not a chaos of simple, isolated data or elements (such as physical stimuli), but rather a *difference*, that of *figure-ground*. A Gestalt is selected and privileged with respect to other Gestalts in the course of Gestalt-formation, and it is set off against a more or less indeterminate, uniform and indifferent background (e.g. that which is coloured against that which is not coloured, warm colours against cold colours, red against yellow, etc.[11]). Figure and ground arise *simultaneously*. The dissolution of this difference does not lead to primitive individual data, but to a monotony in which perception itself disappears.
(b) In the formation of the figure-ground structure we find the *organization* of a *perceptual field*, where organization or order implies a reduction of homogeneity, a reduction of arbitrariness, a differentiation. The dissolution of the field as a whole into isolated elements is not the result of a primitive mode of behaviour, but of higher-level or pathological behaviour.
(c) The process of Gestalt or structure-formation takes place on the one hand in terms of the increasing *differentiation* of a given Gestalt (e.g. in the formation of a system of colours or sounds); this would correspond to what we have called further determination (*Weiterbestimmung*).
(d) The process takes place on the other hand by means of reformation (*Umgestaltung*), by means of the formation of new Gestalts; this would correspond to the redetermination which leads to a change of meaning. In a similar manner, Kuhn[12] compares paradigm change in the history of science with a Gestalt shift, and this is more than a mere metaphor, since the process of Gestalt-formation and transformation has different registers; for example, we also speak of a Gestalt of movement. To the extent that a whole is formed and reformed in the course of development, the continuation cannot be interpreted as a mere accumulation of individual moments. And the fact that the Gestalt process in its primary form is governed by a law of *self-organization* implies that the structure of the world and the structure of behaviour are not reducible to the consciousness *of* these structures. The dialectic of experience and praxis which appears here extends deeper than any possible dialectics of consciousness.

Now, a few special remarks concerning the concept of structure. The figure-ground difference is itself already a 'structural phenomenon' (Koffka). According to one typical definition, structure is a *totality* whose elements are not what they are in isolation, but rather through their relationships to one another within the whole; this allows for *transformations and substitutions*, but not for mere additions and subtractions; it cannot be changed by mere external affection, but is always governed by a law of *self-regulation*.[13] Accordingly, the course of experience can be interpreted as a process of *structuring and re-structuring.* The dialectic of meaning and reality manifests itself at the elementary level in the form of an adaptation of the organism to its environment. According to Piaget, this process occurs between two poles, between the pole of *assimilation*, in which external facts are integrated into structures, and the pole of *accommodation*, in which the structures are modified under the influence of external factors. Empiricism would insist on an accommodation without assimilation, *a priorism* on an assimilation without accommodation, whereas the intermediate view would recognize a reciprocity between organism and environment: 'No subject without influence on the object, no objects without a structuring which is called forth by the subject.'[14] We are thus already beyond subjectivism and objectivism. The dialectic of human praxis would consist in the ability 'of going beyond created structures in order to create others'.[15]

It should be noted that structural analysis is not limited to normal behaviour, that it also extends to pathological phenomena. These are not described as the mere loss of individual functions, but as the *disintegration*, i.e. as the breaking away of partial structures, or as loss of differentiation, i.e. as the simplification of the structure as a whole. The process of coming to terms with the world and the environment continues, but in a distorted and reduced form. We can refer here to the broader circles of phenomenology, for example, the medical-psychological investigations of brain injuries from the school of A. Gelb and K. Goldstein or the linguistic studies of aphasia by R. Jakobson. It seems clear to me that these investigations are also relevant for a social pathology which, as in Marxism, is primarily concerned with the institutional conditions of an atrophied praxis. The recourse to meanings, structures and rules removes the illness from the realm of merely private experience.

These hints must suffice. It goes without saying that the results and methods of the human sciences require a more detailed and differentiated interpretation. Nevertheless, we can see that meaning, Gestalt and structure are appropriate concepts for the interpretation and analysis of the process in which man comes to terms with his world and environment in the light of an open dialectic.

4

In conclusion, I should like to pose one more question, which was already suggested by my initial reflections and which is capable of bringing to light the possible openness of the global process which we call history. I have described the movement of human experience and praxis as a process in which reality becomes meaningful, takes on form (*Gestalt*), on the one hand in the sense of a further determination and differentiation, on the other hand in the sense of a redetermination and restructuring. My question deals explicitly with the connections between the individual phases of this global process and with the laws which regulate the transition from one to another.

An empiricist has no difficulty answering this question, since all he recognizes is a *sequence* of externally connected events, events which are self-contained and isolated, and do not refer beyond themselves.[16] The connection is reduced to the factual *regularity* of the sequence. Here we are confronted with a maximal openness, since everything could also occur in a completely different manner, but there is no sign here of a dialectic in the sense of an inner unity and reciprocity. In contrast, an unambiguous inner connection is given when the individual events are ordered in terms of a unitary *goal*. It is a *positive teleology* if the goal already lies in the nature of things or is projected in the form of a law of reason; this would be the metaphysical or moral form of teleology. It is a *negative teleology*[17] if the goal is at work in the internal *contradictions* of the whole; this would be the dialectical form of teleology as it is found in Hegel and his followers. As we have seen, openness in this context implies a mere 'not yet', in which case it is quite possible that one leaves undetermined the whether, the when and how of the realization of the goal. I shall not try to decide to what extent the Marxian dialectic exhausts itself in this kind of negative dialectic; should this turn out to be the case, then it would indeed be nothing more than 'the necessary expression and the product of the alienation of materialist-social life'; it would be 'the logic of a history which has not yet become human, but is becoming human'.[18] One may call that which would follow dialectics or not: with the end of prehistory and the disappearance of the 'antagonistic contradictions', the pace and laws of the dialectic change; if one thinks of this as an infinite approximation of a goal, it remains a question of a mere 'not yet'.

Against these lines of thought, I would like to pose the general question whether a dialectic for which Hegel's contradiction is the 'motor' (*Springquelle*)[19] is in any sense capable of adequately articulating the inner structure of the process of experience. If the processes of giving meaning, Gestalt-formation and structuring are based on contingent selections, and if these selections always open up specific fields of vision by closing off others, then it is to be assumed that a specific process of structuring does not unambiguously follow from the preceding phases and that while structural systems surely transform themselves into one another, they cannot be totally *superseded* (*aufgehoben*) by one another.

By way of illustration I shall make use of a simple linguistic model. It is one of the basic assumptions of structural linguistics as developed from Saussure that every linguistic unit can be assigned to a syntagmatic axis (principle of succession and contiguity) and a paradigmatic axis (principle of equivalency); it is subject to a linear ordering and enters into a framework of alternatives. This means that every linguistic activity unites an operation of combination and context formation, and an operation of selection and substitution; we combine by choosing, and we choose by combining.[20] Thus, an answer picks up on a question by making a selection within a predetermined frame of reference. This model could, with appropriate care, be applied to other sequences of behaviour.

In order to characterize the situation which appears here I would like to speak of a *coherence* which is more than an empirical contiguity, but less than a necessary consequence. Utterances suit one another or not, i.e. they make reference to rules which are partially context dependent, partially context independent; the latter constitute only the general framework. The transition from one utterance to another is, aside from a relative necessity or arbitrariness, neither necessary nor arbitrary. It is *motivated* by the context and the situation. We have a double field of action, a field within open rules and a field in opposition to contingent rules, whereby the breadth of the field varies. Every contradiction presupposes such a thematic and regulated context – for what should we disagree about otherwise? This logic of coherence lies at a deeper level than any logic of consequence. This is not to downplay the importance of contradictions, but we do have to prevent an inflation of contradictions. And aside from that, the openness is naturally not something which can be taken for granted; this is made clear by disturbances on the immediate linguistic level.[21] The point is that the opening of the boundaries means something other than their overcoming, just as transformation signifies something else than supersession (*Aufhebung*).

A context which is not necessary leaves room for a creativity which not merely unfolds and which does more than merely realize its beginnings, for a creativity which inaugurates something new; the back side of this creativity is the ambiguity of a history in which there is sense, a history in which nonsense can be eliminated, in which there is not, however, the one true sense, and this not because we simply don't know it yet, but because it is in the process of formation. History does not develop according to a textbook. A dialectic which corresponded to this conception of history would not deal with a finality which steers separate elements from outside, and not with a finality which results solely out of the inner contradictions of a whole, but with the 'global and primordial cohesion of a field of experience wherein each element opens onto the others'.[22] An 'incarnate dialectic' of this kind offers the possibility of a concrete freedom which moves in structures but offers no guarantee for an imaginary freedom pure and simple.

Notes

1 Maurice Merleau-Ponty, *The Visible and the Invisible*, trans. Alphonso Lingis, Evanston, Northwestern University Press, 1968, pp. 151, 152.
2 Louis Althusser and Étienne Balibar, *Reading Capital*, trans. Ben Brewster, London, New Left Books, 1970, pp. 19–20, 21.
3 Cf., for example, H.-G. Gadamer, *Wahrheit und Methode*, 2nd edn, Tübingen, Klostermann, 1965, pp. 351 ff.
4 Cf., for example, *Beiträge zur marxistischen Erkenntnistheorie*, 2nd edn, ed. A. Schmidt, Frankfurt am Main, Suhrkamp, 1970.
5 Analytic philosophy also argues against this way of viewing things. Thus, for example, Gilbert Ryle recommends that we replace 'the sabbatical notion of "the Given"' by 'the week-day notion of "the ascertained"' (*The Concept of Mind*, Harmondsworth, Penguin, 1963, p. 226).
6 Karel Kosík, *The Dialectics of the Concrete*, Dordrecht, D. Reidel Publishing, 1976, p. 8. Cf. Marx, 'Ökonomisch-philosophische Manuskripte', in *Marx–Engels Werke*, supplementary volume I, p. 540. This is the complete emancipation of all human senses and properties (via the abolishment of private property) precisely in that 'these senses and properties have become *human*, both subjectively as well as objectively'. On the other hand, this is still said with a view to the 'total human being'.

7 Maurice Merleau-Ponty, *The Adventures of the Dialectic*, trans. Joseph Bien, Evanston, Northwestern University Press, 1973, p. 179.
8 Marx, 'Ökonomisch-philosophische Manuskripte', op. cit., p. 542.
9 Cf. Althusser and Balibar, *Reading Capital* op. cit., pp. 52–3. As critic, Althusser constructs a phalanx which reaches from Descartes over Kant and Hegel to Husserl. Regardless of how one chooses to answer this position, one must say that the critique inspired by Foucault and Lacan with respect to traditional teleological thought invites a reconsideration of this tradition.
10 I am thinking here above all of the Berlin school of Gestalt psychology and its followers (cf., e.g. K. Koffka, *Die Grundlagen der psychischen Entwicklung*, Darmstadt, Wissenschaftliche Buchgesellschaft, 1966, especially pp. 96ff.). As is well known, Husserl's phenomenology had an influence here too.
11 R. Jakobson has explicitly related the structure of the colour system to the structure of the system of linguistic sounds, which likewise is based on a maximal *contrast* (cf. *Kindersprache, Aphasie und allgemeine Lautgesetze*, Frankfurt am Main, 1969). As is well known, structural phonemics was one of the main sources for Lévi-Strauss's structural analyses in ethnology.
12 Thomas Kuhn, *The Structure of Scientific Revolutions*, Chicago, University of Chicago Press, 1970. Cf. especially pp. 111ff.
13 Cf. J. Piaget, *Le structuralisme*, Paris, 1968, ch. 1.
14 Cf. the remarks by Piaget in *Das neue Menschenbild*, ed. A. Koestler and J. R. Smythies, Vienna-Munich-Zürich, 1970, pp. 162f.
15 Maurice Merleau-Ponty, *The Structure of Behaviour*, trans. Alden Fisher, Boston, Beacon Press, 1963, p. 175. An extended discussion of this context can be found in my essay 'Die Offenheit sprachlicher Strukturen bei Merleau-Ponty', in *Maurice Merleau-Ponty und das Problem der Struktur in den Sozialwissenschaften*, ed. R. Grathoff and W. Sprondel, Stuttgart, 1976.
16 Cf. Hume, *A Treatise of Human Nature*, Book III, Part I, section I: 'All beings in the universe, considered in themselves, appear entirely loose and independent of each other.'
17 Cf. Rüdiger Bubner, 'Logik und Kapital', in *Dialektik und Wissenschaft*, Frankfurt am Main, Suhrkamp, 1973, p. 59.
18 For example, G. Markus in *Beiträge zur marxistischen Erkenntnistheorie*, pp. 44f.; note that this interpretation is restricted to the young Marx. Jürgen Habermas, on the other hand, calls dialectic 'not unconstrained intersubjectivity itself . . . but the history of its repression and re-establishment' (*Knowledge and Human Interests*, trans. Jeremy J. Shapiro, Boston, Beacon Press, 1971, p. 59). Authors such as Althusser or Godelier put as much distance between Marx and Hegel as possible in order to get rid of *all* teleological ballast. For Godelier, the fundamental contradiction does not lie within a structure, but between structures which are *irreducible* and which do not stand under the sway of

the law of an 'identity of opposites' (cf. 'System, Struktur und Widerspruch in "*Das Kapital*"', in *Der moderne Strukturbegriff*, ed. H. Naumann, Darmstadt, Wissenschaftliche Buchgesellschaft, 1973).

19 Cf. Marx's casual remarks in *Capital I*, New York, International Publishers, 1967, p. 596, n. 3.

20 Cf. Roman Jakobson, *Aufsätze zur Linguistik und Poetik*, ed. W. Raible, Munich, 1974, p. 119ff.

21 Two basic types of aphasia are interesting in this context. Jakobson orders them to the activity of combining and selecting (ibid., pp. 123ff.), and one can assume that they have their extra-linguistic analogues.

22 Merleau-Ponty, *The Adventures of the Dialectic*, op. cit., p. 205.

CHAPTER 6

The unity of theory and praxis as a problem for Marxism, phenomenology and structuralism

Jan M. Broekman (Leuven)

1

The internal relations between phenomenology, Marxism and structuralism as philosophical movements in the twentieth century can be thematized as problems in the philosophy of culture and as epistemological problems. In the notion of a *crisis*, which has been interpreted in quite different manners in the three movements, we see the culture-philosophical, in the notion of *critique*, also the subject of quite different interpretations, the epistemological component of our problematic.

Both themes, the culture-philosophical as well as the epistemological, the notion of crisis as well as that of critique, are by and large determined by the particular understanding of science in phenomenology, Marxism and structuralism respectively. This becomes very clear when we consider the continual reflection on the theoreticity of theory and the relation of this theory to praxis in these movements. Thus, in each of the different philosophical contexts we encounter the assertion that the separation between theory and praxis is necessarily transcended. The question of the degree to which this separation of the two moments continues to be effective as a constitutive moment in this transcendence is neither answered by the presentation of this transcending, nor does it become visible on the basis of the understanding of science which founds the transcendence. It is no accident that the necessity of this transcendence is justified with reference to the unsolved problem of the relation between the abstract and the concrete. All three movements use this separation of the abstract and the concrete in order to discuss the strengths and weaknesses of the philosophical position in question.

This schema of thought and argumentation is obviously itself indebted to a traditional ontology. Thus, we must pose the critical question whether this traditional-metaphysical moment might not stand in the way of the development of a post-Cartesian epistemology and philosophy of science. Can the variously formulated goals of phenomenology, Marxism and structuralism with regard to such an epistemology be realized as long as this reference functions? Or is it possibly the case that these philosophies can bring about a genuine emancipation only when they have freed themselves from this coercion and this desire?

The question is not without importance. The self-understanding of the philosophical positions developed by Husserl, Marx and the structuralists has always been presented as being rigorous and above all *critical.* Thus, in the foreword to his *History of Marxism* Vranicki can mention 'the prominent role of the principle of critique, which is peculiar to Marxism as the critical thought about the contemporary epoch'.[1]

This critique is necessary and strict, for it has to criticize the bourgeoisie, which, as Lukács says in his lecture 'Functional Change of Historical Materialism', 'never attains a clear insight into the social presuppositions of its own existence'.[2] Only through Marxism as strict critique is it possible for a social form to gain this insight. This critique is presupposition and result all at once, the price paid and the goods bought. For this reason the young Lukács characterizes this critique as *totality* and comes to the conclusion that 'the methodological essence of historical materialism cannot be separated from the "practical-critical" activity of the proletariat'.[3] With this reference to the necessary inseparability of theory and praxis we, as in a circle, return to our point of departure. In practical terms this means that either Marxism as critique breaks with other less insightful forms of social life or that the critique is not yet strict enough and the goal is not attained. Philosophically this means that as long as this inseparability of theory and praxis, concrete and abstract, constitutes the Marxist discourse, it by the same token brings the separation and with it the ontology which lies behind the separation to expression.

Husserl, too, never doubted the radicality, the rigour and necessity of his transcendental-phenomenological approach. He mentions again and again the incomparable originality of the phenomenological point of view, the necessity of a total conversion, a total change of the natural attitude:

> Actually, therefore, phenomenological explication is nothing like 'metaphysical construction'; and it is neither overtly nor covertly a theorizing with adopted presuppositions or helpful thoughts drawn from the historical metaphysical tradition . . . phenomenological explication does nothing but explicate the sense this world has for us all, prior to any philosophizing . . . [It is] precisely the beginning of a radical clarification of the sense and origin of the concepts: world, nature, space, time, psychophysical being, man, psyche, animate organism.[4]

This departure from the metaphysical tradition implies critique, indeed, according to Husserl philosophy 'has grown out of the universal critical attitude toward anything and everything pregiven in the tradition. . . . Only the capacity for a universal critical attitude . . . must be present'.[5] In this lecture, 'Philosophy and the Crisis of European Humanity', which Husserl delivered before the Viennese Kulturbund in 1935, this 'peculiar universality of his critical stance' is referred to not merely as 'a new cognitive stance', but as 'a far-reaching transformation of the whole praxis'. For Husserl critique is clearly bound up with a *synthesis* of theory and praxis. The theoretical attitude of the philosopher is precisely that, an attitude, and he never speaks for a final disengagement of theoretical from practical life or for 'a decay of the concrete life of the theoretician into two isolated life-continuities, which socially would mean the development of two spiritually separate spheres of culture'.[6] The synthesis of theory and praxis, itself a 'new sort of praxis', a 'universal critique', is also capable of yielding a 'fundamentally new humanity', the result of the synthesis of 'theoretical universality and universally interested praxis'. Husserl describes the historical development towards this goal as a process of 'offering one another helpful criticism' – a good formula for emancipatory action![7] Thus, one should not be surprised when Husserl, in the same lecture, has the following to say about his attitude and his transcendental philosophy: 'I would like to think that I, the supposed reactionary, am far more radical and far more revolutionary than those who in their words proclaim themselves so radical today'.[8]

In the contemporary context this self-evaluation is by no means an exaggeration. In his essay 'The Most Recent Attack on Metaphysics', Horkheimer acknowledges the courage and contemporary relevance of this 'last genuine epistemologist', recognizing a genuine achievement with respect to a synthesis of theory and praxis:

> Even in the face of all oppositions between Husserl's approach and the theory represented here (critical theory), his last work with its highly abstract problematic has more to do with the contemporary historical tasks than the supposedly oh-so-contemporary pragmatism or the words, supposedly directed to the 'man at the machine', by many young intellectuals who are ashamed to be such.[9]

Note the word 'approach' (*Denkart*): critical theory and phenomenology have common goals, but pursue them in different manners. This becomes visible in Horkheimer's essay from the same period: 'Traditional and Critical Theory'. As in Husserl, Horkheimer's understanding of critique implies in the first place a break with philosophy's traditional self-understanding. Thus, Kant's notion of critique is still thought in terms of 'the super-individual activity, of which the empirical subject is unaware, and which is thought only in the idealistic form of a consciousness in itself, a purely spiritual instance'. Still, Kant understood that 'behind the discrepancy between fact and theory . . . there is a deeper unity, the universal subjectivity on which individual knowledge depends'. But the transcendental power of this universality remains unclarified, it is by no means articulated in terms of social labour. This has the consequence that the structure of that dependence of individual cognition on this universality also remains obscure. And this obscurity stands in the way of the emancipation of the concrete subject, for in this manner reason can never become transparent to itself, can never – to use Lukács's words quoted above – achieve clarity concerning the social presuppositions of its own existence. This can occur only by means of a break in the form of a 'critical recognition of the categories which govern social life', a recognition which in a dialectical manner directly produces its own transcendence.[10]

The result is, as in Husserl, a new cognitive attitude which can be characterized in terms of totality, a totality above all of theory and praxis: 'We must go over to a conception in which the one-sidedness which necessarily arises through the emphasis on intellectual partial processes within the totality of social praxis, is again transcended.' The realization is not a matter of a reorganization of science and labour but rather the result of a new understanding of the relation between fact and conceptual order. The basic condition for this is insight into the inner structure of bourgeois thought. This thought is 'so constituted that in reflection on its own subject it recognizes with logical necessity the ego which fancies itself autonomous. It is essentially abstract, and its principle is that individuality which, closed off from the process, inflates itself to being the primal ground of the world or to being the world itself.'[11] This autonomy, which was always understood in terms of a tension between factuality and conceptual structure, is transcended in the insight that the facts are socially pre-formed in a twofold manner: once through the historical character of the perceived object and again through the historicity of perception. Both, object and perception, are 'not merely natural, but rather formed through human activity' – only the individual which as the subject of a bourgeois philosophical discourse fancies itself autonomous *must* interpret itself to be receptive and passive in perception. The break with this discourse is itself emancipation from this passivity and leads to a clear insight into the role of thought in social reality. It is only at this point that thought becomes aware of its own function; it is only here that man historically achieves a knowledge of his own activity and thus comprehends the contradiction in his own existence.[12]

The different styles of thought in phenomenology and Lukács's and Horkheimer's Neo-Marxism would seem to make them incommensurable. On the one hand, one finds a reflection concentrated on the achievements of an egology, atomistic reflections, *epoché*, transcendental analyses and statements on the highest level of abstraction; on the other hand, we find insight into the construed character of bourgeois discourse, transcendence of its necessity, social and historically oriented thought, reflection on the totality and statements on a wholly concrete level. But when one pays attention to the *telos* of the two philosophies, they turn out to have surprisingly much in common: overcoming the crisis, necessity of critique, departure from positivism and ahistorical physicalism, post-Cartesian epistemology, emancipatory interest, rigour and radicality of the philosophical approach, unity of theory and praxis.

This comparison has two significant consequences. On the one hand, phenomenology is removed from the orbit of the primarily idealistic tradition of Husserl interpretation. Epistemologically it is probably more important that this example makes clear the degree to which philosophical discourses which are fundamentally differently construed can turn out to have much more in common with respect to their basic principles of organization than one would have expected as long as one philosophized within their respective discourses. In this manner, the absoluteness of the break with traditional ontology and metaphysics made prominent by phenomenology and (Neo) Marxism appears as the necessity of a *coupure épistémologique*'. With this remark we remain within the tension of fact and conceptual order sketched by Horkheimer. But the very same problematic was in these same years the object of Bachelard's *nouvel esprit scientifique*, a dialectical epistemology which is recognized as one of the sources of inspiration for contemporary Parisian structuralist authors such as Foucault or Althusser. According to this *épistémologie non-cartésienne* (Bachelard), statements concerning general kinds of processes in the history of science are to be avoided, since epistemological questions always arise within a specific historical situation, i.e. a specific relation between fact and the respective discourse. The unreflective acceptance of conclusions based on a given state of affairs is thus nothing other than sheer metaphysics, dogmatism, or – in Nietzsche's sharp words – 'people's superstition out of an unimaginable age'. Nietzsche is doing nothing other than taking this epistemology at its word when he says:

> One should use 'cause' and 'effect' only as pure *conceptions*, that is to say, as conventional fictions for the purpose of designation and mutual understanding – *not* for explanation. . . . It is *we* alone who have devised cause, sequence, reciprocity, relativity, constraint, number, law, freedom, motive and purpose; and when we interpret and intermix this symbol-world, as 'being in itself', with things, we act once more as we have always acted – *mythologically*.[13]

According to Bachelard, past and present of a science are not located within an identical historical continuum. The contemporary state of a science produces a very specific interest is the past of this science: precisely this interest must be thematized as a constitutive moment in every historical reconstruction.

Retrospectiveness is thus the highest principle of a theory of science. This theory should refuse to pay homage to the usual evolutionary principles with whose help the progress from the more simple to the more complex is suggested. Only through this awareness can science come to an adequate self-understanding: here too it is impossible to ignore the voice of an emancipatory interest. Critique has become consciousness of the break, the cut (*coupure*). This in turn is connected with the relation of this epistemology to the idea of a crisis. It too is caused by our superstitious belief in historical continuity.

This ideology forces us to construe history as the praxis of denial, the denial of the human, since the continuity of history was represented as sense although it can become a source of meaning only as discontinuity. Wherever this fact remains unclarified, we encounter unclarified contradictions between individual and society, theory and praxis, subjectivity and objectivity, fate and necessity. The subject of history no longer appears as unalterable and autonomous, as the praxis of denial would have it. It changes itself in the course of the historical process along with its self-understanding, its interests and its knowledge. Foucault asserts the same thing when he signals a departure from the traditional relation of the abstract to the concrete: it is not the case that traditional humanism is concrete and this structural epistemology abstract, but rather just the reverse: 'All of these claims on the part of the human person, of existence, are abstract: i.e. cut off from the scientific and technical world which is our real world. . . . But we are trying to connect man with his science, with his discoveries, with his world, which is concrete.'[14]

With this the relation between theory and praxis is transformed into a constitutive unity. Not because, as Kant would have it, knowledge is the product of the activity of the subject and because it is the same regulative principles which guide action, rather it is now realized that knowledge and action, theory and praxis, owe their unity to the discourse whose elements they are, to a discourse which is organized according to much more comprehensive criteria.

Thus, Marxism, phenomenology and structuralism are related to one another not by virtue of their styles of thought, but by their common *telos*: the idea of an overcoming of the crisis, the idea of a rigorous and necessary critique, of a new epistemology, a new historicity is just as common to these philosophical approaches as their emancipatory interest, their attempt to work out the unity of theory and praxis and to revise the traditional relation between the abstract and the concrete. Thus, our initial question as to the degree to which traditional ontology and metaphysics takes part in the constitution of this common *telos* is still pressing.

2

The philosophical analysis of the crisis in the 1930s can be characterized by means of two different positions, namely in terms of

Husserl's *reflective* position and Horkheimer's *dialectical* position. They have in common the fact that the role of epistemology in contemporary culture as well as the theoreticity of the theory in question is, in the form of the *critique*, bound up with this problematic of the crisis.[15]

Although Husserl does characterize the task of his transcendental philosophy as the 'theoretical function of a praxis', the reflective moment remains decisive for him. The separation of theory and praxis, inherited from the Kantian critique of knowledge, constitutes precisely this event of reflection. It determines the schematism of the subject-object relation as well as the epistemological discourse. For in that 'he who philosophizes proceeds from his own ego . . . it is possible to construct an absolutely self-sufficient science of the spirit in the form of consistently coming to terms with oneself and with the world as spiritual accomplishment'.[16]

Horkheimer takes a similar reflexivity as point of departure, but guides it in the course of a further dialectical development on to other epistemological paths: 'The self-knowledge of man in the present is not however mathematical natural science, which appears as eternal *logos*, but the critical theory of society which is impregnated by the interest in rational circumstances'; somewhat more roughly, Horkheimer writes in the same context: 'After all, the reference of hypothesis to fact does not take place in the scholar's head but in industry.'[17]

The power of the reflexive and its epistemological model is already visible in the mere comparison of the two positions. Thus, we must ask whether Husserl was in any way in a position in his Viennese lecture on 'The Crisis of the European Sciences' – which for him is also the crisis of European humanity[18] – to overcome this crisis by means of a philosophical reorientation which in the last resort is dependent on self-reflection. The reorientation which Husserl suggests remains within the traditional discourse of science, theory, *eidos*, *logos* and is in the final resort the discourse of the very physicalism and objectivism which Husserl fought.

Neither is the rupture with the reflective tradition of critique which is called for in this context realized. This tradition was characterized by the attempt to control the orderly process of the experience of the subject. This control took place precisely through the reflecting subject – called the 'transcendental-phenomenologizing ego' in Husserl's transcendental philosophy[19] – which thematizes the process of constitution and is thus able to produce guarantees for the validity of experience. In this manner the justification of knowledge, in isolation from praxis and in contrast to any empiricism or dogmatism, becomes the main moment of epistemological discourse.

The subject should first come to terms with itself before it embarks on praxis. The technique of this coming-to-terms-with-oneself is reflection, and the philosophical foundation of reflection is the apodicticity of the self. This self-confidence makes possible in turn the actualization of the rationality of the subject, something which of course is to occur with respect to praxis in the life-world. In spite of this relation to praxis, reflection remains primary for the philosophy of subjectivity, the connection of the *cogitationes* to the *cogitata* appears in this light almost as a side-effect of *ratio*. One can learn from Kantian philosophy how hard it is not to allow this achievement of connection to become the main point. Hegel's dialectic grows out of this tension, it is to connect reason to itself and to the things. The ambiguity of reason is equally an ambiguity of history.

The fact that the critical path for Kant is already the sceptical path is of great importance in this context: the sceptic, in contrast to the dogmatist, is not prepared to subject his judgment to any other instance. The 'criticist' retains this control over his own judgment, and this holds for the foundations of judgment as well as for the conditions of possibility of this judgment. This critique turns the philosopher once again into judge and legislator. Thus, the philosopher is not merely *dikastés*, i.e. one who is bound to laws and dogmas and whose task it is merely to apply these laws and dogmas correctly according to a pre-given logic. He is rather *krités*, an expert who is to investigate without prejudices or any other presuppositions. He searches for the laws of logic: they are not pre-given to him. He judges the *lege ferenda* and can place the unwritten laws above the written. Kant's metaphor of the court of reason concerns the *dikastérion* less than the *kritérion*. Kant thus assigns to the philosopher as judge and legislator the task of giving and interpreting laws; he has the right to legislate as well as the right to investigate the limits and sense of legislation. He confirms the central position of *knowledge* within the reflective tradition.

The *Critique of Pure Reason* makes it clear that the understanding can have no knowledge of objects unless it itself legislates, for the objects of experience could not be thought otherwise: the source of all legislation of the understanding is the unity of apperception. In the *Critique of Practical Reason* this unity is legally and morally legislative, since it is a matter of the laws of freedom. In the *Critique of Judgment* the context of empirical laws of nature is thought by the reflecting power of judgment as the idea of a goal. In these three *Critiques* reflection conditions the certainty of knowledge as well as critique itself.

In *Beyond Good and Evil* Nietzsche attacks Kant and Hegel by describing the authentic philosopher as 'commander and legislator'. But he gives this Kantian formula a new dimension: the *krités* creates values. This distinguishes him from the *dikastés*, who claims to create value but in fact merely repeats. Every epistemology creates values, traverses the sphere of human values and emotions, and presses valuations into formuli such as objectivity, truth, knowledge.

In his book *Knowledge and Human Interests*, Habermas records three cuts in recent epistemology: (i) Hegel's critique of Kant, i.e. the development from reflection to dialectics, (ii) Marx's idea of epistemology as theory of society, and (iii) Nietzsche's reduction of knowledge to interests. In the course of this development epistemology becomes a theory of science. But even this observation is made from the perspective of a reflective tradition of epistemology. On the last page of the book, Nietzsche is presented as a 'virtuoso of reflection that denies itself', who simultaneously develops the context of knowledge and interest and misinterprets it empiristically. The result is 'the dissolution of the theory of knowledge into methodology', the 'final chapter' in the 'prehistory of modern positivism'.[20] Reflexivity plays the role of criterium here as well as in Habermas's definition of the emancipatory. Emancipation, the heart of that interest which constitutes a unity with knowledge, is defined as an 'act of reflection' which 'changes a life'. One can methodologically ascertain the knowledge-guiding interests of the natural and human sciences only after one has entered 'the dimension of self-reflection':

> It is in accomplishing self-reflection that reason grasps itself as interested. Therefore we come upon the fundamental connection of knowledge and interest when we pursue methodology in the mode of the experience of reflection: as the critical dissolution of objectivism.

Neither Peirce nor Dilthey understood their investigations in this sense as a self-reflection of science, as Habermas notes.[21] This highlights not only the ruling role of reflection in epistemological discourse but also the possibility of a *total* reflection. But there remains a naïvety with regard to the character of this reflection as totality. It is structurally identical to Husserl's idea of a 'new kind of synthesis of *theoria* and *praxis*' and to the Marxist philosopher's idea of a totality of theory and praxis.

Husserl's synthesis is of course the result of a certain, namely reflexive, form of epistemology. His idea of a total reflection of this kind is based on a repeated recapitulation of the same schema: the philosopher objectifies the world by means of his change of attitude, his *thaumazo* turns him into an 'nonparticipating spectator', he becomes the 'surveyor of the world, he becomes a philosopher'. This change comes about by means of the contrast between *doxa* and *episteme*,[22] and thus an imitative power of *theoria* is effective in the thought of the philosopher – philosophical by means of the process of reciprocal, universal-critical stance and more generally by means of a spreading communal movement of education. Positivist objectivism is in contrast a naivety because it can produce no higher levels of reflection. Objectivism cannot see through its own naivety and allows the predominance of a dualistic view of the world. 'Only when the spirit returns from its naïve external orientation to itself, and remains with itself and purely with itself, can it be sufficient unto itself.'[23]

Husserl did not break with the Kantian tradition. Just like positivism, he centralizes achieving subjectivity. His attempt to provide a solution by means of an extension of transcendental philosophy, which was to be more radical than Kant, failed because such a solution can never be the act of an achieving subjectivity. The same holds true of the emancipatory interest which, as the idea of a 'social movement of education', plays a role in Husserl's philosophy. This idea too is normative, it represents an interest, namely an ideal of humanity which has its roots in the history of reflection in Western epistemology. Husserl cannot free himself from this discourse, his critique does not lead him to a *coupure épistémologique* (Bachelard) as the first movement in a new, post-Cartesian epistemology.

This holds true *grosso modo* for the neo-Marxist approaches of Horkheimer and Habermas. The latter often speaks of achievements of the transcendental subject which are of central importance for this subject, of self-preservation and self-reflection. The theses of his Frankfurt inaugural lecture rest upon these principles, and so do his later positions with reference to the problematic of communicative competence. A difference with transcendental phenomenology appears when the dialectic of critique within critical theory refers to social processes: to work, language and interaction. But with this the role of the reflexive becomes problematic in a manner which tends to mislead – and this even more strongly than is the case in phenomenology. On this basis, the break between theory and praxis is hypostasized all over again, for *the foundational character* (*Unhintergehbarkeit*) *of the theoretical in the praxis of work, language and interaction is confirmed in being subject to a complete reflection* (*durchreflektiert*). Thus, a more precise structural analysis of subjectivity is not forthcoming: the first steps towards such an analysis are to be found in Husserl's egology,[24] especially at those points at which the change of attitude, the *epoché*, the theory of transcendental subjectivity as well as the discussion of Kant's epistemology are thematized. But the analysis of work, language or interaction is not carried out, so the structures of communicative action remain without epistemological relevance for Husserl.

It is clear that these differences and commonalities between the two philosophical approaches are to be viewed as the result of the reflective tradition of epistemology. The difference between the philosophical positions which was introduced above, namely the differences between reflective and dialectical positions, was a superficial perception. The dialectical position, at any rate in the form it takes in the writings of Horkheimer and Habermas, remains fundamentally reflective. Both the constitution of human action as well as the problematic of history are forms of the problematic of subjectivity: this was already made clear by Marx.

For Habermas, the mediation of theory and praxis, and especially the institution of their unity, does not take place on the level of cognition, but rather in language, work and interaction, for the subject is always already socialized, i.e. constituted by praxis, and thus never in the position of a neutral subject, an observer of its own reflective processes. Reality is that which can be interpretively experienced within an accepted symbolic. The mediation of theory and praxis thus means: implication. As praxis, the explication of that implicative experience is *theoria* – but, as we have already seen, still in the form of *reflection*.

For Horkheimer too, the problem of critical theory is basically a problem of subjectivity. On the one hand he asserts for precisely this reason that the separation of individual and society is transcended in critical theory. On the other hand, subjectivity is explicated as historicity – in a history which naturally includes both individuality and society. Yet, according to Horkheimer, the thinking subject is not the point at which knowledge and object coincide, the point from which an absolute knowledge would become possible. Individual and society require one another – in an opaque, unconscious society the I cannot take possession of itself. The structure of this need is not simply spun out of thought but takes place in an explication that is fundamentally historical. 'In the course of history men gain knowledge of their action and thus comprehend the contradiction in their existence.'[25] This fundamental role of the historical presupposes an understanding of society in which the individual can spiritualize (*verinnerlichen*) itself. When Habermas emphasizes such processes as work, language and interaction, and Horkheimer historicity, the unity of theory and praxis becomes the problem of spiritualization. The sense of this approach is that this spiritualization cannot occur exclusively within cognition. 'Traditional theoretical thought accepts . . . both the genesis of specific states of affairs and the practical application of conceptual systems with which one deals with them, thus its role in praxis, as external.' This externality is transcended by the process of spiritualization. This transcendence is emancipation, is unity of theory and praxis. 'Reason cannot become self-transparent as long as men act as members of an irrational organism. The organism, as a unity which naturally grows and passes away, is not a model for society but rather a dull form of being from which it has to emancipate itself.'[26]

3

The structural model of knowledge[27] which developed out of aesthetics, phonology and linguistics simultaneously with the reflective-dialectical model, first appeared under the name *structuralism* in Prague. This took place after the turbulent developments in Russian formalism and following a polemic with Marxism. The latter debate has its centre in Trotsky's *Literature and Revolution*, 1924. Following Stalin's *Pravda* letters on linguistics,[28] the discussion between structuralism and Marxism became less antagonistic. The debate took a new turn: today it is a matter of questions of structural thought *within* Marxism.[29]

Structuralism and phenomenology are also less antithetic to one another than is commonly supposed. Patočka's memorial talk for Husserl before the 'Prague Philosophical Circle' on 13 May 1938 demonstrates this community in an impressive fashion. Structuralism, especially in Czechoslovakia, receives a fundamental impulse from the philosophy of the *Logical Investigations*. Logical and pure grammar, as well as material ontologies, become the object of an intense discussion. For Patočka, the structuralist regeneration results directly from Husserl's rediscovery of the Idea as well as from the emphasis on the universal whole as the object of concrete philosophy. 'If the idea was understood as ideal structure in the first place, it is now the idea of the universal, all-encompassing and illuminating whole.'[30]

In this manner Patočka includes structuralism in the history of Western reflection and construes an agreement with regard to ontology between reflective epistemology and structuralism. This assertion remained unchallenged during the period of Czechoslovakian structuralism. But after the work of the historian Foucault, the psychologist Lacan, the anthropologist Lévi-Strauss, after Derrida's investigations of Nietzsche, Husserl and Hegel, and Althusser's Marx interpretation, such an assertion cannot remain unchallenged, for these authors practise within structuralism that which Nietzsche held to be the task of the 'authentic philosopher'. They have identified and pressed into formuli 'former *determinations of value*, creations of value, which have become prevalent, and are for a time called "truths"'; just as Nietzsche said: in the realm of the logical or of the political or of the artistic. Their cognition was *production*, as Nietzsche understood it, or, as Roland Barthes put it, *construction*. 'Creation or reflection are here not an accurate "imprint" of the world, but rather the geniune generation of a world which is similar to the first one, but does not copy it: it makes it comprehensible.'[31]

This is the work of a synthetic structuralism, whereas Patočka's remarks stood under the influence of a concept of structure which belonged to an analytic phase of structuralism. In contemporary, synthetic structuralism, it is less the concept of structure than that of discourse which is of central epistemological significance. Within a discourse, valuations are called truth without being universally valid, ontological truths. Discursivity and conventionality of truth: both call for something other than metaphysical-ontological ontologies.

In this light, the relation of theory and praxis itself appears as a valuation of this sort which became truth, identified and pressed into a formula, and which is now to be thought through anew as a discourse. The theory-praxis relation is to be characterized as a discourse in this sense, within which our problematic of reflexivity, subjectivity, abstraction and concretion can never be solved. It is necessary that we exercise a *coupure épistémologique* also within the realm of the discursive – thus here too. This is the reason why we said that neither Marxism nor

Horkheimer, Habermas or Husserl see the degree to which the distinction between theory and praxis is a constitutive moment of that epistemological discourse. The transcendence of this moment appears to reflection as an *aporie*, the tie to traditional metaphysics as unbreakable, the theoreticity of theory at this point as not open to discussion.

Only when this problematic is relativized as discursivity is it possible to see that the problem cannot be solved via reflection but only by means of a transformation of the problem. Marxism too can free itself from traditional ontological-metaphysical epistemologies only when the theory-praxis problem is transformed; supersession (*aufheben*) cannot suffice. This is surely the background of Althusser's attempt to read Marx with new eyes, to represent him as a reader, to develop a theory of reading and to demonstrate the textual character of every philosophical work, including the works of Marxism.

A reading of this kind rests upon the general idea of *competence*, as do the partial aspects of a competence in the form of a linguistic-lexical (Chomsky), practical-interested, communicative (Habermas), textual (Kristeva) or emancipatory competence. This general concept of competence is merely the transformation of that which functioned as the unity of theory and praxis in a traditional discourse. Peirce, with his semiotic transformation of transcendental philosophy, took this path. Language, work and interaction do not mediate theory and praxis, but rather internalize them in such a manner that the result is an enrichment of competence. In every word, in every work process, in every communication we produce not only language, work and interaction, but also referentially a social structure. The unity of theory and praxis becomes a unity *prior* to all duality by means of this transformation of discursivity. Everything that occurs as a relation of theory and praxis *prior* to this unity belongs to the prehistory of Marxism in just the manner in which Marx characterized history up to now as the prehistory of human society. Only through Marx's transformation of the basic principle of all society does history become humanized.[32] Human society was prehistorical up to now because the modes of production of material life determined the process of life in general. History is humanized only when these economic forms of society are transformed into social formations. These too can be referentially created in processes such as language, work and interaction. The unity of man with these social formations is deproblematized as competence. The social processes no longer have the character of laws of nature or are no longer experienced organizationally as hollow forms of being:

these images are seen through as valuations which are discursively construed as truth and can be transformationally shifted over into other discourses. This shift is the genuine task of philosophy.

Notes

1 P. Vranicki, *Geschichte des Marxismus*, Frankfurt am Main, Suhrkamp, 1972, vol. I, pp. 9ff.
2 G. Lukács, *Geschichte und Klassenbewußtsein*, Neuwied, Luchterhand, 1970, p. 359.
3 Ibid., p. 25.
4 E. Husserl, *Cartesian Meditations*, trans. Dorian Cairns, The Hague, Martinus Nijhoff, 1960, pp. 150–1, 154.
5 E. Husserl, *The Crisis of European Sciences and Transcendental Phenomenology*, trans. David Carr, Evanston, Northwestern University Press, 1970, p. 288.
6 Ibid., p. 286. This is in fact the case in C. P. Snow, *The Two Cultures*.
7 Husserl, *Crisis*, op. cit., pp. 283, 287.
8 Ibid., p. 290.
9 M. Horkheimer, *Kritische Theorie*, Frankfurt am Main, Suhrkamp, 1968, vol. II, p. 96.
10 Ibid., pp. 148ff.
11 Ibid., p. 159.
12 Ibid., p. 161.
13 F. Nietzsche, *Beyond Good and Evil*, trans. Helen Zimmern, Edinburgh, T. N. Foulis, 1907, pp. 30–1.
14 M. Foucault, Interview with M. Chapsal, in *La Quinzaine Littèraire*, 1966.
15 Husserl, *Cartesian Meditations*, op. cit., pp. 154ff.; *Crisis*, op. cit., pp. 332ff.; Horkheimer, *Kritische Theorie*, vol. II, op. cit., pp. 192ff.
16 Husserl, *Crisis*, op. cit., p. 298.
17 Horkheimer, *Kritische Theorie*, op. cit., pp. 147, 145.
18 Habermas puts it differently: 'Husserl was concerned with crisis: not with crises in the sciences, but with their crisis as science' (*Knowledge and Human Interests*, trans. Jeremy J. Shapiro, Boston, Beacon Press, 1971, p. 302).
19 Jan M. Broekman, *Phänomenologie und Egologie*, The Hague, Martinus Nijhoff, 1963, pp. 174ff.
20 Habermas, *Knowledge and Human Interests*, op. cit., pp. 299–300.
21 Ibid., p. 212.
22 Husserl, *Crisis*, op. cit., p. 285.
23 Ibid., p. 297.
24 Broekman, *Phänomenologie und Egologie*, op. cit., pp. 98ff., 122ff.

25 Horkheimer, *Kritische Theorie*, op. cit., p. 160.
26 Ibid., p. 157.
27 Jan M. Broekman, *Strukturalismus*, Moskau, Prag, Paris, Freiburg, Alber, 1971, pp. 47 ff., 61 ff., 76.
28 J. Stalin, *Über den Marxismus in der Sprachwissenschaft* (1950), in F. J. Raddatz (ed.), *Marxismus und Literatur*, vol. III, Hamburg, Rowohlt, 1969.
29 Broekman, *Strukturalismus*, op. cit., pp. 145 ff.
30 J. Patočka, *Edmund Husserl zum Gedächtnis*, Prague, 1938, p. 25.
31 Nietzsche, *Beyond Good and Evil*, op. cit., p. 152; R. Barthes, *Essais Critiques*, Paris, 1964, p. 191.
32 A. Pažanin, *Wissenschaft und Geschichte in der Phänomenologie Edmund Husserls*, The Hague, Martinus Nijhoff, 1972, pp. 174 ff.

CHAPTER 7

Ideology and ideology critique

Paul Ricoeur (Chicago)

I shall begin by describing the phenomenon of ideology, taking into account the variety of forms in which it appears. I shall then deal with an epistemological question which I would like to formulate in the following manner: is it possible to constitute a science of ideology or ideologies which is not *itself* in turn an ideology? Finally, I shall be concerned with a philosophical reflection of a hermeneutical nature; its result will be that ideology must be embedded in our understanding of historicity.

1 The phenomenon of ideology

Our understanding of the phenomenon of ideology must be based on a description. Indeed, it is by no means obvious that 'ideology' is an exclusively negative phenomenon, that it is merely something like a 'false consciousness', a 'deception', a 'distortion' of reality, brought forth by unconscious interests which in turn are traceable to membership in a ruling class. This definition of ideology as a false idea which aims at concealing interests could turn out to be the result of the description, but it is most certainly not an appropriate starting point. The fact is that one cannot understand how a false idea is possible if one does not first comprehend the concept of an idea in general, i.e. the role and importance of ideas and representations within the picture which human beings make of their social existence. One must thus go back behind deception and distortion to the original phenomenon of the symbol, of which 'false consciousness' is a perversion.

Thus, my point of departure is not the Marxist concept of ideology; this concept can at most be the result of my investigation.

I shall proceed in three stages. The point of departure is provided by Max Weber's analysis of social action and social relations. According to Weber, we are confronted with a social action when human behaviour is meaningful for the actor and the behaviour of the one is oriented in terms of that of the other. The notion of a social *relation* adds the idea of the stability and predictability of a system of meaning to this two-sided phenomenon of the sense and reciprocal orientation of an action. It is precisely on the level of significant, reciprocally oriented and socially integrated action that the phenomenon of ideology appears in its complete originality. It is bound up with the necessity that a social group produce an image of itself, present – in the theatrical sense of the term – itself. In what follows I shall take this property of ideology as my point of departure.

Why is this necessary? Jacques Ellul[1] considers the relation which a historical community produces to the act which originally founded that group to be fundamental in this respect. Examples of such founding acts are: the American Declaration of Independence, the French Revolution, the October Revolution, etc. Ideology is thus a function of a distance which separates the social memory from an event which is to be recapitulated in spite of this distance. Its role is thus to spread a creed beyond the small circle of the founders and to perpetuate the initial energy beyond the time of the revolution. Within this distance, which is characteristic of all situations *post festum*, images and interpretations arise; an act of grounding or initiation can only be reactualized by means of an interpretation and a self-presentation. It may well be that there are no groups without this indirect relation to their own formation. Thus, the phenomenon of ideology is a very early development, for with domestication via memory we find the beginning of consensus, but also the beginning of convention and rationalization. But at precisely this moment ideology ceases to be a moving power; it becomes a justification and legitimation. Or, more exactly, it only remains a moving power to the extent that it can simultaneously provide a justification.

This allows us to understand why we find a second property of ideology on this first level, namely dynamism. It is related to what one might call a theory of social motivation. It is for social praxis that which a motive is for an individual project: a motive justifies and gives impulses. Ideology argues in the same manner: it is moved by the will to show that the group which it represents is legitimately the way it is. But one must be careful not to pass judgment against ideology too quickly at this point. Its mediation is irreplaceable; this can be seen in the fact that ideology is always more than mere reflection in that it is also justification and project. This 'generative' property of ideology is visible in its power to provide undertakings and institutions with a belief in the correctness and necessity of their actions.

But how does ideology protect its dynamism? Here we encounter a third property of ideology: simplification and schematization. Ideology is a screen, a code which provides not only a synoptic view of the group but also of history and, in the final analysis, of the world. This code-character is immanent to the justificatory function of ideology; its capacity for transformation and flexibility is preserved only under the condition that the ideas which it offers become opinions and that thought becomes less strict in order to increase social efficacy, as if ideology alone could not only deliver a memory of the founding act but in addition convey the systems of thought themselves. For this reason, anything and everything can become ideology: ethics, religion and philosophy. 'The transformation of a system of thought into a system of faith', says Ellul, '*is* ideology'. The idealization of the picture which the group makes of itself is merely a corollary of this schematization. By means of an idealized picture, the group presents itself its own existence. This picture strengthens in turn the interpretative code; this can be seen in the fact that ritualizing and typifying phenomena appear simultaneously with the first celebrations of the founding.

This third property allows us to recognize what I would like to call the doxic character of ideology, namely: the epistemic level of ideology is that of opinion, of *doxa* in the Greek sense. Or, should one prefer Freudian terminology: it is the moment of rationalization. This is the reason why ideology prefers to express itself in maxims, slogans and catch-words. This is also the reason why nothing is closer to the formular of rhetoric – the art of the probable and persuasion – than ideology. This comparison suggests that social cohesion is only guaranteed when the doxic optimum which corresponds to the average cultural level of the group in question is not overstepped. But once again, the deceptive or pathological should not be put in centre stage too quickly: this schematization, this idealization, this rhetoric is the price which one has to pay for the social efficacy of ideas.

With the fourth property we encounter the negative aspects which are usually associated with ideology. But there is nothing shady about this property in itself. It is connected with the fact that the interpretative code of an ideology is rather something *in which* human beings live and think than a concept *which* they form. To put it a bit differently, ideology is not thematic, but rather operative. It operates behind our backs. We think from its point of view rather than thinking about it. This is the source of the possibility of deception and distortion which has been associated with the notion of the inverted image of our own social position since Marx. But it might be the case that it is not possible for an individual, and even more so for a group, to formulate, thematize and turn everything into an object of thought. This impossibility, which I shall deal with extensively in my critique of *total* reflection, has the consequence that ideology is by nature uncritical. In addition, it would seem that the opacity of our cultural code is a precondition for the production of social messages.

The fifth property sharpens the non-reflective and opaque status of ideology. I am thinking of the sluggishness, the backwardness which seems characteristic of the phenomenon of ideology. The novel can only be assimilated in terms of the typical, whereby the typical itself arises through the sedimentation of social experiences. This is the locus of the disguising function. It makes its appearance with respect to the realities which are in fact experienced by the group, but which cannot be assimilated by the guiding schema. Every group manifests elements of orthodoxy, of intolerance with respect to fringe groups. It may well be that a radically pluralistic, radically permissive society is not possible. At some point we encounter that which is intolerable, which gives rise to intolerance. The intolerable arises at the point at which the novel begins to threaten the group's possibilities of recognizing and rediscovering itself. This property seems to contradict the first function of ideology, which was to maintain the charismatic power of the founding act. But this initial energy is limited and subject to wear and tear. Thus, ideology is simultaneously the effect of wear and resistance to wear. This paradox is tied up with the original function of ideology, namely to perpetuate the act of founding in the mode of 'presentation' or 'representation'. For this reason, ideology is at the same time an interpretation of the real and a barrier against the possible. Every interpretation moves within a limited field; but ideology narrows this field with respect to the possibilities of interpretation which are intrinsic to the original driving power of the process. In this sense one can thus speak of an ideological reticence or even of ideological blindness. But even when this phenomenon appears to approach the pathological, it retains something of its original function. It is inconceivable that awareness takes place outside of an ideological code. Thus, ideology is affected by the schematization which it necessarily exhibits; it becomes rigid, whereas the facts and situations change. This paradox leads us to the threshold of the notorious function of disguising.

At this point our analysis has reached the second concept of ideology. It seems to me that the function of disguising wins the upper hand as soon as the general integrative function – which we have dealt with up to now – is bound up with a specific function of domination with reference to the hierarchical aspects of social organization.

I have preferred to postpone the investigation of this concept of ideology to the second stage of the discussion, since one must first understand the other functions of ideology if one is to see through the crystallization of the phenomenon with reference to the problematic of domination. In explicating this phenomenon, I shall refer to Max Weber once again, to his famous analyses of authority and dominion. Weber notes that all dominion searches for a legitimation, and political systems can be distinguished according to the kind of legitimation they offer. Now, if every claim to legitimacy corresponds to the individual's belief in this legitimacy, then the relation between the claim uttered by the authority and the belief which is correlated with this claim is essentially asymmetrical. I would like to argue that the claim which is maintained by the authority always contains more than the belief which the authority elicits. I would see the irreducible phenomenon of surplus value here, understood in the sense of the surplus of the demand for legitimacy in contrast to the supply of belief. It may well be that this surplus value is the authentic surplus value, since, as we have seen, every authority demands more than our belief can offer. Here ideology turns out to be a continuation of the phenomenon of surplus value and simultaneously a system of legitimizing dominion.

This second concept of ideology is intimately connected with the first in that the phenomenon of authority goes hand in hand with the constitution of a group. The act of founding a group which presents itself ideologically is an essentially political act. As Eric Weil repeatedly emphasized, a historical community becomes a political reality only by becoming capable of making decisions, and this is the source of the phenomenon of dominion. This is the reason why ideology as disguise interferes with all other properties of ideology as integration, especially with the property of opacity which is bound up with the mediating function of ideology. As we have learned from Max Weber, there is no completely transparent legitimation. Even if one does not equate every form of dominion with the charismatic form, every authority is characterized by an essential opacity. No phenomenon confirms so completely the sluggish character of ideology as that of authority and dominion.

Thus, if the mediating role coincides with the phenomenon of dominion, the distorting and disguising character of ideology comes to the centre of attention. But to the degree to which the integration of a group cannot be completely traced back to the phenomenon of dominion, not all properties of ideology which we have read off of its mediating role are taken up into the distorting function.

And that brings us to the third concept of ideology, the genuinely Marxist concept. I should like to show that it achieves its full contours when it is unified with the others. What does it have to offer which is new? Essentially the idea of distortion and deformation via *inversion* or *reversal*. Marx writes: 'If in all ideology men and their circumstances appear upside-down as in a *camera obscura*, this phenomenon arises just as much from their historical life-process as the inversion of objects on the retina does from their physical life-processes.'[2]

I shall ignore the metaphorical character of this mode of expression for the moment. At this point I am more interested in the descriptive content of the Marxist claim. The decisive thing is that ideology is defined by its function as well as by its content. If an inversion occurs, then only because a specific production of human beings is as such an inversion. In Marx – and here he follows Feuerbach – religion exercises this function to the extent that it is not one ideology among others, but is rather ideology pure and simple. It brings about an inversion between heaven and earth and stands man on his head. What Marx is trying to grasp with this model is a universal process in the course of which the real activity, the real process of life, ceases to be the basis and is replaced by that which men say, imagine and think. Thus, ideology is that deception that leads us to take the picture for the reality, the mirror image for the original.

We see that this description is based on a genealogical critique of productions which move from the real to the imaginary. The critique in turn undertakes an inversion of the inversion. To this extent it is by no means free from presuppositions: it considers Feuerbach's reduction of the whole of German idealism and philosophy itself to religion, and religion to an inverted mirror image, to be demonstrated fact. It is not as if Marx were simply repeating Feuerbach, he supplements the reduction on the level of theory by a practical reduction which has the task of revolutionizing the foundations of ideology.

On this level I am concerned to understand the descriptive potential which is set loose by this critique of the genealogy. Its claim to scientific status will be investigated at a later point. To begin with, it appears to me that Marx has *specified* the concept of ideology; but this concept of ideology presupposes the other two. Indeed, how could illusions, phantasms and phantasmagorias have the slightest effect if ideology did not have a mediating function which is incorporated into the social relations from the very beginning as a symbolic constitution in the sense of Mauss and Lévi-Strauss? And this forbids us to speak of genuinely pre-ideological or non-ideological activity. In addition, we would not be able to understand how an inverted notion of reality might serve the interests of a ruling class if the relation between dominion and ideology were not more basic than the analysis which operates with the concept of social classes. That which is novel in Marx is set off against the background of a symbolic constitution of social relations in general and the relation of dominion more specifically. In addition, there is the idea that the justificatory function of ideology can be primarily applied to the relation of dominion which rises out of class differences and the class struggle. We are thus indebted to him for the specific thematization of the ideological mode of functioning with reference to the ruling position of a class. But I am inclined to say that this specific contribution cannot be fully appreciated if one does not tear it out of its fundamental narrowness, i.e. as long as one does not bring the Marxist concept of ideology into connection with the more general concept of ideology against the background of which it stands out as such. The narrowness of the Marxist concept is not the result of the fact that it is connected with the notion of the ruling class, but of the fact that it is defined in terms of a specific content – religion – and not in terms of its function. This restriction is a Feuerbachian legacy, as can be seen in the 'Theses on Feuerbach'. But the possibilities implicit in the Marxist concept are much broader than their application to religion in the first phases of capitalism, an application which – by the way – is quite legitimate, although religion constitutes its authentic significance in a different sphere of experience and discourse. Indeed, the Marxist thesis can be applied to every system of thought which has the same function as religion. This has been fully recognized by Horkheimer, Adorno, Marcuse, Habermas and the members of the Frankfurt School. Science and technology can also appear in the form of ideology within a specific historical period. For this reason, the ideological function must be separable from the ideological content. And if religion allows itself to be co-opted to such a function, standing the relation between heaven and earth on its head, then it is not religion any more, i.e. it is no longer the introduction of the Word into the world but rather an *inverted picture of life*. In this case it really is nothing more than the ideology which Marx discovered. But the same thing can happen to science and technology – and does in fact occur – as soon as the function of justifying the military and economic system of late capitalism hides behind the claim to scientific status.

In this manner, combining the Marxist criterium with the other criteria of ideology can set free the critical potential of just this criterium, under certain circumstances even turning against ideological misuses of Marxism which I shall investigate shortly.

But these secondary considerations must not be allowed to obscure the basic thesis that ideology is an unavoidable phenomenon of social existence, since social reality has always been symbolically constituted, social relations themselves experiencing their interpretation in pictures and presentations.

Thus, our second problem is posed very sharply: what is the scientific status of discourse concerning ideology? Is there a non-ideological position from which one can speak about ideology in a scientific manner?

2 Social science and ideology

The whole dispute concerning ideology presupposes the implicit or explicit rejection of the Aristotelian argument to the effect that argumentation can only take the form of rough outlines in all of those sciences which Aristotle still called political and which modern thinkers have successively called the moral sciences, the *Geisteswissenschaften*, sciences of man, social sciences and critical social sciences. The surprising thing about the contemporary discussion is not only – not so much – *what* is said about ideology as rather the claim to say it from a non-ideological standpoint which is called science. Thus, everything which is said about ideology is subordinated to a supposed science which stands in contrast to ideology. It seems to me that in the antithesis between science and ideology both concepts – simultaneously –

must be put in question. If ideology loses its mediating role, retaining only the mystifying role of a false consciousness, the reason is that it has been contrasted with a science which is thought to have a non-ideological status. But is there really any such science?

I shall distinguish between two stages within the discussion, according to whether science is understood in a positivistic sense or not.

Let us begin with the positivist understanding. My thesis is: it is only in the positivist sense that one can make a sharp division between ideology and science. Unfortunately, the social sciences, especially on the level of general theories, do not meet the positivist criteria of scientificity. In its turn to positivity, Galileo's mathematical physics was able to stamp out the *impetus* of pre-Galilean physics once and for all, and Kepler's, Copernicus' and Newton's astronomy could overcome Ptolemaic astronomy. Social science's relation to ideology would be an exact counterpart to these examples if it were capable of satisfying the same criteria as those positive sciences. The scientific weakness of general social theories is proportionate to the intensity with which they denounce ideology. The fact is that social theory never attains the level of scientificity which would allow it to use the concept of a scientific turning point or scientific revolution in a manner which would clearly set it off from ideology. A young Canadian philosopher, Maurice Lagueux, in a noteworthy essay dealing with 'L'usage abusif du rapport science-idéologie',[3] recently came to the conclusion that only those contributions are to be classified as being scientific 'which *simultaneously* lead to a satisfying explanation of phenomena which were incomprehensible up to then . . . *and* successfully withstand systematic and strict attempts at falsification (verification in the Popperian sense of non-falsification)'. The decisive point here is not the proposal of two different criteria but rather their simultaneous application. A theory can indeed have a very great explanatory value while being only weakly confirmed by strict attempts at falsification. Now, the combination of these two criteria is still lacking and will perhaps always be lacking in the global theories of the social sciences. Thus, one has either theories which are unifying, but not verified, or theories which are well verified but only deal with partial aspects of the phenomenon, for example demography or all mathematically or statistically oriented partial disciplines which for this reason do not make a claim to being integrative theories at all. The representatives of unifying theories, which are less demanding with regard to verification or falsification, generally denounce the ideology of their opponents with bitter arrogance. I should like to provide a few examples of just how easily this can happen.

A typical argument claims that ideology is a superficial discourse that is unaware of its own real motives. This argument becomes even more important when one contrasts the unconscious character of the real motives with the straightforwardly conscious character of public or official motives. But one must admit that the emphasis on the real, even if it is unconscious, by no means guarantees the required scientificity. The transition from the illusory to the real, from consciousness to the unconscious, no doubt has great explanatory value. But this value as such is the real scientific danger. The transition from the one level to the other does in fact satisfy thought, but it leaves us with the belief that the opening up of a field of the unconscious is intrinsically a scientific operation.

This naivety is strengthened by the conviction that we have eliminated the factor of subjectivity by means of a transposition of the explanatory model from the level of conscious rationalization to that of unconscious reality. If one compares Althusser's Marxism with Max Weber's sociology, then we do in fact see that explanation by means of the subjective motives of the actors is replaced by an analysis of structural wholes which are free of all subjectivity. But banning the subjectivity of the historical actors is no guarantee that the sociologist who pursues his science has himself entered a form of discourse without a subject. At this point we catch sight of what I would like to call the trap of science. By means of a semantic confusion which amounts to a sophism, explanation in terms of structures – instead of explanation in terms of subjects – is taken to be a discourse which is not borne by any subject at all. At the same time, this weakens one's vigilance with respect to verification and falsification. This danger is all the more threatening in view of the fact that increasing rationality can even act as a barrier against claims to verification. This is precisely what unmasks this theory as ideology: a rationalization which shoves itself in front of reality.

Various strategies have been developed to disguise this weakness; I shall mention only two of them.

On the one hand, the attempt has been made to make up for the lack of empirical verification by the expansion of formal methods. But this only strengthens the criterium of explanation in contrast to the criterium of verification in a new way. Indeed, if critical thought such as Marxism is pushed on to the level of formalism, it sacrifices all of its strengths. Is not Marx's main charge against the economic thought of his time that it merely builds models 'which have lost all density'?[4]

On the other hand, the attempt has been made to make up for the weakness of individual theories by means of the reciprocal reinforcement of a series of critical disciplines. Here we encounter a kind of cross between a social theory of ideology and psychoanalysis. This cross takes on the form of a chiasma in which one assumes that that which is asserted in one discipline, but only poorly verified, can be more adequately verified in another discipline. As interesting as this cross may be from a non-positivist perspective, its consequences for the criteria of explanation and falsification are detrimental. I would be inclined to say that what one wins on the one side is lost on the other.

The first phase of this discussion has the result that social theories by no means have that authority which would allow them to unmask ideological positions; at any rate, they do not have the authority with which astronomy and chemistry have radically distanced themselves from astrology and alchemy.

But this is not the end of the discussion. One can object that the preceding argument has forced criteria on to social theory which are not proper to it; in other words, that it remained caught up in a positivist conception of the social sciences. This objection is thoroughly justified. Thus, I am quite prepared to keep my eyes open for other scientific criteria for social theory. But here one must be very clear about what one is doing. The abandonment of positivist criteria signifies simultaneously that one has abandoned the separation between science and ideology. One cannot abandon the positivist model and at the same time make use of this model to define an authentic turning point for the separation between science and ideology. But this is precisely what often happens in contemporary discussions of the problem of ideology.

Let us try out the second way. The redetermination of the relation between science and ideology can be postponed to a later stage of my discussion.

With respect to ideology, science can be given a second meaning, namely that of *critique*. This second meaning corresponds to the position of the left-wing Hegelians, who modified the Kantian critique by demanding a genuinely critical critique. Marx did not hesitate – not even after the so-called scientific turn of 1847 – to give *Capital* the sub-title *Critique of Political Economy*.

Here we must confront the following question: can a social science understood as critique, in view of its own criteria for ideology, take up a completely non-ideological standpoint?

I see three difficulties in this question; the third will be of special interest, since the possibility of granting the dialectic of science and ideology an acceptable status depends on its solution.

The first difficulty is this: how is it possible to avoid, in the transformation of critique into a *partisan* science, that quasi-pathological phenomenon which one denounces in one's opponents? In speaking of a partisan science I am thinking above all of the Leninist interpretation of Marxism which Althusser has defended so tenaciously in his book *Lenin and Philosophy*. Althusser defends two theses which are intimately related to one another: Marxism represents the third major turning point in the history of thought; following the first turning point in Euclidean geometry and the second in Galileo's mathematical physics, Marx is in a similar manner able to discover a new continent: that of history. To be sure, history as knowledge and self-knowledge has other predecessors. This may be acceptable. Things get more difficult with the claim that a line, which Lenin called the 'party line', can be drawn between this new science and bourgeois science, thereby constituting a science which is partial in the most literal sense of the word. The danger here is that Marxist science turns into an ideology – ideology in the sense of its own criteria. In this respect, the later fate of Marxism confirms the gloomy premonitions. From being a fruitful working hypothesis, the analysis of social classes – to give only one example – and most especially the thesis that there are fundamentally only two classes, turned into a dogma which blinded Marxism to social upheavals in industrial society.

But even worse than this blindness to reality is the official anchoring of the doctrine in the party, whereby another form of ideologizing makes its appearance. Just as religion is charged with justifying the power of the ruling class, Marxism in turn produces a very problematic justification for the rule of the party. This justificatory function with respect to the power of a ruling group accounts for the ossification of Marxism. It is paradoxical that Marxism after Marx is the best possible example for his own concept of ideology. And for precisely this reason it is worth recalling that Napoleon turned the quite honourable expression 'ideology' into a polemical and derogatory word.

But these fairly pointed objections do not mean that Marxism is fundamentally mistaken. Rather they point out that the critical function of Marxism can only be given free rein when the use of the Marxist works is completely separated from the exercise of power – when one subjects his analyses to an immediate test by means of an application to modern economy, just as Marx himself did with reference to the economic situation of his period – in short, when Marx's *Capital* approaches Nietzsche's *Zarathustra*, about which its author said that it is 'a book for everyone and no one'.

The second difficulty concerns the problem of a non-ideologically grounded explanation of the formation of ideologies.

As the reader will perhaps have noted, my remarks are by and large in agreement with Jacques Taminiaux,[5] although I do not go so far as to view Marx from the point of view of onto-theology. In view of the ambiguity of the expressions 'origin', 'goal', 'subject', etc., I hestitate to undertake such an assimilation. I shall rather point out the mediating role of the Hegelian and Feuerbachian concepts within the Marxian concept formation. Certainly, Marx complements the Feuerbachian critique, but he remains on its line as soon as he speaks of 'ideology'. One must first have interpreted all of German philosophy as a commentary on religion, and religion as an inversion of heaven and earth, in order to go on to understand the critique itself as inversion. He uses the metaphor of the inversion of images on the retina, of head and feet, heaven and earth, reflection and echo, of sublimation in the chemical sense, of fog, etc.[6] As Sarah Kofman has remarked in a work influenced by Derrida,[7] all of these metaphors remain tied to a system of oppositions, namely the oppositions between theory and praxis, reality and representation, light and darkness, all of which confirm the metaphysical origin of the concept of ideology as an inversion of the inversion. Against this background, how can one assert that following the rise of science ideology is no longer thought in an ideological manner? The section of *Capital* concerning the fetish character of commodities gives us little reason for hope in this respect: the phantasmagoric form which the value of the products of labour take on in their transformation into commodities remains a riddle which not only cannot account for the religious illusion, it is built on it, at least in the form of the analysis. After all, religion as the basic form of ideology is more than an analogy; it remains the 'secret' of the commodity. As Sarah Kofman emphasizes, the fetish 'commodity' is not 'the reflection of the real relations, but the reflection of an already transformed, mystified world. The reflection of a reflection, phantasma of a phantasma.'[8] The failure of the attempt to understand the development of the illusion without recourse to metaphors simultaneously documents in reverse manner the difficulty, which Aristotle described again and again, of understanding Platonic participation. He claims that it is a mere metaphor, an empty phrase. Here participation runs in the other direction, not from the idea to its shadowy image, but from the thing to its reflection, but the difficulty is the same.

The reason for this failure can be seen with the help of our first analysis. If it is true that the image-like self-presentation of a social group consists in interpretations which belong immediately to the constitution of social relations, or, to put it a bit differently, if social relations are always of a symbolic nature, then there is no point in trying to derive this self-presentation from something else which would be real in the authentic sense, real activity, real process of life, of which it would be the subsequent reflection and echo. A non-ideological discourse concerning ideology runs into the impossibility of encountering a social reality *prior* to symbolization. This difficulty encourages me in the conviction that one cannot take the phenomenon of inversion as point of departure in speaking about ideology. It is rather the case that inversion must be taken to be a special case of a much more fundamental phenomenon which consists in the symbolically performed institution of the subsequent representation of social relations. Concealment is a secondary event of symbolization. I think that this is the reason for the failure of every attempt to understand social reality as a reality which is initially transparent and only subsequently becomes opaque. In Marx, it seems to me, the more fruitful idea is that transparency does not lie behind us, but before us, at the end of a historical process which can perhaps never be brought to a close. But if this is the case one must have the courage to consider the separation between ideology and science to be a limiting concept, and that means: to dare to make the assertion that at the present time we do not have a non-ideological conception of the development of ideology.

But the greatest difficulty has not been mentioned yet. It is involved in the fact that an absolutely radical critique cannot be carried out. A radically critical consciousness would after all have to be the result of a *total* reflection.

I would like to develop this argument in some detail, an argument, by the way, which applies to every social theory which lays claim to totality, including Marxism.

I shall begin by considering the two models of explanation which Jean Ladrière distinguishes in an important text[9] and which can be easily found in the two fundamental types of interpretation of contemporary Marxism. I should like to show that the presupposition of a total reflection is equally unavoidable in both models. Ladrière says: 'One can suggest two kinds of models of explanation, namely explanation in terms of project and explanation in terms of system' (p. 42). Let us begin with the first model. Max Weber's 'interpretative sociology' belongs here, but also the Marxism of Gramsci, Lukács, Ernst Bloch and Lucien Goldmann. This model makes the 'value freedom' which Max Weber demanded extraordinarily difficult. Explanation in terms of project is necessarily explanation in which the theoretician is included, which thus demands of him that he clarify his own situation and his project with respect to this situation. Here we find the silent assumption of a total reflection.

Does the second model avoid this possible presupposition? It would seem to do so, at least at first glance. Since one does not want to explain action in terms of a project, one does not need a complete analysis of the project, i.e. a total reflection is dispensable. But the inclusion of the scientist in his instrument of interpretation cannot be avoided in explanation of this kind, if it is to be total. According to Ladrière, the critical point of systems theory is bound up with the necessity of developing a theory which deals with the development of systems. 'Here one must necessarily draw on either physical or biological systems (in making use of a cybernetic model, for example), or on theories of a philosophical nature (thus non-scientific theories) such as a dialectical philosophy' (p. 42). In both cases, the demand for completeness corresponds to the demand for a total reflection in the case of explanation in terms of projects. Thus, an entire philosophy is brought into play, 'according to which a complete overview of the system is possible at any time, and according to which the standpoint from which the overview takes place can be explicated and described in an appropriate discourse. We are thus once again forced to appeal to another kind of discourse' (p. 43).

Thus, the second model is no better off than the first. Explanation in terms of projects could only free history from its ideological bonds by silently presupposing the possibility of a total reflection. Systems-theoretical explanation, in turn, presupposes in a different manner that the scientist can reach a defined standpoint from which the totality can be given expression – and this corresponds to the total reflection of the other hypothesis.

These two failures point to the impossibility of an absolutely radical reflection. And a radically critical consciousness would have to be the result of a total reflection.

This is the real reason why social theory cannot completely free itself from ideology. It is not in the position to perform a total reflection and bring the totality to expression in such a manner that the expression is free from all ideological mediation and distortion.

3 The dialectic of science and ideology

The question which poses itself at this point, and which amounts to the proposal of a vote of confidence, is the following: what about the insufficiently thought-out and perhaps incomprehensible opposition between science and ideology?

Should we simply drop it? I must admit that I have often been tempted to solve the problem in this manner. But I do not believe that this would be the correct solution, since taking this path requires us to give up the advantages of a tension which can neither be reduced to a rigid antithesis nor to a ruinous blending.

We should perhaps begin by taking a serious look at the standpoint which proposes to do away with the distinction, especially in light of the therapeutic effects which it brings with it. This is the insight which I have won from the, at least in Europe, unfortunately forgotten book by Karl Mannheim, *Ideology and Utopia*.[10] The value of this book lies in the fact that the author takes seriously the discovery of the backlash of the accusation of ideologizing and shows how the suspicion that an opponent is tainted by ideology recoils on the critic of ideology.

Mannheim accepts Marxism's discovery that ideology is not a purely local error which might be explained psychologically, but rather a thought structure attributable to a group, class or nation. But he charges Marxism with stopping half-way, i.e. with failing to subject itself to the strategy of suspicion and distrust. According to Mannheim, Marxism cannot break the chain reaction. This is made impossible by a fundamental phenomenon, that of the decline of cultural and intellectual unity, that decline which leads to war between every possible discourse and all others. But what happens when one moves from the restricted to the universal suspicion? Mannheim answers that we move from a partisan, war-like science to a peaceful science, namely to the sociology of knowledge, which was grounded by Troeltsch, Max Weber and Max Scheler. What had been a weapon for the proletariat becomes a method of investigation which looks into the social conditions of every mode of thought.

Mannheim generalizes the concept of ideology in the following manner: for him, ideologies are essentially characterized by their failure to coincide with social reality. They are primarily invoked by the ruling classes and denounced by the rising classes; ideologies look back, utopias look forward. Ideologies adapt themselves to reality, they justify and disguise; utopias, on the other hand, mount a frontal attack on reality and bring it to the point of explosion. These differences are certainly important, but they are never decisive, as one can see in Marx himself, who reckons utopian socialism to the ideological phantasms. And it is only history itself which can decide whether a utopia really is what it claims to be, i.e. a new vision capable of changing the course of history.

Let us take this generalized concept of ideology, which is bound up with that of utopia in a most complex manner, as a working hypothesis. My question is: from what point of view does the scientist who is concerned with a theory of general ideology speak? There is no such point of view – this much must be admitted. And we are even farther away from the possibility of such a point of view in this case than in the case of a theory of special ideology for which it is only the other who is a victim of ideology. But in this case the scientist knows that he himself has an ideological bias. In this respect, Mannheim's self-reflection and self-understanding are exemplary, thanks to his unlimited honesty. He knows that Weber's claim to a value-free sociology is a myth. At most, this claim corresponds to a necessary stage:

> What is needed, therefore, is a continual readiness to recognize that every point of view is particular to a certain definite situation, and to find out through analysis of what this particularity consists. A clear and explicit avowal of the implicit metaphysical presuppositions which underlie and make possible empirical knowledge will do more for the clarification and advancement of research than a verbal denial of the existence of these presuppositions accompanied by their surreptitious admission through the back door (p. 80).

But if we are satisfied with this creed, we fall victim to relativism and historicism, and research is stifled. As Mannheim remarks, he who has no presuppositions asks no questions; he who asks no questions formulates no hypotheses and does not investigate anything. The individual scientist is not any better off than society itself: ideologies are deviations from the genuine course of things. But the death of ideology would lead to the most sterile clear-sightedness, since a social group without ideology and utopia, without distance to itself and without self-presentation, would be a society without a general project, the victim of a history which disintegrates into a series of insignificant events.

But how can one make presuppositions when one knows that everything is relative? How can one make a decision which does not amount to throwing dice?

As I have already hinted: Mannheim struggles with this difficulty, demonstrating exemplary intellectual courage. He wants to work out a distinction between relationism and relativism at all costs. But what is the price? The price is an impossible one, namely that all partial ideologies be integrated into a general overview which would prescribe a relative validity to each. This would be a move from a non-evaluative conception of an impartial observer to an evaluative conception which dares to say which ideology is correct and which is not. Once again, we are confronted with the demand for a total knowledge. Mannheim says: 'The sociologically oriented history of ideas is destined to provide modern men with a revised view of the whole historical process' (p. 69). Thus, the weight of the distinction between relationism and relativism is borne by a hesitant Hegelianism. As Mannheim says, one will be inclined to see the change of norms, formations and institutions 'as symptoms and to integrate them into a system whose unity and meaning it becomes our task to understand' (p. 82). And in another place: one must pursue the history of ideas in such a manner that one 'will seek to discover in the totality of the historical complex the role, significance, and meaning of each component element' (p. 83). The author identifies himself with a 'sociological technique for diagnosing the culture of an epoch' (p. 83).

This is the price which the scientist must pay if he is to avoid scepticism and cynicism and be able to evaluate the present, i.e. in order to be able to say: these ideas are valid in this given situation, those other ideas hinder clear vision and change. But in order that we be able to apply this criterium to a given situation, the thinker must have a finished science at his disposal. Indeed, if one is to judge the degree to which reality has been distorted, one must have access to the total social reality. But it is only at the end of a historical process that the judgment concerning the sense of reality itself falls: 'The attempt to escape ideological and utopian distortions is, in the last analysis, a quest for reality' (p. 87). Thus we have fallen into a circle once again, just as in Marx, who said that the real, which one initially opposes to the ideological illusion, can only be recognized when the ideologies have been dissolved in practical action. Here too everything is circular: 'Only when we are thoroughly aware of the limited scope of every point of view are we on the road to the sought-for comprehension of the whole' (p. 93). But the reverse is no less important: 'a total view implies both the assimilation and transcendence of the limitations of particular points of view' (p. 94).

In moving from a partial to a total historicism, Mannheim undertook the infinite task of transcending historicism by means of its own excesses. In this respect it is not insignificant that Mannheim was simultaneously concerned with the social problem of the intelligentsia, since the synthesis of standpoints presupposes a social vehicle which cannot be a middle class, but only a relatively classless stratum which is not all too completely integrated into the social order. This stratum might be Max Weber's 'free-floating intelligentsia'. Thus the theory of ideology itself is based on the utopia of a 'state of mind that has been sociologically fully clarified' (p. 175).

A total synthesis is obviously an impossibility. Have we thus returned to the critique of total reflection without having won any new insights? Must we abandon any claim to truth concerning ideology? I think not.

It seems to me that Karl Mannheim's position can be considered to be a turning point which allows us to form an idea of the direction our inquiry must take.

I think that the possibility of a solution is to be found in a *hermeneutic* discourse concerning the conditions of all historical understanding. Elsewhere[11] I have pointed out the central role of the phenomenon of pre-understanding, following the lead of Heidegger and Gadamer, and emphasizing the fact that its ontological status dominates all genuine problems in the theory of science, problems which the social sciences encounter under the title of prejudice, ideology, the hermeneutic circle, etc. All of these problems and difficulties have the same origin, although they are all distinct from one another. In the final analysis they are the result of the structure of a being which is never in the sovereign position of a subject and thus capable of distancing itself from the totality of its own conditions and conditionedness. In the current context, I did not plan to take the less complex path of an argumentation which from the very beginning moves on the level of an ontology of pre-understanding, in order subsequently to deal with the oppressive question concerning theories of ideology, as it were, from above. I have preferred to follow the long and difficult path of a philosophical reflection on the conditions of a knowledge of ideology and the possibilities for confirming a social scientific explanation of ideology. In this manner I encounter once again, in the failure of a total reflection, the necessity of another discourse, namely that of the hermeneutics of historical understanding.

4 Habermas's ideology critique

In order to concretize the preceding discussion by means of an additional example, and in order to show that the *critique* of ideology is in turn an element of the effort to come to terms with the historical situation, I shall discuss Jürgen Habermas's analysis of the concept of ideology and the critique of ideology. I shall begin with the essay 'Knowledge and Human Interests'[12] from 1965; at a later point I shall come back to the book which bears the same title.

The concept of interest contradicts any claim on the part of the theoretical subject to situate itself above all interests; Habermas sees precisely this pretension at work in Plato, Kant, Hegel and Husserl. The task of a critical philosophy consists in unmasking the subliminal interests intrinsic to the pursuit of knowledge.

The concept of interests allows the introduction of the concept of ideology in the sense of an allegedly disinterested knowledge which serves to conceal an interest behind a rationalization which is not unsimilar to Freud's.

It is important to see that there is not merely *one* interest, but a pluralism of spheres of interest. Habermas distinguishes three basic interests, each demarcating a sphere of scientific research, i.e. a species of science.

First, there is the technical or instrumental interest which brings forth the 'empirical-analytic sciences'; it guides these sciences in the sense that the significance of possible empirical assertions lies in their technical exploitability: the relevant facts of the empirical sciences are constituted in the prior organization of our experience in the behavioural system of instrumental action. This thesis, which is related to Dewey's and Peirce's pragmatism, will later be important for understanding what Habermas, following Marcuse, holds to be the modern ideology, namely science and technology themselves. The most immediate possibility of ideologizing is based on the correlation between empirical knowledge and the technical interest, Habermas defining the latter more precisely as a 'cognitive interest in technical control over objectified processes' (p. 309).

But there is a second sphere of interest which is no longer technical but rather practical in the Kantian sense of the term. In his other works, Habermas contrasts communicative with instrumental action. The practical sphere is the sphere of interpersonal communication. The 'historical-hermeneutic sciences' correspond to this sphere. The signification of assertions produced in this realm no longer refers to possible prediction and technical exploitation, but to the understanding of sense and signification. Understanding itself takes place in the interpretation of opinions which are exchanged in everyday language, in the interpretation of traditional texts, and finally in the internalization of norms which institutionalize social roles.

Habermas finds hints of this distinction between two types of interest in Marx. More precisely: he sees this distinction at work in the famous distinction between the 'forces of production' and the 'relations of production', the latter being the institutional forms within which productive activity occurs. Indeed, Marxism is based on the opposition between force and form. The forces of production are to bring forth a self-productive humanity; but the relations of production are responsible for a division of producing subjects into antagonistic classes. Habermas sees an outline of his own distinction here, according to which the phenomena of domination and violence, the dissimulation of power relations within ideologies and political action of liberation fall into the sphere of the relations of production, but not into that of the forces of production. Thus, one must be clearly aware of the distinction between the spheres of instrumental and communicative action if one is to understand the phenomena analysed by Marx. But this is just what Marxism itself cannot do, since it subsumes the forces and relations under one and the same concept of production. To this extent, it clearly belongs to the history of positivism, to the history of forgetting reflection, although it implicitly belongs to the history of coming to awareness of that reification which hinders communication.

But we have not yet spoken of the third interest, which Habermas calls the emancipatory interest. The critical social sciences are correlated with this interest. These sciences are *essentially* critical; this distinguishes them not only from the empirical-analytic sciences of social processes, but also from the historical-hermeneutic sciences which stand under the practical interest. It is the task of the critical social sciences to discover ideologically frozen relations of dependency behind the observable regularities of the empirical social sciences. Thus, it is an emancipatory interest which guides the critical approach; Habermas also ties this interest to self-reflection. This self-reflection, as he writes in the essay from 1965, frees the subject from dependence on hypostatized 'powers' (p. 310). As we see, this interest is the interest which animates the philosophies of the past; it is common to philosophy and the critical social sciences, but ontology buried it behind a completed reality. This interest becomes active only within a critical reflection which criticizes the silently effective knowledge interests and demonstrates the dependence of the theoretical subject on empirical conditions which are related to institutional imperatives.

Thus, this detour leads us to the genuine concept of ideology. The concept of ideology plays the same role in the critical social sciences that the concept of the misunderstanding plays in a hermeneutics of traditions. Schleiermacher, prior to Gadamer, tied hermeneutics to this latter concept. Hermeneutics arises where there are misunderstandings. But hermeneutics is based on the conviction that the understanding which precedes the misunderstanding is capable of integrating the misunderstanding within itself by means of the movement of question and answer, i.e. by means of the dialogical model. Misunderstanding is, if one will, homogeneous with understanding; for this reason, the latter need not recur to explanatory schemata, which are rejected as improper claims of 'methodologism'.

The situation is completely different in the case of the concept of ideology. What is the difference? In this context Habermas makes repeated use of the parallel between psychoanalysis and the theory of ideology. This parallel is based on the following criteria:

(a) In the Frankfurt School, and in those lines of thought which can still be called Marxist in a broad sense of the term, distortion is always traced back to the repressive action of an authority, i.e. to violence. 'Censorship', understood in a Freudian sense here, is a key concept, since it is a matter of a political concept which, after having been adopted by psychoanalysis, is reintroduced into the field of critical social science. The link between ideology and violence is decisive, since it allows factors to appear in the realm of reflection which, although not foreign to hermeneutics, are not emphasized by it, namely the factors 'labour' and 'domination'. Thus, in a broadly Marxist sense we may say that the phenomenon of class domination appears within the realm of human labour, and that ideology expresses this phenomenon of domination in a manner which will be thematized shortly. In Habermas's language: the phenomenon of domination appears in the realm of communicative action; language is distorted here in its function on the level of communicative competence. For this reason, a hermeneutics which holds on to the ideality of meaning finds its limit in a phenomenon which only affects language because the relation between the three factors – labour, power and language – is disrupted.

(b) Since the linguistic distortions do not stem from the use of language itself but rather from its relation to labour and power, they cannot be recognized as such by the members of the community. This lack of recognition is a specific property of ideology. In order to understand it phenomenologically, one must make use of psychoanalytical concepts: of the illusion which is distinct from error, the projection which constitutes a false transcendence, the rationalization which after the fact justifies motives by giving them the appearance of rationality. In order to say the same thing within the realm of critical social science, Habermas speaks of a 'systematically distorted communication', of 'pseudo-communication' which is fundamentally distinct from a mere misunderstanding.

(c) If this lack of recognition cannot be successfully dealt with on the level of dialogue, then the overcoming of ideology must take a detour through explanatory mechanisms, since the mechanisms of understanding are insufficient. This procedure brings into play a theoretical apparatus which cannot be derived from any possible hermeneutics which would merely continue the spontaneous interpretation of everyday discourse on the level of systematic inquiry. Here too, psychoanalysis offers a good model: this example is developed in the third part of *Knowledge and Human Interests* and in the essay 'Der Universalitätsanspruch der Hermeneutik'.[13]

Habermas adopts Alfred Lorenzer's suggestion that psychoanalysis be interpreted as a 'language analysis', according to which the 'understanding' of sense takes place by means of the 'reconstruction' of a 'primal scene'. This 'primal scene' is linked to two other scenes, the symptomatic scene and the artificial scene of the situation of transference.

To be sure, psychoanalysis remains within the realm of understanding, which culminates in the patient's becoming aware of his real situation; in this sense, Habermas calls it a depth hermeneutics. But the understanding of sense requires the detour through a 'reconstruction' of the 'process of de-symbolization' which psychoanalysis follows back in the reverse direction, i.e. in the sense of a 're-symbolization'. Thus, psychoanalysis is not entirely foreign to hermeneutics; it would rather seem to be a borderline experience, in view of the explanatory power which appears in the 'reconstruction' of the 'primal scene'. In other words, in order to understand the *what* of the symptom, its *why* must be explained. The theoretical instrumentarium which defines the conditions of possibility of explanation and reconstruction comes to the fore in this phase of the explanation: topical, economic and genetic concepts. With reference to the triad Ego/It (or Id)/Super-Ego, they are, says Habermas, linked to the sphere of communication via the dialogical process by means of which the patient is brought to self-reflection. 'Metapsychology,' Habermas concludes, 'can only be established as meta-hermeneutics.'

Unfortunately, Habermas does not have much to say about the manner in which the explanatory schema of psychoanalysis is to be transposed to the level of ideology. I think that the distortions of communication which go along with the social phenomena of domination and violence are in turn phenomena of de-symbolization. Habermas often uses the happy expression 'excommunication', which reminds one of Wittgenstein's distinction between public and private languages. At this point one would have to make clear the precise sense in which the understanding of these phenomena requires a reconstruction in which one would rediscover specific elements of the 'scenic' understanding. One would at least have to show why understanding requires a moment of explanation, namely because the sense can only be understood if the origin of the non-sense is explained. Finally, one would have to show that this explanation makes use of a theoretical instrumentarium similar to the Freudian topic or economic, i.e. concepts which can neither be derived from dialogical experience within normal language nor from an interpretation of texts which is based on immediate understanding.

These are the basic characteristics of the concept of ideology: the effects of domination on discourse, a dissimulation whose key is not available to consciousness, and the necessary detour through the explanation of causes.

5 Critique of ideologies and hermeneutics

I would like to offer the following remarks concerning the concept of the *critique* of ideology, which has replaced that of the *science* of ideology.

I suggest that we follow the sequence of theses which I have used in the schematic presentation of Habermas's approach.

(a) I shall begin with the theory of interests which is the foundation of the critique of ideologies. One can ask what authorizes the expansion of the thesis that every form of investigation is guided by an interest which provides a frame of reference for the meanings of the realm of investigation. One can also ask why there are precisely three interests (and not two, or four), why these interests are rooted in the natural history of humanity, marking man's emergence from nature and taking form in the realms of labour, domination and language. One would have to ask why knowledge and interest come together in self-reflection, and how the unity of knowledge and interest manifests itself in a dialectic which recognizes the historical traces of the repression of dialogue and reconstructs that which was suppressed.

Are these 'theses' subject to empirical justification? No, for then they would be subject to the yoke of the empirical-analytic sciences, which are said to be guided by *one* interest, namely the technical interest. Are these theses a theory in the sense of a network of explanatory hypotheses which make possible the reconstruction of the primal scene? No, for then they would become regional theses and would once again be legitimated only by a *single* interest, perhaps by the emancipatory interest; its justification would thus be circular.

Mustn't one thus admit that the discovery of these interests and of their relation to the triad labour/domination/language is derived from a philosophical anthropology which is similar to Heidegger's analytic of *Dasein* and especially to the hermeneutics of care? If that is the case, then these interests are neither observable nor are they theoretical entities such as the Ego, the Super-Ego and the It (or Id) in Freud, but rather 'existentials'. Their analysis belongs to a hermeneutics to the extent that they are simultaneously 'obvious' and 'completely concealed'.

To be sure, one can call the analysis of interests a metahermeneutics if one assumes that hermeneutics is above all a hermeneutics of discourse or even an idealism of linguistic life; but we have seen that this simply is not the case and that the hermeneutics of pre-understanding essentially coincides with a hermeneutics of finitude. This is the reason why I am inclined to say that the critique of ideology cannot base its legitimacy on hermeneutics, but rather on the triad labour/domination/language. But both claims intersect within the hermeneutics of finitude, which is the main source of the link between the concepts of prejudice and ideology.

(b) At this point I would like to return to the connection between critical social science and the emancipatory interest in Habermas's work. We have sharply contrasted this privilege of critical social science as opposed to the historical-hermeneutic sciences, i.e. those sciences which are inclined to recognition of the authority of the traditions and not to revolutionary rebellion against 'oppression'.

The question which heremeneutics poses to ideology critique is the following: can ideology critique lay claim to an interest in emancipation which yields a scientific status which is just as clearly circumscribed as is that of the historical-hermeneutic sciences? This distinction is asserted in a rather dogmatic manner, as it were, to widen the gulf between the emancipatory and the human-scientific (*geisteswissenschaftliche*) interest. But Habermas's concrete analyses belie this dogmatism. It is most noteworthy that the distortions which psychoanalysis describes and explains are interpreted as being distortions of communicative competence. Everything points to the fact that the distortions over which ideology critique has jurisdiction arise on this level. We recall that Habermas reinterprets Marxism on the basis of a dialectic of instrumental and communicative action. At the innermost reaches of communicative action, human relations suffer a reification which makes this action itself unrecognizable to the protagonists of communication. Thus, the distortions (those which psychoanalysis discovers as well as those which are denounced by ideology critique) are distortions of man's communicative competence.

Is this reason enough to regard the emancipatory interest as being clearly circumscribed? This would appear not to be the case, especially if one takes into account the fact that – understood positively – this interest aims at nothing other than unrestricted and unlimited communication. The emancipatory interest would in fact be abstract and lifeless if it did not refer to that level at which the historical-hermeneutic sciences are constituted, i.e. to the level of communicative action. If this is the case, can a critique of the distortions of communicative experience be separated from this experience itself? It is the task of the hermeneutics of tradition to remind the critique of ideology of the fact that it is only on the basis of a creative interpretation of his cultural legacy that man can develop his emancipatory projects and anticipate an unrestricted and unlimited communication. If we had no experience of communication – regardless of how restricted and defective it might be – we could hardly wish that this experience be available to all persons at all levels of social institutions. It seems to me that a critique can never be the first or last instance; one criticizes distortions only in the name of a consensus which we cannot anticipate emptily, as an ideal point of orientation, as it were, and we cannot criticize if this ideal is not intuitively available somewhere. One such exemplification consists precisely in the capacity to bridge the cultural distance in the interpretation of those works which are our legacy from the past. One who is not capable of interpreting his past is perhaps also incapable of concretely projecting his emancipatory interest.

(c) We come now to the third point, which concerns the abyss between misunderstanding and pathological or ideological distortion. I should like to direct our attention to an aspect of the theory of ideology which has nothing to do with the parallel between psychoanalysis and the theory of ideology. A large part of Habermas's work is concerned not with ideology in an abstract sense but rather with contemporary ideologies. When the theory of ideology is developed this concretely within the framework of a critique of the contemporary situation, it manifests aspects which call for a concrete – as opposed to a merely theoretical – rapprochement between the emancipatory and the communicative interests.

What is the dominant ideology of our time, according to Habermas? His answer is similar to that of Marcuse and Jacques Ellul: it is the ideology of science and technology. I shall not deal with Habermas's specific arguments here, restricting my remarks to that which is essential. It seems to me, namely, that the theory of ideology is integrated into the field of hermeneutics all over again.

According to Habermas, modern industrial society has replaced the traditional legitimations and the convictions which served to justify power by the ideology of science and technology. And indeed, the modern state no longer represents the interests of a ruling class: it deals with dysfunctions in the industrial system. The function of ideology is no longer that of justifying surplus value by disguising its mechanism, as was still the case in the liberal capitalism Marx described, and this quite simply because surplus value is no longer the source of productivity. The essential aspect of the system is now the production of rationality itself. What must be legitimated is thus the maintenance and growth of the system itself. The scientific-technical apparatus which has become an ideology serves precisely this end, i.e. the legitimation of the relations of domination and inequality which are necessary if the industrial system is to remain functional. Thus, contemporary ideology is quite different from the ideology which Marx described: the latter reigned only for a short span of time and by no means possesses a temporal universality. There is also no such thing as a pre-bourgeois ideology, and bourgeois ideology is expressly tied to the camouflage of domination under the legal cloak of the free contract.

If one accepts this description of modern ideology, then the following question must be posed: what does 'interest' mean in this context? It means that the sub-system of instrumental action has ceased to be a sub-system, and that its categories have inundated the sphere of communicative action. This is the essence of the famous 'rationalization' of which Max Weber spoke: rationality not only conquers ever new realms of instrumental action, it also subjects communicative action to its own structures. Max Weber described this phenomenon as 'disenchantment'; Habermas, on the other hand, describes it as the obliteration of the distinction between the level of instrumental action, which is also the realm of labour, and the level of communicative action, which is also the realm of norms, symbolic exchanges, of personality structures and rational decision-making procedures. In the modern capitalist system, which seems to coincide with the industrial system, the ancient Greek question concerning the 'good life' is abandoned in favour of the functionality of a manipulated system. But the problems of communication – especially the wish to subject important political options to public discussion and democratic decision – have not disappeared; they still exist, but in repressed form. Precisely because their elimination does not occur automatically, and because the need for legitimation remains unsatisfied, an ideology which legitimates the authority of the system is required; this is the reason why technology and science have taken on an ideological role today.

But in this case the hermeneutician's question to the ideology critic is the following: assuming that ideology today consists in the disguising of the distinction between the normative realm of action and the bureaucratic realm, what can be done for the emancipatory interest, such that this interest does not remain a mere wish? And what is to be the ground for the reawakening of communicative action if not the creative renewal of the cultural legacy?

6 Conclusion

In conclusion, I should like to make a few suggestions that might give the pair of concepts science and ideology an acceptable sense.

First suggestion: all objectifying knowledge concerning our place in history, in a social group, a cultural tradition or a society is preceded by a *belongingness* which can never be the object of an exhaustive reflection. Prior to taking up a critical distance, we belong to a history, a class, a nation, a culture, this or that tradition. In accepting this belongingness, we also accept ideology in the first sense discussed above, i.e. as the mediation of images and self-presentations. Thanks to this mediating function, we also participate in the other functions of ideology (dissimulation, distortion, falsification). But we now know that the ontological condition of pre-understanding makes impossible a total reflection which puts us in the favourable position of a non-ideological knowledge.

Second suggestion: even if objectifying knowledge is always posterior to belongingness, it can still constitute itself in a relative autonomy. The critical moment which makes itself felt in it is fundamentally only possible on the basis of that *distance* which belongs to the historicity of *Dasein*.

I want to emphasize the fundamental necessity of including the critical standpoint in that movement which leads us back to the structure of that pre-understanding which constitutes us and which we ourselves are. Hermeneutics itself makes a critical distinction between pre-understanding and prejudice necessary. This problem, which Heidegger only brushes upon and which Gadamer developed, refers us to the central point of the distance and the distancing which is not only (as in the case of text interpretation) temporal but in the genuine sense an active distancing. That one gains a distance is one of the conditions of historical understanding. I should now like to pursue this line of thought a bit further. The mediation of the text is in this respect a very fruitful example. Understanding an utterance means above all treating it as something uttered and, in its textual form, as something distinct from its author. This distancing is an element of reading, which can only bring us close to that which lies at some distance from us. It seems to me that textual hermeneutics contains very valuable hints for an adequate working out of ideology critique, since every distancing is, as Karl Mannheim showed in his generalization of the Marxist approach, a distancing from oneself. For this reason, every ideology critique must be accompanied by a straining of one's self-understanding: this strain presupposes a critique of subjective deception. In short, my second suggestion is: distancing, dialectically opposed to belongingness, is the condition of possibility of ideology critique, not *outside* of or against hermeneutics but rather within it.

Third suggestion: even if ideology critique is able to partially free itself from its original rootedness in the pre-understanding, even if it can thus organize a knowledge or, as Ladrière puts it, pass over into theory, this knowledge still cannot become a total knowledge. It is and remains condemned to partiality: its *incompleteness* rests on the original and inviolable hermeneutic condition to the effect that distancing itself is a moment of belongingness. If one forgets this unavoidable condition, it is impossible to avoid the backlash of ideology on knowledge concerning ideology. Here the theory of ideology is subject to the constraint of incompleteness and non-totality, which in turn has its hermeneutic origin in the conditions of understanding.

I thus accept Habermas's thesis that all cognition is determined by an interest and that ideology critique – as we have seen – is guided by an emancipatory interest in an ordered and unlimited communication. But one has to see that this interest itself functions as ideology or utopia. We do not know which, since it is only the further course of history which distinguishes between fruitless and creative dissension. We must not only keep both the ideological as well as the utopian character of ideology critique in view, but also – perhaps above all – be aware that this interest is organically bound up with the other interests, namely with the interest in material exploitation and the interest in historical understanding. Thus, the emancipatory interest is never completely isolated in the system of interests, so that even on the level of knowledge there is not a sharp separation.

My third thesis can be summarized in the following manner: the critique of ideology which is guided by a specific interest does not transcend its tie to the original belongingness to history, to society, etc. To forget this original reference is to fall prey to the illusion of a critical theory which lays claim to absolute knowledge.

My fourth suggestion is merely deontological. It concerns the *correct use* of ideology critique. The preceding discussion indicates that the critique of ideology is a task which must be taken up again and again, a task which never comes to an end. Knowledge can tear itself away from ideology again and again, but the latter always remains a framework, an interpretative code thanks to which we are not free-floating intellectuals, but are borne by what Hegel called 'morality' (*Sittlichkeit*). My last suggestion is deontological: since today nothing is more pressing than the unremitting endeavour to gain a distance from our historical substance in order to take possession of it anew.

Notes

1 J. Ellul, 'Le rôle médiateur de l'idéologie', in *Démythisation et Idéologie*, ed. E. Castelli, Paris, 1973, pp. 335–54.
2 K. Marx, *Feuerbach: The First Part of 'The German Ideology'*, London, Lawrence and Wishart, 1973, p. 24.
3 M. Lagueux, *Culture et Langage*, Cahiers du Québec, Montréal, 1973, pp. 197–230.
4 Ibid., p. 219.
5 J. Taminiaux, 'Sur Marx, l'art et la vérité', *Revue philosophique de Louvain*, vol. 72, 1974, pp. 311–27.
6 Cf. Marx, *The German Ideology*, op. cit., p. 24.
7 S. Kofman, *Camera obscura. De l'idéologie*, Paris, Editions Galilée, 1973.
8 Ibid., p. 25.
9 J. Ladrière, 'Signes et concepts en science', *L'articulation du sens* (Bibliothèque des Sciences Religieuses), 1970, pp. 40–54.
10 K. Mannheim, *Ideology and Utopia*, New York, Harcourt Brace Jovanovich, 1955.
11 P. Ricoeur, 'Herméneutique et critique des idéologies', in *Démythisation et Idéologie*, op. cit., pp. 25–64.
12 J. Habermas, *Knowledge and Human Interests*, trans. Jeremy J. Shapiro, Boston, Beacon Press, 1971, pp. 301ff.
13 In *Hermeneutik und Ideologiekritik*, Frankfurt am Main, Suhrkamp, 1971, pp. 120ff.

PART II

Practical philosophy

CHAPTER 8

Life-world and the historicity of human existence

Ludwig Landgrebe (Cologne)

1 Introduction

The complex of problems which is indicated by the title 'life-world' is more or less omnipresent in contemporary discussions, if not always under this title. With regard to its relations to the problem of history and historicity, it is not only the often unnoticed background of all attempts to develop a philosophical anthropology, but also of the methodological discussions within American and German sociology as well as of the debates with structuralism and with the development of a systems theory of society. Inasmuch as all of these are concerned with human behaviour and action, the problem must be understood as one of the central problems of practical philosophy and its question concerning the fundamental principles of action.

All of these discussions are oriented in terms of Husserl's last book, *The Crisis of European Sciences and Transcendental Philosophy*.[1] This book not only introduced the expression 'life-world' into the discussion, but also the explication of the problem of the life-world and its significance for the history of the Western sciences. This is not the place to go into the various positions which have been developed on the basis of Husserl's late work and into the discussion of the *aporias* to which it leads. Gerd Brand has discussed these positions in the first part of his book *Die Lebenswelt*[2] and his critique follows above all the arguments of Merleau-Ponty, whose interpretation and critique of Husserl's phenomenology is the most influential in the international discussion. It is noteworthy that in his critique Brand can appeal to Husserl's own statements in reflections, some of which remain unpublished. It is indeed hard to understand how some of these reflections can be consistent with the basic concepts of Husserl's work and with the manner in which he himself characterized this work up to the very end. The fact that one can argue with Husserl against Husserl in this manner shows that the criticisms of his work do not rest on simple misunderstandings which can be easily cleared up.

2 The problematic of the life-world in the contemporary discussion

We shall begin by summarizing a few fundamental aspects of the critical reception of Husserl's problematic of the life-world, those aspects which concern a central point in the understanding of Husserl's phenomenology and which appear in all critics in one form or another. Brand (op. cit., p. 17) discusses the misunderstanding which takes the life-world to be a 'natural and original', we could also say an 'intact' (*heile*) world which existed prior to the rise of philosophy and science. This is a misunderstanding which has also been criticized by Hans Blumenberg: 'The life-world by no means exhibits the fullness and opulence of a mythical paradise, nor the innocence characteristic of such a world'; it is rather a matter of a 'limiting idea which serves the construction of an a-historical beginning of history, an "a-theoretical" prehistory'.[3] We shall see how significant this problem of prehistory is in the final phases of Husserl's thought and how the correct understanding of this 'pre-' requires reflections which Husserl himself did not carry out, but which turn out to be necessary on the basis of his analyses.

After dealing with this misunderstanding, Brand points out (p. 16) that Husserl, for the first time in the history of philosophy, pinpoints a problem in something which up to then had not even been seen because of its very obviousness; it is so close to us that we overlook it. This is the fact that we always live in a world which we presuppose as a matter of course as the ground of our questions, and that all achievements of science refer back to this world out of which they receive their sense. Husserl's goal is to make this very self-evidence with which the existence of the world is accepted 'understandable'. This acceptance is what Husserl in the *Ideas* called the 'general thesis of the natural attitude'. That which is accepted here is the existence of the 'concrete world' in which we always live. All attempts to understand this world, first in mythology, then in science and philosophy, all interpretations which are developed on the ground of this world, 'flow back into the concrete world and belong explicitly or implicitly to the concrete world' (Brand, op. cit., p. 20). Thus, phenomenology has the task of explicating and analysing this obviousness of the existence of the concrete world for us in the manner in which it exists for us. In this context Brand invokes Husserl's idea of an ontology of the life-world. The 'life-world' as this concrete *a priori* is nothing other than the world itself, but now in its immanent reference to the ego: 'The I "has" the world as ground for all existents, and this having is an "I can". In this having the world we say: I can understand this and that in this and that manner, I can develop my understanding of it, discrepancies may appear, but in the unity of the world I can restore the harmony of experience' (Brand, op. cit.). For this characterization Brand can refer to an unpublished manuscript of Husserl's: '"World" is the name of the ability to systematically experience and preserve the identical existential sense through experience, eliminating discrepancies and replacing them with that which is correct.' Brand adds: 'The fact that we have the world as an "I can" manifests itself in conduct as the actuation of an ability.' 'The I is thus as such that which makes being-in-the-world possible'. Thus – again in the words of an unpublished manuscript – 'every existent [is subordinate to] the concept of the world, the law of the world, which is not the concept of something or everything, not a universal concept, but a "concept" in a new sense, which as a universal rule governs the being of all things in their conceptuality, thus in their specific forms.' Brand comments on this passage as follows: 'The I is not a subject which as subject – perhaps even as the subject of pure consciousness – stands over against a world; world and I are intertwined in an I which is an I-in-the-world, which Husserl calls "world-experiencing life".'

Thus, the life-world exists as the concrete world in which we live and which we relate to in our experience; the indivisible correlation of I and world is the universal and absolute theme of phenomenology – a thesis which Husserl seems to confirm when he states (*Crisis*, pp. 132ff.) that the problem of the life-world is not one problem among others, but rather a universal philosophical problem. In addition, there is his reference to the fact that all enlightenment and confirmation of world experience moves in the medium of language as a process in-the-world:

> One is conscious of civilization from the start as an immediate and mediate linguistic community. . . . Thus men as men, fellow men, world – the world of which men, of which we, always

> talk and can talk – and, on the other hand, language, are inseparably intertwined; and one is always certain of their inseparable relational unity, though usually only implicitly in the manner of a horizon (*Crisis*, pp. 358–9).

It thus seems clear that: 'in the final analysis there is only one single apodictic evidence, that of world-experiencing life . . . [and] thus only one single apodictic necessity. The material *a priori*, the universal and thus necessary prior givenness, now understood as that which I can always come back to as that which encompasses all else, is that of the intertwining of world and I' (Brand, op. cit., p. 104).

But Brand can also appeal to the fact that Husserl again and again speaks of a 'universal correlational *a priori* of I and world'. His critical question concerns the legitimacy with which Husserl can shift the 'apodicticity from the intertwining of I and world to the I alone' as the 'primordial intentional ground of my world'. But in this objection Brand ignores Husserl's reference to the 'total problem of the universal historicity of the correlative manners of being of humanity and the cultural world and the *a priori* structure contained in this historicity' (*Crisis*, p. 369). This means that 'universal historicity' is the fundamental structure of the 'correlational *a priori*' of the 'life-world'. Husserl uses the expression 'historicity' (*Historizität*) as synonymous with the word *Geschichtlichkeit*. We must thus show how the root of all the paradoxes which Husserl himself worked out and which Brand cites is to be found along with the key to their solution in the problem of the relation between life-world and historicity. Husserl was not able to work out this solution systematically and thus could not carry out the revision and specification of the concept of 'transcendental subjectivity' which is necessary in this context.

In ignoring this reference and assuming that it is already clear what we are to understand by 'transcendental subjectivity', Brand argues against Husserl's programme of the transcendental–phenomenological reduction as the reduction to the absolute self-certainty of the 'transcendental ego'. Husserl himself repeatedly formulated the paradoxes which this step gives rise to, also in the *Crisis*: 'How can a component part of the world, its human subjectivity, constitute the whole world, namely constitute it as its intentional formation? The subjective part of the world swallows up, so to speak, the whole world and thus itself too. What an absurdity!' (*Crisis*, pp. 179–80). Husserl dissolves the paradox by means of the distinction between the mundane and the transcendental ego. Brand attacks just this distinction (pp. 105ff.), and he is not alone in doing so. Already in Göttingen, Husserl's students and followers rejected the programme of the phenomenological reduction and Husserl's turn to 'idealism'. In his comments on the first versions of Husserl's *Encyclopaedia Britannica* article on phenomenology, Heidegger expressed his reservations concerning this distinction, and the critique of this distinction is, as it were, a *locus communis* of the international Husserl discussion. As we have already mentioned, this discussion is greatly influenced by Merleau-Ponty, and Brand too accepts his arguments: the reflection disregards itself and displaces itself on to the level of an invulnerable subjectivity which is beyond all being and time and thus beyond givenness (Brand, op. cit., p. 109). Merleau-Ponty sharpens this critique, referring to the fact that the first and original opening to the world through the sensing body gives rise to an understanding of the world which can never be exhausted by reflection.[4] Lübbe criticizes Husserl for the fact that whereas his goal is a concrete determination of 'intersubjective reality', i.e. of the 'concrete *a priori*', 'since he is not philosophically acquainted with this society, since he thinks that he must reach the human sphere of universal intersubjectivity taking off from the phenomenologically reduced ego, he confronts himself with the insoluble task of constituting "humanity" out of the acts and contents of consciousness'.[5]

That transcendental phenomenology could not find the way to clarify the 'life-world' because 'the phenomenological approach remains within the bounds of the analysis of consciousness' is also the tenor of Habermas's critique in his *Logic of the Social Sciences*.[6] Here we can only give a very simplified sketch of his very subtle discussion. It brings in the problem of the relation between 'transcendental subjectivity' and history, which Brand had ignored in his theses concerning the life-world as the concrete *a priori*. Habermas, like the American sociologists, understands by 'life-world' the socio-cultural surrounding world (*Umwelt*). Husserl too sometimes calls the life-world the 'world of culture', and Habermas can appeal to this. Habermas is not directly concerned with Husserl, but rather with the phenomenologist Alfred Schütz's[7] project of an understanding sociology and with the consequences which his American followers have drawn from it. Habermas points out the following difficulty in this project: an understanding sociology requires universally binding and in this sense transcendental rules in accordance with which it can describe and analyse the various life-worlds. These rules would constitute the *a priori* of empirical research.

The manner in which Habermas evaluates phenomenology's ability to realize this goal can be seen in his discussion of the Schütz disciple Cicourel, who 'views the experimental investigation of the transcendental structure of life-worlds to be the precondition for a reliably measuring social research'. But the attempt to experimentally investigate that which is the presupposition of all experimentation amounts to a 'misunderstanding of the phenomenological approach'. 'The entire force of phenomenology rests on the reflective presentification of a productive subjectivity and cannot be given an external orientation in experiments. If phenomenological description is to have any sense at all, it is to be found in the fact that its results can be confirmed in the step-by-step recapitulation of the reflective meditations, but cannot be intersubjectively tested' (*Logik*, p. 118). In these meditations, 'the phenomenologist always takes the experience of his own life-world as point of departure, in order to gain access to the achievements of sense-instituting subjectivity by means of abstraction and generalization' (ibid., p. 119). For Schütz too, the point of departure for the reconstruction of the life-world was the biographical situation (ibid., p. 114):

> In this manner, the constitution of the life-world in its abstract generality may be open to investigation, *but we do not encounter a specific historically concrete life-world here* [my emphasis], unless it be that of the phenomenologist himself. We can of course phenomenologically describe the fact that there are in general only life-worlds which are inalienably individual. But this abstract statement does not help us over the barrier which separates a phenomenological description of the social structure of the life-world in general from the investigation of each possible individual life-world, be it that of the individual or of a social group. The generalization of one's own experience, the point at which Schütz as a good Husserl disciple stops, is not sufficient here (ibid., p. 119).

In order to bridge this gap between the abstract universal and the individual particular, the sociologist must abandon the phenomenological presuppositions and move over to the ground of linguistics:

> He could then understand those rules of interpretation in terms of which the actor defines his situation and his own understanding for what they are – as rules of a communication which guides action (ibid., p. 119).

> Thus, we can understand the structure of individual life-worlds only in terms of socially institutionalized communication; but one learns its specific rules by means of systematic participation and not, as Schütz would have it, by means of phenomenological intuition (ibid., p. 120).

This is Habermas's critique. Its significance lies in the fact that he has focused attention on the historicity of the individuality of the life-worlds and that is precisely the question we are concerned with. But Habermas did not see that this is also the basic problem of the late Husserl. Life-worlds change according to the historical-social conditions. But, on the other hand, according to Husserl the 'life-world' is the *a priori* of history, i.e. the invariant which is common to all given individual life-worlds and is the basis of all of their variations. How can we grasp this universal structure when our understanding itself only appears under the historical conditions of that life-world on the basis of which this understanding itself is possible? To put it in a different way: these 'life-worlds' as the respective surrounding worlds of a group are 'contingently' empirically given in their own unique character and are open to investigation as such. Doesn't it follow that phenomenological reflection on the constituting accomplishments of 'transcendental subjectivity' must leave behind its own ground in order to take up in its project of a concrete *a priori* that which it cannot simply 'spin out' of itself, which can only be given in an historical-contingent manner? This is the sense of Habermas's objection (cf. also ibid., p. 124), and it is formulated in one of the reflections which were to serve the further specification and supplementation of the first and second parts of the *Crisis* text:[8]

> When we methodically and systematically bring to recognition the *a priori* of history, is this itself a facticity of history? Does it not then presuppose the *a priori* of history? The *a priori* is related to the being of mankind and the surrounding world that is valid for it in experience, thinking, and acting. But the *a priori* is something ideal and general, which on the one hand refers to men themselves as objects and on the other hand is a structure within men, in us who form it. . . . But we come back again to the fact that historical facts (including the present fact that we are) are objective only on the basis of the *a priori*. Yet the *a priori* presupposes historical being? . . . Does this not then apply to all science. . . ? Does it not derive from an idealization which is itself

> the historical sphere, and does it not presuppose the *a priori* of history, which itself derives from an idealization?[9]

Of course, at this point one can pose the same question: how can it presuppose history when it is precisely history's *a priori*? More precisely: how can it presuppose history, when on the other hand the *a priori* as condition of possibility of history must be presupposed? We shall see that this is the *central problem* of our investigation.

Let us take another look at Habermas's critique with reference to the problem of coming to terms with the structure of individual life-worlds. One can only learn their rules by means of systematic participation, not in phenomenological reflection. This assumes that these rules can be read off of linguistic formulations and that these formulations can be understood without further ado, or at least with the aid of translations. But is this really so obvious? Grace A. de Laguna obviously saw this difficulty and formulated it as the *dilemma of the anthropologist* who wants to move from a survey of foreign life-worlds to universal propositions concerning the existence of man and his human world, the 'life-world': he cannot understand the foreign world by means of the concepts of his own world. 'On the other hand, if he could gain entrance to their world and view it from within as do his alien subjects, he would understand it no better than they do.' But 'it is equally true that to gain an understanding of his own *Lebenswelt* he must, by withdrawing from it, see it from without. How can this be possible?'[10] De Laguna did not answer the question. Habermas could attempt to give an answer in terms of his thesis of the *a priori* of language which he developed in *Knowledge and Human Interests* and 'Technique and Science as "Ideology"',[11] but this would not do away with de Laguna's dilemma. We cannot go into this in any more detail here; our question is rather whether it is not precisely the paradoxes which Husserl himself encountered in the course of his work on the *Crisis* which indicate the manner in which the dilemma can be solved, if only we consequently follow them back to their ground. Provisionally, we can say that the methodological presuppositions for answering de Laguna's question are to be found in the correctly understood method of transcendental-phenomenological reduction to the apodictic self-certainty of the 'transcendental ego' – thus in precisely that step which is generally rejected.

The argument for this assertion is complex. We shall begin with two critical points which came up in the course of our discussion of the critical reception and reinterpretation of Husserl's introduction to the problem of the life-world: (i) in Brand's neglect of the problem of the 'universal historicity of the correlational mode of being of humanity and cultural world', and (ii) in the double sense in which Habermas uses the word 'life-world', on the one hand as the multiplicity of individual different socio-cultural surrounding worlds and on the other hand as the singularity of that which all of these surrounding worlds formally have in common such that they can be compared to one another as different worlds. Habermas can appeal to Husserl for this double usage. If these critical points have come up in the reception of the Husserlian concept of the life-world, the reason must lie in the manner in which Husserl himself introduced these problems in the *Crisis*. Thus, our first step will be to subject the problematic of the life-world to an analysis which demonstrates the discordances in this introduction, in order to then sketch the outlines of their systematic solution.

3 Husserl's introduction of the concept of the life-world and its *aporias*

We can begin with a few general remarks concerning the character of Husserl's *Crisis*. Like all other books which Husserl himself published after the *Logical Investigations* (thus, *Ideas I*, *Cartesian Meditations*, *Formal and Transcendental Logic*), this book was conceived as an introduction to transcendental phenomenology. This new introduction was to demonstrate the historical necessity of phenomenology in the contemporary world situation, and deals with the task of the philosopher in the light of this situation. This present is characterized as an epoch of the crisis of the European spirit and its sciences. But it is more. It is the crisis of the modern world in general, since European science and technology was the basis of the transformation and consolidation of the world into the *one* world of universal interdependency which we know today. This world seems to be in a state of what Nietzsche called *active* nihilism. This crisis can only be overcome by means of a reflection on its origin in the modern history of European thought. This reflection is, as it were, the *anamnesis* that is required for every diagnosis. It is the topic of the first two parts of the book, which appeared in separate form in 1936 in Belgrade, and which at that time was distributed only outside of Germany. This historical reflection demonstrates the thesis that the root of the crisis is to be found in the 'objectivism' of the modern sciences. Under 'objectivism' Husserl understands the conviction which goes back to Descartes that the world which we command by means of exact mathematical natural science is the one true world. This conviction neglects the fact that the world as men experience and understand it prior to the development of this style of scientificity is not shown to be a mere appearance by this science, but is rather the ground on the basis of which we continue to live with one another. This acquaintance and familiarity with the world prior to all science, the self-evidence of life in this world, is forgotten and ignored in objectivism. Objectivism is the amnesia of the 'life-world'. In the light of this situation, the first task of philosophy is not to be found in the classical transcendental-philosophical question concerning the conditions of scientific knowledge, but rather the question concerning the transcendental functions of consciousness on the basis of which it 'has' its world prior to all science. Accordingly, the development of modern European philosophy is presented as a struggle between objectivism and transcendental philosophy. The stages of this struggle are unfolded in the course of a recapitulation of the development from Descartes to Kant.

When the problem of the life-world is introduced in the third part (III A) of the work, and its investigation held to be a path to the most fundamental transcendental functions of consciousness, the connection between the problem of the life-world and the historical grounding of the necessity of transcendental-phenomenological reflection seems to be clear. But it is precisely this connection which remains obscure in the context of the work. The exposition of the problem of the life-world does link up with the discussion of the concept of the transcendental and of Kant's significance as a precursor of transcendental phenomenology, which constitutes the last two paragraphs of part two, beginning with a critical discussion of Kant: his transcendental-philosophical approach is limited by the fact that it essentially involves ignoring the life-world. The reason why Kant must ignore the life-world is to be found in his inadequate concept of sensibility, which does not do justice to kinaesthetic corporeal functions. Against this background, he could not see the most fundamental constitutive functions of the 'last functioning' (*letztfungierenden*) subjectivity and misinterpreted the sense of 'inner perception' in an empiristic and psychologistic manner.[12] Following this link to part two, the exposition of the problem of a science of the life-world begins in section 34 without any reference to the previous historical reflections.

It might thus appear as if the return to history has served its purpose at that point and can be laid *ad acta*, since it has opened the way to the discovery of the necessity of a science of the life-world, and as if this science can then be worked out independently in evidences which are possible at any time and under any circumstances. After all, the theme of this science of the life-world is to be the common ground of all human surrounding worlds, a ground which can be discovered and comprehended as that which is invariable and permanent, independent of all historical change. Could it be a mere contingent historical fact that the 'life-world' was first discovered in this specific historical situation? This would not affect the unconditioned universality and necessity of the scientific propositions concerning the life-world as the universal concrete *a priori* of this fact, and the science of the life-world could aspire to be a *philosophia perennis*. Or is there an inseparable connection between life-world and the historicity of human existence? The introduction of the problem of the life-world in the *Crisis* does not provide an answer to this question.[13]

The fourth part of the work (III B) links up again directly with the second part and investigates the role of 'objectivism' in the philosophical development following Kant and especially in psychology. This discussion, like the lectures on phenomenological psychology from the 1920s, stands under the sign of Husserl's struggle against the psychologistic misinterpretation of the transcendental constitutive functions, a struggle which Husserl began in the *Logical Investigations*. Contemporary philosophers seem to have so little interest in psychology that they are no longer aware of the fact that it was precisely the struggle against psychologism which brought Husserl to the transcendental-phenomenological reduction. This context too remains in the background in the *Crisis*. The fourth part makes no reference to the previous introduction of the problem of the life-world. This is surprising, since the return to the life-world served the function of pointing the way to overcoming objectivism, and with the historical demonstration of the necessity of transcendental phenomenology, with its development of the problem of the life-world, phenomenology was to be introduced as a foundational science, a science which serves the fundamental responsibility and justification of life, *our* life in this historical situation. As such, it poses the question whether the path which modern history has taken is the correct one, or whether this path must be changed. This question has occupied Husserl's attention ever since the end of the First World War. He speaks of a situation of collapse which is a consequence of the way objectivism 'empties' technique and technology of all 'sense' and 'alienates' man from his world. Loss of sense involves becoming questionable not in the sense of reduced efficiency, but in its 'significance for life'. In this context Husserl thinks of our loss of faith in progress with its expectations based on the omniscience of technology and the domination of nature. As the First World War demonstrated, technology has not brought about a better world, but rather ever-new catastrophes; it has destroyed other ancient cultures without being able to offer the members of these cultures a genuine replacement. Husserl recalls the responsibility which Europe must bear as the source of this development. In the 1930s, of course, he knew nothing of the threat of atomic annihilation, of the destruction of the environment and of the 'limits of growth'. If he had lived to experience all this, it would have been a confirmation of his thesis concerning objectivism as the effacement of the life-world.

It is an achievement of textual philology which has yielded insight into the reasons for these gaps in the thought structure of the *Crisis*. It was years after the publication of the volume that proof was found that the part dealing with the life-world was inserted later and is thus only poorly integrated into the text as a whole. Husserl did not plan to publish the manuscript in this form and continued to work on improvements up to his death. The reflections which are published as supplements to the main text document his attempt to improve and develop it. Here we can find some hints as to how the *aporias* which remain in the main text can be cleared up. Thus, the work itself is a torso which documents Husserl's very preliminary groping his way among the problems, and this accounts for the confusing structure of the section dealing with the life-world and thus also for the conflicting reception.

Claesges has subjected this structure to an exhaustive analysis.[14] Here we can only discuss a few points of his critique. It should not be forgotten that Husserl's programme for an analysis of the life-world has its historical precursor in the positivistic demand for a 'natural concept of the world' (Avenarius). 'It is basically the demand that the original reality of human experience become the object of a theory, that reality which is no longer thematized when it is physicalistically-physiologically explained.'[15] The certainty of this original reality is thus nothing other than what Husserl called the 'general thesis of the natural attitude' in the *Ideas*. It is the belief in the existence of the world. Only by means of the transcendental reduction can it be thematized as 'belief in this pregiven world which is common to all', the 'constant ground of validity, an ever available source of what is taken for granted, to which we, whether as practical men or as scientists, lay claim as a matter of course' (*Crisis*, p. 122). Thus, 'life-world' is nothing other than the name for this correlate of the 'natural attitude' conceived in its full concretion. The 'belief in the world' of the natural attitude is not an empty certainty of an 'external reality', but a belief that has its own inner structure, highly differentiated and full of content. As given in this certainty, the world is the given 'life-world'.

This is all that we can say here concerning the systematic context within which Husserl unfolds the problem of the life-world. But this is enough to make it clear that the problem of the life-world can only be seen in and through the transcendental reduction. And if most interpreters still reject this transition to transcendental-phenomenological reflection, this rejection can find support in the manner in which the problem is introduced in the *Crisis*.

We must now take a closer critical look at this introduction and the resulting structure of the section dealing with the life-world. The problem of the life-world is not a special problem, one problem among others. It must be regarded as the universal philosophical problem, as *the* problem in terms of which the fundamental philosophical science can be understood (*Crisis*, pp. 132ff.). We must therefore investigate the specific character of this science of the life-world. The fact that this question stands in the context of the critique of objectivism as the root of the crisis, along with the fact that objectivism is said to rest on an 'effacement' or 'forgetting' of the life-world, suggests that the scientific character of the fundamental philosophical science of the life-world be determined by means of a contrast with the scientific character of the 'objective', that is, the exact sciences. Science aims at 'objective', i.e. universally valid, propositions. As such, they should be testable by anyone at any time, be it in the form of verification or falsification. In contrast, the things of the world as experienced prior to and apart from all science always appear in changing subjective perspectives. Husserl demonstrated this time and again by means of the example of sense perception, in the reflective analysis of the functions of the senses of seeing, hearing, touching, of grasping, etc., which are the necessary medium of our first representations of the world around us. The science of the life-world thus has to deal with this subjective aspect of appearing. It must describe, without admixture of 'explanations', regardless where they come from, the way in which this subjective aspect 'makes things there for us' and has done so all along in a manner which everyone can confirm in his own case. Thus, the question is: 'Can there be, next to objective truth, yet a second truth, the subjective?' (*Crisis*, p. 175). This world, as we always 'have' it in our experience, turns out to be a continual change into ever-new perspectives. The science of the life-world would thus have to deal exclusively with the task of comprehending 'precisely this whole merely subjective and apparently incomprehensible "Heraclitean flux"' (*Crisis*, p. 156). This science is initially introduced as a postulate, as the postulate 'of that novel universal science of subjectivity as pre-giving the world' (*Crisis*, p. 147). At this point the question of 'the correct comprehension of the essence of the life-world and the method of a "scientific" treatment appropriate to it, from which "objective" scientific treatment, however, is excluded' (*Crisis*, p. 123) becomes pressing. How can it be in a position to produce propositions which, if it is to be a science at all, must make the same claim to universal validity as do the objective sciences, such that their truth is subject to an intuitive control by anyone at any time? This demand cannot refer only to the world which *we* and in which *we* can live, be it as individuals or as a specific group of human beings. What 'can be undertaken scientifically, as something that can be established once and for all and for everyone?' (*Crisis*, p. 139).

It seems clear that that which is called for here cannot be won by means of a universal comparison, not in terms of actually accessible life-worlds, present and past. Indeed, it cannot be won by empirical means at all, but only in terms of worlds projected in the play of free fantasy as it occurs in, for example, science fiction. This is the procedure of 'eidetic' variation; it starts with empirically given worlds and experimentally replaces the given structures by others, until it encounters limits beyond which the result of the variation can no longer be termed a 'world'. This procedure of eidetic variation thus guarantees that a series of fundamental structures of the life-world can be isolated, structures which necessarily and universally must be thought of as moments of all conceivable worlds if they are to be thought of as worlds by us at all, i.e. if they are to be comparable with that with which our experience acquaints us as world. But Husserl points out that this procedure is by no means a specifically philosophical task: 'In a certain way, concern with this sort of thing belongs continually even to [one type of] objective investigation, namely that of historians, who must, after all, reconstruct the changing, surrounding life-worlds of the peoples and periods with which they deal' (*Crisis*, p. 147). This is also true for comparative cultural anthropology and hermeneutic sociology. They too require – as Habermas has pointed out – the universally binding and in this sense transcendental rules according to which the various life-worlds can be described, analysed and compared. These rules would be the *a priori* of empirical research. We can thus see that 'the life-world does have, in all its relative features, a *general structure*. This general structure, to which everything that exists relatively is bound, is not itself relative. We can attend to it in its generality and, with sufficient care, fix it once and for all in a way equally accessible to all' (*Crisis*, p. 139).

> The world of life, which as a matter of course takes up into itself all practical structures (even those of the objective sciences as cultural facts. . .), is, to be sure, related to subjectivity throughout the constant alteration of its relative aspects. But however it changes and however it may be corrected, it holds to its essentially lawful set of types, to which all life, and thus all science of which it is the 'ground', remain bound (*Crisis*, p. 173).

The theme of the philosophical science of the life-world is thus 'what is formal and general, what remains invariant throughout all alterations of the relative' (*Crisis*, p. 142), the invariant style of all worldly life. It is an *a priori* for all empirical investigation of the various life-worlds, for it is the common structure, the product of the eidetic variation of all empirically available life-worlds. As such it is the condition of possibility of comparison and differentiation. 'Only through recourse to this *a priori*, to be unfolded in an *a priori* science of its own, can our *a priori* sciences, the objective-logical ones, achieve a truly radical, a seriously scientific grounding' (*Crisis*, p. 141). Since they arise on the basis of this *a priori* constitution of the life-world, it must be understood as the 'universal pre-logical *a priori*'. Since 'the world is the universe of things' for us, the elaboration of this *a priori* could become 'the task of a life-world ontology, understood as a concretely general doctrine of essence for these *onta*' (*Crisis*, p. 142). Needless to say, this cannot be an ontology in the sense of pre-Kantian metaphysics. Husserl obviously has in mind an ontology in the sense of the regional ontologies which he discusses in *Ideas II*. By means of eidetic variation they produce the categories of every region of beings in their essential typicality. 'Even without any transcendental interest – that is, within the "natural attitude" . . . – the life-world could have become the subject matter of a science of its own, an ontology of the life-world purely as experiential world' (*Crisis*, p. 173).

This remark has had a decisive influence on the manner in which the problematic of the life-world has been generally interpreted, namely as the theme of an ontology of the concrete *a priori*. This is, however, to ignore Husserl's statement that this is not the goal of his introduction to the problem of the life-world, that what is at issue is 'a task which is much greater' (*Crisis*, p. 142).

For this task, the life-world 'proves to be a mere "component", so to speak, within concrete transcendental subjectivity; and correspondingly its *a priori* shows itself to be a "stratum" within the universal *a priori* of the transcendental [in general]' (*Crisis*, p. 174). The reason why this statement has been ignored is to be found to some extent in the almost casual manner in which Husserl speaks of the 'great task'. In comparison, the programme of an ontology of the life-world seems to be immediately plausible. After all, it is capable of taking up the results of empirical comparisons in anthropology, cultural history and sociology, developing the principles on the basis of which the scientific claim to universal validity on the part of these comparative sciences can be guaranteed. What is the point of the additional question concerning transcendental constituting subjectivity? This question can only be answered after we have seen the *aporias* to which the Husserlian programme leads.

The first *aporia* concerns the title 'ontology' itself. Ontology has the task of determining the fundamental distinctions in the modes of being of the *onta* which we find in the world. But understood in this sense we can only call it an ontology of the life-world if 'world' means nothing other than the sum total of beings we distinguish in this manner, the totality of beings. But is the world itself a being like the multifarious beings *in* the world? Only in this case would the title 'ontology' be legitimate. And this is precisely what Husserl denies; there is

> a fundamental difference between the way we are conscious of the world and the way we are conscious of things or objects. . . . Things, objects . . . are 'given' as being valid for us in each case . . .

> but in principle only in such a way that we are conscious of them as things or objects *within the world-horizon*. Each one is something, 'something of' the world of which we are constantly conscious as a horizon. . . . The world, on the other hand, does not exist as *an* entity, as an object, but exists with such uniqueness that the plural makes no sense when applied to it. Every plural, and every singular drawn from it, presupposes the world-horizon (*Crisis*, p. 143).

This concept of the world as horizon is not an ontological concept.

> The determination of the life-world as horizon is guided by a transcendental perspective, for this concept of the horizon is itself the result of a reflection on the correlation of life-world and the subject who experiences the life-world. And here the distinction between that which is there for the subject of experience and that which is there for the philosophical reflection is at work. In contrast, the determination of the world as the 'totality of beings', as the sum total of *onta*, belongs to a purely ontological perspective. Thus, the concept of the life-world in Husserl's work is an ontological-transcendental hybrid (Claesges, op. cit., p. 97).

This hybrid nature of the concept of the life-world manifests itself in Husserl's claim that it is the concept of the world as the 'universe of things', i.e. as the sum total of all beings, which alone determines the sense of talk about the world in natural life (cf. *Crisis*, p. 142). This concept of the world is a concept which results from philosophical abstraction. The natural understanding of the world does not speak in this manner. Thus, a concept which results from philosophical reflection is projected back into the pre-philosophical understanding. The description as horizon is more appropriate for the manner in which the world is there for the natural understanding. This concept of world as horizon unites the continually shifting openness on the one hand and the limitations on the other in a manner which undercuts the Kantian antinomies, since these antinomies arise only when the world is understood as 'totality' or sum total of all beings. This totality is certainly not an 'object' which can be found among the objects of possible experience. There must be a mode of access to this horizontal structure on the basis of which statements about it can be confirmed with evidence. But the claim that this confirmability requires the transition to transcendental-phenomenological reflection and that the concept of the horizon is a transcendental concept, this must first be shown. One might object that this horizonal structure has been discovered independently from Husserl's phenomenology in Gestalt psychology's discovery of the figure-ground relation, and that Husserl himself was led to his concept of the horizon by the concept of 'fringes' in W. James's psychology. Thus, the thesis of the necessity of the transition to transcendental phenomenological reflection must be argued for.

In the first place, it is clear that *the reflection in which the horizonal structure of the world is thematized must be of a fundamentally different sort than the reflection in which the 'onta' in the world are compared and distinguished* and in which the concepts of the highest species of being and the categories which define them are developed. *An 'ontological' reflection of this kind does not thematize the world horizon* within which all of its operations take place. If then 'horizon' is the name of the manner in which we are already aware of the world in our prescientific life, and if this life-world is to be the 'concrete universality' (Husserl also calls it the social-historical cultural world), then this universality cannot be understood in the sense of the sum total of all beings. For this reason, there cannot be an ontology of the life-world.

We shall not deal with the question whether ontology in this sense can be developed in a 'scientific' manner such that its propositions can be confirmed in evidence by anyone at any time. It should not be forgotten that the project of regional ontologies in the *Ideas* was oriented in terms of the division of the major groups of sciences into physical and biological natural sciences on the one hand and 'sciences of the spirit' (*Geisteswissenschaften*) on the other – a division which is the result of a specific historical constellation and in this sense cannot lay claim to universal validity.[16]

If the science of the life-world we are searching for cannot be developed in the form of an ontology, what character must it have? The answer to this question can only be given on the basis of *an even more fundamental aporia*. It concerns the following state of affairs: on the one hand the theme of the philosophical science of the life-world is to be the invariant style of worldly life which is the standard for all worlds, i.e. a fundamental structure which is common to them all. On the other hand, the life-world is to be 'concrete universality'. Husserl also characterized this as the 'universe of in principle intuitability', as the realm of the primal evidences in which we 'have' our world prior to all philosophy and science. The examples which Husserl gives for the manner in which all understanding between subjects of quite different worlds is based on these primal evidences (e.g. between the physicist, who lives in the special world of the physical sciences, and one who understands nothing of this world (*Crisis*, p. 125) or between the European and the member of a more or less archaic culture (*Crisis*, p. 139)) make clear the manner in which this 'universe of in principle intuitability' is to be understood. But this commonality which Husserl appeals to here is not yet the concrete universality of the specific cultures which come into contact with one another in this manner; it is merely the structure which is common to them all. Thus, the *aporia* concerning the sense in which Husserl calls the life-world a concrete universality is more than the problem of the character of the science of the life-world. This *aporia* presents itself in the form of the *question how the two determinations of the life-world, on the one hand as concrete universality, on the other hand as the 'universe of in principle intuitability' are compatible with one another*. How must we understand the life-world such that these can both hold, each in its own way? More clearly: how can we talk about the world as life-world in an appropriate manner?

We have already seen that in this context world cannot be understood by means of the ontological concept 'totality of beings'. This is not the manner in which 'natural' life understands its world prior to all sciences and philosophy. Rather, the concept of the world as horizon, as 'total horizon', is more appropriate. To be sure, this concept too is not a concept of natural life, but it is more appropriate to the manner in which this life is from the very beginning acquainted with its world. Natural life is a 'life of interests', interested in its specific goals and guided by considerations of the manner in which the things of this world can serve or hinder its projects. It knows that others have other projects and goals which under certain circumstances can collide with its own, and it knows that the others act according to other intentions which may be unknown or unintelligible to it: 'That is beyond my horizon'. It thus knows that it has its own limited perspectives on the world, whose limits can, however, be changed and broadened by communication and learning. And this is precisely the state of affairs which is meant by the word 'horizon' in a very normal sense of the word. Thus, talk about a variety of environments or surrounding worlds is immediately intelligible. Every individual has his or her surrounding world, and within it his or her 'special worlds', the intimate 'world' of the family, the 'professional world', the world of hobbies, sport or politics, if the individual is politically active. He can play his 'roles' in each of them, often shifting roles many times during the day. All of this takes place on the ground of the world in which he lives in his epoch, in his encompassing group, and in this sense the determination of his world as concrete universality in the sense of a total horizon can be immediately intelligible to him. It refers to his own self-identity in which he performs these shifts of role.[17] He has as such, in all special worlds in which he plays his role, his world as the total horizon which encompasses all special horizons which are determined by his specific life interests. With reference to this total horizon his world is *one* world. In this context it is intelligible that Husserl speaks of the absolute *singularity* of the world, for this signifies nothing other than *the manner in which every individual has his world*.

On the other hand, it also seems to be obvious and immediately comprehensible that life-worlds can be compared with one another. This comparison is made possible by that which is invariant in all worlds, and this can be nothing other than that which allows us to speak of having the world as horizon and to say that even those who live within different world horizons have a common world. To have a common world means to be able to communicate with one another with reference to this world. Thus, the invariant in all conceivable worlds must be that which in spite of all differences among these worlds must be present as a common structure which serves as the basis for the initiation of communication. This is that fundamental structure of the world which manifests itself in sensuous-corporeal, kinaesthetic motility as the condition for having impressions in the first place. Being able to communicate with one another about such impressions is an essential moment of communication. Only on this basis is an active creature recognized as a human being, i.e. as 'one of us', and only with reference to actual and possible 'ones of us' can we meaningfully speak of having a world or of a common world. The capacity to think, the faculty of speech and a kinaesthetically functioning corporeality belong inseparable together; the capacity to think can only develop in linguistic articulation, and this is *also* a kinaesthetic-corporeal function.

These are the *fundamental conditions of possibility of having a world* and of being able to compare worlds. The comparative shift from one world to the other rests on the 'universe of intuitability', i.e. on those structures common to all life-worlds which refer to their relation to the kinaesthetic corporeality of sensibility. Intuition must be understood here in the broader sense of intercourse with that which is given in our world by means of sensible–corporeal functions. Communication begins not only with the 'look at that!' but also with the 'dig in!', 'do this or that!' In this elementary manner communication is already *possible prior to language*, and words with deictic 'occasional' meaning are the first elements in the transition to linguistic communication.

In this sense, we can make the compatibility of the two determinations of the life-world as 'concrete universality' and 'universe of intuitability' intelligible: *every world is intrinsically concrete universality, but it is a 'universe of intuitability' with reference to that which makes it comparable with other worlds*. This is the title for the fundamental modes of having a world and of the ability to compare worlds – conditions which appear to be so self-evident that we need not expressly name or thematize them. *This is the basis of all comparisons of life-worlds*, be it a matter of the world of a person or that of a limited group of persons: thus, the comparisons of the cultural historian, the cultural anthropologist and the empirical comparisons of sociological research, especially when it, in the form of systems theory of functional structure, attempts to understand various realms of action in terms of concepts which allow us to compare various cultural systems such as economy, administration, politics and religion. In their unthematic recourse to these apparently so banal and self-evident universal conditions of their own activity, they stand on the *ground of the 'natural attitude'* whose general form is that of 'living into the horizon of the world' without thematizing this horizon as such:

> All our theoretical and practical themes . . . lie always within the normal coherence of the life-horizon 'world'. World is the universal field into which all our acts, whether of experiencing, of knowing, or of outward action, are directed. From this field, or from objects in each case already given, come all affections, transforming themselves in each case into actions (*Crisis*, p. 144).

4 The *aporias* as a transcendental–phenomenological problem and the task of the transition to transcendental phenomenological reflection

The preceding discussion had the task of discovering the reason for the merely partial and discontinuous reception of Husserl's introduction of the problematic of the life-world and of showing that it is to be found in the *aporias* to which this introduction gives rise. This discussion was oriented in terms of the thesis that the self-evident 'universally human' does not suffice for the dissolution of these *aporias*, that this requires the transition to transcendental–phenomenological reflection, which puts into question these self-evidences of the 'natural attitude'. In this sense, Husserl called his approach the most radical scepticism, in which, as it were, scepticism overcomes itself by demonstrating that that which is supposedly relevant is precisely the absolute.[18] We have here again the arguments which speak against the necessity of such a transition to transcendental phenomenological reflection: have we not already dissolved the *aporias*, have we not already answered the central question 'how can we speak in an appropriate manner about the world as life-world?'? Doesn't all that Husserl said about the life-world have a good sense which is open to confirmation by everyone? This would also hold for the conception of the life-world as horizon, although that is said to be a transcendental concept. If world is the universal field in which all of our actions take place, and if it is given with the general thesis of the natural attitude, what reason can we have to abandon this attitude and undertake the 'completely different task' for which the life-world is only one 'stratum in the concrete *a priori* of transcendentality'? Can we say anything more about the concrete *a priori* as the common ground of the possibility of having a life-world of any kind than what we have already called banal and self-evident?

In the text of the *Crisis* Husserl introduced this transition from the natural to the transcendental phenomenological attitude as a possibility which replaces the 'ontological' approach, which remains on the ground of the natural attitude, a possibility which is realized by an act of the will. He says nothing about the compelling motives for this transition, just as in the lectures on *First Philosophy* the question concerning the motive for the reduction remains unanswered.[19] But the demand for this shift would be justified if it could be shown that it is by no means the case that all *aporias* concerning the problem of the life-world have been dissolved. We mentioned earlier two central points which were neglected in the reception of the problematic of the life-world. The first is the ambiguity in the use of the word, according to which life-world is spoken of on the one hand in the singular as *one* common world and on the other hand in the plural as a multiplicity of life-worlds. The other is the failure to pay enough attention to Husserl's reference to the 'total historicity of the correlational mode of being of humanity and cultural world'. This thesis thus concerns the problem of the link between life-world and historicity. If the life-worlds are not only themselves caught up in historical change but also appear and disappear in the course of history, and if the passing of an individual is also the passing of his own individual life-world as his horizon, do we really find in the 'universal in principle intuitability' as that which is common to all life-worlds something transhistorically invariant and permanent which as the *a priori* of history is not subject to change and concerning which propositions of transhistorical validity would be possible? Not merely the old search for laws of history, but also sociological systems theory and structuralism are on the lookout for insights which make possible knowledge of historical change and overcome 'historical relativism'. Our clarification of the problem of the life-world up to this point has not even posed these problems, to say nothing of showing how they might be answered. If it should turn out that the answers can only be found by means of a shift to the transcendental-phenomenological attitude, then its necessity would have been demonstrated.

Husserl himself first poses these questions explicitly in the supplement to the text of the *Crisis*. This is not to say that he did not deal with them earlier. Decisive aspects of this problematic were worked out as early as 1931, when Husserl was working on a revision of the *Cartesian Meditations*. They are now published in volume XV of the *Husserliana*. In this context the important texts are no. 22: 'Teleology', no. 23: 'The Historical Mode of Being of Transcendental Subjectivity. Its Veiled Manifestation in Human History and Natural History' (pp. 371, 378ff.) and no. 38: 'Temporalization and the Monad' (p. 666ff.).[20]

The discussion of the shift to the transcendental-phenomenological mode of reflection will thus have to proceed in a completely 'undogmatic' manner, taking up the questions which remain open. It cannot cling to the entrenched formulations which Husserl repeatedly uses – in the *Crisis* too – to introduce the reduction; it is precisely these formulations which have often been the object of critique.

The first of the *aporias* which are our point of departure here concerns the sense in which we speak of life-world on the one hand in the singular, on the other hand in the plural. It is connected with the question how the two descriptions 'concrete universality' and 'universe of intuitability' are compatible with one another. Talk of concrete universality can be given in initial clarification in terms of the manner in which the individual has its world as *one* world, as total horizon in contrast to the special worlds. It is his world, because his body with its sensuous-kinaesthetic functions is his body, he alone having control of its kinaesthesias: he must exercise them. Thus, the body is the zero-point of his orientation, around which his world is centred.

This explicates the possibility of speaking of the life-world both in the singular and in the plural with respect to the manner in which every individual has this world as his own, one world in his multifarious interests. The singularity of the world is correlative to the one whose world it is. This is surely self-evident, and does not give rise to *aporias*. They arise when one considers the fact that this individual singularity (life-world in the singular) is such for *every* individual which has it as this single world. But it is also true of the life-world of a people or, more generally, the life-world of a more or less limited group with its specific individual stamp. All of these life-worlds are life-world in the singular. But on the other hand, *the* life-world is to be that which they all have in common. In contrast to this singular they seem to be life-worlds in the plural. In this case, that which they have in common would be the universal, and the specific individual worlds would be the particular. 'Life-world' would be the sum total of all these particulars. But that would be an ontological concept of the world all over again, a concept which does not correspond to the manner in which we have the world: 'The world does not exist like an existent, like an object, but in a singularity for which the plural is meaningless.' But how is this relation to be characterized? We can describe it very roughly, and without going into the details of the theory of intersubjectivity, in the following manner. Within the horizon of the world, which every individual has as the one and only world, others are also there for him. Each of them has his or her world as his or her 'concrete universality', and just as the others are there for him in the horizon of his world, he is there for them in the horizon of their own respective world. As concrete universality, it is *one* world for every individual, a world which includes in itself its various special worlds. They can be different for every individual, no one shares all of the interests of another, so their concretion is never precisely the same. The result is the fundamental distinction between one's own and the alien. But that which allows them to *coexist* in spite of all differences is the common life-world. That which allows it to be a common world is that which is invariant in all of these different individual concrete universalities. This is not only true of contemporaries with their historically specific worlds; it is also true of those worlds which for us are past and which we know as past. It is possible for us to speak of a specific world of earlier human beings and to 'project' ourselves into this world by means of comparisons, as long as this world has left behind remains, monuments or, best of all, texts which are the result of the activities of 'the likes of us', activities which presuppose an active corporeality, guided by intentions and goals, and of actors who as corporeal creatures have their 'fate' between birth and death and are thus in the final analysis formed by an interest in their lives which they share with us. In this sense we can speak of that which makes possible the life-world common to *all* human beings as a universe of in principle intuitability. It is the ground to which all individual life-worlds are referred and on the basis of which they unfold their respective individual concrete universality. Thus, it is also the ground of their development, and as the *a priori* of this development it is the *a priori* of history. All *aporias* in the concept of the life-world can in the final analysis be traced back to *this* property, and once it has been made intelligible we shall have done justice to Husserl's demand that we take account of the total historicity of the life-world, thereby making the following thesis intelligible: 'History is the great fact of absolute being.' In this context we can only give a few hints concerning this manner of dissolving the *aporias*.

The first question in this context is the following: this *a priori* of the life-world is characterized as the universe of intuitability with reference to that which makes all individual life-worlds comparable with one another. But understood in this way this 'universe' itself is not yet the concrete life-world common to all individual life-worlds, but rather, as the 'ground', is merely a fundamental structure of the one and only world and of all the specific individual life-worlds which unfold on this basis. Thus, the concept of this fundamental structure is not the concept of a universal whose specifications would be the individual life-worlds; their universal concept would be 'concrete universality in general'. Thus, it is Husserl's talk of the life-world as the universe of intuitability which has led to this logical embarrassment.

On the one hand, he speaks as if this universe were present everywhere in the same manner, something which is everywhere, accessible at every moment and in this sense a universe of intuitability – thus the question, 'how is it possible that it took so long to discover it?' – on the other hand, it is said that it is by no means accessible in this manner, but rather is an *a priori* whose concept is the result of a comparative reflection. Only when we have clarified the nature of this reflection will the sense in which the world can be spoken of in the singular be intelligible.

The reason why 'universe of intuitability' exhibits this confusing ambiguity is to be found in the manner in which Husserl introduces the problem of the life-world, namely by means of a contrast between the fundamental philosophical science he calls for and 'objective' science. This is the basis for the first property which Husserl accords the life-world, the property of being the universe of intuitability in contrast to the 'true' world in the sense of objective science, a world which is the result of a theoretical–logical substruction. Needless to say, this description is not meant in a negative sense; it is merely a reference to the methodological abstraction by means of which exact science gains access to its field of research. They are thus 'substructions' *bene fundata*. In contrast, the life-world is a realm of 'original evidences', and the task is to follow the way back to the 'primordial evidences' in which the world is continually pregiven. Sense perception, in which the given is 'experienced as "the thing itself", in immediate presence' (*Crisis*, pp. 127–8) is the source of these primordial evidences. If intuitability is understood in the sense of sense perception, this leads us to understand that which is intuited in it as the realm of the things which are 'purely and simply' (*schlicht*) given in sense perception, those things to which we can return everywhere and at any time. As the sum total of that which everywhere and always exists 'in itself', it would be that which one generally calls the permanence of nature in contrast to all historical change. In this sense the world is conceived as a stratified structure of regions of being, whose lowest region, on the basis of which all others are erected, would be the region 'material thing'. But as we have already seen, an ontological conception of the world, as its totality, does not correspond to the manner in which we originally have our world, namely as horizon. All distinctions with respect to this world concern its horizonal structure and not a hierarchy of orders of being.

If we are to understand the universe of intuitability as a horizonal structure of the world which permeates all other structures, its 'intuitability' in the sense of 'self-giving' cannot be understood in the sense of pure sense perception, as if this were the final and immediate mode of access to the world. Husserl, however, never rejected this point of view. But the having of the life-world never takes place by means of pure sense perception, whose correlate is the 'material thing'. To be sure, Husserl did demonstrate that sense perception is by no means mere 'receptivity', that it is the 'sense activity' of corporeal-kinaesthetic functioning. But he only investigated this functioning with reference to its contribution to sense perception and knowledge in the context of the question how that which becomes the object of the objective sciences is constituted in this functioning. Thus, the investigations in *Ideas II* continue to move in the framework of the traditional 'theory of knowledge'. This neglects the fact that at the most primitive levels of life the kinaesthetic functions occur in the form of instinctive drives and are guided by very elementary interests. And even at more developed stages, it is always specific interests which initiate the process of perception. In the immediacy of our having the world there is no such thing as this pure perceptual thing. Perception is always guided by the interests of the life-world, the conspicuous as attractive or repulsive and perhaps frightening awakens an interest in taking a closer look, in turning away or in flight, etc. Thus, as the Gestalt psychologist Koffka has shown, the original sense qualities are not those which are ordered according to sensory fields, but rather the beneficial and the detrimental, which permeate the sensory fields. If the concept of intuitability or the intuition which corresponds to it are understood this concretely in its complex intentional structure, then we can indeed say that the universe of intuitability is a fundamental structure which permeates all life-worlds, the realm of sensory presence with its primordial evidences. But in its relation to that which unfolds on this basis, this realm is not something that we simply *have*; it is something that we *acquire*. The first and most original confrontation with that which is 'given' occurs in intuition understood in this broad sense, and this is our first acquaintance with the world. It begins genetically at a very early stage in learning controlled movement which is steered by an individual centre, i.e. in a reflexivity which is not initially an explicit consciousness of oneself as an 'I', but rather a pre-reflexive relation to oneself. Even for the smallest child as a living organism, the world is *one* world, an as yet quite restricted horizon of all its actions, which are guided completely by its elementary needs and emotions. As horizon it is referred to the body as the 'zero-point' of all orientation and is also 'concrete universality' within the limits of its restricted horizon – from the perspective of an adult, of course, a potential universality, a promise for the future. But even within this restricted horizon there is much in common with the adult: desire, pain, disappointment, satisfaction, joy, fear and hope, and it is the duty of the adult to interest himself in and participate in them in order to broaden the narrow world horizon. And while the actions and reactions in this region also have the character of elementary passions which are repressed in the course of further development, they can always come to the surface at a later date. This elementary sphere of behaviour is not a foundation which simply disappears under that which is erected upon it. It constitutes the horizon to which all 'higher actions' have a living relation and with reference to which they are determined.

If the world is not something which we simply have, just as 'humanity' is not constituted by a few specific essential properties, the life-world can correspondingly only be spoken of as a *world in the process of becoming*. This is already implicit in the concept of the world as horizon. And the functioning of the senses is also not to be considered to be once and for all determined, since it exists only in a tension between further development and atrophy. Marx too spoke of the possibility of the development of the senses, and the word 'culture' can legitimately be understood in the sense of a refinement of sensation.

5 The *a priori* of the life-world as the universal problem of the history of conscious experience – transcendental and empirical history

What are the implications of this discussion for the concept of the life-world as that of the *a priori* of all transformations and variations? If life-world is fundamentally a world in process, how can it exhibit a determinate invariant structure? But only if there are invariants is it possible to speak of the world as *one* single world and of a world history of humanity. And it must be possible for the philosophical science of the life-world to specify these conditions in a universally valid manner. It is not sufficient to refer to the unalterable basic faculties of human nature, which are, after all, the condition for it being possible to pose not only this question but any question at all in an intelligible manner. But if it turns out that these basic faculties are not constants, that they are capable of further development or atrophy, then there is no firm basis for universally valid propositions. In such a situation, the only proposition which could be formulated concerning this *a priori* would be that it is the *πάντα ῥεῖ*, that everything is caught up in the process of becoming and that nothing is permanent. Husserl's talk of a Heraclitean flux seems to point in this direction. In this case the last word would be the *aporia*: 'Does not all science develop on the basis of an idealization which is itself in history, does it not presuppose the *a priori* of history, which itself develops out of an idealization?'

The thesis which was to be demonstrated here was that this *aporia* can only be dissolved by means of the shift to transcendental-phenomenological reflection. It must begin with the critique of silent presuppositions whose validity is accepted as self-evident. In spite of all differences, it shares with traditional transcendental reflection the fact that it poses the question concerning the *quid juris* of such presuppositions. In the course of this investigation the critique must pay special attention to the points at which the notion of this *a priori* has manifested *aporias*, and this was the case in the attempt to clarify the ambiguous sense of the talk about a universe of intuitability. On the one hand, it is to be that which is everywhere available and immediately accessible; on the other hand, it is to be the *a priori* whose concept can only be formed on the basis of a universal comparison. In order to clarify this situation, we must begin by asking: *in what manner is this universe present and available*? Obviously only in the execution of kinaesthetic functions, in seeing, hearing, grasping as the source of the primordial evidence in which we become acquainted in an elementary manner with our world as the world which exists for us. These functions are guided by interests and their execution is controlled and 'steered' in a generally pre-reflexive manner. This can be seen in terms of the example of the way in which a child practises goal-directed movements. It is not the execution itself which the child has in view, but that which it wants to obtain by means of it. The execution is, as Husserl says, 'anonymous'. It is thematized in reflection. On a higher level of development, this thematization can take the form of deliberation. 'You could have done it differently or better.' The process of this execution is thus understood as a possibility which can be compared with other possibilities. Only at this point is the performance lifted out of its anonymity and subjected to rational considerations. Thus, the reflection in which the performances are recognized to be *a priori* is always the result of a process of comparison. And if it yields the concept of the 'universe of intuitability', this is *the same universe which was previously available in a self-evident and anonymous manner*, without being subject to rational reflection. It is precisely this manner of *leaving the functions which constitute the horizon in anonymity* which Husserl views as that 'living into the horizon of the world' which is characteristic of the 'natural attitude'. But if this ground of the life-world is that with which we are most familiar, that which we have always already laid claim to, then its discovery in reflection must have been possible all along. Why did it take so long? Husserl never explicitly posed and answered this question; but the fact that his discussion of the crisis of modern society led him to this ground indicates how this question must be answered and where the motives for this kind of reflection are to be found.

Within natural life reflection is not something that occurs without any motive. It appears when the normal direct performance of actions, at the lowest level of kinaesthetic movements, are inhibited or fail to yield the expected results. At this point we stop to 'think things over' as a part of everyday life: 'Can you do that?', 'Why didn't it work?'. *Reflection is never a turning back to 'states of consciousness'* – as such they are always the result of performances – but always reflections on these performances and on the ability to carry them out. *Reflection is always reflection on what one is capable of doing*, and on the limits and obstacles of these abilities. *What, then, motivates the 'universal' philosophical reflection on the ground of our life-world*? This reflection presupposes a universal comparison, i.e. the historical look back at all of the ways of having a life-world which are accessible to us. It presupposes all that the comparative sciences have discovered. Husserl pursued broad ethnological studies as preparation for his analysis of the life-world, entering into a correspondence with Lévy-Bruhl. He by no means expected that his phenomenology could simply 'spin out' these possibilities. Like every other philosopher, he made use of all that these sciences of man, his society and history have discovered. That these sciences and their comparative methods exist, that is a fact which belongs to the 'concrete universality' of our 'modern' life-world and determines its horizon. Their results 'flow back' into it and are available to everyone in the form of books, a fact that is obvious to everyone.

This obviousness cannot be shaken by the fact that only our Western history has brought forth this style of comparative science of man and his world. No other of the great world cultures has developed this kind of science. But why should this fact call for further reflection? Research into the history of thought can easily show how this came about. Among others, this specific culture arose in the course of the 'history of humanity'. It developed ways in which to compare this culture and its development with others. In doing so it has pointed out the differences and shown that the style of behaviour in these cultural life-worlds varies from case to case, just as the norms which govern behaviour differ from case to case and cannot be reduced to a common denominator. Thus, 'history' signifies constant change in which there is nothing permanent, and the result is an absolute relativism. Indeed, the exhaustion which is characteristic of a sceptical relativism is the basic mood which permeates most highly developed and methodologically perfected sciences. But, on the other hand, modern technology with its highly developed means of communication have brought all peoples and cultures on earth so close together that nothing which happens in one of them can remain without effect on the others. Precisely this sceptical exhaustion cannot do justice to this world situation. What is needed in such a situation is the specification of norms which are binding on all such that this common life does not fall back into a Hobbesian 'state of nature' of the war of all against all for the natural resources which this common earth has to offer.

This is the world situation, the situation of our common life-world in which universal reflection on this universal commonality is motivated and necessary. That this reflection cannot be of a kind with the comparative sciences is clear from the fact that it is just these sciences which have led us into the *aporias* of relativism. That which they take to be self-evident is what Husserl called the general thesis of the natural attitude. All of these sciences are sciences on the ground of the world, whose existence is presupposed. They are facts in this world as the concrete universality of our life-world. As such they presuppose the existence of this world as a continual process of becoming in which there is nothing permanent, that is, a history of this world in which the development of 'humanity' is only a brief and 'late' moment in the great cosmic process, and 'humanity' in this process is only an insignificant nothing. Thus, it is presupposed that there 'is' this history to which this brief moment belongs.

But where and how 'is' there this history, and what justifies us in speaking of it? After all, 'history' exists only for those who stand in it and can recall that which recently occurred in the process of this history and can inform themselves about earlier events by means of information which has come down to us in various forms. And they can theoretically reconstruct even earlier events as cosmic history, events which lie before the beginning of human history. In this situation, the natural understanding will say: this cosmic process of nature is after all earlier than and older than man. He is only a transient creature in its immeasurable ages. Husserl spun out this argument: 'Is humanity with its cosmos, to which also the world of the stars belongs, "contingent"?', and answered, 'This is a temporal mode of speech. We stand in transcendentality. I am, time constitutes itself in terms of me!' ('Temporalization and Monad', *Husserliana* XV, pp. 666f.).

This requires some discussion. The first sentence indicates that this talk on the part of the natural understanding presupposes that there simply is this process of the world and its time, to which everything which we can talk about belongs. And this is nothing other than the general thesis of the natural attitude. Transcendental-phenomenological reflection begins with its 'bracketing' and 'suspension'. In putting it out of play, he who reflects stands 'in transcendentality'. Who is this 'we' who stand in it? These are the reflecting philosophers who can communicate with one another about this reflection. This is by no means to deny that they continue to have their position and time *within* this process of the world; it is merely to say that they do not accept this process as something self-evident, that they thematize it in reflection. But how can this reflection do anything other than underline the fact that it takes place on the ground of this world? But here one should consider the results of this standing in transcendentality. It is the result of the first step of the reflection, of the transcendental reduction. It leads to the apodictic self-certainty of the 'I am'. The significance of this has generally been misunderstood: the critique has generally been that this line of thought inevitably leads in the direction of a subjective idealism. There can be no doubt that many of Husserl's formulations give aid and comfort to this misunderstanding. But this misunderstanding fails to see that what is at issue is the fact that reflection is a reflexive relation which cannot be simply observed here and there, that reflection is always a matter of the one who reflects. Reflection is something which each must carry out for himself. One can also follow the reflections of another if they have been given linguistic expression. This following is *his* ability, and in this he remains individual and isolated. Thus, the reflection on the apodictic self-certainty which can be expressed in the 'I am' is reflection on the 'absolute fact', since with its 'it is thus' the first point of reference is given in terms of which there is the world as horizon. The reduction makes us aware of the fact that *we can never speak of world in general*, that *we must always ask for whom it is the world.* If we today speak of *one* world, we must remember that it was not always as such the horizon for all who lived in the past. If world as this continually changing horizon is fundamentally world in process, *it is as this one world the result of this process.* It is the one world for us, for modern society. But the fact that we can speak of a 'for us' means that it is a 'for everyone'. The commonality of one world as horizon is not suspended over the individuals which have it in common; it is the result of a history of the formation of this horizon, a history which presupposes the many individuals who in their with-one-another and against-one-another, in their own movements and their individual differences which are given through their respective life histories, constitute the common horizon.

The *a priori* of this formation is the 'universe of intuitability'; but the concept of it can only be formed in reflection on the sensory-kinaesthetic performances, a reflection which can only be a 'self-reflection' on one's own performances, since only in such self-reflection are the performances given 'intuitively', i.e. as they themselves. What this reflection brings to light is nowhere to be found as an observable fact in the world. What is observable is the common style of behaviour and its regularities which are guided by traditions and norms. In this world the comparative sciences of man remain on the ground of the world. Here they find process and development, the differences among the life-worlds, here they find the development from lower to higher modes of having a world by means of comparison with that which has been achieved to date. They do not ask how they came to have the concept of behaviour in the first place and how their talk about behaviour can be intelligible. To be sure, the assumption that all of this is generally intelligible is not illegitimate, but they are incapable of giving an answer to the question concerning the ground of the legitimacy of this assumption, since this ground is not that which can be observed here or there and because they think that reasoning must make reference only to that which is observable in the world if it is to be scientific. But *the 'self' that performs is not observable; only in reflection is it there for itself, and this self is the final source of all possible evidences.* Thus, the neglect of the life-world is a neglect of oneself, and it is precisely in order to combat this neglect that we reduce to the primordial fact of the I-am. But since this I-am is an 'I-am-there',[21] and since being-there (*Da-sein*) signifies having a world as horizon, my own world is included in this primordial fact. To bracket the thesis of the world is to see that this primordial fact is the absolute fact, since it is only in terms of its world horizon that that which we can in any sense understand as a human life-world is available: 'I am, and time constitutes itself in terms of me.' That is: only in the self-reflection on this primordial fact do we discover that which allows us to legitimately speak of the formation of a common world, its becoming and its history. Only this reflection brings to light the *a priori* of the functions of this subjectivity which had remained anonymous up to then and which are the conditions of possibility of having a common world as a process towards unity. And these functions too are nothing permanent; they unfold and develop themselves. Since they are not to be found as facts in the given finished world, being conditions of possibility of discovering facts in the first place and of being able to look back on a world which has already developed, *they are transcendental conditions, and the look back on their process of development is a transcendental history of conscious experience.*[22]

In order to give an initial impression of its first steps, we can close by discussing the question of the relation of transcendental history to factual-empirical history. As Husserl once noted, the actual empirical is the mode in which transcendental history appears in or is 'reflected in' the world (*Husserliana* XV, p. 491). The word 'appearance' is not to be understood in a Kantian sense here, rather in the sense that that which can only be experienced as 'it itself' in one's own self-reflection on one's own performances 'manifests' itself in a manner accessible to all in the world of the observable facts of human behaviour. They are the *a priori* of the developmental processes of the life-world and its history. Their comprehension as *a priori* is, however, itself a result of their transcendental genesis. In this sense Husserl speaks of genetic phenomenology as an archaeology of consciousness.

But if its performances are pre-temporal and pre-historical, and if they can first be discovered in reflection, where and what are they prior to this reflection? Husserl's answer that they are anonymous is inadequate, for this anonymity must be or have been something if we are to legitimately speak of its being discovered by reflection. *What is the connection between the two properties anteriority (Voranliegen) and anonymity*? What allows us to say that they are already at hand and in what sense can this be said? Here we must recall just what it is that reflective thematization itself already knows itself to be: it knows itself to be related to that which has just occurred as performance and it knows itself to be an awareness *post facto*, in that it, as it were, hurries after that which has already taken place and attempts to get a grip on it. Thus, this awareness after the fact ontifizes (*ontifiziert*): we say, it 'is' or it 'was' this or that. But in this kind of reflection, that on which we reflect as just performed becomes a 'before'. But this is not to order it in a flow of time which is already present; this flowing takes place in the living 'There' of the performance, in the living present.

All temporal determinations are referred to such an absolute 'There'. The functions which can be described as syntheses of temporalization and on the basis of which there 'is' time for us, are lifted out of their anonymous passive process by means of reflection, and in their thematization they are ontified. We say, it 'is', or 'is' this or that. Its description occurs in statements in which that which is described is designated as, e.g. retention, protention, etc. This designation refers to what they mean. Designation is meaning intention. As references they refer to that in which the intention is fulfilled. According to Husserl, fulfilment is intuition – self-giving, and it occurs only in a recapitulation (*Nachvollzug*). *Only in this relation between original 'living' anonymous performance and the reflection which refers back to it are temporal relations constituted.* Thus, we cannot say that we are dealing with a process which falls into a presupposed flow of time; this flow forms itself in the respective 'There' of the performance and in its relation to the reflective recapitulation. There is not in addition to this a flowing and becoming as a form which is filled with changing contents. That this flowing and more generally this process which we call 'history' 'exists', this presupposes that an individual is 'There' with its others, an individual who wants to hold on to this being-there in self-presence in such a manner that it becomes communicable. 'Holding on to' means making it subject or predicate by use of the usual expressions and familiar words of language. *The being-there (Da-sein) of the one who so reflects is thus the ultimate presupposition for there 'being' a flowing at all and thus time and history*. What this might be in the absence of any reference to this being-there is a meaningless question, as is the question what the world is without reference to the individual or individuals for whom it is the world; sense is always sense-for. As the meaning of the words we use it fulfils itself in the 'There' of the one who hears or reads and who achieves the fulfilment of their meaning in this recapitulation. Ontifizing we can say that this flowing is only a flowing as long as it is correlative to those who not merely co-accomplish (*mitvollziehen*) this flowing but in this co-accomplishment already have a pre-reflexive acquaintance with this accomplishment. Thus, a 'self' is presupposed as performer. As Husserl says: 'The flow is to be temporalized *a priori* by the "last functioning" ego. This temporalizing itself flows; the flowing always is in advance; but the I too is in advance.'[23] But he notes that this talk of the I is not literal. Transcendental–genetically, I-consciousness is the result of a process. It is preceded by the pre-reflexive self-reference in the control of the capacities for kinaesthetic self-locomotion by the self as its performer.

Thus, we are not confronted with two things here, with a flowing of time and an experience of this flowing; the flowing is itself self-experience, since flowing cannot occur in any other manner than as centred in terms of the being-there of the experiencer. Seen in this light, with reference to the functions and performances of the self of these performances, the flowing, since it is only discovered in transcendental reflection, is transcendental genesis as the history of the experience of consciousness. *Consciousness itself is this history. It is not consciousness of a history but rather the locus of its formation*. This is to say that history only exists where it is recalled or reconstructed as one's own prehistory. But this prehistory as one's own always implies the history which is 'sedimented' therein, a history which includes the experiences of the others as that which forms the horizon of the concrete life-world in which the reflecting individual in its 'There' finds himself. The transcendental history of consciousness and empirical history are thus not two different things; they are one and the same but viewed from different levels of reflection. Empirical history, as it is presented by the empirical sciences, accepts the relativity of its process as something final, which can only lead to the scepticism or relativism. Transcendental history, which is opened up in reflection on the transcendental functions on the basis of which there can be something like history for us, leads to the absolute in all relativities, to the existence of that being for whom there is history and for whom history takes the form of its own historical world. It can thus comprehend history as 'the great fact of absolute being' (*Husserliana* VIII, p.506).[24] An absolute fact, since the 'There' of those *for* whom history exists is absolute facticity. They have not picked it out; they find themselves in it as the place from which they cannot withdraw, in which they with their respective life histories have to live and act. Within this 'There' it is decided whether this is a 'successful' life or a failure. If this 'There' is *our* There in our world which has become *one* world, our task is to pay heed to what this demands of us. We have seen that the absolute boundary of our world horizon is the *earth* (a transcendental determination) with its limited possibilities, which sets an absolute limit to all that we are capable of doing – even with the aid of technology. It is an absolute demand, beyond all relativity, that man settle within these limits in such a manner that all individual life-worlds cannot only *live*, but live in such a way that their individual variety is respected.

Notes

1 Edmund Husserl, *The Crisis of European Sciences and Transcendental Philosophy*, trans. D. Carr, Evanston Northwestern University Press, 1970.
2 Gerd Brand, *Die Lebenswelt*, Berlin, Walter de Gruyter, 1971.
3 Hans Blumenberg, *Lebenswelt und Technisierung unter Aspekten der Phänomenologie*, Sguardi su la Filosofia Contemporanea, no. 51, Turin, 1963, p. 14.
4 Cf. Landgrebe, 'Merleau-Pontys Auseinandersetzung mit der Phänomenologie Husserls', in *Phänomenologie und Geschichte*, Gütersloh, Mohn, 1968, pp. 167ff.
5 H. Lübbe, *Bewußtsein in Geschichten*, Freiburg, Rombach Verlag, p. 79.
6 Supplementary volume to the *Philosophische Rundschau*, 1967.
7 Cf. Alfred Schütz, *Collected Papers I–III*, The Hague, Martinus Nijhoff, 1962–6. Concerning Schütz's relation to Husserl, cf. 'The Problem of Transcendental Intersubjectivity in Husserl', in *Collected Papers III*.
8 Cf. Husserl, *Die Krisis der europäischen Wissenschaften und die transzendentalen Phänomenologie*, The Hague, Martinus Nijhoff, 1962. See the text-critical remarks concerning 'Beilage II', p. 551.
9 Cf. Husserl, *Crisis*, op. cit., p. 349–51.
10 Grace A. de Laguna, *On Existence and the Human World*, New Haven, Yale University Press, 1966, p. 222.
11 Cf. Landgrebe, *Über einige Grundfragen der Philosophie der Politik*, Schriftenreihe der Rheinische-Westfälische Akademie der Wissenschaften, 1968.
12 Cf. Landgrebe, 'The Phenomenological Concept of Experience', *Philosophy and Phenomenological Research*, vol. XXXIV/1, 1973, pp. 13ff.
13 For an extensive discussion of this problematic, see P. Janssen, *Geschichte und Lebenswelt*, The Hague, Martinus Nijhoff, 1970, especially pp. 98ff. and 171ff.
14 U. Claesges, 'Zweideutigkeiten in Husserls Lebensweltbegriff', in *Perspektiven phänomenologischer Forschung*, The Hague, Martinus Nijhoff, 1972.

15 H. Lübbe, 'Positivismus und Phänomenologie', in *Bewußtsein in Geschichten*, op. cit., p. 49.
16 Cf. Landgrebe, 'Seinsregion und regionale Ontologien in Husserls Phänomenologie', in *Der Weg der Phänomenologie*, Gütersloh, Mohn, 1963, pp. 113ff.
17 We cannot go into details here. Husserl merely touches on this problem in the main text of the *Crisis*. In later reflections (*Krisis*, Beilage XVII) it is given an extensive treatment. Cf. W. Marx, 'Lebenswelt und Lebenswelten', in *Vernunft und Welt*, The Hague, Martinus Nijhoff, 1970.
18 Cf. A. Aguirre, *Genetische Phänomenologie und Reduktion. Zur Letztbegründung der Wissenschaft aus der radikalen Skepsis im Denken E. Husserls*, The Hague, Martinus Nijhoff, 1970.
19 Cf. Landgrebe, 'Husserls Abschied vom Cartesianismus', in *Der Weg der Phänomenologie*, op. cit., pp. 163ff.
20 Cf. Landgrebe, 'Faktizität und Individuation' in *Sein und Geschichtlichkeit, Festschrift für Volkmann-Schluck*, Frankfurt am Main, Klostermann, 1974.
21 Cf., concerning this 'There' as an absolute determination, *Husserliana* XV, p. 533.
22 Cf. Landgrebe, 'Phänomenologie als transzendentale Theorie der Geschichte', in *Phänomenologische Forschung*, vol. 3, 1976.
23 From a manuscript from the year 1931, quoted from K. Held, *Lebendige Gegenwart*, The Hague, Martinus Nijhoff, 1966, p. 101.
24 Cf. Landgrebe, 'Meditation Concerning Husserl's Words: "History is the Great Fact of Absolute Being"', *Southwestern Journal of Philosophy*, vol. V/1, 1974.

CHAPTER 9

Marx's critique of morality as an introduction to the problem of his philosophy as a whole

Ivan Urbančič (Ljubljana)

1 Introductory remarks

(1) One might say that Marx is a philosopher of the practical, productive activities of man. But the search for a special practical philosophy in his work is in vain, we do not find an ethics or moral philosophy as a special philosophical discipline; indeed, we do not even find the possibility of working out an ethics from his point of view. The same holds for all other philosophical disciplines such as ontology, epistemology, axiology, aesthetics and logic. If this is the case we must ask whether Marx is a philosophical thinker in the first place, for what is left of philosophy when we remove all of its disciplines? This question is thoroughly legitimate when it is considered in the light of the traditional definition of European philosophy. All the more so, since the Marxists themselves, who hold themselves to be the legitimate heirs of Marx, talk about a specifically Marxist ethics, aesthetics, epistemology, etc., especially in those countries in which Marxism is the ruling ideology. We cannot go into these Marxist theories here. But it seems to me that they miss the centre of Marx's thought. We shall see why this is the case in the course of the following discussion.

In rejecting the very possibility of a special philosophical ethics from the Marxist point of view, we are not asserting that there is in fact no longer any such thing as morals or ethics or practical philosophy, nor do we wish to say that there is in fact no such thing as a proletarian or socialist ethics. This is a different question and requires its own discussion. But is it legitimate to assert the possibility in principle of a *Marxist* moral philosophy on the basis of the factual existence of a proletarian or a socialist morality?

(2) The discussion will take the following path:

(a) If we wish to discuss Marx's critique of morality, moral consciousness or moral philosophy, we must first sketch some of the main elements of the basic structure of moral consciousness in the way that this moral consciousness or moral philosophy appears from the Marxist point of view. We need not exegetically collect all of Marx's claims concerning morality and moral consciousness; we shall rather attempt to develop the problematic in terms of the 'spirit' of his thought. In doing so, we shall take Kant's moral philosophy as our example.

(b) We shall then proceed to the centre of Marx's critique in order to gain an insight into the essence and origin of his critique of moral philosophy. This requires that we briefly discuss the basic standpoint of Marxist thought as a whole in order to see clearly why a new foundation of moral philosophy and indeed of philosophy itself in the traditional sense is no longer possible. Only on this level of our discussion will it be possible to say something about the relationship between Marxism and phenomenology.

(c) Finally, we shall have to ask whether we can accept the basic stance of Marx's thought without further ado. If we take the Marxist critique not only of moral philosophy but of philosophy itself seriously, how can we honestly pursue philosophy today?

2 Moral consciousness, moral philosophy

How and where does the basic structure of moral consciousness manifest itself? An initial characteristic: moral consciousness necessarily views itself as distinct from and standing opposed to factual reality. This difference and opposition is thematized by traditional philosophy as the opposition between is and ought. Thus, ideal moral norms and values such as freedom, equality, justice, honesty, etc., necessarily stand in opposition to reality for moral consciousness or for moral philosophy, while simultaneously being thought to be completely independent from this reality.

We said that this opposition between morality and reality is *necessary* for moral consciousness, for if freedom, equality, etc. themselves were already realized in reality, they could no longer count as duties or norms for the actor; if justice were already reality, the demand for justice would have no real sense. Moral consciousness, which moral philosophy merely systematically and consequently formulates and justifies, always confronts the actor with a demand, i.e. an imperative according to which he should act, thus realizing ideal morality. Moral consciousness represents this demand as a duty, and this is the second characteristic of moral consciousness. The moral demand that morality be fulfilled or realized in reality is *ipso facto* a demand that reality be changed in such a manner that reality is assimilated to morality, and not vice versa. For moral consciousness, the sense of this moral action lies in the attainment of a happiness of which only man as a reasonable being is worthy. The ultimate fulfilment, the complete realization of morality in reality, would amount to the dissolution (*Aufhebung*) of the opposition between is and ought, thus the dissolution of moral consciousness and thus a universal happiness. But for moral consciousness such a complete fulfilment of morality lies in the infinitely distant future. Morality is thus an infinite task.

We can understand moral philosophy as a systematic formulation of moral consciousness, and as such it attained its highest form in Kant. The Europe of the post-Kantian era has not seen the development of a moral philosophy comparable to Kant's.

The highest law of Kantian moral philosophy is the categorical imperative, which has two forms. The first, from the *Critique of Practical Reason*, is: 'So act that the maxim of your will could always at the same time be valid as a principle making universal law.' The second, from the *Groundwork*, is: 'Act in such a way that you always treat humanity, whether in your own person or in the person of any other, never simply as a means, but always at the same time as an end.'[1]

This highest law of morality is derived from Reason, from the 'rational will which in its own maxim is simultaneously universal legislator'. According to Kant, all moral concepts have their origin in reason. The highest law of morality is *a priori*, is thus independent from any *reality* external to it, be it a concrete individual, society or nature. It is simultaneously also universally valid, valid for all rational creatures regardless of their concrete empirical differences. But it is not forced upon these individual rational creatures from without and thus affords each of them his complete autonomy. According to Kant, this autonomy of the rational will is the ground of man's freedom as a rational creature.

Moral consciousness, whose basic structure we have sketched, leads to an insoluble antinomy. The development of the oppositions of this antinomy is also itself a critique of moral consciousness, a critique from the standpoint of this consciousness itself. Hegel developed this kind of critique in great detail in the *Phenomenology of Spirit*.[2] We cannot discuss this Hegelian critique here; although it is radical and thorough, from the Marxist point of view it is inadequate. Marx takes another path.

According to the Marxist analysis of the capitalist epoch of world history, we must begin with the strange fact (i) that Marx by no means primarily criticizes moral consciousness from the standpoint of consciousness or thought, and thus does not confront the old moral philosophy with a new one, for the simple reason that for him this would be senseless; (ii) that the division, the opposition between ought (morality) and is (social reality) turns out to be mere appearance from his point of view, behind which is concealed an indissoluble identity of the two, an identity which necessarily, according to the very principle of moral consciousness itself, must remain hidden to this consciousness; (iii) that there is no essential difference between morality and immorality.

Thus, if there is indeed a specific identity between moral consciousness or moral philosophy and the given historical reality – which must be demonstrated – then moral philosophy must in a certain sense be a manifestation of this reality itself, although according to its self-understanding it stands in opposition to this reality, is completely independent of it. The lofty, *a priori* moral 'ought' as a whole is thus nothing other than a specific self-revelation of this reality itself, although the consciousness of this ought knows nothing of this fact. If we follow Marx we can say: moral consciousness or moral philosophy does not know that it is not what it appears to itself to be, and is what it appears not to be. And further: if moral philosophy (moral consciousness) is such a self-revelation or, as Marx says, an ideal expression of the given reality, and if this reality is capitalist, thus for Marx a reality which is, as it were, inverted, then its ideal expression is also, as it were, inverted. In spite of its own appearance, it does not stand in opposition to this reality but rather affirms and confirms nothing other than this inverted reality. In this respect Marx's critique allows of no exceptions. There is no form of moral consciousness (be it understood as 'humanistic morality' or as 'class morality', 'Christian morality', 'proletarian morality' or 'socialist morality') which is not subject to his critique.

In the face of such theses one must surely ask: does Marx preach amorality? But this question misses its mark. It does not see that preaching amorality by no means leaves the level of moral consciousness. But because with his first step Marx breaks through the level of moral consciousness as consciousness, he preaches neither morality nor some sort of amorality.

In order to understand these theses, we shall have to take a closer look at Marx's critical analyses.

3 The Marxian critique

According to Marx, the existing reality is the all-encompassing process of capital. The process of capital is not just any process in the world or in society; it is a historical mode of the entire social production and reproduction. It thus includes everything and gives everything the imprint of its own character. In short: the process of capital bears and informs this entire epoch of world history. By mode of production is meant the totality of social relations of production. Within the totality of these relations, the relation of exchange plays the decisive role, for it is the foundation of all others. We shall have to take a closer look at Marx's analysis of commodity exchange.

In the *Grundrisse* Marx writes:

> Indeed, in so far as the commodity or labour is conceived of only as exchange value, and the relation in which the various commodities are brought into connection with one another is conceived as the exchange of these exchange values with one another, as their equation, then the individuals, the subjects between whom this process goes on, are simply and only conceived of as exchangers . . . there is absolutely no distinction between them. . . . Each of the subjects is an exchanger; i.e. each has the same social relations towards the other that the other has towards him. As subjects of exchange, their relation is therefore that of *equality*. . . . Furthermore, the commodities which they exchange are, as exchange values, equivalent, or at least count as such (the most that could happen would be a subjective error in the reciprocal appraisal of values), and if one individual, say, cheated the other, this would *happen not because of the nature of the social function in which they confront one another*, for this is *the same*, in this they are *equal* (p. 241).[3]

The last part of the quotation requires some explanation. Marx first speaks of the complete equality of subjects or individuals – of human beings – in the process of commodity exchange. Viewed from the moral standpoint, the relation of equality among individuals is the content of a moral maxim. In the last part of the quotation Marx explains the sense of cheating in such a relation of exchange. When cheating occurs, equivalents are not exchanged. To be sure, cheating is something morally negative. It only appears when someone, perhaps with great powers of persuasion, gives the other less than he receives in return while convincing him that he has received equal value. But for the pure, paradigmatic structure of the relations of exchange, which is the foundation for the whole process of capital, such cheating is something merely accidental which, as Marx himself points out, is even weakened and foiled in the further development of this process. But this means that the process of exchange as a whole as the relation of equality already corrects cheating on its own, forces the cheater to respect the moral law of equality. Thus, one can already suspect that the capitalist reality of social relations in its paradigmatic form is identical with morality.

This connection between the process of capital and morality is nicely illustrated by the following remark from the 'Preface' to the *Situation of the Working Class in England* by Engels:

> Although it is not expressly listed in the recognized textbooks, it is a law of modern political economy that the more capitalist production develops the less it can tolerate the small practices of cheating and swindling which are characteristic of its earlier phases. . . . Indeed, these tricks and dodges are not as lucrative in a larger market in which time is money and where a certain level of commercial morality develops, not out of any enthusiasm for morality, but simply in order not to lose time and effort uselessly. And this is precisely the way things developed in England in the relation between the industrialist and his workers.[4]

In short, cheating, injustice, etc. is something merely accidental in the general relations of exchange, an accidental transgression of the norm which is already effective in this reality itself. Moral consciousness with its ought necessarily corrects only this sort of accidental transgression of this basic structure. In so doing, this moral correction, this ought or morality, establishes *precisely this* basic structure of exchange, which first makes the process of capital as a whole possible, as a duty.

In addition, the Marxist analysis of the act of exchange shows that this act also guarantees the individual complete freedom and autonomy.

For example, Marx writes:

> Out of the act of exchange itself, the individual, each one of them, is reflected in himself as its exclusive and dominant (determinant) subject. With that, then, the complete freedom of the individual is posited: voluntary transaction; no force on either side; positing of the self as means, or as serving, only as means, in order to posit the self as end in itself, as dominant and primary (*übergreifend*). . . . The general interest is precisely the generality of self-seeking interests. Therefore, when the economic form, exchange, posits the all-sided equality of its subjects, then the content, the individual as well as the objective material which drives towards the exchange, is *freedom*. Equality and freedom are thus not only respected in exchange based on exchange values but, also, the exchange of exchange values is the productive, real basis of all *equality* and *freedom*. As pure ideas they are merely the idealized expressions of this basis; as developed in juridical, political, social relations, they are merely this basis to a higher power (*Grundrisse*, pp. 244–5).

We can already see that Marx – in his analysis of the simple structure of the exchange of commodities – simultaneously finds the elements of morality. It turns out that everyone who takes part in the exchange of commodities takes the other as well as himself not merely as a means, but by the same token as an end in himself. In this way he does his duty in just the manner demanded by the second version of the moral categorical imperative in Kant's moral philosophy. To be sure, the maxim of his action can equally serve as a universal law. But since the relation of commodity exchange is the reality of the society which is based on the process of capital, this categorical moral 'ought' is neither independent from nor opposed to nor separate from this reality. To be sure, this remains completely hidden from moral consciousness. We shall see the reason for this shortly. In addition, Marx's analysis shows us that the universal interest appears in the relation of commodity exchange only as the universality of egoistic interests. Egoism is the general rule. But even Kant's categorical imperative has given rise to the objection that it is merely a form of universal egoism.[5]

In addition, we see that for Marx the entire process of commodity exchange in its developed form is already the real system of freedom.

Marx formulates this in the following manner: 'Since money is only the realization of exchange value, and since the system of exchange values has realized itself only in a developed money system, or inversely, the money system can indeed only be the realization of this system of freedom and equality' (*Grundrisse*, p. 246).

Although it may sound fantastic, from Marx's critical standpoint classical political economy turns out to be a special form of moral consciousness or moral philosophy; indeed, moral philosophy turns out to be merely a special aspect of political economy. But this structural identity of morality and reality remains hidden from moral consciousness or moral philosophy. They cling to the appearance of their complete independence from and opposition to reality by obstinately demanding the realization of morality in reality.

Following the Marxist analysis, we encounter two different kinds of consciousness or knowledge. The first kind of consciousness or knowledge is moral consciousness or moral philosophy; the second sees and recognizes the status of the first as mere appearance, thus sees deeper, sees into the hidden foundations of the first, both in its form as normal, everyday consciousness and in its systematic formulation in moral philosophy. We shall call the first positive consciousness or knowledge, the second critical knowledge. This Marxist or critical knowledge thus penetrates into the foundation of positive knowledge. Marx formulates this in the following manner:

> In the course of science, it is just these abstract attributes which appear as the earliest and sparsest. . . . In present bourgeois society as a whole, this positing of prices and their circulation etc. appears as the surface process, beneath which, however, in the depths, entirely different processes go on, in which this apparent individual equality and liberty disappear. It is forgotten, on one side, that the *presupposition* of exchange value, as the objective basis of the whole of the system of production, already in itself implies compulsion over the individual, since his immediate product is not a product for him, but only *becomes* such in the social process, and since it *must* take on this general but nevertheless external form; and that the individual has an existence only as a producer of exchange value, hence that the whole negation of his natural existence is already implied; that he is therefore entirely determined by society; that this further presupposes a division of labour etc., in which the individual is already posited in relations other than that of mere *exchanger*, etc. . . . What is overlooked, finally, is that already the simple forms of exchange value and of money latently contain the opposition between labour and capital etc. (*Grundrisse*, pp. 247–8).

Thus, that which appears superficially to moral consciousness and national economy as the system of equality and freedom turns out, in the deeper vision of reality, as the system of inequality and bondage, of coercion. This look into the depth level, this critical knowledge, is not simple, but rather must discover at least two more strata beneath the surface of positive knowledge. As the surface, moral consciousness remains forever and necessarily where it is, i.e. on the surface, and thereby knows itself to be opposed to reality and pays no further attention to it as such. The deeper look of critical knowledge discovers *first* that there is no opposition or independence here at all, that reality – viewed paradigmatically – is rather already the precise fulfilment of morality itself, i.e. the system of equality and freedom; and, one might add, of brotherhood as well, since indeed every single subject treats both himself as well as every other person not as a mere means but also as an end in himself. But when it looks even deeper, critical knowledge discovers that in a still deeper stratum, this real system of equality, freedom and brotherhood is actually its own negative, namely a system of inequality, bondage (coercion) and egoism.

How is this look into the deeper strata below the surface of positive consciousness, how is this critical knowledge itself possible, how is it possible to see through all prior knowledge – not merely moral philosophy but along with it also all previous philosophy including the sciences – as a mere surface and to investigate its foundations? This possibility cannot be simply assumed as something self-evident, as something which was already at hand somewhere in finished form merely waiting for its discoverer – Marx.

But before we try to give an answer to this question we must describe at least four of the main aspects of this unusual context of surface (thus, all of previous positive knowledge) and the deeper strata which lie below it, and explain the peculiar nature of this context.

The first thing that we see is that morality turns out to be unmorality when viewed from the Marxist standpoint. All ideal elements of morality reveal themselves to this deeper view to be the opposite of what they appeared to be. There is a symptomatic objection to this assertion: were morality in fact unmorality, then an honest relation to one's fellow men would be the same as a dishonest relation, robbery would be the same as honest labour, telling the truth would be the same as lying, etc. Objections of this kind are certainly possible and indeed justified within their own limits; we must understand them. But they also clearly give witness to the fact that their authors simply have not understood what Marx is talking about, they cannot break through the level of everyday moral consciousness. They latch on to the abstraction and do not see the concrete relations. Moral consciousness can only correct the *deviation*, the small, accidental case of cheating, but cannot change the basic structure of the relation of exchange, since it is identical with it; by the same token, moral consciousness does not see that precisely the complete fulfilment of its principle, its imperatives, is even more problematic for the deeper view. This ridiculous objection arises on the basis of a simple unreflective transfer of the assertions of the critical depth analysis to the surface of moral consciousness, where it appears as a call for amorality and becomes the object of moral indignation. This only signifies that moral consciousness stubbornly remains on its own level. But at the same time it must be emphasized that if one takes the Marxist analysis as point of departure, one cannot simply reject moral consciousness or moral philosophy, indeed, not even philosophy itself. This would be pointless, since as long as the basic structure of social reality remains unchanged, positive consciousness necessarily corresponds to it as its ideal expression. This is also true of the science of national economy (and for philosophy). To want to have commodity production, exchange value and the free market while doing away with 'classical' political economy is, according to Marx, nonsense. It is only the other side of the same coin when someone who has heard the thesis that morality is unmorality asks if we should continue to educate our children in the spirit of morality. As if we had any choice in the matter.

But again, this cannot mean that one must simply close one's eyes to the fact that moral consciousness is a mere appearance. This can be seen clearly in Marx's critique of the socialists:

> What this reveals, on the other side, is the foolishness of those socialists (namely the French, who want to depict socialism as the realization of the ideas of *bourgeois* society articulated by the French revolution) who demonstrate that exchange and exchange value etc. are *originally* (in time) or *essentially* (in their adequate form) a system of universal freedom and equality, but that they have been perverted by money, capital, etc. Or, also, that history has so far failed in every attempt to implement them in their true manner. . . . The proper reply to them is: that exchange value or, more precisely, the money system is in fact the system of equality and freedom, and that the disturbances which they encounter in

> the further development of the system are disturbances inherent in it, are merely the realization of *equality and freedom*, which prove to be inequality and unfreedom. It is just as pious as it is stupid to wish that exchange value would not develop into capital, nor labour which produces exchange value into wage labour. What divides these gentlemen from the bourgeois apologists is, on one side, their sensitivity to the contradictions included in the system; on the other, the utopian inability to grasp the necessary difference between the real and the ideal form of bourgeois society, which is the cause of their desire to undertake the superfluous business of realizing the ideal expression again, which is in fact only the inverted projection (*Lichtbild*) of this reality (*Grundrisse*, pp. 248-9).

Thus, for Marx it is 'silly and stupid'

1 not to see that the actual capitalist system or money system is the real fulfilment of the system of equality and freedom;

2 for this reason to want to realize the ideal of equality and freedom all over again;

3 to think that exchange and exchange value in its original form is the original form of the system of freedom and equality and that it has merely been falsified by money or the capitalist;

4 to think that exchange value does not develop into capital;

5 not to see that the disturbances of the system of exchange and exchange value, namely inequality and unfreedom, are immanent in this system;

6 not to see that the ideal is merely an expression or photograph of reality and thus in complete correspondence with it, corresponding in a twofold fashion: in the first place as the positive and then as the negative of the original.

Thus, we see that moral consciousness corresponds to reality in a twofold fashion. On the one hand it is an ideal expression of reality and is thus structurally identical to it; on the other hand, however, in the light of a still deeper stratum of reality, it corresponds to it as a reversed, negative image of itself: morality, beneath the surface of moral consciousness, reverses itself into unmorality; or, put into the language of economics, the relation of exchange of equivalent exchange values reverses itself in the hidden depths which lie behind this mere appearance into an exchange of non-equivalents. We must ask how it is possible that the exchange of equivalent exchange values becomes a mere appearance beneath which *the same* act occurs as an act of exchanging non-equivalents, and all this without any cheating.

What kind of act of exchange is this? This specific act, which is decisive for the entire system of capital, is the exchange of labour power as a commodity for other commodities of the same value. The only commodity available to the worker is his own labour power. He sells his labour power for a specified time, he exchanges it as a commodity for another commodity of the same value. The quantity of the value of labour power is basically determined by the cost of its reproduction, which is in principle analogous to the determination of the quantity of the value of any other commodity. We cannot follow the Marxist analysis into more detail here. It would appear that here too, in the exchange between the worker and the capitalist, equivalents have been exchanged. But labour power is a commodity whose use produces other, new commodities, it produces value. Marx shows that in the agreed-upon span of time labour power produces more value than the capitalist gave for it in the form of other commodities or money as the universal commodity. But it is the capitalist, and not the worker, who controls this surplus value, which remains strictly invisible to both parties in the act of exchange between the worker and the capitalist. And it is precisely the surplus value which turns the equivalence into a non-equivalence. This is the foundation for all of the reversals we have described; it lies in this *social relation* and only there. This relation is the foundation of all other social relations of production. It includes 'the entire negation' of the natural existence of man, as Marx says, his reduction to mere labour power as a commodity; thus the whole *essential impoverishment* of man, the reduction of his entire developed *essential wealth* and his *essential bounty* to the *essential poverty* of mere labour power as a commodity is already contained in this social relation of production (cf. *Grundrisse*, p. 248, lines 6–7). Its epochal significance first becomes visible at this point: it is the foundation of the whole world epoch of capital. In the discovery of the simple moments of the social relations in the act of exchange between the worker and the capitalist lies the seed of the entire Marxist critique of existing reality.

Before taking the next step towards the question of the basic possibility of such a discovery and critique, we must clarify something else.

4 Relations of production – powers of production

If one asks what Marx actually means by reality, the answer seems easy enough. It is generally thought that for Marx reality is the whole of society with all that belongs to it. But this answer does not correspond to the Marxist view, because it is not precise enough. According to this answer, the powers of production would also belong to social reality. But this is not the case.

In the preface to the *Critique of Political Economy* Marx writes:

> In the social production of their existence, men inevitably enter into definite relations, which are independent of their will, namely relations of production appropriate to a given stage in the development of their material forces of production. The totality of these relations of production constitutes the economic structure of society, the real foundation, on which arises a legal and political superstructure and to which correspond definite forms of social consciousness. The mode of production of material life conditions the general process of social, political and intellectual life. It is not the consciousness of men that determines their existence, but their social existence that determines their consciousness.[6]

Marx summarizes his entire analysis of existing reality in these short sentences. For Marx, moral consciousness is a specific form of social consciousness that corresponds to the economic structure of society, i.e. to the real basis or to social existence. The economic structure, the real basis, social existence thus all mean the same thing, namely the whole of the given *relations of production* which correspond to a specific level of the development of the powers of production. Thus, *reality* signifies actually and only the *economic* structure, *social existence*, and by no means the powers of production themselves. There is thus an important distinction between the relations of production and the powers of production, a distinction which is decisive for Marx's entire thought: The powers of production are understood merely as the 'material' *base*, as the foundation of the relations of production, thus of social being as the real basis, and cannot be confused with this real basis or understood to be simply included in it. Social being as the whole of the relations of production *corresponds*, according to Marx, to the powers of production. This is the reason why Marx, as we have seen, writes: 'The mode of production of material [= actual] life conditions the general process of social, political and intellectual life.' Precisely this *mode* of production is the decisive factor; the relations of production are thus the real basis of society. For this reason, the powers of production are not the real theme of Marx's analysis of social existence or of the real basis in general, they remain external to the analysis of the capitalist *mode* of production. This is not to say that his original understanding of the essence of these powers of production did not play an important role in his critical analysis of the capitalist *mode* of production (the capitalist world). On the contrary, this understanding determines and supports *every* step of this critical analysis of social being and its ideal expression, i.e. all social forms of consciousness (e.g. legal, political, religious, moral, philosophical, economic forms of consciousness, the consciousness of the human sciences and even of the natural sciences). All of these forms of consciousness together are positive consciousness or positive knowledge. This knowledge as a whole is in principle to be characterized in the same manner as we have characterized moral consciousness in our discussion; it is an ideal expression of the real social basis or of social existence, thus of the existing relations of production, and is thus also in principle an apology for them. Marx does not shrink back from this consequence.

The distinction and opposition between the relations of production and the powers of production is however not an absolute and eternal one; it is rather a historical appearance which for this reason is subject to supersession (*Aufhelbung*). Marx's theory of revolution turns on this point. Because the powers of production are subject to a continual development, they come into conflict with the given, relatively stable relations of production on the basis of the distinction between the two. This gives rise to a contradiction which is in turn cancelled by a revolutionary change of the existing relations of production, i.e. of the real basis of society. According to Marx, in the course of the capitalist epoch this difference as a contradiction develops up to its extreme limits, whereby the possibility of a radical, revolutionary change is made possible and necessary, a necessity which itself stems from the continual development of the powers of production. Thus, when we speak of a *distinction* between the *relations of production* (= the real basis, the economic structure of society, social existence) and the *powers of production*, we must not lose sight of this historical character.

5 The basic standpoint of critique

The discussion thus far leads us to the question: how is Marx's analysis of social reality itself, as well as the analysis of moral consciousness and in general consciousness that is bound up with this reality, in principle possible at all? Furthermore, what is the origin of the possibility of viewing as such the *reversals* within this reality as well as the reversals in the corresponding ideal expressions of this reality?

In order to answer these questions, we must penetrate to the core of Marxist thought, to the point from which a survey of the whole will perhaps be possible.

We have already given an answer to what appears to be the same question in our reference to Marx's theory of surplus value. This theory opens the way to insight into the necessity of the reversals within social reality as well as morality. This theory itself amounts to insight into the real ground of the entire hitherto existing positive knowledge, which was and had to be hidden to this knowledge.

But our current question concerns the possibility in principle of just this Marxist theory, so the apparent answer cannot count as an answer to our question. How could Marx gain insight into the reversals in social reality, what is the standpoint from which the relation of commodity exchange between capitalist and worker, and above all the decisive element of this relation, the production of surplus value, appears in the manner that Marx saw and described? Marx's personal genius is not sufficient. An in principle new standpoint, which leaves behind all existing positive knowledge, and from which moral philosophy and reality turn out to be what Marx saw them to be, is required. Only from such an in principle novel standpoint is this new, *critical* knowledge and thereby the relentless critique of existing reality possible. There is not really an opposition in the sense of a theoretical controversy between the 'old' positive knowledge and critical knowledge, because critical knowledge stands on an entirely different level. Marx does not enter into a theoretical debate with this or that theory of the 'old' philosophy on *its* level, and he need not do so; he sees in them simply the ideal expression of the given social reality, and he sees that theoretical refutations of such ideal expressions of reality in abstraction from this reality itself are meaningless. Thus, critical knowledge must have an in principle new standpoint.

There is, however, the widespread opinion that Marx assumes the standpoint of the working class or of the proletariat. Although this thesis is taken to be self-evident, it is false; besides, it is pointless, since according to Marx it is not merely a question of abolishing the capitalist class but by the same token of abolishing the working class or proletariat. Such theses simply do not take seriously Marx's demand for the revolutionary abolishment (*Aufhebung*) of the class structure of society and do not see that the two antagonistic classes are both the result of the ruling relations of production. The assertion that Marx assumes the standpoint of the proletariat or of the working class is *ipso facto* the assertion that he assumes the standpoint of the existing social relations of production, and that is simply absurd. The fact that for Marx the proletariat is the vehicle of that movement which leads to the abolishment (*Aufhebung*) of the class structure of society and thus also to its own abolishment as proletariat merely shows that Marx does not and could not assume the standpoint of the proletarian class.

On the other hand, certain historical theories concerning the threefold origin of Marx's thought are widespread. According to these theses, the new standpoint of Marxist critical knowledge is somehow dependent on its historical origin, namely on Hegel's philosophy, classical political economy and utopian socialism. But a new standpoint could never be developed on this basis. It is true, of course, that all of these played a very great role in Marx's thought, but they were not decisive. Marx holds that all three theories assume the standpoint of positive consciousness as the ideal expression of the real social relations of production and are thus in principle uncritical with reference to their real basis. Marx worked out this claim in detail, and he never could have done so if his critique of the three historical 'components' of his thought were not carried out from an in principle different standpoint which made his *specific* (and no longer merely philosophical) *critique* of all three possible. Thus, his basic standpoint simply could not have been derived from his historical studies.

Thus, the question concerning the fundamental standpoint of Marx's thought remains open. In the absence of an answer to this question, we cannot know how we should react to Marxist thought today, we cannot know the degree to which it is valid for us, what its relations to phenomenology are, etc. It is thus highly important that we find an answer to this question.

Let us be clear about the problem. We have asked how it is in principle possible that Marx should see through the whole of hitherto existing positive consciousness or knowledge, especially moral consciousness, as an ideal expression or picture of the existing relations of production, i.e. of the real social basis, with all of the inversions we have seen to be at work in this knowledge and in the real basis. We are obviously confronted with two modes of consciousness or with two completely different types of knowledge. The one is positive, traditional knowledge, the other is Marx's critical knowledge itself. Figure 9.1 illustrates this structure.

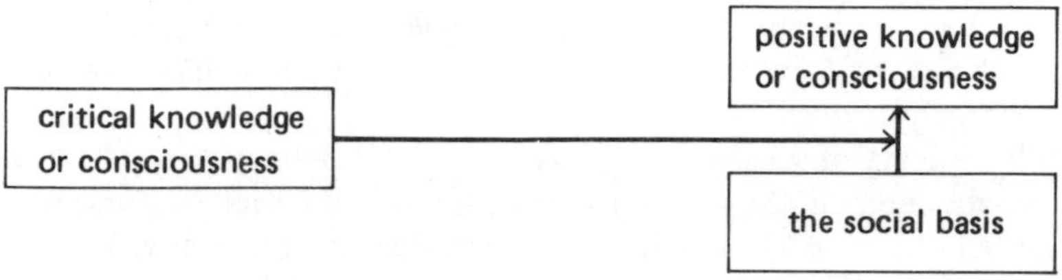

Figure 9.1

Critical knowledge comprehends positive knowledge and its real basis in their specific interrelations; these two constitute its object. The question concerns the ground of this critical knowledge itself. In purely formal terms, we have the following two possibilities:

(a) Critical knowledge or consciousness itself is grounded in the real social basis. But it is already clear that this cannot be the case. Should the ground of critical knowledge or consciousness itself turn out to lie in the real social basis, then according to Marx himself it could never be critical with regard to this positive knowledge and its social basis; it would be simply impossible as such.

(b) Critical knowledge or consciousness could be grounded in itself. But this could be true only in a very specific sense, and not in the sense in question. This self-grounding of critical consciousness *as consciousness* would only be possible against the background of the Cartesian *cogito, ergo sum*. This proposition embodies the principle of the absolute self-grounding or self-certainty of consciousness and by the same token its complete independence from any and every external reality. This is the absolute foundation of philosophy from Descartes to Hegel and on to Husserl. We have found this independence from external reality at work in Kantian moral philosophy. But with his very first step, Marx left behind any such self-grounding and self-certainty of consciousness as consciousness, of knowledge as knowledge, and in this manner discovered that this absolute independence and self-grounding is a mere appearance, behind (beneath) which lies concealed the fact that this knowledge is completely dependent upon social reality or the real basis as its ideal expression, as photograph to original.

This insight has the result that Marx's critical method cannot recapitulate the path or method of transcendental philosophy from Descartes to Hegel and Husserl; he can no longer assume the basic standpoint of this philosophy.

If our theme bears the title 'phenomenology and Marxism', and if 'phenomenology' means Husserl's transcendental phenomenological philosophy, which returns to the Cartesian standpoint of the absolute self-certainty of consciousness, then we have to say that Marx's thought has absolutely nothing in common with this phenomenology and is at no point compatible with it. When this is clearly seen, we have to agree with Martin Heidegger's remark that Husserl's philosophy does not allow the possibility of a fruitful dialogue with Marx.

Thus, critical knowledge, Marx's knowledge, is not self-grounding, its fundamental standpoint is not to be found immanent to this thought itself. If it reflects upon itself concerning the *conditions* of its existence – and it does indeed do so – it cannot take itself to be independent and self-grounding, but rather must see itself as referred to its own material conditions. And this is precisely the direction our inquiry must take. What is the material condition of the existence of critical knowledge or critical consciousness? For Marx, this condition is embodied by the actual *powers of production* which – as we have already seen – are not the real basis of society or of social existence.

We must pay careful attention to the fact that the material powers of production are not only the condition and ground of critical knowledge, but also the condition of the real social basis – the relations of production – and also of the ideal expression of this basis, i.e. positive consciousness or positive knowledge. Figure 9.2 illustrates this structure.

The powers of production are condition and ground of critical knowledge as well as of the real social basis and the positive knowledge which corresponds to it as its ideal expression. There are no reversals in these powers of production. But their immense wealth is negated by the given social relations of production or the real social basis, and reduced to a single relation, to commodity and exchange value (cf. the quotation from the *Grundrisse*, p. 248). This negation and reduction is identical to the negation and reduction of the use value of objects

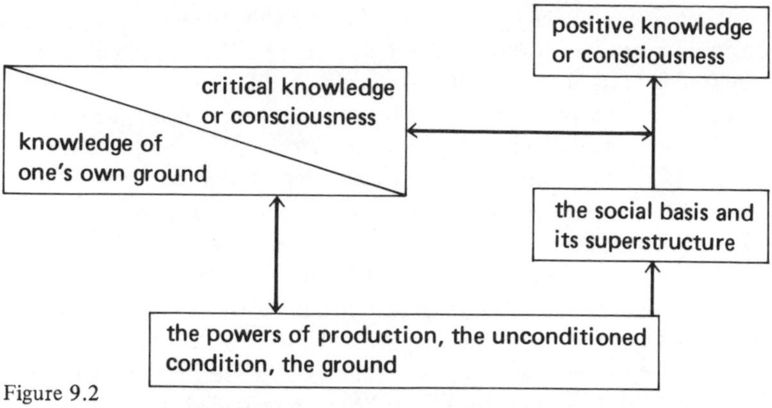

Figure 9.2

to mere commodities or that of the *essentially human powers* to mere labour power as a specific commodity. Modern powers of production, which have really developed the entire *essentially human wealth*, encompass the real human individuals as species-beings as well as the entirety of their means of production along with real nature as their own *possibility*. Viewed from the point of view of the 'material' powers of production, nature appears as their possibility. The 'materiality' of the powers of production does not signify a 'matter' in the sense of traditional materialism, but is only intended to point to the fact that in accordance with the Marxist understanding the powers of production are understood as *real*, i.e. not as something merely 'spiritual' or merely 'subjective'; this 'materiality' means as much as 'reality', but not in the sense of traditional philosophy. 'Materiality' thus encompasses not merely the 'material' (in a narrow sense) but also the 'spiritual' (e.g. the knowledge of the modern sciences).

The crucial insight at this point is that only the real social basis, social being or the existing relation of production – which are for Marx one and the same – yield the negation and reduction of the immense real wealth of the developed powers of production to a mere 'abstraction', as Marx puts it, to capital or to value as exchange value. This reversal occurs in the relations of production, not in the powers of production themselves. A thing is not valuable or a commodity on the basis of natural properties inherent to it as a thing, but only as a social relation – this is for Marx an abstraction which appears as a property of the real thing. This is precisely what Marx means by fetishism, and this is why he holds it to be a 'mystification'.

What does this have to do with our problem? How is critical consciousness or critical knowledge itself possible? To be sure, critical knowledge is founded in the powers of production, has its ground in them. *But critical knowledge is what it is, namely critical knowledge, only with reference to or in correlation with the existing real basis and positive knowledge as the ideal expression of this basis*. When it is removed from this correlation with the object of its critique (e.g. under the presupposition of a genuine revolutionary transformation of the existing social relations of production, which as a whole constitute social existence) critical knowledge ceases to be critical knowledge. And what remains of it can only be a moment of the powers of production themselves. So it would appear, at least. It is of great importance that this state of affairs be comprehended in terms of the whole of Marxist thought. Critical consciousness or critical knowledge constitutes itself as critical only with reference to the existing positivity. This positivity must however be understood strictly as the real basis or as the whole of the relations of production, i.e. of social being along with the positive consciousness or knowledge that corresponds to it. But since the ground and thus the basic standpoint of critical knowledge is to be found only in the powers of production, which as such are recognized in this knowledge as the foundation of its critique of existing reality, this critical knowledge is – once the existing structures have been abolished by a revolution – nothing more than knowledge of its own real foundation and is thus in principle an *un-critical* knowledge. But when it has 'become' uncritical with respect to the powers of production – and that means, really, 'always has been' instead of 'becomes' – this knowledge cannot be understood to have sunk back to the level of the old positive knowledge. We must distinguish two moments in critical knowledge. The first is the critical moment with respect to the real social basis, the second is the uncritical moment with respect to its own real ground – the powers of production; in its uncritical moment it appears to belong to the powers of production themselves. *Only* as this second moment would the new knowledge survive the transformation of the existing social positivity (i.e. the capitalist relations of production) by a revolutionary act. Such an act would also abolish the break or contradiction between the powers of production and the social relations of production (i.e. the real social basis); critical knowledge would have no object for its critique and would itself cease to exist. Consciousness or knowledge would be nothing more (!) than the universal consciousness or knowledge of the wealth of universal production for the universal satisfaction of universal needs. There would – according to Marx – be only *one single* science, the science of man.

We have seen that the powers of production play a fundamental role in Marx's thought. His original understanding of the essence of the powers of production determines and carries his entire analysis of the process of capital and thus of the entire capitalist epoch, although the powers of production themselves are not the real theme of this analysis.

The main problem in interpreting Marx's entire thought is thus not his analysis of the process of capital as a whole or the specific aspects of this analysis, is not his critique; the problem concerns his original understanding of this unconditioned condition, the real powers of production. And the problem concerns *these* powers not in the form of mere value, of the commodity or of capital, although in the context of the existing positivity they appear as reduced to such, but in that which was and is concealed by this form of capital, the powers of production in their fully developed wealth. To paraphrase Marx, we might say that to liberate the powers of production from their narrow bourgeois form is to lay open their actual *human* wealth.

6 The problem of Karl Marx's philosophy

On the assumption that the basic standpoint and the foundation of Marx's thought as a whole lies in the real powers of production, it remains to ask what this really means. The first central moment of the powers of production is according to Marx man as a conscious productive power, the really (sensuously) effective individuals who in and through their universal *production*, understood as the genuine expression or activation of all of their *essential powers*, satisfy their universal needs and thus continually develop themselves as ends in themselves. Really producing and enjoying in this manner, they are essentially *social* and in the final analysis *species-being*, the beings (*Wesen*) of the species. All objects, individually and as a whole, belong to the species-being or the species as their own objective reality, externalized in production. The immense wealth of the developed powers of production (including nature) is for Marx the externalized wealth of man (of his satisfaction) as the species-being. Consciousness or knowledge is understood only as the conscious species which knows itself. Thus, by the whole of the powers of production Marx means exactly that which he essentially means by species. The self-conscious species is the authentic, real objective subject of the whole.

We must understand the *concept of species*, which Marx took over from Feuerbach and often uses in his early writings, against the background of his later works. Understood in this manner, the species is no longer a 'static' concept of the essence of man in the sense of Feuerbachian metaphysics. *The species is the whole of the given, historically developed powers of production in conjunction with the relations of production which correspond to them* (and not understood in opposition or contradiction to them). Being (*Sein oder Wesen*) as *species* in Marx's early writings can thus only be understood in this sense, since the powers of production in their real actualization, i.e. in production, are *ipso facto* the actualization or the genuine manifestation of the totality of essentially human powers in which all historically developed needs and modes of satisfaction are included. Man as the self-conscious species and totality of his essential powers is thus not separated as subjectivity from his actual objects as objects of the actualization of his essential powers.

But our inquiry cannot stop here. We must inquire into the inner structure of the powers of production. According to Marx, we must distinguish three inseparable moments within the powers of production. They are:

(a) the factually effective human individual as the self-conscious, subjective productive power with all of the wealth of his productive activities, essential capacities and satisfactions;
(b) the whole of the means of production; and
(c) the factual, actual *production* itself as the unity of the first two elements. It is only in and through production that the first two elements are real, exist.

We must be very clear about this simple situation. If man is understood as a productive *power*, then he, as this power, has reality (being) only in the real actualization or manifestation of this essential power, otherwise not. The real actualization of productive power is production. On the other hand, the sensuous-material object is only real when human productive power works on it. Here we can see that production is of *decisive* significance in the context of the powers of production as a whole, that it is only through production that the other moments of the powers of production – man himself and his object – attain reality, i.e. *real being*. Production is *self-determining*. It is very important that this be seen clearly, since that by means of which man (the real-effective individual) and his object really exist is *production alone*, which is essentially to be understood as the actualization or manifestation of all human essential powers. Marx expressly says that production is the *condition* of human experience. It goes without saying that objects do not exist without production. *This* existence, *this* real being is posited and determined by production, and for this reason we say that production *posits and determines being*. Man, understood according to his essence as productive power, necessarily produces in order to be real at all, and for this reason he cannot be something static. He is subject only as the being that necessarily produces, his *production* is his *objective subjectivity*, from which he has his real being.

What about the *means of production*? In the context of the *developed* powers of production the means is that which one usually calls the unity of modern science and modern technology, and which Marx understands *instrumentally* as means. They are means, because it is *by means of* them that man manifests and actualizes his essential powers. In being understood instrumentally in this manner, modern science and technology are also understood anthropologically. Modern *production* as the decisive moment of the powers of production is thus mediated by these means, modern science and technology, and is only possible as so mediated. Production can only be characterized *as modern* (developed, as Marx puts it) in terms of its dependence on the unity of modern science and technology, which itself was developed in the course of the continual development of the powers of production.[7] These means, i.e. modern science and technology, suddenly receive a decisive role in the context of modern, i.e. developed production. Modern science/technology cannot be merely a means of the actuation of essential human powers, they become the determining condition of this actuation. Modern, developed *production*, which Marx essentially understands as actuation and manifestation of all essential powers, is now with historical necessity necessarily dependent on modern science/technology in such a way that science/technology affects production itself, indeed – and this is the decisive point – *determines* it. In no previous epoch of world history was production so completely determined by the exact natural (and social) sciences, never was production so *technical* in the modern sense of the term, as is the case today. This is the point, and the only point, at which our modern epoch of world history distinguishes itself from all previously known epochs. The consequence is that the decisive and determining moment is no longer production as the actuation and manifestation of essential human powers, but rather science/technology – and this with historical inevitability. It determines the *mode of being* of everything which is touched by modern, technically conditioned production, and thus determines the mode of being of man himself. The *capital*-instrumentalist as well as the *anthropological*-instrumentalist understanding of science/technology necessarily miss this decisive significance of modern science and technology. But the fact is that this understanding governs man's *attitude* towards that production which is determined by modern science/technology. This attitude is exhausted by strained attempts to gain control of modern science/technology, and the production which is conditioned by it, as mere means, an enterprise which can never succeed once their *epochal* significance has become determining for being itself. And our theme here is the 'practical' conduct of man.

Marx does not see this entire state of affairs at all, and from his basic standpoint it is *not even visible*. How is it possible that modern science/technology, and no longer production as the actuation of essential human powers, determines the real being of man and objects? This remains outside of the field of vision which Marx's basic standpoint opens up. Marx can view modern science and technology *in principle only* as a means, can understand them only anthropologically-instrumentally, but not as *determining being itself*. From his standpoint he can only repeatedly voice the demand that modern science/technology be merely a means subject to and ruled by man. But this only serves to increase the tension in human conduct.

Let us return to our problem. If we now ask what is going on in moral philosophy, also known as practical philosophy, we must come to the following conclusion: although we have contrasted the basically *affirmative, uncritical* moment in Marxist thought with the critical moment, his critical thought, whose basic elements we have sketched, has blocked itself off once and for all from the possibility of making positive use of traditional moral philosophy and of philosophy in general in his own affirmative thought. His affirmative, uncritical thought is thought of the powers of production or of the human species as a whole.[8] It is thus – following Marx – in principle impossible to take over any elements from traditional philosophy or from consciousness as the ideal expression of capitalist reality into the new 'Marxist' positive thought. Why? Because the philosophy of the old style, regardless when it arose, turns out from Marx's standpoint to be a mere ideal expression or image of the real basis as the totality of the relations of production based on exchange value and capital. And as such this traditional philosophy has no meaning outside of this specific reference to the existing real basis. It is thus useless for the new positive thought of the powers of production. Philosophy is abolished as such in being realized. But this only means that it must be grounded in the described reality itself, and not in itself, not in consciousness, in the *ego cogito, ergo sum*.

From the Marxist standpoint it is senseless to want to develop a specifically 'Marxist' ethics. 'Marxist' aesthetics, logic, epistemology, etc., for this attempt can only produce monsters; all such attempts, and many Marxists have set out on this road, are fantastic mixtures out of some poorly understood ideas from Marx and elements of traditional positive consciousness. From the Marxist standpoint, such attempts turn out to be nothing other than a new kind of apology for the long since existing relations of production, which merely appear in a slightly changed form. The old philosophy, or rather philosophy of the old type, is thus fruitless – when viewed from the Marxist standpoint, that is. This is not to say that we may or ought simply to forget or reject it, that we should no longer teach and learn it, or investigate this or that aspect of it. Quite the contrary: we *must* study it, perhaps more intensively than ever before. However, doing so is not genuine philosophy. But even if we were to elaborate new philosophical systems, this would not be genuine philosophizing according to Marx.

Once we have reached this point, it would seem that our options for philosophical thought are reduced to two possibilities. We must either dogmatically accept the basic Marxist position without reservations, or we must reject it completely as something which is completely invalid and continue to philosophize in the old style in peace, to move along the well-marked paths of philosophy, i.e. to repeat the old, already abandoned positions of philosophical thought, thus keeping up the appearance of the 'development of the discipline'.

The possibility of a third way for contemporary thought could perhaps reveal itself only if we should encounter something at the core of Marxist thought which in principle cannot be grasped and explained with Marxist conceptual tools, i.e. is fundamentally not even visible from his standpoint. But this something must also elude the grasp of the conceptual tools of the old philosophy which Marx criticized, for we would otherwise fall back into the old style of philosophical thought: it must be *novel.*

But why should we even attempt an investigation of this sort? What is the source of the thrust of our discussion up to this point? Is this merely a historicism and scholarly industry, or are there perhaps deeper reasons for such an investigation? Our general topic here is practical philosophy. This title points to human *conduct*. The question is thus how we ourselves, as concrete human beings here and now, conduct ourselves, how we can exist at all once we have seen and reflected upon the real meaning of the situation we have uncovered in our discussion, a meaning which touches the deepest roots of our life and being. *That* is what has been at issue all along.

We ask – following Marx to the deepest roots of his thought – what is his own, new, positive thought; how are we to understand it? We said that this new positive thought is the thought of the powers of production or of the species. What is the relation between this *novel thought* and the powers of production? But this question is itself misleading. If we are not constantly aware of the fact that for Marx this new consciousness of thought or knowledge is always the consciousness, etc., of the concrete, materially sensuous, effective individual – man – as the central moment of the powers of production themselves, we might unknowingly fall back into the old philosophy or metaphysics, simply overlooking its novelty in the attempt to explain this new kind of relation in the old style. Marx also calls the species as a whole simply *being* (*das Sein*), and speaks of a relation between thought and being when he says, 'Thought and being are thus to be sure *distinct*, but by the same token in *unity* with one another.'[9] (We must understand the species or being in the sense elaborated.)

From the basic Marxist point of view we are thus barred from accounting for the novel relation between thought and being in the old philosophical or metaphysical manner. We cannot say that this relation between thought and being is a picturing relation or a constitutional relation (the latter for example in the sense of Husserl's philosophy). This is out of the question because for Marx this new thought *as* thought is only *one* among a multiplicity of other real relations between human beings and being as the whole of the objective species, only *one* way among others in which the real world is appropriated, others being, e.g. sensation, feeling, willing, working, enjoying, loving, hating, etc. Marx discusses this in the *Paris Manuscripts*:

> Man appropriates to himself his manifold essence in an all-sided way, thus as the whole man. Every one of his *human* relations

> to the world – seeing, hearing, smelling, tasting, feeling, thinking, perceiving, sensing, wishing, acting, loving – in short, all the organs of his individuality, which are immediately communal in form, are an appropriation of the object in their *objective* relation (*Verhalten*) or their relation to it. This appropriation of *human* actuality and its relation to the object is the *actualization of human actuality*. It is therefore as varied as are the *determinations* of the human *essence* and *activities*. It is human *efficacy* and human *suffering*, for suffering, humanly conceived, is a satisfaction of the self in man.[10]

Thus, the relation of man to real being is grasped in its totality only when one understands it as *production*. As we have already seen, the factual, real externalization of the essential human powers, their actuation, is production. This 'being' is not thereby turned into an 'abstraction' all over again; it is rather the whole of the powers of production in their actuation and movement, precisely in production.

At this point in our considerations we are again suddenly confronted with something completely unexpected. As we have seen, modern science/technology plays a decisive role in the developed powers of production, such that they determine and bear production as a whole; in this manner they are determinative of being itself and not mere means. If they are understood as means, this is an utter impossibility, so they are forced back into the role of means, but they can never be displaced from their epochal-new decisive role. The tension rises even higher, and this state of affairs simply cannot be seen through and thought out from the Marxist standpoint. But the old philosophy is just as impotent, since Marx has already critically seen through the positivism of its principle with respect to the existing real basis of society (the existing relations of production).

How and from which standpoint is this state of affairs to be thought through?

Something unexpected arises on another side too. The novel positive thought as Marx would have us understand it has turned out to be a moment of the powers of production themselves, it is not external to them. But it is also undeniable that man, who is really effective in this manner as species-being, along with the totality of his real objects, is to be thought as the whole in precisely this manner. Marx's own new positive thought is a thought of the totality of the powers of production in connection with the relations of production which do not contradict them, both understood as the species or as real being. But *this* thought (*'Marxist'* thought), which thinks man in his relation to being or the world in *this* manner, obviously is not and cannot be identical with that thought or consciousness which is included and enclosed in every process of production itself. These are two totally distinct modes of consciousness (and thus of thought, of knowledge).

This 'Marxist' thought is not absorbed without remainder into the powers of production themselves, since a distance, a difference is required if these powers of production are to be thought as a whole. It is this difference which makes it possible to view the powers of production as a whole, i.e. as a world. The point that distinguishes these two modes of thought is very simple. The first ('Marxist') mode of thought thinks the *totality*; the other thought, enclosed in the powers of production, never thinks the totality, remaining merely a moment of concrete production; in this precise form it appears in the developed powers of production in the form of the modern sciences (on the assumption that they have been freed from their alienated form). Marx also calls the whole of the powers of production *being* and in so doing speaks of a relation between thought and this being. To repeat the quotation: 'Thought and being to be sure are thus *distinct*, but by the same token in *unity* with one another.' Marx describes the *unity*. But the question concerning the nature of the *difference*, and the circumstance that it is precisely this difference that 'allows' factual man according to his own nature not to be merely productive power and not to exhaust himself therein, were simply skipped over by Marx. And given his standpoint this was necessary and irrevocable. Marx simply skips over the question of how the difference between this new thought and being is to be thought in its decisive significance for concrete-factual man, what the sense of this difference might be. The fact that man can see himself in his totality in the sense of the powers of production or the species is evidence for the fact that the human being is not absorbed without remainder in the productive power or the species. But Marx does not ask what this is.

For Marx, the human being is the species or the totality of all his essential powers and thus the authentic productive power. But we discover a strange 'surplus' in this human being, a surplus which does not express itself as productive power and is thus not visible from the Marxist standpoint.

This 'surplus' is even more clearly visible from another angle. Although for Marx man is essentially the species as the totality of all of his essential powers (the essential powers are his essence – that is what we have to hear) – *he dies*. Man as the individual species-being is *mortal*. And the only thing Marx has to say to us about human mortality is: '*Death* seems to be a harsh victory of the species over the particular individual and to contradict the species' unity, but the particular individual is only a *particular generic being* and as such mortal.'[11] Marx takes this contradiction between the species and the individual to be a contradiction between man and being (as the totality of the powers of production), since in the context of this quotation Marx also calls the whole of the species, whereby the whole of the powers of production is to be understood, 'being'. Thus, this distinction between being and man appears in spite of their essential unity, in spite of the fact that man as concrete individual is only the specific, individualized and concretized species, is only a specific productive power. Marx is obviously not very concerned about the absolutely unavoidable finitude of this individual, his inevitable death; he simply neglects this facticity in favour of the species, i.e. in favour of the totality of the powers of production and of production along with the satisfactions which belong to it. Thus, he can also write:

> The individual and generic life of man are not *distinct*, however much – and necessarily so – the mode of existence of individual life is either a more *particular* or more *general* mode of generic life, or generic life a more *particular* or *universal* mode of individual life. As *generic consciousness* man asserts his real *social life* and merely repeats his actual existence in thought just as, conversely, generic existence asserts itself in generic consciousness and in its universality exists explicitly as a thinking being.[12]

Thus, Marx thinks that the entire distinction between the individual and the species consists in the fact that the individual is merely a more specific or more general concretization of the species itself; as a concrete individual man is merely a *specific* species-being. The fact that he must, as such, die, this is for Marx a trivial accident; and for this reason the distinction between the concrete individual and the species is in Marx basically no distinction at all. They constitute a unity, and this is all that matters for Marx.

But in spite of this asserted unity, there is 'something' proper to every concrete individual, something which simply cannot be inherent in the species. This is the absolutely unavoidable finitude and mortality of the individual, his facticity. Concrete, factual individuals die, the species does not: the species is fundamentally a *death-less* being. If the concrete individual man were to see only the species-being in himself, nothing but productive power, he would completely lose sight of his death, his mortality. And this is precisely what is impossible for an individual living his real life. Marx simply ignores this human facticity when he asserts that man's individual and species life are nevertheless not different. Such an assertion is blind to the entire, all-encompassing realm of the facticity of the individual, which extends into every moment of this individual life and stamps it as a human life; it neglects this realm in favour of the species understood as the whole of the powers of production. This occurs in spite of the fact that Marx wanted to thematize precisely the concrete human individual, liberating it from its reduction to mere labour power as a commodity which includes all other reductions. But his original understanding of this human being as species or as the totality of the powers of production blinds him to the facticity of man which manifests itself most clearly in his mortality. And this facticity of mortality is not unimportant. It is decisively present in one way or the other in all human production, in all human satisfaction, in every expression of human life. It is not something theoretical, nor something practical, not a thing at all, not even a thing of thought (*Gedankending*). It is thus more than questionable whether human activity can become visible *as human* when this facticity is systematically ignored. But it is also by no means clear just what kind of thought might be adequate to this fact of death in relation to life. Our topic here is contemporary 'practical philosophy', and this topic, when understood correctly, might well move in the realm we have sketched, although it is also misleading.

Marx certainly knew – as does each of us – that human beings die, that the concrete individual is mortal in the sense that its life comes to an end. But Marx overlooks the simple fact that man *lives* as a mortal creature. And this is by no means equivalent to the mere statement that the individual dies at the end of its life. And it may well be that when we speak of the life-world, this simple fact that man *lives* as a mortal creature will be seen to be the basic structure of the life-world, fundamental for all other structures. From his standpoint Marx necessarily overlooks the fact that the facticity of every human act of production, satisfaction and enjoyment is qua *human* act essentially determined by human *mortality*. This human mortality, with which every human being *lives*, cannot be ignored as something towards which this creature is indifferent, which is merely accidental, for it itself *belongs* to the human being. How this is to be adequately thought remains unclear, since the new positive thought which Marx projects is of no help at this point. However, neither can the traditional philosophy and metaphysics circumscribe that point from which this problem can be attacked. Neither the old styles of thought nor Marxist thought offers us an appropriate *topos*. We thus find ourselves in a u-topia; we are displaced. It would seem that it is the whole of philosophical thought to date which ties us to this u-topia and leaves us without any orientation.

Thus, talk about practical philosophy is insidious, it can mislead us; to be sure, it speaks most decisively about what it is to be human, but can we still try to think about what it is to be human in a practical–philosophical manner after all that has been said? What have we said? In the first place, that we do not have the option of returning to the old philosophy or to positive knowledge as a whole. But we encountered three unexpected problems, problems which remain invisible, unexplainable and thus obscure for the Marxist standpoint. The first is modern science and technology, which is taken to be a means and yet turns out to be *determinative of being itself*. The second is that essential difference or distance to being as species in the sense of the totality of the powers of production which is intrinsic to man as man. The third is that facticity of mortality, according to which man *lives* as a mortal, such that mortality must belong to the essence of man himself. All of these are questions, questions for which I do not have any ready-made answers. But genuine questions are of greater value for thought than ready-made answers.

The fundamental constellation of human life today is an unbridgeable schism and thus a difference between that subjectivity which is active in this or that manner and the facticity of mortality. It is unimportant whether this subjectivity be called spirit, will to life, will to power, realm of values, species, totality of essential powers, totality of powers of production or whatever. This discrepancy, this difference in the essence of humanity, must first be experienced. And for precisely this reason, the basic position of Marx's thought remains valid for us today, *but not in any dogmatic sense*.

Notes

1 Immanuel Kant, *Kant's Critique of Practical Reason and Other Works on the Theory of Ethics*, trans. T. K. Abbott, London, 1909, p. 119; *Groundwork of the Metaphysics of Morals*, trans. H. J. Paton, New York, Barnes & Noble, 1948, p. 91.

2 G. W. F. Hegel, 'Spirit sure of itself. Morality', VI C.
3 Karl Marx, *Grundrisse*, trans. Martin Nicolaus, New York, Vintage Books, 1973.
4 Frederick Engels, *Zur Lage der arbeitenden Klasse in England*, in *Marx-Engels Werke*, vol. 22, Berlin, Dietz Verlag, 1963, p. 316f.
5 Cf. A. Schopenhauer, *Preisschrift über die Grundlage der Moral*, II, §7.
6 Karl Marx, *A Contribution to the Critique of Political Economy*, trans. S. W. Ryazanskaya, Moscow, Progress Publishers, 1970, pp. 20–1.
7 According to Marx, one can view the historical development of modern technology and science from two different sides. In the first place, modern technology certainly was developed under the conditions of the process of capital, and in this development capitalist competition plays an important role. But for capital, science–technology (which itself appears as a form of capital) is an – always important – *means* of its self-realization. Since capital is the genuine subject of the capitalist world epoch, modern science–technology is the *means* which it posits for its own self-realization; it is thus a means for the goal of the faster quantitative growth of capital. Thus, in the capitalist world epoch modern science–technology has a *capital–instrumentalist* character.

On the other hand, modern science–technology – freed from its narrow form as capital, thus essentially – is a means that man himself (who is the actual subject) posits for the actuation of his essential powers; thus, it is the means for the mediation between man and his object or actual object. Thus, Marx understands modern science–technology essentially *anthropologically–instrumentally*. Only as such is it a moment of the powers of production.
8 This is demonstrated in an especially instructive and revealing manner in the *Paris Manuscripts*, in the chapter 'Private Property and Communism' and in other places. But it should be noted that one cannot read the early works of Marx alone, but must understand them in the context of his later works.
9 Karl Marx, *Pariser Manuskripte, III*, *Marx-Engels Werke*, Supplementary volume I, Berlin, Dietz Verlag, 1967, p. 539.
10 Ibid., pp. 539f.
11 Ibid., p. 539.
12 Ibid.

CHAPTER 10

Behavioural norm and behavioural context

Bernhard Waldenfels (Bochum)

With norm and context I have chosen two perspectives in terms of which human behaviour can be viewed and interrogated. The decisive aspect for me is the reciprocal relations between them. Under *behavioural norm* (or behavioural rule) I understand, in accordance with normal usage, a general behavioural prescription, i.e. one which is not restricted to a unique situation, a prescription which is given expression in the reciprocal expectations of the given actors and which simultaneously serves as the justification or ground of the corresponding conduct. Under *behavioural context* I understand the sum total of behavioural acts, be it of one's own acts or those of the others, simultaneous or successive, to which the conduct in question is internally related; this context has, to use Husserlian language, a noematic and a noetic side. Thus, context is a narrower concept than situation in that the latter contains all of the relevant circumstances of behaviour. The behaviour or conduct I am interested in here is, of course, a significant event which can be characterized as intentional or rule-governed, and is not to be understood behaviouristically.[1] This kind of concept seems to me to be neutral and flexible enough to open up the field of problems I shall discuss.

The first question I shall deal with is: is it in principle possible to give a complete justification of an action by means of an argument which justifies or grounds the *norms* to which the actor appeals? The negative answer to this question leads to a further question: doesn't the *context* of the action also play a role in the attempt to vindicate the action and, if this is the case, what would this role be and what kind of justification do we find here? Thus, I consider the context not merely as a precondition for understanding utterances and actions. The fact that meaning is to a great extent context-dependent is one of the truisms of hermeneutics and the pragmatics of language: one cannot 'tear utterances out of their context'; the concrete sense of sentences depends on specific situations. My claim is much stronger: the context is involved in the process of coming to terms with one another, it determines the very possibility of producing a consensus and indeed is essential to the productivity of human conduct in general.

This dual set of questions corresponds to alternative theoretical approaches. On the one hand one can opt for the possibility of giving a complete justification and grounding of human behaviour by appeal to norms; that which does not measure up to the norm falls victim to critique or is shoved off into a peripheral zone of 'indifference'. Tendencies in this direction can be found in recent critical theory and in Habermas's universal pragmatics, and it is fully realized in Apel's transcendental hermeneutics or transcendental pragmatics. I say tendencies, since what we find here are developing theories whose future direction is not entirely clear. If my critique seems to be somewhat overdrawn, there are good reasons for this.[2] What I want to avoid is any appearance of participating in a tug of war: transcendental on the one side and empirical on the other; on the contrary, I think that the attempt to undercut the opposition between *a priori* and *a posteriori*[3] deserves more attention; similar tendencies are to be found in phenomenology. But I doubt that a normatively oriented reconstruction of the course of human development can lead to a satisfactory intermediate position, and I wonder if the initial Marxism has not ended up in all too neo-Kantian waters – which would be only *one* sort of revision and surely not the most satisfying. To give a clear formulation of the critical point in advance: under these presuppositions the context of behaviour is minimized to being the mere boundary conditions for the application of norms.

My alternative approach aims at giving the context of behaviour a central role in the analysis and justification of behaviour. This results in a shift of accent: universal norms are merely the framework for the productivity of a conduct which continually develops new contexts and derives specific motives from them.

This alternative approach is open to the obvious charge that the question concerning validity is minimized or even repressed in the recourse to *existing* norms and rules. In this context one could develop an extensive front in which certain varieties of phenomenology and hermeneutics, linguistic philosophy following the late Wittgenstein, the historically differentiated philosophy of science of Thomas Kuhn, Luhmann's systems theory as well as so-called structuralism (where contextuality with a linguistic accent plays an especially important role) would find their places, and a common front of this sort would not be so far-fetched. This is an astonishing variety which hardly allows for a unitary for or against, but perhaps it can yield some central points of view such as that of contingent sense configurations and systems of rules which are subject to transformation but cannot become the embodiment of a perfect rationality (*sich nicht 'aufheben' lassen*).

I shall close this introduction with a few rather general remarks which should cast some light on the broader horizon of my question. It would hardly be productive to attempt a frontal confrontation between the relativity of the context and the absoluteness of norms. This approach would not only be all too simplistic, yielding little more than a renewal of disputes which have been played through time and again: the crucial thing here is to arrive at a productive balance. There is a very great difference between applying norms to univocal contexts and developing them out of ambiguous contexts. A theory of human praxis and history which emphasizes application is quite different from one which sees development to be the essential phenomenon.

In this respect, it seems to me that recent critical theory has all too naïvely taken up the traditional distinctions between facticity and normativity. Here critique means that one subjects the factually existing to an ideal measure – with the result that human knowledge and action appear merely as a process which univocally moves towards an anticipated goal, realizing this goal step by step as long as things go well. There is of course a great difference between a pregiven law which is immanent in the things and a self-legislated law which is intrinsic to human activity; but in both cases, in the final analysis reason is elevated above the contingency of the factual. Doesn't this kind of approach fail to do justice to the productivity of human conduct and to the openness and ambiguity of the historical process?

In contrast, a primary orientation in terms of the context of behaviour and its ambiguity signifies the relinquishment of a *univocal hierarchy* of cognitive and practical goals; the vertical mediation finds its counterpart in a horizontal mediation, an open mediation on a middle level. This simultaneity and successiveness do not obey a law of continual ascent but rather a law of the series, a nexus which does not rule out progress, but one which does make talk about *the* one and only unitary progress questionable.

This is a field in which phenomenology can carry on a critical (and self-critical) dialogue with Marxism – in the expectation that the latter will more decisively distance itself from the more extreme claims of the Hegelian tradition, at least more decisively and differently than critical theory has done to date. This may lead to new difficulties, but it is important that we make the effort.

1 The normative justification of behaviour

A critical theory which lives up to its name has to prove itself in the art of making distinctions; this is also true for the question concerning the justification of behaviour. The demarcations and divisions which follow have the task of determining the point at which validity claims make their appearance, of determining the procedure by means of which validity is checked and of demonstrating the capabilities of this procedure. It will turn out that the manner in which the lines are drawn has important implications. I shall give only a brief sketch of Habermas's well-known theory in order to clearly mark out the point of departure for my own critical considerations; it goes without saying that I shall leave unmentioned a great deal that is plausible and worthy of serious consideration, since it belongs in other contexts.[4]

I shall begin with communicative action as the locus of the mediation between different levels and regions. In Habermas's work, of course, the autonomy of communicative action is derived from the distinction between work and interaction; this distinction was drawn with a critical eye on Marx, who is thought to have mixed the two under the title 'social praxis' (*KI*, p. 62). Later, under Apel's influence, the opposition between the constitution of objects and the validity of sense is brought in to clarify the initial distinction (*P*, p. 166); this is the point at which our own considerations begin. In the most recent projection of a 'universal pragmatics', the problematic is almost exclusively concentrated on the questions of validity which are posed on the communicative level; the distinction between the various levels is thus presupposed.

(a) *The double structure of linguistic communication*. Ordinary communication moves on two levels. We come to an understanding *about something*, i.e. we thematize objects which we identify and about which we predicate something; this occurs in independent sentences with propositional content. We come to an understanding *with someone*, i.e. we assert states of affairs or question, recommend, promise something; this occurs in dominating performative sentences, which determine the pragmatic contextual sense of the dependent sentences (for example: I promise you that . . . ; I assure you that . . .). *In that* we assert or recommend something, we make an implicit claim to truth or correctness. Thus, communicative action is the locus of *claims to validity*. The double structure involves a reference backward (b) and a reference forward (c).

(b) *The constitution of objects in experience*. Communicative action refers us *back* to a prior region of objective experience in which that about which an understanding is possible is constituted.[5] In this context, *constitution* signifies the categorial structuring of possible objects of experience, the projection of a material *a priori* 'which enables us to open up reality by objectivating it' (*P*, p. 166; cf. *HL*, p. 209). The region of experience is *prior to all validity claims*; the only distinction here is that between the objectivity of experience, i.e. of an experience which can be shared intersubjectively, and mere 'subjectivity', i.e. merely supposed experience. Already at this early stage of the argument one can wonder if this is not an all too mono-empirical way of seeing things, whether namely the possibility of *sharing* experiences doesn't say too little concerning the possibility of gaining common experience; 'identical meanings' (cf. *UP*, p. 8) are not sufficient for common meanings – here one can learn more (in spite of all the problems) from Husserl than from Kant, especially with reference to what 'social praxis' in Marx might mean.

According to Habermas, the constitution of experience unfolds in two fundamental regions: in the region of *things and events*, which correspond to sense experience (and observation), and the region of *persons and utterances*, which corresponds to communicative experience (and understanding). The two modes of experience are distinguished by their differing relations to action. The things of sense experience are also objects of *instrumental* action. Their objectivity is confirmed in the success of that action which is grounded in experience; our experiences are corrected by reactions on the side of reality. This region thus remains truth-indifferent. The persons of communicative experience on the other hand are at the same time and primarily partners in *communicative* action, participants in interactions. Communicative experience itself extends into a realm of validity claims, since it presupposes communicative action; understanding presumes agreement.

(c) *Reflection on validity in discourse.* Since communicative action only raises validity claims and does not itself redeem them, it refers *forward* to a higher region, to the so-called discourse. Here it is not the objects of experience which are thematized; the *validity claims* of theoretical opinions and practical recommendations in which we come to an understanding concerning the objects of experience are thematized reflectively; the critical examination of claims leads to their redemption or dissolution.

This discourse is a kind of dialogue within the *epoché*: the experiences and actions of communicative praxis are suspended, their intrinsic validity claims left undecided. This suspension makes possible an isolation of questions of validity from questions of genesis (*HL*, pp. 117, 200); this is to yield a conscious *disengagement* from the context of experience and action (*P*, pp. 174–5; *HL*, p. 117).

The goal of this examination procedure is the reasonable consensus, its method is that of argumentation, i.e. supplying reasons. The discourse itself as the implementation of the procedure embodies the ideal conditions under which validity claims are redeemable and a well-grounded consensus attainable, namely the 'unlimited and domination-free dialogue'. If we would only communicate with one another long enough in this manner, the result would be a consensus which *per se* would be a true consensus (*HL*, p. 139).

(d) *Theoretical and practical discourse.* There is a certain difference between two forms of discourse.[6] Theoretical discourse (examination of opinions) presumes experiences, which as such are *eo ipso* objective, i.e. universal. The universal is, as it were, encountered. Practical discourse (examination of recommendations for action) on the other hand takes interests and needs as its point of departure, and they are not *eo ipso* universal, but rather possibly *universalizable*. The universal must be produced. Practical discourse aids this process by examining the validity claims of norms (this claim aims *eo ipso* at universality), and only accepts those norms which suggest actions in which the demands of universalizability are satisfied. In the case of essentially particular interests we would be referred to compromise, a result of judicious action and negotiation against the background of a balance of power.[7]

Thus, the justification of practical conduct takes place by means of the justification of behavioural norms; the criterium of legitimacy is universalizability. So much for the first result. Now we shall move on to the consequences for a theory of praxis and historical progress.[8]

(e) *Conception of praxis.* As I noted in the introduction, communicative action occupies a middle position. If we consider communicative action in practical contexts, namely as an exchange of recommendations for action and as a shared decision procedure, it signifies nothing more than *the application of pre-established norms to pregiven situations.*

The *process of arriving at decisions* can be reconstructed in the form of a practical syllogism which connects the 'posited goal and the information concerning means within the situational context' (Apel, I, op. cit., p. 69). The universal premises (norms) of this syllogism can be examined and justified in practical discourses, the particular premises (situation as the sum total of initial conditions) is theoretical discourses. *Carrying out the decision* would be a matter of instrumental action, which falls under criteria for success; this would produce a result which once again would take its place as a pregiven situation for new projects. The *decision itself* would consist in volition as the mediation between normative 'ought' and practical 'can', between that which was justified in the reflection on validity and that which can be tested in instrumental action. Above and beyond these there would remain only an existential and an empirical remainder. An existential remainder: the justification of volition is not the volition itself (cf. Apel, II, op. cit., p. 412; also Habermas, *HL*, p. 139); an empirical remainder: factual circumstances such as limited time and the conflict of interests can make a complete justification impossible, such that engagement in the concrete situation involves risks (Apel, II, pp. 426ff.) but this does not impinge on the in principle redeemability of the validity claims.

Praxis as communicative action thus moves completely and exclusively within the framework of that which is *normatively required* (*quaestiones iuris*) and the *factually possible* (*quaestiones facti*). But these two are not rigid factors, as we shall see.

(f) *Conception of progress.* Historical progress moves on the two corresponding levels (cf. Habermas, *P*, pp. 182ff.; *HL*, p. 270ff.), on the one hand the level of instrumental action, where *success* is decisive and where it is a matter of survival, on the other hand on the level of communicative action, where decisions concerning *truth and correctness* must be made and where it is a matter of the proper life; here discourse is the tribunal. Leaving scientific-technical progress aside, progress consists in the gradual dissolution (*Aufhebung*) of the contradiction between a *real* and an *ideal* communication community, i.e. in the universalization of morality. Thus, the *direction* of the development is already determined; the only thing that remains open is whether and when and how the goal will be reached; this would be the empiristic remainder which would globally correspond to the moment of decision. In this sense Habermas earlier propagated an 'empirically controlled philosophy of history in practical intent'. Apel obviously oscillates between Hegel–Marx on the one, Kant–Peirce on the other side. Whereas he on the one hand speaks of a possible dissolution of the dialectical contradiction between real and ideal communication community (Apel, II, op. cit., pp. 430f.), in another place he speaks of a 'regulative principle' on the basis of which the idea of progress 'could not count on something empirical ever corresponding to the idea' (Apel, I, op. cit., p. 75) – one would be left with an 'eternal ought'.

Apel's postulate extends into the history of science, for example when he objects to Thomas Kuhn: we must postulate that a later theory (such as Einstein's) has surpassed an earlier (such as Newton's) (Apel, I, op. cit., p. 46). *Must* we really? But the, compared to Hegel, faint-hearted manner in which progress is conceived and the degree to which the productivity of human action is lost sight of is shown by the style of the polemic against Gadamer's hermeneutics: the insistence on 'understanding better' (Apel, I, op. cit., p. 50) – as if that were the point! And if it is a matter of progress over against Homer's epics or Plato's dialogues, wouldn't it be a matter of '*doing* it better', of surpassing by means of one's own production or in a higher form of production? One should either demand more or less.

To summarize: in the theory of communicative action which has just been sketched, the context of behaviour only plays a marginal role in comparison to the norms of behaviour. Viewed *structurally*, we have a vertical mediation: validity-free constitution of objects in experience – validity claims in communicative action – examination of validity in discourse; and viewed *genetically* we have a corresponding ascent or progressive movement. The context, i.e. the lateral relation of conduct to conduct, appears as a mere marginal condition for the appropriation and application of norms, whereas the normative justification liberates itself from this context and in doing so produces the universalization.

The limits of this way of approaching things announces itself in striking blank spots. Even when it is not a matter of blind spots, but rather of a deliberate focus of attention, one must ask whether this is not in conflict with the comprehensive claims of the theory. I shall list a few points which seem to be worth further examination and which lead away from an all-too-global confrontation:

(i) The problem of thematization (choice of theme, constancy of theme, change of theme) is – as far as I can see – never seriously taken up by Habermas, although shared thematization is immediately relevant for a complete theory of communication. It seems to me that Habermas parries Luhmann's objections a bit too quickly in this respect (objections which are grounded in the phenomenological work of Husserl and above all Gurwitsch and Schütz). Is the reason that this problematic simply does not fit into the general approach? Indeed, thematization neither fits into the realm of that which is here called experience and given the index of objectivity, nor in the realm of universal validity claims; a theme is, as Frege says about *Sinn*, neither purely subjective nor the object itself. On the other hand, that thematization which opens up a thematic field does have a great deal to do with the context of behaviour, as we shall see.

(ii) Universal pragmatics limits its analyses to speech acts as 'elementary utterances' in the singular. This involves a deliberate abstraction from *complementary acts* such as question–answer as well as from the *variable context* of specific speech situations, such as contingent, linguistic and extra-linguistic boundary conditions as well as personality and role structures (*HL*, pp. 101–8; *UP*, p. 216, n. 67). The linguistic restriction to individual sentences as the basic units of language[9] finds its pragmatic counterpart in the basic units of speech. The reason for this restriction is called by name: 'The restriction is the result of the aspect of conditions of validity' (*UP*, p. 31). If one restricts oneself to the intelligibility and acceptability of utterances (ibid., p. 59), one can abstract from the way in which utterances are linked together, from that which we have called context. But can one then claim to deal with the '*universal* presuppositions of communicative action' or the 'universal conditions of possible agreement' (ibid., p. 1)? Is everything that does not belong to the 'universal basis of the validity of speech' (ibid., p. 5) thereby merely empirical–contingent and thus the subject matter of a purely empirical pragmatics? Isn't this restriction an expression of the traditional schema of validity versus mere facticity, a schema which belongs to a transcendental philosophy which stands in need of revision? Is the concept of coming to terms with one another (*Verständigung*) (ibid., pp. 3f.) not conceived in much too narrow a manner when it ignores shared common thematization and the manner in which utterances interlock with one another? The co-ordination of question and answer, to use the most obvious example, surely has its place in the universal structure of speech situations, or better, in the formation of structure and the creation of situations. The variability of the context does not mean that the context itself is a mere variant of an invariant structure. Shoving the analyses of context and conversation into the merely empirical realm takes the bite out of such investigations.

(iii) It is no accident that the exemplary sketch of discursive justification procedures usually appeals to a very *narrow class of speech acts*; we find a definite partiality for assertions, recommendations and warnings (cf. *LdD*), obviously because validity claims play a major role in such examples. But what about questions, requests, promises – are they perhaps not justifiable in the same manner?

(iv) This leads to the suspicion that the concept of justification itself has been conceived too narrowly, such that it covers only normative justification. The question 'Why do you act the way you do?' is surely not identical with the question: 'With what right do you act that way?'[10] Critical theory tends to give primacy to the model of the court, where concrete motivation takes a back seat to legitimation, quite in contrast to the case of deliberation or consultations, the second field in which classical Aristotelian rhetoric finds application.[11] In addition, it seems to me that Habermas's concept of motivation is anything but clear. On the one hand, he speaks of 'empirical motives' which belong to the data of the situation, not to the reasons (*LdD*, p. 385); on the other hand, he talks of a 'rational motivation' (ibid., p. 386), and not as a special or limiting case, but rather as the ideal case. Correspondingly, in the so-called discourse we are to give reasons why we act in one way or the other in a given situation (*HL*, pp. 116–18) – without any differentiation or restriction concerning the why. This means that so long as the behaviour is capable of being justified, as opposed to being merely explained, it is subject to a normative justification of a universal character, which is always potentially a total and final justification. This one-sided fixation on universal validity claims and the resulting exaggeration of such claims is perhaps the reason for the deficient conception of praxis and the all-too-simple-minded faith in progress.

The alternative approach which I shall sketch in the following pages can also be read as a complementary attempt, but only if at the same time the emphasis is shifted and the general lines of questioning are shifted; for context is not an empirical adornment to the seriousness of the normative.

2 The context of behaviour

I began by defining the context of behaviour as the sum total of behavioural acts to which a given action is internally related. Before taking a closer look at this, I would like to sketch the problem which underlies this situation as sharply as possible.

That all conduct is embedded in a context is something that no one would deny; the question is *how* the context is to be conceived and dealt with in a theory of conduct. If one presupposes the classical dichotomy: here questions concerning right, there questions concerning fact, then every given utterance as act of uttering is itself a fact which can be theoretically determined and understood, taken into account practically and steered. But to the extent that it, as an assertion or recommendation, raises a validity claim, it is justified or not (true or false, correct or incorrect), it becomes the object of agreement or rejection. If this dichotomy is exhaustive, then the context must be reckoned to the data of the situation, i.e. it belongs to the boundary conditions for the application of norms, both for the actor and for the examiner. My alternative is this: the context opens up an intermediate realm which eludes the division into a sphere of the purely factual (facts raise no claims) and a sphere of the purely normative (counterfactual claims), since it has to do with *situated claims*. The 'purely factual' and the 'purely normative' are limiting notions which are essentially the *result* of a twofold process of factualizing and idealizing, and both processes presuppose the intermediate realm and are limited by it. It is thus not a matter of transcending the gap between idea and fact by means of something which is beyond idea and fact and which would yield the total mediation of the two, but rather of undercutting the division by means of a realm which lies this side of idea and fact, a realm in which sense is produced, but under contingent conditions.

(a) *Combination and selection*. I shall begin my reflections by, as I have already done elsewhere, discussing a schema from structural linguistics which seems to be capable of overcoming certain bottlenecks. A theory of language such as Saussure's, which does not assume ultimate *elements*, working instead with ultimate *differences*, is forced to grant the context (understood here in the broadest sense) a central influence, since wherever something can only exist by setting itself off from others the idea of a positive something which is merely 'embedded' in further contexts disappears. Context is no longer merely a matter of the concretion of products, but a matter of the production itself; and production is itself fundamentally a continuation and extension of contexts. Let us take a closer look.

In Saussure we find the distinction between two axes of language, a *syntagmatic* axis, where linguistic units are serially ordered (e.g. h-o-u-s-e), and a *paradigmatic* axis, where units are exchanged for one another (e.g. *h*-ouse, *l*-ouse, *m*-ouse). In the modified version of Roman Jakobson,[12] which abandons the mere linearity of the significant, this signifies that every linguistic unit is subject to a double principle. On the one hand there is a principle of sequentiality and coexistence; to this extent, every linguistic operation is simultaneously *combination and context formation*, it deals with units which belong together. On the other hand, there is a principle of alternativity; in this respect every linguistic operation is simultaneously *selection and substitution*, it deals with equivalent units. This holds for the levels of sound formation, word formation, sentence formation and finally for the formation of sequences of sentences, whereby the freedom of selection grows. An example for the last level would be question and answer: the question opens up a limited field and the answer takes up this opening by making a selection within this predetermined field. Combination and selection cannot be separated. When one of the two moments is weakened, this leads to speech and communications disturbances; combination without selection yields compulsive behaviour within a *closed* context, selection without combination an arbitrary, incoherent behaviour within a *completely open context*.[13] Between these two pathological extremes there is a scale of context dependency. One can think, for example, of the typical distinction between questions which call for words as answers (yes/no) and questions which call for sentences as answers, or of the relation between spontaneous and ritualized utterances and actions, which varies according to the degree to which a society or a culture is conventionalized. One could distinguish between corresponding types of speech, parallel to the way in which Jakobson co-ordinates the fundamental stylistic figures of metonymy and metaphor with corresponding types of texts. To be sure, this leads into the empirical realm, but it is a structurally preformed empirical realm.

(b) *Variety of contexts*. If we are to make the linguistic schema productive for behaviour as a whole, the concept of context must be differentiated and broadened. The breadth and depth of variation of behaviour would correspond to a corresponding variety of contexts. I shall restrict myself to a few hints here. As we have already seen, within the realm of *linguistic* behaviour one can construct a scale which moves from phonemic, semantic and syntactic contexts up to the pragmatic context of series of utterances. Just how this scale can be carried over to *extra-linguistic* behaviour such as bodily expressions and actions (thus, e.g., in the search for ultimate units of movement, the '*Kinemen*', and in the establishment of a grammar of expression) is another question; at the very least, we must pose the problem of context formation and transformation in the case of extra-linguistic behaviour. *Formally* we would have to distinguish in each case between a more intimate and a more distant, actual and habitual, personal and anonymous-typified context, and there is every reason to think that one would have to go much further. Finally, as we have already suggested in connection with Jakobson, in every case we are confronted not only with a *successive sequence* of behavioural acts and utterances, but also with a *simultaneous intertwining* of forms of behaviour and utterance. Only within this poly-dimensionality does behaviour become a text, a 'fabric' in which linguistic and extra-linguistic, one's own behaviour and that of others continually mesh with one another. I have tried to show what this implies for a theory of communication in another context.[14] In restricting myself here to the successive connections between behavioural expressions, this is a deliberate simplification which is accounted for and justified by the questions under discussion here.

Generalizing the linguistic schema, we can say the following: all conduct picks up on actual conduct by making choices from modes of conduct which are possible within the given situation. We now have to inquire into the kind of connection and into the criteria for selection. Question and answer, which always also include a practical component, can serve as a model here.

(c) *Empiristic model*. According to the empiristic model in its classical Humean form, we merely ascertain and, on the basis of empirical hypothetical laws, explain that *b* follows *a*. The behavioural connection with its context is reduced to an *empirical contiguity*, to the mere regularity of a sequence of facts. The selection is correspondingly reduced to a *statistical frequency* or *increasing probability* in the individual case. We are confronted with purely factual questions. According to this approach it makes no sense to talk about an inner connection between question and answer, to characterize the question as the question as to. . . , to characterize the answer as the answer to. . . The same holds for the co-ordination of actions and generally for the way in which actions hang together. Husserl would object that a question inaugurates a sense which can be fulfilled or disappointed; Wittgenstein would reply that human behaviour is constituted by rules which the future course of conduct can follow or fail to follow. The context of fulfilment and the context of rule-governed conduct, each in its own way, go beyond mere ascertainable contiguity. This is all that I can say concerning the empiristic model in this context.

(d) *The normative model.* According to this model, which constitutes our critical partner in this dialogue, there is the additional factor that the fact that *b* follows *a* or not is derived from norms and grounded. The connection between *a* and *b* in this case could be characterized as that of *axiological consequence* (or inconsequence). The criteria for selection are provided by the norm which, under specific circumstances, depending on the situation and context, calls for or forbids a specific mode of conduct. Thus, the factual questions are supplemented by validity questions, whereby the claim to validity always involves a universal claim to validity pure and simple.

My objections concern the conditions and limits of the normative derivation, especially the *range* of the practical syllogism.

(i) First an observation: every specific norm is reducible to the if-then form. 'If one has taken out a loan, one should repay it within the time limit prescribed' (this is Habermas's example in *LdD*, pp. 386f.). Without this general form we would only have singular imperatives which would themselves be in need of a justification.

(ii) A recommendation can only be derived from norm and situation when the situation is so *univocally* determined or univocally ordered that the action in question is the *only* action which satisfies the norm. This is true, at least to some extent, for the example which Habermas (one-sidedly) selected. If among the data of the situation we include the fact that I have committed myself to a specific action under specific circumstances (e.g. to the repayment of the loan), then the decision has already fallen; the only thing that remains is adhering to the decision and carrying it out. And if it, as is the case in many everyday situations, is a question of routinized decisions, we are confronted with prefabricated series of actions with, as it were, action-phrases which – as in clichés – are in fact strongly codified, but for precisely this reason are not very surprising.

(iii) The context of the action which implicitly or explicitly appears in the minor premise of the practical syllogism (for example: I have borrowed money) is not itself justified in the procedure in question; it thus constitutes an unjustified remainder (just as in the case of empiristic explanatory procedures, where the factual assertion is not itself explained within the same explanation). But here we are confronted with the decisive problem of an anterior *determination of the question and the theme* which first makes specific norms applicable. 'Whoever says *A* must also say *B*' – *if* he says *A* in the first place. The decision as formation and transformation, as 'definition' of a situation, is not derivable from norms, since the norms first come into play when a specific situation is given. I cannot resist citing Luhmann in this context: 'The question concerning reasons arises only on the basis of contingency. The subject must first be thought of as contingent selectivity before it can ground its "this way and no other". And the selections, and not merely the justifications, to say nothing of the truths, become problems in intersubjectively constituted contexts of interaction.'[15] The problem is quite far-reaching; one could bring in Husserl's objections to Kant, whom Husserl criticizes for having skipped over an important level; the question concerning the legitimation of worldly (mundane) experience presupposes the constitution (formation) of a world. Can one refer this world-formation to a preliminary pre-communicative realm? This will hardly do: the 'definition' of the situation itself implies social agreement and rules, since its contingent character cannot be subordinated to a purely purposive-rationally steered process of adaptation. This objection seems to be so obvious that I wonder if a misunderstanding is not at work here.

Be that as it may, if the justificatory procedure encounters an inner limit, such that an exhaustive justification of a given course of conduct cannot be produced by recourse to mere norms and facts, we must wonder if there is not an *open connection* between question and answer or more generally between phases of behaviour, a connection which goes beyond the alternatives we have discussed up to now.

(e) *The coherence of behaviour within contexts*. In order to characterize the connection between or the transition from one piece of conduct to another, I would like to speak of a coherence in a specific sense which means more than empirical contiguity but also less than axiological consequence. It would stand for the *compatibility* between conduct *b* and conduct *a*. In addition to the criteria true/false, correct/incorrect, we now have the criterium *suitable/unsuitable*: something is relevant, 'pertinent' in a specific connection or not. We can see that this is an independent criterium from the fact that when we talk past one another an answer can simultaneously be true as an assertion and unsuitable as an answer ('Where is Munich?' – 'It is raining in Munich') and from the fact that when our actions do not 'hang together' an action can obey all the norms but still be out of place (the wrong gift, superfluous advice, protesting too much, etc.).[16] We thus have various possible combinations: (i) true/pertinent, (ii) true/not pertinent, (iii) false/pertinent, (iv) false/not pertinent; for actions one can easily construct the corresponding combinations with correct/incorrect. Of course, this does not exclude the possibility that something be suitable on one level while being all the more unsuitable on another level. We are familiar with deliberate incongruences in art (blatant in surrealism) and other contexts. Here we can see the poly-dimensionality of the context, which was mentioned earlier, at work, allowing a polyphony of expression and thus background and underground resonances and dissonances.

So much for the connection and cohesion of conduct, now to selection. Selection comes into play because and to the extent that conduct *merely* fits to other conduct. To be sure, the field of possibilities is restricted by the context and by rules, the possibilities are not arbitrary. But on the other hand, conduct only very rarely fits to the situation and context the way a key fits a lock or the way the letters fit into the squares of a crossword puzzle; this kind of prefabricated context is hardly a suitable paradigm. Normally there is a whole series of answers which are both suitable and normatively legitimate ('Munich is in Europe, in Germany, in Bavaria. . .'). Thus, the transition from question to answer is usually neither arbitrary not practically necessary, but rather merely *motivated*, i.e. in this situation and taking account of the relevant rules, this or that speaks more or less for a specific answer. Rolling dice and the security of complete rationality are limiting cases; to turn them into normal cases would be to land in the pathological (here one need only study the existentialist Sartre with his perilous alternatives): 'as long as we are alive, our situation is open, which implies both that it calls up specially favoured modes of resolution, and also that it is powerless to bring one into being by itself'.[17] To come back to the linguistic once more, Saussure speaks of a 'relative motivatedness' within the arbitrariness of the linguistic system.[18] Finally, we should recall Husserl's account of horizonal implications and suggestions, which move in a field of open determinateness and thus create 'motivated possibilities' (*Ideas*, § 47), as well as Wittgenstein's conception of open rules which allow a certain latitude for progressive application and thus require not just discovery (*Finden*) but also invention (*Erfinden*).

(f) *Double justification of behaviour*. Conduct which not merely applies norms but simultaneously forms and transforms contexts makes a double justification possible. In the first place we have a *justification in terms of the context*. Here specific *motives* are given with reference to the demands of the context and situation. Question, request and demand raise as such specific claims, pose a 'demand' (*Zumutung*) (Husserl) which I can respond to or not. If I say that I said this or that because I was asked, this is *one* kind of justification in which the validity of that which I said is not in question. Here one could refer to the theory of narrative explanation (Danto), where events are taken up into the explanation. In addition, there is *justification in terms of norms*. It is only here that *general justificatory reasons* are given with reference to the demands which come from the norms themselves.

Since motivation and justification are not coextensive, a *total* justification which would transform a motivation into a completely 'rational motivation' is impossible. If one still insists on the demand for total legitimation of conduct, one reduces practical conduct to moral action and is thus left with only the tail end of practical philosophy. Concrete action would no longer allow of justification.

Conduct that moves in contexts and is codetermined by them involves only *open rules*; within the rules there is a certain latitude, a manoeuvre space which the rules themselves cannot fill in.[19] But this means that the context may no more be overloaded than the norm; if the norm taken by itself is not context-forming, the context alone is not norm-building. Coherence in the context and conformity with respect to norms complement one another.

(g) *The two-fold order (Regelhaftigkeit) of behaviour.* To the extent that rules are at work, we must make distinctions with reference to the conditions they are subject to on the basis of their if-then form. In the first place, there are *context specific* rules which refer to specific contexts of varying extent. These rules are contingent; here there is a certain latitude with respect to the rules themselves, not only within the rules. Here one could think of specific linguistic rules, of perceptual schemata, social forms, professional rules, rituals and so forth. On the other hand, there are – and here I am in agreement with Apel and Habermas – rules which are *context neutral*, which refer to any and every context. Such rules are essentially unrevisable, since this would bring conduct into contradiction with itself and negate the conditions of meaningful and ordered conduct itself. The model of argumentation which finds application here is already present in Aristotle, in Book IV of the *Metaphysics*. In this case we are dealing with what it means to be rule-governed in the first place in logical and moral realms, and in a sense also in linguistic realms, where so-called linguistic universals in Jakobson's sense cannot be completely denied the character of empirical universality.

Context-specific rules constitute only a *mobile* framework which more or less restricts possible selections, but itself rests in turn on selections and thus is formed and transformed in contexts, whereas the context-neutral rules provide a *fixed* framework which owes it universality to its lack of specificity. The important thing is to keep sight of the difference and avoid putting too much weight on the universal framework. What is ruled out is a *concrete universal system* of rules. The universal rules make possible a critique of contingent rule systems, but they do not allow that these be transcended (*aufhebt*) in a universalizing reflection, be it definitively or approximatively, since with the dissolution of the context the concretion disappears. Contingent systems of rules allow for *transformations*, but they cannot be transcended in the direction of the non-contingent.

(h) *Application to praxis and history*. I would like to close with a few suggestions concerning the *productivity* of praxis and the *ambiguity* of the course of history, both of which receive too little attention in critical theory.[20]

If one accepts the approach suggested here, praxis (including theoretical and poietic praxis) would be more than a mere application of norms and rules to situations and contexts which are the evolutionary result of a pre-communicative process of constitution. Praxis would signify structuring, forming, organization, articulation of reality, i.e. an – always shared – creation of contexts and situations against the background of pregiven contexts and situations. This would lead in part to *new* situations within the traditional framework (= the differentiation, further determination in the light of open rules), in part to *novel* situations which explode the traditional framework (= restructuring, reformation, redetermination involving an implicit transformation of the rules). This process occurs at a deeper level than that of any possible universal normativity.

Correspondingly, the development does not involve a univocal orientation towards *one* goal which can be approached via critique and by overcoming the gap between the factual and the normative; it is rather a matter of an ambiguous process which is dependent upon contingent selections, exhibits ruptures and discontinuities, and develops contingent rule systems which cannot be ordered as elements in a super-system. Here we find progress within the limits of a unitary thematic and to the extent that the results accumulate and allow a hierarchical ordering, but we cannot find progress pure and simple; here we find sense (and non-sense), but not *the* sense (and nonsense). This process would admit horizontal mediations: transformations, translations, but not a vertical mediation in the sense of a reflective integration, which would inevitably lead to either a vacuum or paralysis.

The unfinished character of the world would correspond to a motivated conduct and a situated thought which moves in contexts without degrading them to being the boundary conditions for universally valid norms. If emancipation is possible and necessary here, it is an emancipation *within* the context; but perhaps we don't have words for this.

Notes

1 Cf. my essay 'Die Verschränkung von Innen und Außen im Verhalten. Phänomenologische Ansatzpunkte zu einer nicht-behavioristischen Verhaltenstheorie', in *Phänomenologische Forschung*, vol. 2, 1976.

2 I have the impression that, for example, Dallmayr's attempt to bring Habermas and phenomenology or hermeneutics closer to one another is all too indirect, thought-provoking as this attempt is.

(Cf. *Materialien zu Habermas' 'Erkenntnis und Interesse'*, ed. W. Dallmayr, Frankfurt am Main, Suhrkamp, 1974.)

3 Cf. J. Habermas, 'What is Universal Pragmatics?' in *Communication and the Evolution of Society*, trans. Thomas McCarthy, Boston, Beacon Press, 1979, pp. 24–5. This work will be referred to in the text as *UP*.

4 I shall be referring to the following works of Habermas: *Knowledge and Human Interests*, trans. Jeremy J. Shapiro, Boston, Beacon Press, 1971 (referred to in text as *KI*); to the two contributions in J. Habermas and N. Luhmann, *Theorie der Gesellschaft oder Sozialtechnologie*, Fŗankfurt, Suhrkamp, 1971 (referred to in text as *HL*), especially pp. 101ff., 171–221; to 'Zur Logik des theoretischen und praktischen Diskurses' (referred to in text as *LdD*), in M. Reidel (ed.), *Rehabilitierung der praktischen Philosophie*, vol. II, Freiburg, Rombach, 1974; to 'A Postscript to *Knowledge and Human Interests*', in *Philosophy of the Social Sciences*, vol. 3, 1973, pp. 157–89 (referred to in text as *P*).

5 Cf. Husserl's distinction between the full judgment (*das Geurteilte*) and the object about which the judgment predicates (*das Beurteilte*) (*Ideas I*, §94).

6 There is an intimate interplay between the two forms if one (as Habermas does in *UP*) binds the different validity claims more tightly to one another; the types of discourse differentiate themselves in this case only by means of their thematic accent.

7 Cf. Habermas, *Legitimation Crisis*, trans. Thomas McCarthy, London, Heinemann, 1976, pp. 111–12.

8 In the following I shall also make reference to K.-O. Apel, *Transformation der Philosophie*, 2 vols, Frankfurt am Main, Suhrkamp, 1973. (References will be made via volume and page numbers.) I shall avoid playing off earlier essays in the book against later ones. This can be done, but it would weight our discussion down with a false alternative, namely with an alternative, as it were, between hermeneutical and transcendental hermeneutics.

9 This is, by the way, no longer quite so self-evident and has been, for example, abandoned in textual linguistics; cf. Broekman's contribution on the theory of meaning in this volume.

10 Cf. A. R. White (ed.), *The Philosophy of Action*, Oxford, Oxford University Press, 1968, pp. 12ff.: 'Explanations of Action'.

11 Cf. the work of Ch. Perelman.

12 Cf. 'Zwei Seiten der Sprache und zwei Typen aphatischer Störungen', in R. Jakobson, *Aufsätze zur Linguistik und Poetik*, ed. W. Raible, Munich, Nymphenburger Verlagshandlung, 1974.

13 Cf. ibid., pp. 123 ff.

14 Cf. my lecture at the International Phenomenology Congress, Munich, 1976, 'Der Sinn zwischen den Zeilen', published in *Phänomenologische Forschung*, vol. 8, 1979.

15 From J. Habermas and N. Luhmann, *Theorie der Gesellschaft oder Sozialtechnologie*, pp. 326f.

16 Cf. Grice's conversation postulates (cf. S. Kanngießer in *Sprachpragmatik und Philosophie*, pp. 296ff.). The speech act theories of Austin and Searle take such situations and contextual aspects into account; but success of this kind involves more than 'validity' in the normative sense. On the other hand, this theory touches the context of a linguistic action when it allows the 'illocutionary' act to end in understanding and separates it from the 'perlocutionary' effect. (Cf. my essay 'Der Sinn zwischen den Zeilen'.)

17 M. Merleau-Ponty, *Phenomenology of Perception*, trans. Colin Smith, London, Routledge & Kegan Paul, 1962, p. 443.

18 F. de Saussure, *Grundfragen der allgemeinen Sprachwissenschaft*, Berlin, Walter de Gruyter, 1967, pp. 156 ff.

19 Concerning practical 'indetermination' of linguistic forms of communication, cf. Kanngießer, *Sprachpragmatik und Philosophie*, op. cit., pp. 328ff.

20 Cf. my essay in this volume, 'Towards an Open Dialectic' (Chapter 5).

CHAPTER 11

'Meaning in the use' OR On the irrelevance of the theory of meaning for practical philosophy

Jan M. Broekman (Leuven)

Since Nietzsche it has become a commonplace that language is not merely a neutral medium of human communication and action. Our strategies for speaking are so constructed that they realize a specific interpretation of the relation between language and reality. Here we can catch sight of the central importance of such strategies – unitary forms of discursivity are presupposed and simultaneously realized by the confirmation of these presuppositions in actual speech.

But this interest rarely comes clearly to light; it generally remains concealed in the naïve understanding of the essence of language and in man's undeniable mastery of his linguistic abilities. The virtues of language are thematized neither in speaking nor in the projection of specific speech strategies. Human discursivity seems to lie concealed in the mastery of the words and expressions of a language. This would hold not only for natural language but also for technical and artificial languages. They are always present to the speaker as a specific normality, and this self-evidence has a normative effect – as a normativity which concerns not merely the use of words but also the background interpretation with respect to the relation between language and reality.

In this context Wittgenstein's formulation in the *Tractatus* is a triviality: 'The totality of propositions is language' (4.001). This thesis is the common background for both the picture theory of the *Tractatus* and the use-theory of language in the *Philosophical Investigations*. Seen in this light, both theories of language appear as expressions of one and the same principle concerning the interpretation of language and reality.

In the *Investigations* Wittgenstein writes:

> But how many kinds of sentence are there? Say assertion, question, and command? – There are *countless* kinds, countless

> different kinds of use of what we call 'symbols', 'words', 'sentences'. And this multiplicity is not something fixed, given once for all; but new types of language, new language games, as we may say, come into existence, and others become obsolete and get forgotten (§23).

As in the *Tractatus*, this organistic conception of language is possible because there are smallest units of language which in their totality constitute language itself and in one way or the other contain the logical structure of reality. This is also true for the discussions in the *Philosophical Grammar*, where even a late manuscript (1936) merely expresses some hesitation with regard to the question whether an elementary proposition is merely one whose logical analysis shows that it is not composed from other propositions by means of truth functions. Wittgenstein stresses the problematic of analysis and fails to reflect upon the notion of the elementary proposition itself, i.e. upon the proposition as the supposed building-block of language.

A general characteristic of contemporary theory of meaning appears at this point. It is based on a theory of language which takes it to be constructed out of smallest units, becoming a totality via the joining together of these units. On the level of meaning these 'smallest units' are words or propositions (Frege, Wittgenstein, Husserl), *sémes* (Greimas), phrases (Kristeva). One of the limits of linguistics and the philosophy of language becomes visible here: the realm of the linguistic rule stops, as it were, with the proposition – the *connection* of propositions in discursive structures and texts has barely been thematized up to now. The semantic analysis of types of conversation, rhetorical figures and specific modes of argumentation has hardly freed itself from the fundamental ideal of the 'smallest unit'. This remains the case even when Wittgenstein notes in the *Philosophical Grammar*:

> In reflecting on language and meaning we can easily get into a position where we think that in philosophy we are not talking of words and sentences in a quite common-or-garden sense, but in a sublimated and abstract sense. As if a particular proposition wasn't really the thing that some person utters, but an ideal entity (§77).

The unity or even ideality that is put into question here is itself based on the idea of the 'smallest unit'. This is also true of considerations with regard to the continuation of a series of propositions, as well as with regard to the question whether propositions can follow from other propositions, how this phenomenon can be continued and to what degree of complexity this is the case. The problem of the continuation of a series of propositions does not lead to a genuinely syntagmatic approach as long as the limits of the linguistic approach to meaning as well as the relation to other kinds of approach to language have not become the theme of a philosophy of language. Even Wittgenstein stops at this limit: 'Wouldn't this be what we'd have to say: it's only when a proposition exists that it follows from it. It's only when we have constructed ten propositions following from the first one that ten propositions do follow from it' (*Phil. Gram.*, II, §3). Clearly, Wittgenstein's theory of meaning which is summarized in the famous sentence from the *Philosophical Investigations*: 'the meaning of a word is its use in the language' (§43), is to be understood in this context. This is also true when Wittgenstein understands the 'use-theory' syntactically, as in the *Philosophical Grammar*:

> We say: the essential thing in a word is its *meaning*. We can replace the word by another with the same meaning. That fixes a place for the word, and we can substitute one word for another provided we put it in the same place (§22).
>
> I want to say the place of a word in grammar is its meaning (§23).

In both cases, the presupposition according to which – as the *Tractatus* puts it – language is the totality of propositions, is accepted without discussion.

This observation is even more important when one considers that we are not dealing with a relatively arbitrary theory of meaning by a specific author here. Bringing this presupposition to light as such puts the position of the theory of meaning in Western philosophy in question all over again. As Dummett has put it:

> Because philosophy has, as its first if not its only task, the analysis of meaning, and because, the deeper such analysis goes, the more it is dependent upon a correct general account of meaning, a model for what the understanding of an expression consists in, the theory of meaning, which is the search for such a model, is the foundation of all philosophy, and not epistemology as Descartes mislead us into believing. Frege's greatness consists, in the first place, in his having perceived this . . . he starts from meaning by taking the theory of meaning as the only part of philosophy whose results

> do not depend upon those of any other part, but which underlies all the rest. By doing this, he effected a revolution in philosophy as great as the similar revolution previously effected by Descartes (M. Dummett, *Frege*, London, 1973, p. 669).

The same assessment holds for Wittgenstein:

> Frege's new perspective was not wholly shared by Russell, who was in many ways so close to Frege in philosophical outlook. Russell was to a considerable extent still under the influence of the ancient tradition, in which epistemological considerations are primary. The first philosopher to adopt Frege's perspective was Wittgenstein: the difference between him and Russell is brought out sharply if we compare the *Tractatus* with *The Philosophy of Logical Atomism*; many of the same doctrines are argued for in the two books, but in Russell's work they take on an epistemological guise which is wholly lacking from the *Tractatus*. The *Tractatus* is a pure essay in the theory of meaning, from which every trace of epistemological or psychological consideration has been purged as thoroughly as the house is purged of leaven before the Passover (Dummett, *Frege*, op. cit., p. 679).

It is interesting that the philosophical revolution that Dummett describes here did not lead to a correlative shift from a theory of the smallest units of language to a theory of language in which the text and discourse stand at the centre of attention. Both perspectives, the traditional epistemological perspective as well as Frege's and Wittgenstein's theory of meaning, retain this notion. The revolution is apparently not as radical as it would seem at first glance. Neither the discussion of Frege's distinction between sense and reference, nor his differentiation concerning sense, tone and power with respect to reference, neither the combination of propositions with truth functions and logical calculi nor the emphasis on the *analytic* character of the analysis of propositions lead to a discussion of this idea. This is also true of Dummett's discussion of Frege's philosophy. Dummett too simply assumes the self-evidence of certain presuppositions:

> A sentence is, as we have said, the smallest unit of language with which a linguistic act can be accomplished, with which a 'move can be made in the language-game': so you cannot *do* anything with a word . . . save by uttering some sentence containing that word . . . the sense of a word consists in a rule which, taken

> together with the rules constitutive of the senses of the other words, determines the condition for the truth of a sentence in which the word occurs. The sense of a word thus consists – wholly consists – in something which has a relation to the truth-value of sentences containing the word . . . in a certain sense, therefore, sentences have a primacy within language over the other linguistic expressions. . . . Frege's clear apprehension of the central role of sentences was the first step, not merely to a workable theory of language, but to one which was even plausible (Dummett, *Frege*, op. cit., pp. 681ff.).

In this text we find at least *three* moments which are tied up with the idea of the smallest unit: (i) Words constitute the *content* of sentences. The truth function of a sentence is connected with this content, and it is only in this connection itself that the relation of language and reality is analysable, i.e. articulatable. (ii) Words joined together in sentences make it possible for us to *do* something *with* language – saying something and doing something are equated with one another here, and the condition of possibility of both activities is the sentence. Sentences are true or false, one can do something with them, i.e. in the final analysis: say something. This instrumentalistic conception of language dominates the later speech act theory, which for this reason could not lead to a theory of the text and discursivity. (iii) The way in which we represent and use truth is also bound up with the idea of the smallest unit, since the truth function of a *sentence* is dependent on the presuppositions with reference to the character of a sentence which we have discussed.

These hidden consequences are still present when Dummett conceives the theory of meaning as a use-theory:

> the theory of meaning for the language, taken as a whole, must be correlated with the practice of speaking the language. . . . A grasp of the sense of a word is manifested by the employment of sentences containing the word. It is this conception, which is part (but only part) of what the later Wittgenstein intended by his slogan 'Meaning is use', to which Frege came so close but never actually formulated (Dummett, *Frege*, op. cit., p. 682).

This problematic also has nothing to do with the question of the degree to which philosophy is dominated by epistemology or the theory of meaning; it rather points to the question concerning how we conceive of truth itself, how we conceive of our place in the world. Differences between the various theories of meaning with respect to the idea of a smallest unit are of little importance in this context. The important thing is *that* this approach is taken up in the first place, always intimately connected with the natural descriptivity of the relation of language and reality. We may well suspect that the philosophy of language cannot relativize the representational character of language as long as it considers language as a compound of smallest units.

In addition, and this is a second characteristic of the contemporary theory of meaning, we note the fact that Dummett's revolutionary turn from epistemology to the theory of meaning has not turned out to have genuine practical-philosophical relevance. The political dimension of the theory of meaning is extremely thin. Peirce's ideal of a 'logical socialism' might be taken to be an exception, but the question is whether this exception is really the result of a priority of the semiotic in his philosophy.

All of this is quite surprising when one considers the fact that every practical decision – the decision of a judge, a politician, a technician or of a simple everyday human being – is to be understood as a process of the allocation of meaning. There is not a decision which is not the result of the establishment of semantic dominances, and such an establishment always appears as an important *discursive* event. But as long as language is conceived as a process of representation, meanings cannot be understood as the result of a production. The genuinely emancipatory character of a theory of meaning thus remains hidden. The question is whether man can liberate himself within his own linguistic relation to the world as long as he attributes a representational character to this language. In doing so he robs himself of the possibility of clarifying the structure of discursivity as such. This kind of account would only be possible as a discursive event, perhaps only as a theory of the philosophy of language. But the result of our discussion would be that a fundamental moment of every theory or philosophy contributes to the fact that discourses are developed in which precisely this structure is *not* brought to light. A central concern of every reflection on the contemporary theory of meaning would thus be to uncover the interests which lead to this kind of obfuscation.

From here it is only a short step to the consideration that the theory of meaning in its contemporary form is the product of a discursive strategy. It would have a prime interest in disguising this fact, and it can only succeed in doing this by presenting itself as a representation of a pre-existing reality instead of as a strategy, i.e. in the final analysis as a *politicum*. Thus, the political insignificance of the theory of meaning is the result of its own theoreticity.

This principle is, for example, at work in the fact that the theory of meaning is based on a theory of language which understands language in terms of meaning and then presents meaning as the result of the use of language. This use of language is thus understood fundamentally as the use of words and sentences *in* a language, i.e. not as discursivity and textuality. And should one for once speak of discursivity in the context of the use-theory, this discourse is in turn understood as a combination of sentences. Speech concerning discursivity is presented as a meta-linguistic event, such that the differentiation of various levels of language obfuscates the multiple reflexivity of natural language. The theory of meaning results from this differentiation of levels and not from the strategies of natural language.

Thus, the discussion of the theory of meaning leads necessarily to more general questions concerning human discursivity and its metaphysical foundations. The self-evident manner in which we strive for truth in our discourse seems to be completely transcended (*aufgehoben*) in the *analyticity* of that discursivity. We must therefore pose the question *how* we make use of truth and *whether or not* we risk the truth. Nietzsche: '"How much truth can a spirit *endure*, how much truth does a spirit *dare*?" – this became for me the real standard of value . . . every achievement of knowledge is a consequence of courage, of severity toward oneself, of cleanliness toward oneself' (*Will to Power*, p. 536). On this basis, Nietzsche characterized his philosophy as an experimental philosophy. What appears here is a new assessment of philosophical discourse, an assessment which casts a new light on the structure of linguistic strategies and the resulting speech situations.

Three steps might contribute to getting rid of the political insignificance of the theory of meaning, which is the result of a specific strategy of this theory: A. the introduction and realization of Kristeva's distinction between phenotext and genotext with reference to human discursivity; B. a subsequent investigation of the relation between transformation and production as discursive processes; C. a consideration of the dynamics of meaning.

A. The distinction between phenotext and genotext opens up new possibilities for the understanding of a theory of meaning. Such possibilities result from the fact that the relation between the two levels of the text is not to be thought as a difference between levels which are the result of a restriction of a language's reflective possibilities on the basis of which complexities of meaning then arise, but rather as a *relation of production*.

> The text is not a linguistic phenomenon, in other words it is not a structured signification which is presented in a linguistic corpus seen as a flat structure. It is its *engendering*, an engendering inscribed in that linguistic 'phenomenon', that pheno-text which is the printed text, but is only readable when one ascends vertically through the genesis of: (1) its linguistic categories, and (2) the topology of the signifying act. Signifiance will thus be this engendering which one can doubly grasp: (1) as engendering the tissue of language; (2) as engendering the 'I' that is placed in position to present signifiance. What is opened in this vertical is the (linguistic) operation of the generation of the pheno-text. We will call this operation a geno-text. . .to analyze a signifiant production as textual would come down to demonstrating how the process of the signifiant system's production is manifest in the pheno-text (J. Kristeva, *Semeiotike*, Paris, 1969, p. 280).

This demonstration of the production relations on the various levels of the text amounts to a fundamental reorientation of philosophy: idealist epistemology, which appears in traditional theory of language in the form of the speaker–hearer situation, is fundamentally relativized. To treat meaning as a textual phenomenon is to conceive of the surface structure of language (phenotextuality) merely as one of the possible – generally socialized – spheres of action for meaning. The increase in complexity with reference to the structure of meaning implies relativizing the linguistic power of the speaking subject. The 'I' of the speaker, which utters meaning as a surface phenomenon, is itself a function of language. With this we have left behind the conception of language as realization of sentences or words within propositional units which was so necessary for Frege, Wittgenstein, etc., and which made it possible for us to speak of meanings in the first place.

> What we call a *geno-text* is an abstract level of linguistic function which, far from reflecting the *sentences'* structures, effects their anamnesis in preceding and exceeding them. It is thus a matter of a signifiant function which, while being wholely effected in *language* [*langue*], is not reducible to the *speech* [*parole*] manifested in what is called normal communication. The geno-text operates with analytico-linguistic categories . . . whose limit is not

> to generate a *sentence* (subject-predicate) for the pheno-text, but a *signifiant* taken at different stages of the signifiant function process. This sequence in the pheno-text can be a word, a string of words, a nominal sentence, a paragraph, a 'non-sense', etc. To posit the geno-text is thus to aim at cutting through the structural position – a *transposition* (Kristeva, *Semeiotike*, op. cit., p. 282).

A theory of meaning which presents itself in the form of a theory of action or use merely conceptualizes phenotextuality, and thus mistakes the surface structure of language for language in general. This is the manner in which subjectivity attempts to pose as the centre and ruler of discursivity. The speaker–hearer model of the speech process is the result of a prior reduction and of the development of a specific strategy of speech which opens the door to self-confirming structures of discursivity. The traditional theory of meaning is, as we have seen, such a structure.

B. Continuous transformations take place within language. These are not restricted to the 'smallest units' such as words and sentences; they are just as relevant for textual and discursive units. These units have *materialiter* not merely a linguistic but also a social character. This fact is brought to light, for example, in George Steiner's *After Babel* (1975). For Steiner, language is a historical process, thus a complex of translations. These translations take place between natural languages as well as within one and the same language. Culture, tradition is by and large to be understood as a labour of translation – a labour on and with words and sentences, texts, speech situations and modes of speech. Steiner explains that the wealth of languages is not to be explained biologically, is not to be understood in terms of a few universal principles, is not to be understood merely as a social, but also as an individual event, irreducible to a speaker–hearer model and to communication. The general idea of translation manifests an inner-linguistic dynamic which appears as understanding, as the compatibility of two or more mother tongues, as the possibility of seeing a variety of aspects of the world, as the topology of culture and the exchange of themes and material in literature, as the poly-interpretability of the fundamental relation between language and reality.

All of this concerns the culture–historical dimension of that which is called translation, but which in a broader sense should be understood as transformation. The metaphysical dimension of the problem announces itself in the same catchwords in the works of Walter Benjamin. In his essay 'The Task of Translation' (1923) he writes: 'Translation is a form. . . . The question of the translatability of a work is ambiguous. It can mean: will it ever find a competent translator among its readers? or, and more authentically: is it essentially translatable.' Thus, for Benjamin the concept of translation is a relational concept. But he does refer to the fact, and here the metaphysical dimension manifests itself, that

> certain relational concepts retain their good, perhaps indeed their best sense when they are not referred exclusively to human beings. . . . Correspondingly, one would also have to consider the translatability of linguistic works even when they are untranslatable for human beings. And will that not in fact be the case to a certain extent if we assume a strict concept of translation?

The success of a translation is neither dependent upon the talent of the translator nor on the simultaneous command of various speech strategies on the part of the reader of a given original and the correlative image-like translation. The process of translation is not the manifestation of an individual act of the will, but rather of:

> the kindred nature of languages. . . . Where can we search for the kinship between two languages if not in a historical kinship? At any rate, neither in the similarity of literature nor in that of their words. All trans-historical kinship of languages rests rather on the fact that in each of them as a whole one and the same thing is meant, but which no single language can attain. . . . Whereas all individual elements, the words, sentences, contexts of different languages exclude one another, these languages complement one another in their intentions themselves.

Language is so related to language, linguistic original to its image, that the translator appears as a receiver of sense and meaning, not as ruler. He must understand himself as a transformation moment in that process of sense – otherwise he understands nothing. Benjamin points to one of the dangers of translation here, a danger which has nothing to do with some human-arbitrary activity, but with the very structure of human existence: 'that the gates of such an extended and regimented (*durchwalteten*) language close and lock the translator into silence'. To avert this danger is to refuse to conceive the sense of the text as the mediacy of language – at this point Benjamin's reflections on language approach those of Martin Buber. The immediacy of language can only be experienced by one who can hear language not merely as the intention of the speaker, but also as revelation.

> Wherever the text immediately, without mediating sense, belongs in its literal sense to the true language, truth or doctrine, it is simply untranslatable. No longer, of course, for reasons proper to the text, but rather for reasons concerning language itself. Language demands a so boundless trust from the translation that just as the text unites language and revelation without tension, the translation unites literalness and freedom in the form of the interlineal version. For to some extent all great writing, most of all holy texts, contain between the lines their virtual translation. The interlinear version of the holy text is the model or ideal of all translation.

But: while the event of translation or transformation may not take place absolutely according to the will of the subject, while untranslatability as the peculiarity of language, the immediacy of that language, may dominate – such dominance is primarily to be understood and thought through as an element of a theory of meaning. It is not merely to be found on the constitutional side of the linguistic, but rather to be considered as the production of semantic dynamisms which rarely come to light phenotextually. This means that the work of translation has already taken place when we are confronted with a phenotext. The translation has already become textual as linguistic labour, has thus entered the realm of the production of meaning and is thus responsible for the transcendence (*Aufhebung*) of the dominance of the sentence or word as the 'smallest unit' along with its connotations for the philosophy of consciousness. Thus, when the labour of transformation enters the region of the production of meaning and thus of texts, this is bound up with a change of attitude with regard to the philosophical interpretation of text and meaning, i.e. language. Kristeva:

> If the signifiant work constantly operates on the line swinging from the pheno-text to the geno-text and vice versa, the textual specificity resides in the fact that it is a translation of the geno-text into the pheno-text, disclosable to the reader through the opening of the pheno-text onto the geno-text . . . to say this in brief, every practice that would apply the Freudian precept 'Wo Es war, soll Ich werden' (Where It (= Id) was, Ego is to

become) to the work, would be textual (Kristeva, *Semeiotike*, op. cit., p. 280).

At least four processes play a role in the process of producing meaning in the text: there are processes of *repression* – this is the point at which the psychoanalytical dimension breaks into semiotics; there are *syntactical* processes – as the theory of combination, this linguistic dimension is primarily topological; there is also the development of *phenomena of power* – this is the point at which the sociological dimension breaks into semiotics; and finally there is the phenomenon of the *distribution of scarcity* – scarce positions, scarce possibilities of meaning, etc. are distributed in the economic sense in the realm of the text. The amazing thing is that with reference to the semiotic these four processes are continually transformed into one another and together constitute a unitary structure for the production of meaning. Repression, topology, power and distribution continually pass over into one another, constitute their own phenomenality in the text. Literary hermeneutics deals primarily with the reconstruction of such processes.

A thought that is exclusively concerned with transformations cannot clarify the peculiarity of productivity as it has been presented here. This kind of thought is indeed capable of analysing the historical processes in the various texts and linguistic processes, but it cannot uncover the dominances which produce specific units of meaning within that historical process. In addition, an exclusively transformational thought *requires* the construction of language as compounded from 'smallest units' such as words or sentences. This necessity can only be explained by the analysis of the process of production in the text. We may thus suspect that in the final analysis the concept of transformation is to be taken up into the concept of production, as a specific linguistic process within the more encompassing dimension of a production of texts.

It should be recalled that in a case like this one transcends (*aufhebt*) two classical dominances of the theory of meaning: the *dominance of the linguistic*, a dominance which is expressed most clearly in the priority of grammar, as well as the *dominance of the components native to the philosophy of consciousness* with the linguistic idea of the 'smallest unit'. Both dominances are characterized as the discursive strategy of a theory of meaning which turns out to be a theory of representation. But neither units of meaning nor textual units are representations of a reality which is not a linguistic reality – or reality as language.

Texts exercise a sign function in texts *as* texts, both in the pheno-genotextual totality and in that specific totality of linguistics and social science which we call the 'speech situation'. Texts are thus also exceedingly complex as objects of philosophical reflection and must be thought in a highly differentiated manner. Fragments of genotexts become phenotexts, especially those which can themselves exercise a sign function there. In phenotextuality they also serve as a sign for the genotextual. The role of the quotation is very interesting in this context: among its many discursive functions, a quotation is always also a sign: a sign that one wants to produce a discursive unity with the quoted in order to lead the reader there too. For the reader the quotation serves as a sign that he is to shift to a discursive level which is determined not merely by the text, but also by the quoted texts in the text. The semiotic and these special structures of discursivity co-determine one another here to such an extent that a very special textual topology arises, one which can take on universal characteristics. In view of the obvious complexity of this phenomenon, a merely phenotextual understanding would be completely naïve.

But this textual topology involves a tension between the symbolic and the semiotic. The tension is caused by the simultaneous and continuous effect of the processes mentioned above: repression, power, syntax and distribution. This too can be shown by means of the example of the quotation. The sign function of the quotation in the text or in a discourse can lead immediately to an order within language which is completely dominated by this sign, which has a paralysing effect. The quotation then becomes an isolated moment of syntax, becomes the denotation of a so-called object, becomes the established truth of a discourse, in short: a symbol. The indeterminacy and indeterminability of the semiotic comes in conflict with the established determinacy of the symbolic. For the members of a social group who understand this symbol phenotextually, the sense of the symbol is evident and established. The sense of the semiotic cannot be measured, evades any established evaluation, even a social one. As Kristeva says:

> One can encipher semiotics, the sonagraph gives us the frequencies of the least cry. But one cannot measure meaning – semiotics has no discrete signifiable and localizable unities. A topology can give an image, but it would not indicate its heterogeneous contradiction

> with the symbolic (J. Kristeva, 'The Subject in Political and Practical Language', in *Psychoanalysis and Politics*, p. 63).

This symbolic element is also the cause of a sense which the object has given itself as subject of a discourse. Subjectivity appears in this context precisely as a symbol. The semiotic is called upon to displace, move aside, shift this symbolic sense. This occurs *within* the discourse, it is there that the thetically codified sense of the other is disordered (*déréglage*) by my word: this appears as the praxis of meaning in the text, in discourse. This praxis is political to the highest degree – it is precisely this tension which makes the meaning of the theory of meaning practically relevant.

> In the discourse of the speaking subject, it is the shock of another's discourse that calls for semiotics, heterogeneous to meaning, to displace the symbolic meaning the subject has become accustomed to considering his own. Since every linguistic act is called forth by (or is the call of) an addressee, every enunciation should be a practice, in the sense of being a disordering of the coded thetic meaning by a semiotic rhythm stirred up by the other (ibid.).

This relevance is made accessible by the dialogical event of the alienating effect of the semiotic on the symbolic. This process would have to be redescribed as a dynamics of repression, as a syntactical-topical event, as the distribution of scarce possibilities of sense, as the power of the indeterminable against the power of the determinable.

But one should distinguish between the political within linguistics and the strategy of linguistics within the totality of the sciences. Both are obviously closely bound up with one another, but the processes sketched out here must be considered as strategies within linguistics, i.e. as the auto-constitution of a discourse. Curiously, linguistics is also characterized by the fact that it can be presented conjunctively, since this process of constitution is also part of a more encompassing strategy of linguistics within society and the sciences. These two moments stand in an obvious opposition to one another. Kristeva presents this opposition in the form of a conjunction:

> every linguistic enunciation should be a heterogeneous contradiction between the communicable thesis and the specific semiotic rhythm, prior to the ephemeral constitution of a new signifiant structure; every enunciation should include symbolic time and its emptying out which is a time zero of meaning giving way before rhythm;

> every enunciation should have an incommensurable aspect in which the subject signifies the flashes of rhythm wherein he is lost. *Should, but is not* (ibid.).

The hidden idealism of our thought and our institutions gives rise to a levelling equalization of the tension between semiotics and the symbol. It disguises the breach:

> Accessory to this idealism, linguistic science offers us a systematic vision of language full of meaning, without emptiness, without process, without a practice: thus without a subject in process . . . *another discursive practice* arises . . . indicating another relation to sociality, and thus to politics. For it, the social contract and language system are not some common measure but a limit to be brought into play (not dissolved). This discourse does not speak in the name of sociality, nomination, or language: it expands them before reformulating them. Politics is assumed, as is language's structuring limit, to be destructured by the semiotic play where the unary subject is placed in process (ibid., pp. 63, 68).

C. In spite of this covering over, in spite of this concealment of the breach, in spite of the construction of a theory of meaning which passes itself off for a theory of representation in order to conceal its discursive strategy, it is possible to thematize the dynamics of meaning. This becomes clear when one grounds the theory of meaning in a theory of the text or in a more encompassing theory of discursivity. But even a theory of language which does not make use of the idea of the 'smallest unit' cannot suppress this characteristic of the theory of meaning. In the first place it is the processes of repression, syntax and topology, of the exercise of power and distribution, which make that dynamic visible. They demonstrate that every theory of meaning is a theory of dynamics. And even if one recurs to the second kind of theory of language it becomes clear that meanings are not the result of combinatory games with ontologically hypostatized linguistic units, but moments of a dynamic which unites language and world. This unification makes itself felt in the concept of the speech act. The distinction between language and world or reality is overcome (*aufgehoben*) in this dynamic of meaning – or should one perhaps rather say that meanings arise precisely at the point at which this distinction is overcome? Speech acts are not the 'smallest units' of language and action. They receive their significance first in the necessary analyticity of the discourse. A process of this type is systematically concealed by a theory of meaning oriented towards the idea of representation. In discursivity, understood as the class of speech acts determined by external principles of organization, one speaks of an *infinite series* of such speech acts. For this reason, the dynamic of meaning is here characterized by the connection between the reduction and the increase of complexity of every significant speech act. In this context it would be interesting to transfer systems-theoretically that which has been said here about the theory of discourse to the problematic of the description of the 'world'. As Luhmann writes in an essay concerning 'complexity':

> The development of the world can neither be understood as the movement from the simple to the complex, nor as the movement from the indeterminate to the determinate. In its relational structure, our concept of complexity is too complex to have its minimum or opposite in the simple; there can only be more or less satisfactory solutions to the problem of selection in various contexts. In addition, determinate and indeterminate complexity condition one another reciprocally to the realm of sense experience, since the determinate is constituted within a horizon which remains indeterminate (N. Luhmann, *Soziologische Aufklärung*, vol. II, p. 212).

The systems-theoretical perspective is legitimate both for the theory of language which is the foundation for that theory of meaning and for linguistics. On the other hand, this approach leads to understanding increase of complexity and reduction as processes which *counteract* one another. The two processes cannot occur *simultaneously*: 'Increase of complexity requires not merely growth but also a more exact structural selection, and thus in the process of their execution in the processes of the system a continual reduction of complexity with respect to other possibilities' (Luhmann, *Soziologische Aufklärung*, op. cit., p. 207). Semiotically, however, this 'simultaneity' of the two processes is the central dynamic moment at which the symbolic is transcended (*aufgehoben*) such that sense and meaning can arise. Kristeva formulates this in the following manner, as we have already seen:

> In the discourse of the speaking subject, it is the shock of another's discourse that calls for semiotics, heterogeneous to meaning, to displace the symbolic meaning the subject has become accustomed

> to considering his own. Since every linguistic act is called forth by (or is the call of) an addressee, every enunciation should be a practice, in the sense of being a disordering of the coded thetic meaning (Kristeva, 'The Subject in Political and Practical Language', op. cit., p. 63).

The order of the symbolic in discourse is thereby transformed by the claim of the other. Rather than excluding one another, reduction and increase of complexity require one another in this process. The institution of sense and constitution of meaning take place in the process of just such displacement.

But the disordering of the symbolic in discourse through the word of the other need not necessarily, in the positive sense, arouse and summon; this process can also be co-opted in the process of the totalizing exercise of power and become a catastrophe for the other. This possibility is not explicitly mentioned by Kristeva, but it is also bound to the labour of alienation and is thus a political moment of the linguistic. In this case we cannot celebrate a liberation: *exile* becomes the paradox of the 'simultaneity' of the increase of complexity and reduction of sense. This situation has been described in many autobiographies by South African writers. The reduction of life to a *single* meaning goes hand in hand with an enormous increase in complexity. But precisely this situation is that of the disappearance of all meaning. James Olney describes this in his *Tell Me Africa*: 'There is no explanation where there is no meaning, no meaning where there is no ordering except the arbitrary and the political' (p. 273). Reality shrinks, it becomes the word of the other, which cannot have a liberating effect because it cannot tear itself away from the symbolic and thus cannot allow an authentic sense to arise in speech. 'For the black South African there is no choice between "reality" and the "proclamations of others" because there is no difference between them: . . .reality *is* the "proclamation of others"' (p. 265). The overcoming of such a word by flight from the speech situation is *exile*. In this situation, exile is the last possibility of life – or should one say: to survive? Olney points out that it is only in exile that such autobiographies can be written:

> The arbitrary, artificial, and sterile order imposed by a political, racist dictatorship – the categories and classifications of apartheid: white, Indian, Coloured, African – produces, because it is a man-made scheme, no meaning. 'Perhaps', Peter Abrahams

> says of his reason for leaving South Africa, 'Perhaps life had a meaning that transcended race and colour. If it had, I would not find it in South Africa' (*Tell Freedom*, p. 370) (p. 272).

Autobiography and exile are in this sense identical – this identity provides us with an important metaphor for that situation which is forced upon us in the strategic insignificance of the theory of meaning, but which appears so harmless in many circumstances. This insignificance is a practical-philosophical problem of the first order. Mphahlele, author of *Down Second Avenue*, comes to the significant conclusion 'that coherent answers, if they exist, will be found only in exile, where life can be determined by some logic other than the logic of politics'. Olney comments: 'When, from his own experience, a man can reconstruct no more than the pattern of apartheid and, as an artist, can imitate nothing more than political fact, he is at a dead-end' (p. 274). Do not misunderstand this! This insignificance is a fact not only for the exiled, oppressed author, but also for the oppressors. Only: they are hardly aware of it, they do not think they are in exile; they thing that they have the connection between complexity and reduction in hand, they think they are at their symbolic position in the discourse. This makes clear the extent to which the disordering (Kristeva) and the difference between the symbolic and the semiotical is a *necessity* which can only be realized by the overcoming of the practical-philosophical insignificance of the theory of meaning. This realization is simultaneously the history of the need for the other – the dynamic of the dialogical includes precisely the dynamic of the semiotic.

CHAPTER 12

Merleau-Ponty's critique of Marxist scientism

John O'Neill (Toronto)

1 Waiting for Marx

It is impossible to think of modern political history apart from the Russian revolution. At the same time, it is hard not to be ambivalent towards the history and politics of Marxism itself. In the days before Communism ruled a major part of the world, one could believe that Communism would shunt all forms of political and economic exploitation into the siding of prehistory. In those days Marxism was emancipatory knowledge wonderfully scornful of the 'iron laws' of history and economics. This is not to say that Marxist critique failed to recognize the weight of historical structures. Indeed, we owe Marx much of the credit for a structuralist analysis of historical development. By the same token, there has always been an uncertain relation between Marxist analysis of the determinism of historical structures and its prophecy of a proletarian fulfilment of historical law. Prior to the actual experience of the revolution, it was easy enough to think of it as a temporary, albeit violent, intervention on the side of justice against a moribund but destructive ruling class. But the revolution is itself an institution and it soon acquires a history of its own, leaders and enemies, priorities and policies that could not be foreseen. In view of these complexities, Communist practice inevitably hardened and Marxism soon became the intellectual property of the Party, abandoning the education of the proletariat in favour of slogans and dogma. This is the context of what we call Marxist *scientism*.[1] That is to say, once Marxism became Party knowledge and a tool for the industrialization of Soviet society, Marxism identified with economic determinism and the values of scientific naturalism at the expense of its own radical humanism. This is variously described as the difference between

Communism and Marxism, the difference between theory and practice, or the difference between the early, Hegelianized Marx and the later, scientific Marx.[2]

Today socialism and capitalism are equally in question in so far as the same ideology of technological domination underlies their apparently opposed political and ideological systems. In other words, we can no longer assume that Marxism challenges capitalism and justifies the sufferings of revolution unless we can be sure that Marxism possesses the philosophical resources for rethinking the logic of technical rationality and the Party practices that have forced this logic upon the proletariat in the name of the revolution. The task we are faced with is a reflection upon the very *logos* of Western rationality. It is only against this broad background that we can understand the historically specific goals and ambitions of Western Marxism. In particular, it is in this way that we can best understand the phenomenon of recent attempts to rethink Marxism in terms of Hegelian phenomenology in order to liberate Marxist praxis from the limitations of positivist knowledge.[3] To rethink Marxism, however, means that we put it in abeyance as the only 'other' answer that we have to the uncertainties of our times. In other words, it means that in the first place we need to examine the categories of Marxist thought such as man, nature, history, party and revolution, in order to recover a proper sense of their dialectical relations so that they are not organized around a simple logic of domination. What this will involve is a recovery of the relation between the already meaningful world of everyday life and the specific practices of science, economics and politics through which we attempt to construct a socialist society mindful of the historical risks and responsibilities of such a project. In short, by placing Marxism in abeyance while we rethink the meaning of socialism we educate ourselves into a permanently critical attitude towards the Party and History as guarantors of socialist rationality and freedom.

Merleau-Ponty's critique of Marxist scientism cannot be well understood unless we situate it in the intellectual history of France and the post-Second World War rejection of Communism by left-wing intellectuals who at the same time turned to the revival of Marxism.[4] This renaissance of Marxist thinking in part reflected the task of catching up with Central European thought – Korsch and Lukács – as well as with German phenomenology – Hegel, Husserl, Heidegger, not to mention Weber and Freud. The task was to separate the radical humanist philosophy of Marx from the Engels–Lenin orthodoxy of positivism and scientism.[5] In practice this meant reading Hegel anew and on this basis interpreting Marx's early writings. Merleau-Ponty was among many like Sartre and Hyppolite[6] who listened to Alexandre Kojève's lectures[7] on Hegel's *Phenomenology of Mind*. It was not until the mid-1950s that the rift between Communism and Marxism – a difficult distinction for outsiders, let alone insiders – became wide open. Apart from other broken friendships, the friendships of Merleau-Ponty and Sartre and of Sartre and Camus were destroyed in the wake of *Humanism and Terror*, *Adventures of the Dialectic* and Camus's *The Rebel*.[8] Later, in his *Critique de la raison dialectique*, Sartre attempted to learn from this the 'lesson of history', as he himself puts it, in a massive effort to construct an adequate Marxist history and sociology.

It is much easier for us thirty years after the Second World War to consider capitalism and socialism as subcultures of industralism rather than mortal antagonists. But in 1945 it was possible to hope that Communism was the solution to the capitalist syndrome of war and depression. For left-wing intellectuals in Europe the Soviet war effort and the Communist resistance promised a renewal of life once peace came. But peace never came, except as what we call the Cold War. In such an atmosphere, intellectual attitudes were forced to harden. Thus capitalists and socialists increasingly blamed one another for all the violence and oppression in the world. The price of loyalty either to socialism or capitalism became a blind and uncritical faith.

The argument of *Humanism and Terror* is especially difficult to understand if the radical alternative forced upon French politics by the Cold War split between the USA and the Soviet Union is accepted without question. In 1947 there was still a chance, at least in the mind of a non-Communist left-wing intellectual like Merleau-Ponty, that France and Europe would not have to become a satellite either to the USA or the Soviet Union. The hopes of the Resistance for immediate revolutionary change after the war had withered away in the tripartist tangles of the Communists, Socialists, and Christian Democrats. In March 1947 the Truman doctrine was initiated and in April the Big Four discussions on Germany failed. The introduction of the Marshall Plan in June of the same year, condemned by Molotov's walkout on the Paris Conference in July, hastened the breakdown of tripartism. Suspicion of the anti-Soviet implications of the Marshall Plan caused many on the left to look towards a neutralist position for Europe, but made them uncertain whether to build this position around the Socialist Party, which had failed so far to take any independent line, or the Communist Party, which could be expected to follow a Soviet line. But the drift was towards a pro-Western, anti-Soviet European integration led by the centre and right elements of the French Third Force, including the Gaullists. Within two years, the formation of the Brussels Treaty Organization, the North Atlantic Treaty Organization, and the Soviet Cominform brought down the iron curtain of which Winston Churchill had spoken in his Fulton Speech in March of 1946.

The intellectual French left was in an impossible situation which no combination of Marxism or existentialism seemed capable of remedying. French capitalism was bad, but American capitalism was even more anathema to the left, if only because it was in the rudest of health internationally, though perhaps not at home. At the same time, French socialism was anything but independent and its chances looked no better with Communist help. In such a situation it was impossible to be an anti-Communist if this meant being pro-American, witnessing the Americanization of Europe, and foreswearing the Communists who had fought bravely in the Resistance. On the other hand, it was not possible to be a Communist if this meant being blind to the hardening of the Soviet regime and becoming a witness to the Communist brand of imperialism which broke so many Marxist minds. It is not surprising that many on the left as well as the right were unable to bear such ambiguity and therefore welcomed any sign to show clearly which side to support, even if it meant a 'conversion' to the most extreme left and right positions.

I want to argue that in *Humanism and Terror*[9] Merleau-Ponty does more than illustrate the fateful connection between revolution and responsibility as it appears in the drama of the Moscow Trials. I think it can be shown that Merleau-Ponty develops a theory of the relations between political action, truth and responsibility which is the proper basis for understanding his approach to the problem of the relation between socialist humanism and revolutionary terror. *Humanism and Terror* was prompted by Koestler's dramatization of the Moscow Trials in *Darkness at Noon*. Merleau-Ponty's reply to Koestler's novel takes the form of an essay in which he develops a phenomenology of revolutionary action and responsibility in order to transcend Koestler's confrontation of the Yogi and the Commissar. The argument depends upon a philosophy of history and truth which draws upon Merleau-Ponty's phenomenology of perception, embodiment and intersubjectivity. Here I shall restrict myself to the political arguments without entering into the structure of Merleau-Ponty's philosophical thought which in any case is better revealed in a certain style of argument rather than through any system.[10]

> Politics, whether of understanding or of reason, oscillates between the world of reality and that of values, between individual judgment and common action, between the present and the future. Even if one thinks, as Marx did, that these poles are united in a historical factor – the proletariat – which is at one and the same time power and value, yet, as there may well be disagreement on the manner of making the proletariat enter history and take possession of it, *Marxist politics is, just like all the others, undemonstrable*. The difference is that Marxist politics understands this and that it has, more than any other politics, explored the labyrinth.[11]

It is typical of Merleau-Ponty to speak factually whereas he is addressing an ideal that his own work brings to reality. It needed Merleau-Ponty among others to take Marxist thinkers through the labyrinth of politics for them to understand the true nature of political trial and error. The philosopher of ambiguity,[12] as Merleau-Ponty has been called, prefers to raise questions rather than offer answers. This is not because he is nerveless but precisely because he wishes to bring to life the historical presumptions of Marxist thought. It is not literally the case that Marxists consider their knowledge undemonstrable. From the *Communist Manifesto* to the Russian Revolution there is a fairly straight line – at least doctrinally. But in fact such a line represents a colossal abstraction from the doctrinal debates and historical contingencies that shaped these debates and in turn were interpreted through them. Merleau-Ponty believed it was possible to discern in the terrible reality of the Moscow Trials the places where the life of Marxist thought was larger than the simplistic moral antithesis of the Yogi and the Commissar. Of course, Merleau-Ponty's purpose is easily misunderstood. Koestler's *Darkness at Noon* is certainly true to Soviet practice from the time of the Trials to the later revelations in the Cominform Campaign against Tito, the Rajk-Kosov trials, the Soviet labour camps and mental hospitals. Like many on the left, Merleau-Ponty himself had to open his eyes to Communist practice. Yet at the same time he begins to rethink Marxist philosophy of history and politics along the lines that have led to a renaissance of Marxist-Hegelian thought while only the most blind could have held on to the romance with Soviet institutions.

In *Humanism and Terror* Merleau-Ponty is concerned with revolution as the genesis of political community and with the dilemma of violence which in the name of fraternity becomes self-consumptive. This is the moral dilemma to which the Yogi responds by spiritualizing political action and which the Commissar handles by objectivizing his conduct in the name of historical forces. These alternatives, as posed by Koestler, are rejected by Merleau-Ponty on the grounds that they lose the essential ambivalence of political action and revolutionary responsibility. The science and practice of history never coincide. Because of this contingency, political action is always the decision of a future which is not determined uniquely by the facts of the situation. Thus there enters into political conduct the need to acknowledge responsibility and the fundamental terror we experience for the consequences of our own decisions as well as for the effects of other men's actions upon ourselves.

> We do not have a choice between purity and violence but between different kinds of violence. Inasmuch as we are incarnate beings, violence is our lot. There is no persuasion even without seduction, or in the final analysis, contempt. Violence is the common origin of all regimes. Life, discussion and political choice occur only against a background of violence. *What matters and what we have to discuss is not violence but its sense or its future*. It is a law of human action that the present encroaches upon the future, the self upon other people. This intrusion is not only a fact of political life, it also happens in private life. In love, in affection, or in friendship we do not encounter face to face 'consciousness' whose absolute individuality we could respect at every moment, but beings qualified as 'my son', 'my wife', 'my friend' whom we carry along with us into common projects where they receive (like ourselves) a definite role with specific rights and duties. So, in collective history the spiritual atoms trail their historical role and are tied to one another by the threads of their actions. What is more, they are blended with the totality of actions, whether or not deliberate, which they exert upon others and the world so that there does not exist a plurality of subjects but an intersubjectivity and that is why there exists a common measure of the evil inflicted upon certain people of the good gotten out of it by others.[13]

Yet Merleau-Ponty refuses to draw the sceptical conclusion that violence and conflict derive from the essentially antisocial nature of the human passions. In his essay on Montaigne[14] which allows us to anticipate here his differences with Sartre, he interprets Montaigne's scepticism in terms of the paradox of embodied consciousness, namely, to be constantly involved in the world through perception, politics or love and yet always at a distance from it, without which we could know nothing of it. The sceptic only withdraws from the world, its passions and follies in order to find himself at grips with the world having, as it were, merely slackened the intentional ties between himself and the world in order to comprehend the paradox of his being-in-the-world. Scepticism with regard to the passions only deprives them of value if we assume a total, Sartrean self-possession, whereas, we are never wholly ourselves, Merleau-Ponty would say, but always interested in the world through the passions which we are. Scepticism and misanthropy, whatever the appearances, have no place in Marxist politics for the reason that the essential ambivalence of politics is that its violence derives from what is most valuable in men – the ideas of truth and justice which each intends for all because men do not live side by side like pebbles but each in all.

Marxism does not invent the problem of violence, as Koestler would suggest, except in the sense that it assumes and attempts to control the violence which bourgeois society tolerates in the fatalities of race, war, domestic and colonial poverty. The Marxist revolutionary is faced only with a choice between different kinds of violence and not with the choice to forgo violence. The question which the revolutionary poses is not whether any one will be hurt but whether the act of violence leads to a future state of society in which humanist values have been translated into a common style of life expressed as much in low levels of infant mortality as in solipsistic, philosophical and literary speculation. If consciousness were a lonely and isolated phenomenon, as it is pictured in the individualist tradition of philosophy and the social sciences, and above all in Sartre, then the Yogi's horror at a single death is enough to condemn a whole regime regardless of its humanist or socialist aims. But this is an assumption which Marxist-Hegelianism challenges. We never exist even in splendid philosophical isolation let alone social isolation. We exist through one another, in specific situations mediated by specific social relations in which we encroach upon others and are committed by others so that our intentions are rarely entirely our own any more than their results. In these exchanges were necessarily prevail upon one another and one generation necessarily commits the future.[15]

The Marxist revolutionary starts from the evident truth of the embodied values of men and of the evil of human suffering. Only later does he learn that in the course of building the economic foundations of a socialist society he has to make decisions which subject individuals to forms of violence upon which the future of the revolution may depend. Marxism does not create this dilemma; it merely expresses it. Koestler, on the other hand, poses the problem in such a way as to miss the essential ambivalence of the subjective and objective options of the Yogi and the Commissar. The values of the Yogi are not simply the reverse of those of the Commissar because each experiences an internal reversal of the subjective and objective values whenever either is assumed as an absolute end. It is for this reason that Commissar Rubashov, once imprisoned, experiences the value of the self in the depths of its inner life where it opens up to the White Guard in the next cell as someone to whom one can speak. The tapping on the prison walls is the primordial institution of human communication for whose sake Rubashov had set out on his revolutionary career.

In the debate over the alternatives of industrialization and collectivization there were facts to support the various arguments of Stalin, Bukharin and Trotsky. But their divergences arose within the very Marxian conception of history which they all shared. Each regarded history as a reality made through action in line with yet altering the shape of social forces, just as a landscape is progressively revealed with each step we take through it.

> History is terror because we have to move into it not by any straight line that is always easy to trace but by taking our bearings at every moment in a general situation which is changing, like a traveller who pushes into a changing countryside continuously altered by his own advance, where what looked like an obstacle becomes an opening and where the shortest path turns out the longest.[16]

But the leaders of a revolution are not on a casual stroll. They walk on the wild side and must accept responsibility for the path they choose and to be judged by it as soon as they open it up. For this reason Merleau-Ponty argued that the Moscow Trials have to be understood in terms of the Marxist philosophy of history in which history is a drama open towards the future in such a way that the significance of the action at any point of time is never unequivocal and can only be established from the futurist orientation of the men in power. The

Trials therefore never go beyond the level of a 'ceremony of language' in which the meaning of 'terrorism', 'wrecking', 'espionage', 'defeatism', 'responsibility' and 'confession' has to be sensed entirely in the verbal exchanges and not through reference to an external ground of verification.

The Trials reveal the form and style of the Marxist revolutionary. The revolutionary judges what exists in terms of what is to come; he regards the future as more vital than the present to which it owes its birth. From this perspective there can be no purely subjective honour; we are what we are for others and our relation to them. So often in the Court Proceedings the 'capitulators', while presenting themselves in the light of enemies of the Party and the masses, at the same time hint at the discrepancies between the subjective and objective aspects of their careers. Their statements are to be understood not as formulations of the facts alleged in them except reflectively and by means of certain rules of translation. Consider the following exchange between Vyshinsky and Bukharin:

Vyshinsky: Tell me, did Tomsky link up the perpetration of a hostile act against Gorky with the question of the overthrow of the Soviet government?
Bukharin: In essence he did.
Vyshinsky: In essence he did?
Bukharin: Yes, I have answered.
Vyshinsky: I am interested in the essence.
Bukharin: But you are asking concretely...
Vyshinsky: Did your talk with Tomsky provide reason to believe that the question of a hostile act against Alexei Maximovich Gorky was being linked up with the task of overthrowing the Stalin leadership?
Bukharin: Yes, in essence this could be said.
Vyshinsky: Consequently, you knew that some hostile act against Gorky was under consideration?
Bukharin: Yes.
Vyshinsky: And what hostile act in your opinion was referred to?
Bukharin: I gave no thought to the matter at all at that time and I had no idea...
Vyshinsky: Tell us what you did think.
Bukharin: I hardly thought at all.

Vyshinsky: But was it not a serious matter? The conversation was about what?

Bukharin: Permit me to explain in a few words. Now, *post factum*, now, during the investigation, I can say...

Vyshinsky: Not during the investigation but during your conversation with Tomsky.

Bukharin: But this was only a fleeting conversation, a conversation which took place during a meeting of the Political Bureau and lasted only a few seconds.

Vyshinsky: I am not interested in how long this conversation lasted; you could have spoken to Tomsky for a whole hour somewhere in a corner, therefore your arguments are of no importance to me. What is important to me are the facts, and these I want to establish.[17]

It is not possible to understand these verbal plays apart from the Hegelian-Marxist expressions of the hypostases through which the logic of social forces reveals the essence of a situation or fact and its relevance for revolutionary action.[18] They will otherwise only seem to be the result of a corrupt legal process and as such the pure expression of Soviet terror. If *Humanism and Terror* were merely engaged in an *ex post* justification of Stalinism then Merleau-Ponty would simply have been doing bad historiography. But he understood himself to be involved in trying to comprehend Stalinism *ex ante* or from the political agent's standpoint, in other words, in the subjective terms of a Marxist philosophy of history and not just a Stalinist rewrite.

2 Responsible history

It is, then, Merleau-Ponty's interpretation of the Marxist philosophy of history that must concern us. His method of presentation in this case, as elsewhere, involves the familiar alternatives of determinism and voluntarism. As a complete alternative, determinism is incompatible with the need for political action, though it may be extremely effective in the rhetoric of politics to be able to reassure one's comrades that history is on their side; and similarly, a voluntarism that does not take into account the social preconditions of revolution is likely to waste itself in abortive action. Political reflection and political action occur in a milieu or interworld which is essentially ambiguous because the facts of the situation can never be totalized and yet we are obliged to act upon our estimation of them. Because of the double contingency of the openness of the future and the partiality of human decision, political divergences, deception and violence are irreducible historical phenomena, accepted as such by all revolutionaries.

> There is no history where the course of events is a series of episodes without unity, or where it is a struggle already decided in the heaven of ideas. History is where there is a logic *within* contingence, a reason *within* unreason, where there is a historical perception which, like perception in general, leaves in the background what cannot enter the foreground but seizes the lines of force as they are generated and actively leads their traces to a conclusion. This analogy should not be interpreted as a shameful organicism or finalism, but as a reference to the fact that all symbolic systems – perception, language, history – only become what they were although in order to do so they need to be taken up into human initiative.[19]

Marxism is not a spectacle secure from its own intervention in our common history. Marxists need a philosophy of history because human history is neither open in an arbitrary way nor so closed that we are relieved of the responsibility of reading its signs and implementing our own chances. The future is not stillborn in the present nor does the past lie unalterably upon the present. Between the past and the future there is the presence of ourselves which is the chance we have of testing our limits. In the human world men cannot be the object of their own practice except where oppression rules – that is to say, where some men subject others to the rule of things. Yet men need leaders as much as leaders need men. Thus there arises for Marxism the dreadful problem, once men are determined to be free, of how it is free men are to be led along the path of freedom. For freedom is not the absence of limits which would make knowledge and leadership unnecessary. Freedom is only possible in the real world of limits and situated possibilities which require the institution of thoughtful and responsible leadership.[20]

In confronting the problematic of freedom and truth, Merleau-Ponty reflected upon man's options in terms of Max Weber's response to the historical task of understanding. He saw in Weber one who tried to live responsibly in the face of the conflicting demands of knowledge and action. This was possible, in the first place, because Weber understood that history is not the passive material of historiography any more than the practice of historiography is itself free of historical interests and values. There is no neutral material of history. History is not a spectacle for us because it is our own living, our own violence and our own beliefs. Why then are revolutionary politics not an utterly cynical resort to violence and nothing but a sceptical appeal to justice and truth? For the very reason, says Merleau-Ponty, that no one lives history from a purely pragmatic standpoint, not even he who claims to do so. Scepticism is a conclusion which could only be reached if one were to draw – as does Sartre – a radical distinction between political knowledge and political action. But allowing that we only experience things and the future according to a probable connection does not mean that the world lacks a certain style or physiognomy for us. We live in terms of subjective certainties which we intend as practical and universal typifications that are in no way illusory unless we posit some apodictic certainty outside the grounds of human experience. We do not experience uncertainty at the core of our being. The centre of our experience is a common world in which we make appraisals, enlist support and seek to convince sceptics and opponents, never doubting the fundamental permutation of subjective and objective evidence.[21]

If we accept the Marxist view that there is meaning in history as in the rest of our lives, then it follows that Marxist politics are based upon an objective analysis of the main trends in history and not simply on the will of the Communist Party. In other words, there is a materialist foundation to Marxist politics. At the same time, the trends in history do not lead necessarily to a socialist society. History is made through human action and political choices which are never perfectly informed and thus there is always a contingent factor in history. It is necessary to avoid construing these materialist and ideological factors too crudely. Marxian materialism is not the simple notion that human history consists in the production of wealth; it is the project of creating a human environment which reflects the historical development of human sensibility. Similarly, the Marxist claim that ideological systems are related to economic factors is not a simple reductionist argument; it is the claim that ideological factors and the mode of production are mutually determining expressions of a given social order. At any given moment the mode of production may be the expression of the ideological superstructure, just as the physical movements of the body may express a person's lifestyle. But in the long run it is the economic infrastructure which is the medium of the ideological message – just as our body is the structure underlying all our moods. Because we do not inhabit the present as a region totally within our survey, nor yet as a zone of pure possibility, history has familiar contours for us, a feel that we recognize in our daily lives where others share the same conditions and the same hopes. This daily life is something we shape through our desires and which in turn acquires an institutional reality which conditions the future limits and possibilities that are our life chances. In short, we bring a lifestyle to political action, a lifetime of suffering, with others and for others, and together, for better or worse, we decide to act. But it is neither an open nor a closed calculation. It is more like the decision to live from which we cannot withdraw, a decision which we never make once and for all and yet for which we are uniquely responsible. And like the decision to live, the choice of a politics entails the responsibility for the contingency of violence which is the 'infantile disorder' in our private and public lives.

> One can no more get rid of historical materialism than of psychoanalysis by impugning 'reductionist' conceptions and causal thought in the name of a descriptive and phenomenological method, for historical materialism is no more linked to such 'causal' formulations as may have been given than is psychoanalysis, and like the latter it could be expressed in another language. . . .
>
> There is no one meaning of history; what we do always has several meanings, and this is where an existential conception of history is distinguishable from materialism and spiritualism. But every cultural phenomenon has, among others, an economic significance, and history by its nature never transcends, any more than it is reducible to, economics. . . . It is impossible to reduce the life which involves human relationships either to economic relations, or to juridical and moral ones thought up by men, just as it is impossible to reduce individual life either to bodily functions or to our knowledge of life as it involves them. But in each case one of the orders of significance can be regarded as dominant: one gesture is 'sexual', another as 'amorous', another as 'warlike', and even in the sphere of coexistence, one period of history can be seen as characterized by intellectual culture, another as primarily political or economic. The question whether the history of our time is pre-eminently significant in an economic sense, and whether our ideologies give us only a derivative or secondary meaning of it

> is one which no longer belongs to philosophy, but to politics, and one which will be solved only by seeking to know whether the economic or ideological scenario fits the facts more perfectly. Philosophy can only show that it is *possible* from the starting point of the human condition.[22]

The foundations of Marxian history and politics are grounded in the dialectic between man and nature and between man and his fellow men. It is the nature of human consciousness to realize itself in the world and among men; its embodiment is the essential mode of its openness towards the world and to others. The problems of conflict and co-existence only arise for an embodied consciousness driven by its basic needs into the social division of labour and engaged by its deepest need in a life and death struggle for identity through mutual recognition and solidarity. Embodied consciousness never experiences an original innocence to which any violence would do irreparable harm; we experience only different kinds of violence. For consciousness only becomes aware of itself as already engaged in the world, in definite and specific situations in which its resources are never entirely its own but derive from the exploitation of its position as the child of these parents, the incumbent of such and such a role, or the beneficiary of certain class and national privileges. We rarely act as isolated individuals and even when we seem to do so our deeds presuppose a community which possesses a common measure of the good and evil it experiences.

The problem which besets the Marxist theory of the proletariat is that the emergence of truth and justice presupposes a community while at the same time the realization of a genuine community presupposes a concept of truth and justice. The Marxist critique of the liberal truth as a mystification which splits the liberal community starts from the exposure of its lack of correspondence with the objective relations between man in liberal society. By contrast, Marxism claims to be a truth in the making; it aims at overthrowing liberal society in the name of an authentic community. However, the birth of Communist society is no less painful than the birth of man himself and from its beginnings Communism is familiar with violence and deception. It might be argued that the violence of Marxist revolutionary politics arises because the Party forces upon the proletariat a mission for which history has not prepared it. The proletariat is thus the victim of the double contingency of bourgeois and Communist deception and exploitation. The constant shifts in Party directives, the loss of socialist innocence, the reappearance of profit and status in Communist society may be appealed to as indications of the failure of Marxism to renew human history. Merleau-Ponty was aware of these arguments and indeed explicitly documents them with findings on conditions in the Soviet Union, including the shattering discovery of the labour camps.[23]

Nevertheless, Merleau-Ponty argued that the proper role of Marxist violence is as the midwife of a socialist society already in the womb of capitalist society. The image is essential to his argument. For it intended to distinguish Marxist violence from historically arbitrary and authoritarian forms of violence.[24] The image of birth suggests a natural process in which there arises a point of intervention which is likely to be painful but is aimed at preserving a life which is *already there* and not entirely at the mercy of the midwife. In the language of the *Communist Manifesto*, the argument is that the birth of socialist society depends upon the full maturation of capitalism which engenders a force whose transition from dependency to independence is achieved through a painful transition in which dramatic roles are assigned to the bourgeoisie, the proletariat, and the Party. There are, of course, features of the imagery of birth that lead to outcomes rather different from those which Merleau-Ponty wishes to draw. The human infant achieves maturity only after a long period of tutelage in which if anything social dependency becomes far more burdensome than umbilical dependency, as we have learned from Freud. Understood in this way the image involves a greater political dependency of the proletariat upon the Party and its commissars than is compatible with the aims of socialist humanism. Merleau-Ponty's ideal for the childhood of the revolution is the period of Lenin's frank and open discussions with the proletariat, concerning the reasons for New Economic Policy. This was a time when words still had their face meaning, when explanations for changes of tactics were given which left the proletariat with an improved understanding of events and with heightened revolutionary consciousness.

> Marxist Machiavellianism differs from Machiavellianism insofar as it transforms compromise through awareness of compromise, and alters the ambivalence of history through awareness of ambivalence; it makes detours knowingly and by announcing them as such; it calls retreats retreats; it sets the details of local politics and the paradoxes of strategy in the perspective of the whole.[25]

Marxist violence is thus an integral feature of the theory of the proletariat and its philosophy of history. To be a Marxist is to see meaning taking shape within history. Anything else is to live history and society as sheer force. To be a Marxist is to believe that history is intelligible and that it has a direction which encompasses the proletarian control of the economic and state apparatus, along with the emergence of an international brotherhood. Whatever the lags on any of these fronts, it is the Marxist persuasion that these elements delineate the essential structure or style of Communist society. It is this structure of beliefs which determines the Marxist style of historical analysis and political action.

Even before he turned to Max Weber for his conception of responsible history, Merleau-Ponty had anticipated those adventures of the dialectic which had made it necessary to rethink Marxism as a philosophy of history and institutions. Unless this task is undertaken, Marxism must either continue to hide from its own history or else see its universal hopes thrown into the waste of historical relativism. Only an absolutely relativist conception of history as the milieu of our own living can keep alive what Merleau-Ponty called 'Western' Marxism.

> History is not only an object in front of us, far from us, beyond our reach: it is also our awakening as subjects. Itself a historical fact the true or false consciousness that we have of our history cannot be simple illusion. There is a mineral there to be refined, a truth to be extracted, if only we go to the limits of relativism and put it, in turn, back into history. We give a form to history according to our categories; but our categories, in contact with history, are themselves freed from their partiality. The old problem of the relations between subject and object is transformed, and relativism is surpassed as soon as one puts it in historical terms, since here the object is the vestige left by other subjects, and the subject – historical understanding – held in the fabric of history, is by this very fact capable of self-criticism.[26]

We have to understand how it is that Marxism which arises as a movement within history can be the fulfilment of history rather than a phase subject to its own laws of historical transition. How is it possible that men who are driven by material circumstances in general and the proletariat in particular are capable of the vision of humanity freed from exploitation and alientation? However these questions are answered, we have to face the fact that the proletariat is given direction by the Communist Party and that with respect to this relationship we face new questions about Marxist knowledge and the freedom of the masses. In his analysis of these questions Merleau-Ponty extended his reading of Weber through Lukács's studies in Marxist dialectics.[27] In terms of this reading Merleau-Ponty came to a reformulation of Marx's historical materialism. If materialism were a literal truth it is hard to see how the category of history could arise. For matter does not have a history except by metaphorical extension. Men live in history. But their history is not external to themselves in the same sense that the history of a geological strata might be available to observation. Men inhabit history as they do language.[28] Just as they have to learn the specific vocabulary of Marxism, so they have to bring their everyday experiences of poverty, power and violence under the notion of the 'proletariat' and to interpret their experiences through the projection of 'class consciousness' and 'revolution'. Thus 'class consciousness' does not inhere in history either as a pre-existing idea or as an inherent environmental force. What we can say is that despite all its contingencies the history of society gathers into itself the consciousness that is dispersed in all its members so that it fosters their consciousness as civic knowledge:

> As a living body, given its behavior, is, so to speak, closer to consciousness than a stone, so certain social structures are the cradle of the knowledge of society. Pure consciousness finds its 'origin' in them. Even if the notion of interiority, when applied to a society, should be understood in the figurative sense, we find, all the same, that this metaphor is possible with regard to capitalist society but not so with regard to pre-capitalist ones. This is enough for us to say that the history which produced capitalism symbolizes the emergence of a subjectivity. There are subjects, objects, there are men and things, but there is also a third order, that of relationships between men inscribed in tools or social symbols. These relationships have their development, their advances and their regressions. Just as in the life of the individual, so in this generalized life there are tentative aims, failure or success, reaction of the result upon the aim, repetition or variation, and this is what one calls history.[29]

Despite its detours and regressions, Merleau-Ponty retains his conviction of the overall meaning of human history as an emancipatory process but allows for the successes and failures in this project to lie in one and the same historical plane. History is the growing relationship of man to man. This does not mean that all previous societies are to be judged by today's standards because at every stage history is threatened with loss and diversion. What we can properly regard as today's developments really only takes up problems that were immanent in the previous period. Hence the past is not merely the waste of the future. If we can speak of an advance in history it is perhaps only in the negative sense that we can speak of the elimination of non-sense rather than of the positive accumulation of reason. The price we must pay for history's deliverance of reason and freedom is that freedom and reason never operate outside of the constraints of history and politics. Therefore Marxism cannot simply claim to see through all other ideologies as though it alone were transparent to itself. Indeed, Marxism is itself open to the danger of becoming the most false ideology of all inasmuch as its own political life will require changes of position that can hardly be read from the state of its economic infrastructure.

If Marxism is not to degenerate into a wilful ideology and yet not claim absolute knowledge, it must be geared to the praxis of the proletariat. But this is not an easy matter since the proletariat does not spontaneously realize its own goals and by the same token the Party cannot easily avoid a specious appeal to the allegedly objective interests of the proletariat. If like Sartre we force the distinction between theory and praxis, then the Party is either reduced to a democratic consultation of the momentary thoughts and feelings of the proletariat or else to bureaucratic cynicism with regard to the gap between the present state of the proletariat and the Party's idea of its future. So long as we think of consciousness as a state of individual minds then we cannot get around the problem of locating the synthesis of knowledge in an absolute consciousness, called the Party. This means that the proletariat is really not the subject of its own deeds but the object of what the Party knows on its behalf. To understand Merleau-Ponty's critique of Sartre's 'ultrabolshevism' we need to have some notion of how they were divided even over a common philosophical background. The opposition between Sartre and Merleau-Ponty derives in the first place from their fundamentally opposite phenomenologies of embodiment. For Sartre the body is a vehicle of shame, nausea and ultimate alienation caught in the trap of the other's look.[30] In Merleau-Ponty the body is the vehicle of the very world and others with whom together we labour in love and understanding and the very same ground to which we must appeal to correct error or overcome violence. In

Sartre the body is the medium of the world's decomposition, while in Merleau-Ponty the body symbolizes the very composition of the world and society. In each case there follow radically different conceptions of political life. In Merleau-Ponty, the extremes of collectivism and individualism, labour and violence are always historical dimensions of our basic social life. To Sartre, nothing unites us to nature and society except the external necessity of scarcity which obliges us to join our labour and individual sovereignty into collective projects which are always historically unstable.

> The 'master', the 'feudal lord', the 'bourgeois', the 'capitalist' all appear not only as powerful people who command but in addition and above all *Thirds*; that is, as those who are outside the oppressed community and *for whom* this community exists. It is therefore *for* them and *in their freedom* that the reality of the oppressed class is going to exist. They cause it to be born by their look. It is to them and through them that there is revealed the identity of my condition and that of others who are oppressed; it is for them that I exist in a situation organized with others and that my possibles as dead-possibles are strictly equivalent with the possibles of others; it is for them that I am a worker and it is through and in their revelation as the Other-as-a-look that I experience myself as one among others. This means that I discover the 'Us' in which I am integrated or 'the class' *outside*, in the look of the Third, and it is this collective alienation which I assume when saying 'Us'. From this point of view the privileges of the Third and 'our' burdens, 'our' miseries have value at first only as a *signification*; they signify the independence of the Third in relation to 'Us'; they present our alienation to us more plainly. Yet as they are nonetheless *endured, as in particular our work, our fatigue are nonetheless suffered*, it is across this endured suffering that I experience my being-looked-at-as-a-thing-engaged-in-a-totality-of-things. It is in terms of my suffering, of my misery that I am collectively apprehended with others by the Third; that is, in terms of the adversity of the world, in terms of the facticity of my condition. Without the Third, no matter what might be the adversity of the world, I should apprehend myself as a triumphant transcendence; with the appearance of the Third, 'I' experience 'Us' as apprehended in terms of things and as things overcome by the world.[31]

In Sartrean Marxism it is therefore the role of the Party to unite an ever-disintegrating proletariat to which it plays the role of the other or Third analogous to the role of the capitalist as the Other who unites the atomized labour of the workshop or assembly line. In effect, Sartre constructs the Party as the sole source of historical intelligibility because he denies any basis for intersubjectivity to arise at other levels of conduct. The result is that Sartre is obliged to idealize the notions of fact, action and history as nothing but what is determined by the Party. Hence the Party is subject to permanent anxiety since it is deprived of any middle ground between itself and a proletarian praxis from which it might learn to formulate, revise and initiate plans that do not risk its whole life. Because he can only understand expression as pure creation or as simple imitation, Sartre loses the real ground of political communication.

> If one wants to engender revolutionary politics dialectically from the proletarian condition, the revolution from the rigidified swarm of thoughts without subject, Sartre answers with a dilemma: either the conscious renewal alone gives its meaning to the process, or one returns to organicism. What he rejects under the name of organicism at the level of history is in reality much more than the notion of life: it is symbolism understood as a functioning of signs having its own efficacy beyond the meanings that analysis can assign to these signs. It is, more generally, expression. For him expression either goes beyond what is expressed and is then a pure creation, or it copies it and is then a simple unveiling. But an action which is an unveiling, an unveiling which is an action – in short, a dialectic – this Sartre does not want to consider.[32]

Properly speaking, praxis is not divided between theory and practice but lies in the wider realm of communication and expression. Here Merleau-Ponty's argument already anticipates Habermas's later correction of Marx's confusion of the emancipatory orders of labour and symbolic interaction.[33] The everyday life of the proletariat makes the notion of a class a possibility long before it is formulated as such. When the occasion for the explicit appeal to class consciousness arises, its formal possibility does not lie in the power of the Party's theoreticians but in the ordinary capacity of men to appraise their situation, and to speak their minds together because their thoughts are not locked behind their skulls but are near enough the same in anyone's experience of exploitation and injustice. Of course, the Party has to give these thoughts a political life, to realize their truth as common achievement in which the proletariat and the Party are mutually enlightened.

> This exchange, in which no one commands and no one obeys, is symbolized by the old custom which dictates that, in a meeting, speakers join in when the audience applauds. What they applaud is the fact that they do not intervene as persons, that in their relationship with those who listen to them a truth appears which does not come from them and which the speakers can and must applaud. In the communist sense, the Party is this communication; and such a conception of the Party is not a corrollary of Marxism – it is its very center.[34]

Thus we see that the heart of Marxism is not just the communalizing of property but the attainment of an ideally communicative or educative society whose icon is the Party. At the same time, this ideal society of labour and speech is obliged to resort to violence since its truths reflect only a reality that has to be brought into being. Marxist truth is not hidden behind empirical history waiting to be deciphered by the Party theoreticians. Ultimately, the issue here is the question of the education of the Party itself in its role of educating the masses. It was first raised by Marx himself in the *Third Thesis on Feuerbach*. If the Party is not above history then it is inside history like the proletariat itself. The problem is how to relativize the opposition between Party and proletarian consciousness so that their mutual participation in history is not organized in terms of a (Party) subject and (proletariat) object split. The argument between Sartre and Merleau-Ponty parallels the difference between the political practices of Lenin and Stalin, at least insofar as Merleau-Ponty like Lukács can argue for a period in Lenin's own use of the Party as an instrument of proletarian education and party self-critique. In his book, *Lenin*,[35] Lukács argues with respect to Lenin's political practice much the same thing that Merleau-Ponty later espoused, namely that it must not be confused with *realpolitik*.

> Above all, when defining the concept of compromise, any suggestion that it is a question of knack, of cleverness, of an astute fraud, must be rejected. 'We must,' said Lenin, 'decisively reject those who think that politics consists of little tricks, sometimes bordering on deceit. *Classes cannot be deceived*.'

> For Lenin, therefore, compromise means *that the true developmental tendencies of classes* (and possibly of nations – for instance, where an oppressed people is concerned), which under specific circumstances and for a certain period run parallel in determinate areas with the interests of the proletariat, are exploited to the advantage of *both*.[36]

In the postscript to his essay on Lenin, Lukács repeats the argument for the unity of Lenin's theoretical grasp of the political nature of the imperialist epoch and his practical sense of proletarian politics. In trying to express the living nature of that unity in Lenin's own life, Lukács describes how Lenin would learn from experience or from Hegel's *Logic*, according to the situation, preserving in himself the dialectical tension between particulars and a theoretical totality. As Lenin writes in his *Philosophic Notebooks*, 'Theoretical cognition ought to give the Object in its necessity, in its all-sided relations, in its contradictory movement, in- and for-itself. But the human Concept "definitively" catches this objective truth of cognition, seizes and masters it, only when the Concept becomes "being-for-itself" in the sense of practice.'

It was by turning to Hegel that Lenin sought to find a way to avoid making theory the mere appendage of state practice, while reserving to practice a more creative political role than the retroactive determination or revision of ideology. But this meant that Marxist materialism could never be the simple enforcement of political will, any more than political will could be exercised without a theoretical understanding of the specific class relations it presupposed. Thus Lenin remarks that:

> The standpoint of life, of practice, should be first and fundamental in the theory of knowledge. . . . Of course, we must not forget that the criterion of practice can never, in the nature of things, either confirm or refute any idea *completely*. This criterion too is sufficiently 'indefinite' not to allow human knowledge to become 'absolute', but at the same time it is sufficiently definite to wage a ruthless fight against all varieties of idealism and agnosticism.

Of course, in these later Hegelian formulations Lenin is modifying his own version of Engels's dialectical materialism as set forth in *Materialism and Empirio-Criticism*, thereby rejoining the challenge set to this work by Lukács's own *History and Class Consciousness*, as well as Karl Korsch's *Marxism and Philosophy*, both published in 1923. Lukács's essay on Lenin was published on the occasion of Lenin's death in 1924. What died with Lenin was Orthodox Marxism, although its dead hand was to be upon socialism for another thirty years or more. But while it is clear that scientific socialism was not ready for Lukács, the same must be said of the West, where only today is the critique of scientific praxis entering into a properly reflexive or critical social science. What *History and Class Consciousness* made clear was that living Marxism is inseparable from its idealist and Hegelian legacy. The Hegelian concept of totality furnishes a matrix for the integration of ethics and politics through the restless dynamics of man's attempt to measure his existential circumstances against the ideal of his human essence, which he achieves through the struggle against self and institutional alienations. The Hegelian Marxist totality is thus the basis for the integral humanism of Marxist social science.[37]

What Merleau-Ponty adds to Hegelian Marxism from his own phenomenology of perception is an unshakeable grasp of the 'interworld' (*intermonde*) of everyday living and conduct which is far too dense and stratified to be a thing of pure consciousness. This is the world of our species-being, a corporeal world whose deep structures of action and reflection are the anonymous legacies of the body politic.[38] The interworld is never available to us in a single unifying moment of consciousness or as a decision whose consequences are identical with the actor's intentions. But then none of us thinks or acts outside of a life whose ways have moulded us so that what 'we' seek is never entirely our own and therefore borrows upon the very collective life which it advances or retards. Thus we never have anything like Sartre's absolute power of decision to join withdraw from collective life. What we have is an ability to shift institutions off centre, polarizing tradition and freedom in the same plane as creativity and imitation. Our freedom, therefore, never comes to us entirely from the outside through the Party, as Sartre would have it. It begins inside us like the movements of our body in response to the values of a world which it opens up through its own explorations and accommodations. It follows that Sartre's conception of the Party in fact expropriates the spontaneity of all life in the name of the proletariat, having first separated the proletariat from what it shares with men anywhere engaged in struggle for life.

> The question is to know whether, as Sartre says, there are only *men* and *things* or whether there is also the interworld, which we call history, symbolism, truth-to-be-made. If one sticks to the dichotomy, men, as the place where all meaning arises, are condemned to an incredible tension. Each man, in literature as well as in politics, must assume all that happens instant by instant to all others, he must be immediately universal. If, on the contrary, one acknowledges a mediation of personal relationships through the world of human symbols, it is true that one renounces being instantly justified in the eyes of everyone and holding oneself responsible for all that is done at each moment. But since consciousness cannot in practice maintain its pretension of being God, since it is inevitably led to delegate responsibility – it is one abdication for another, and we prefer the one which leaves consciousness the means of knowing what it is doing.[39]

The universality and truth towards which political consciousness aims are not intrinsic properties of the Party. They are acquisitions continuously established and re-established in a community and tradition of knowledge for which individuals in specific historical situations call and to which they respond. Understood in this way, history is the call of one thought to another, because each individual's work or action is created across the path of self and others towards a public which it elicits rather than serves. That is, history is the field which individual effort requires in order to become one with the community it seeks to build so that where it is successful its invention appears always to have been necessary. Individual action, then, is the invention of history, because it is shaped in a present which previously was not just a void waiting to be determined by the word or deed but in a tissue of calling and response which is the life of no one and everyone. Every one of life's actions, in so far as it invokes its truth, lives in the expectation of an historical inscription, a judgment not only of its intention or consequences but also of its fecundity which is the relevance of its 'story' to the present.

> History is the judge – not History as the Power of a moment or of a century – but history as the space of inscription and accumulation beyond the limits of countries and epochs of what we have said and done that is most true and valuable, taking into account the circumstances in which we had to speak. Others will judge what I have done because I painted the painting

> to be seen, because my action committed the future of others; but neither art nor politics consists in pleasing or flattering others. What they expect of the artist or politician is that he draw them toward values in which they will only later recognize their own values. The painter or politician shapes others more than he follows them. The *public* at whom he aims is not given; it is a public to be elicited by his work. The others of whom he thinks are not empirical 'others', nor even *humanity* conceived as a species; it is others once they have become such that he can live with them. The history in which the artist participates (and it is better the less he thinks about 'making history' and honestly produces *his* work as he sees it) is not a power before which he must genuflect. It is the perpetual conversation woven together by all speech, all valid works and actions, each according to its place and circumstance, contesting and confirming the other, each one recreating all the others.[40]

Merleau-Ponty returns Marxist politics to the flux of the natural and historical world, rejecting its compromise with the ideas of objectivism which have made the tradition of rationality an enigma to itself. Henceforth, politics must abide in the life-world where Husserl found its roots and from there it must recover its own ontological history.

Today history is hardly more meaningful because of the advent of socialism in the Soviet Union or elsewhere. Indeed, the potential nuclear confrontation of world ideologies has brought human history to new heights of absurdity. Marxism has become a truth for large parts of the world but not in the sense it intended. The question is what conclusion we should draw from this. Writing in 1947 and the decade following, Merleau-Ponty was afraid that the West would try to resolve the Communist problem through war. To this he argued that the failures of Communism are the failures of Western humanism as a whole and so we cannot be partisan to it, far less indifferent. The Marxist revolution can lose its way. This is because, as Merleau-Ponty puts it, it is a mode of human conduct which may be true as a movement but false as a regime. But it is the nature of political action to offer no uniquely happy solution. Political life involves a fundamental evil in which we are forced to choose between values without knowing for certain which are absolutely good or evil. In the Trojan wars the Greek gods fought on both sides. It is only in modern politics that, as Camus remarks, the human mind has become an armed camp. In this situation Merleau-Ponty wrote to overcome the split between good and evil which characterizes the politics of crisis and conflict. Above all, he raised the voice of reason which, despite scepticism and error, achieves a truth for us that is continuous with nothing else than our own efforts to maintain it.

> For the very moment we assert that unity and reason do not *exist* and that opinions are carried along by discordant options which remain below the level of reason the consciousness we gain of the irrationalism and contingency in us cancels them as fatalities and opens us to the other person. Doubt and disagreement are facts, but so is the strange pretension we all have of thinking the truth, our capacity for taking the other's position to judge ourselves, our need to have our opinions recognized by him and to justify our choices before him, in short, the experience of the other person as an *alter ego* in the very course of discussion. *The human world is an open or unfinished system and the same radical contingency which threatens it with discord also rescues it from the inevitability of disorder and prevents us from despairing of it*, providing only that one remembers that its various machineries are actually men and tries to maintain and expand man's relations to man.
>
> Such a philosophy cannot tell us *that* humanity will be realized as though it possessed some knowledge apart and were not itself embarked upon experience, being only a more acute consciousness of it. But it awakens us to the importance of daily events and action. For it is a philosophy which arouses in us a love for our times which are not the simple repetition of human eternity nor merely the conclusion to premises already postulated. It is a view which like the most fragile object of perception – a soap bubble, or a wave – or like the most simple dialogue, embraces indivisibly all the order and all the disorder of the world.[41]

Notes

1 The critique of Marxist scientism was first advanced for English readers (if we leave aside the earlier and then untranslated work of Karl Korsch, *Marxism and Philosophy*, and Georg Lukács, *History and Class Consciousness*) by Karl Popper in his *The Open Society and its Enemies* and *The Poverty of Historicism*. I have examined this debate in John O'Neill (ed.), *Modes of Individualism*

and Collectivism, London, Heinemann, and New York, St Martin's Press, 1973.

2 In a number of essays I have argued for the unity of Marxist humanism and science. See my 'For Marx Against Althusser', *The Human Context*, vol. 6, no. 2, Summer 1974, pp. 385–98; and 'The Concept of Estrangement in Early and Late Writings of Karl Marx', in my *Sociology as a Skin Trade, Essays Towards a Reflexive Sociology*, London, Heinemann, and New York, Harper & Row, 1972, pp. 113–36; and 'Marxism and Mythology', ibid., pp. 137–54.

3 George Lichtheim, *From Marx to Hegel, and other Essays*, London, Orbach & Chambers, 1971.

4 George Lichtheim, *Marxism in Modern France*, New York and London, Columbia University Press, 1966; and *From Marx to Hegel*, London, Orbach & Chambers, 1971.

5 Alfred Schmidt, *The Concept of Nature in Marx*, London, NLB, 1971.

6 Jean Hyppolite, *Studies on Marx and Hegel*, ed. and trans. John O'Neill, New York, Basic Books, and London, Heinemann, 1969.

7 Alexandre Kojève, *Introduction to the Reading of Hegel*, New York, Basic Books, 1969.

8 Richard Crossman (ed.), *The God that Failed*, New York, Harper & Row, 1949; Michel-Antoine Burnier, *Choice of Action*, trans. Bernard Murchland, New York, Random House, 1968.

9 Maurice Merleau-Ponty, *Humanism and Terror, An Essay on the Communist Problem*, trans. and with an introduction by John O'Neill, Boston, Beacon Press, 1969.

10 John O'Neill, *Perception, Expression and History: The Social Phenomenology of Maurice Merleau-Ponty*, Evanston, Northwestern University Press, 1970; and Maurice Merleau-Ponty, *Phenomenology, Language and Sociology, Selected Essays*, ed. John O'Neill, London, Heinemann, 1974.

11 Maurice Merleau-Ponty, *Adventures of the Dialectic*, trans. Joseph Bien, Evanston, Northwestern University Press, 1973, p. 6. My emphasis.

12 Alphonse de Waelhens, *Une philosophie de l'ambiguité, L'existentialisme de Maurice Merleau-Ponty*, Louvain, Publications Universitaires de Louvain, 1967.

13 Merleau-Ponty, *Humanism and Terror*, op. cit., pp. 109–10. My emphasis.

14 Maurice Merleau-Ponty, 'Reading Montaigne', *Signs*, trans. Richard C. McLeary, Evanston, Northwestern University Press, 1964; John O'Neill, 'Between Montaigne and Machiavelli', in my *Sociology as a Skin Trade*, op. cit., pp. 96–110.

15 John O'Neill, 'Situation, Action and Language', in my *Sociology as a Skin Trade*, op. cit., pp. 81–93.

16 Merleau-Ponty, *Humanism and Terror*, op. cit., pp. 100–1.

17 Report of Court Proceedings in the Case of the Anti-Soviet

'Bloc of Rights and Trotskyites', Moscow, 2–13 March, 1938. Published by the People's Commissariat of Justice of the USSR, Moscow, 1938.

18 Nathan Leites and Elsa Bernaut, *Ritual of Liquidation, The Case of the Moscow Trials*, Glencoe, Ill., The Free Press, 1954.

19 Maurice Merleau-Ponty, *Themes from the Lectures at the Collège de France, 1952–1960*, trans. John O'Neill, Evanston, Northwestern University Press, 1970, pp. 29–30.

20 John O'Neill, 'Le Langage et la décolonisation: Fanon et Freire', *Sociologie et Sociétes*, vol. 6, no. 2, November 1974, pp. 53–65.

21 John O'Neill, *Making Sense Together, An Introduction to Wild Sociology*, New York, Harper & Row, and London, Heinemann, 1974.

22 Maurice Merleau-Ponty, *Phenomenology of Perception*, trans. Colin Smith, London, Routledge & Kegan Paul, 1962, pp. 171–3.

23 Merleau-Ponty, 'The USSR and the Camps', *Signs*, op. cit., pp. 263–73.

24 'There is indeed a Sartrean violence, and it is more highly strung and less durable than Marx's violence', *Adventures of the Dialectic*, op. cit., p. 159.

25 Merleau-Ponty, *Humanism and Terror*, op. cit., p. 129.

26 Merleau-Ponty, *Adventures of the Dialectic*, op. cit., pp. 30–1.

27 Georg Lukács, *History and Class Consciousness, Studies in Marxist Dialectics*, trans. Rodney Livingstone, London, Merlin Press, 1971.

28 John O'Neill, 'Institution, Language and Historicity', in my *Perception, Expression and History*, op. cit., pp. 46–64.

29 Merleau-Ponty, *Adventures of the Dialectic*, op. cit., pp. 37–8.

30 Jean-Paul Sartre, *Being and Nothingness*, trans. and with an introduction by Hazel E. Barnes, New York, Washington Square Press, 1969, pt III.

31 Sartre, *Being and Nothingness*, op. cit., pp. 544–5.

32 Merleau-Ponty, *Adventures of the Dialectic*, op. cit., p. 142.

33 'In his empirical analyses Marx comprehends the history of the species under the categories of material activity *and* the critical abolition of ideologies, of instrumental action *and* revolutionary practice, of labor *and* reflection at once. But Marx interprets what he does in the more restricted conception of the species' self-reflection through work alone. The materialist concept of synthesis is not conceived broadly enough in order to explicate the way in which Marx contributes to realizing the intention of a really radicalized critique of knowledge. In fact, it even prevented Marx from understanding his own mode of procedure from this point of view.' (Jürgen Habermas, *Knowledge and Human Interests*, trans. Jeremy J. Shapiro, Boston, Beacon Press, 1971, p. 42. Cf. Jürgen Habermas, *Theory and Practice*, trans. by John Viertel, Boston, Beacon Press, 1973, ch. 4, 'Labor and Interaction: Remarks on Hegel's Jena *Philosophy of Mind*'.)

34 Merleau-Ponty, *Adventures of the Dialectic*, op. cit., p. 51.
35 Georg Lukács, *Lenin, A Study on the Unity of his Thought*, London, New Left Books, 1970.
36 Lukács, *Lenin*, op. cit., p. 79.
37 This much has been established in the academic debate over the early and later writings of Marx. One would have thought that it is no longer arguable that Marxism can be separated from its Hegelian sources. Yet, recently this argument has reappeared in the influential contributions to critical theory developed by Habermas and by the structuralist readings of Marx fostered by Althusser. I have considered these arguments in my essays, 'Can Phenomenology be Critical?', and 'On Theory and Criticism in Marx', in my *Sociology as a Skin Trade*, op. cit., pp. 221–36 and pp. 237–63.
38 John O'Neill, 'Authority, Knowledge and the Body Politics', in *Sociology as a Skin Trade*, op. cit., pp. 68–80.
39 Merleau-Ponty, *Adventures of the Dialectic*, op. cit., p. 200.
40 Maurice Merleau-Ponty, *The Prose of the World*, trans. and with an introduction by John O'Neill, Evanston, Northwestern University Press, 1973, p. 86.
41 Merleau-Ponty, *Humanism and Terror*, op. cit., pp. 188–9.

BIOGRAPHICAL INFORMATION

Jan M. Broekman: Born 1931 in Voorburg (Netherlands). Studied sociology and philosophy in Leiden and Göttingen; dissertation on Husserl ('Phänomenologie und Egologie', 1963). Has taught at the Social Academy of the Hague and at the University of Amsterdam. Since 1968 professor of philosophy with special attention to the philosophy of law and contemporary philosophy at the University of Leuven. Additional publications: *Strukturalism* (1974) (translated into Dutch, English, German and Spanish), as well as numerous studies concerning aesthetics, the foundations of psychiatry, social philosophy and the philosophy and theory of law. Editor of the series 'Kolleg Rechtstheorie' (Alber Verlag) in West Germany. Broekman is concerned with a synthesis of structuralism and dialogical thought (Buber), making use of his phenomenological training and inspiration from Marxism.

Fred Dallmayr: Born 1928 in Ulm (Germany). Studied law and political science in Munich (Ph.D. 1955), in Brussels, Turin and at Duke University. Since 1961 he has taught in the USA and is currently professor for political science at the University of Notre Dame. Against the background of phenomenology and hermeneutics, Dallmayr attempts to locate a historically differentiated level of dialogue with Marxism and critical theory. Cf. 'Phenomenology and Marxism', in G. Psathas (ed.), *Phenomenological Sociology* (1973); 'Phenomenology and Critical Theory: Adorno', in *Cultural Hermeneutics* (1976); editor: *Materialien zu Habermas, 'Erkenntnis und Interesse'* (Frankfurt am Main, Suhrkamp, 1974). Recent publications include *From Contract to Community* (1978); *Beyond Dogma and Despair* (1981) and *Twilight of Subjectivity* (1981).

Ludwig Landgrebe: Born 1902 in Vienna. Studied in Vienna and Freiburg. Dissertation under Edmund Husserl (*W. Diltheys Theorie der Geisteswissenschaften*, 1928). Assistant to Husserl. Habilitation in Prague (*Nennfunktion und Wortbedeutung*, 1935). Lecturer in Prague until 1939. First work on the Husserl archives in Leuven,

1939–40. Following the war he taught in Hamburg and Kiel; since 1956 professor in Cologne and head of the Husserl Archives in Cologne. 1970 Emeritus. Landgrebe's attempt to carry Husserl's work forward lays special emphasis on historicity. This and his participation in the Commission on Marxism of the Protestant Study Council accounts for his repeated discussion of the Marxist theory (cf. *Phänomenologie und Geschichte*, 1968). Additional publications: *Phänomenologie und Metaphysik* (1948); *Philosophie der Gegenwart* (1952) (English translation 1966); *Der Weg der Phänomenologie* (1963); *Über einige Grundfragen der Politik* (1969); editor: *E. Husserl, Erfahrung und Urteil* (1948).

John O'Neill: Born 1933 in London. Studied sociology, political science and economics at the London School of Economics, the University of Notre Dame and Stanford University. Has taught at various American universities. Since 1969 professor of sociology at York University, Toronto. O'Neill is concerned with a 'reflexive sociology' (cf. *Sociology as a Skin Trade*, 1972; *Making Sense Together*, 1974; *Hegel, Marx and Ourselves*, 1975), which joins Marxist approaches, including those of critical theory, with a phenomenology of language, corporeality and sociality which is strongly influenced by Schütz and above all by Merleau-Ponty (cf. *Perception, Expression and History: The Social Philosophy of Merleau-Ponty*, 1970). He has translated or edited Baran, Hyppolite and Merleau-Ponty; he is editor of *Philosophy of the Social Sciences* and co-editor of *The Human Context*.

Ante Pažanin: Born 1930 in Vinišće, near Split. Studied philosophy, German and sociology in Zagreb, Göttingen, Münster and Cologne. Dissertation in Cologne under Landgrebe and Volkmann-Schluck (cf. 'Wissenschaft und Geschichte in der Phänomenologie E. Husserls', 1972). Assistant and instructor in Sarajevo, since 1963 professor of philosophy at the Faculty for Political Sciences of the University of Zagreb; since 1972 assistant general director of the Inter-University Centre, Dubrovnik. Pažanin attempts, above all in the realm of practical philosophy, to connect Marxist and Husserlian lines of thought in the sense of a thought which repeatedly develops its categories out of history anew. Additional publications: *Osnove filozofije* (Foundations of Philosophy), 1970; *Marx i materijalizam* (Marx and Materialism), (1972); *Filozofija i politika* (Philosophy and Politics), 1973; studies concerning practical philosophy. Translations of Bloch and Marx. Editor of the series 'Politička misao'.

Paul Ricoeur: Born 1913 in Valence. After studying in Rennes and Paris, philosophical aggregation 1935. 1948–56 Professor of the history of philosophy in Straßburg, after 1956 professor of philosophy at the Sorbonne and in Paris-Nanterre. He currently teaches at the University of Chicago. Leader of the Husserl Archives in Paris. Under the influence of Marcel and Jaspers (cf. *K. Jaspers et la philosophie de l'existence*, 1947 (along with M. Dufrenne); *G. Marcel et K. Jaspers*, 1948) and Husserl (translation and commentary of *Ideas I*, 1950), Ricoeur developed a philosophy of the will (The Philosophy of the Will: I. *The Voluntary and the Involuntary* (1950), II. *Fallible Man* (1960), III. *The Symbolism of Evil* (1960)). This phenomenological approach led beyond itself in the interpretation of symbols to a hermeneutics which takes the path through the ambiguity and meaning-shifts of language (*The Conflict of Interpretations*, 1974; *The Rule of Metaphor*, 1977). As a contributor to the journal *Esprit* Ricoeur was continually confronted with questions dealing with social and historical praxis, and thus also with Marxism (cf. *History and Truth*, 1965). In later works the ideology-critical Marx is placed beside Freud and Nietzsche as members of a 'school of mistrust' whose justification and limits must be tested.

Marek J. Siemek: Born 1942 in Krakow. Studied philosophy in Warsaw under, among others, Baczko, Kołakowski and Schaff. Studied in Paris in 1971. Currently professor at the Institute for Philosophy of the University of Warsaw. Publications: *Spontaneity and Reflection: The Problem of Freedom in Fichte's Philosophy* (Polish 1967, German 1970); *Friedrich Schiller* (Polish, 1970); Habilitation: *The Idea of Transcendental Philosophy in Fichte and Kant* (Polish, 1977). Co-editor of a series concerning the philosophy of the German Enlightenment and of Schiller's letters. Translations of Heidegger, Althusser and Lukács. Member of the editorial staff of the monthly journal *Człowiek i Swiatopoglad*. Siemek's main interest concerns the philosophy of German idealism, Marxism in the past and present as well as phenomenology and post-phenomenological hermeneutics. He represents a Marxism as a dialectical-critical philosophy of culture and historicity.

Ivan Urbančič: Born 1930 in Robic, near Kobarid, Slowenia. Following an electro-technical apprenticeship, studied philosophy and sociology in Ljubljana; 1970 Ph.D. in Zagreb under Sutlić; further study of phenomenological and hermeneutic philosophy 1968–9 in Vienna, 1971–2 and 1975 in Cologne under Volkmann-Schluck. Since 1971 Urbančič has taught, and is now professor at the Institute for Sociology and Philosophy of the University of Ljubljana. His research deals with problems and possibilities of contemporary thought in the horizon of a broadly understood phenomenology (especially Husserl, Heidegger) against the background of the completion of European philosophy in the nineteenth century (Marx, Nietzsche, Dilthey), and with the history of philosophy in Slowenia. Publications: 'Radikalizacija in konec europske moralne filozofije' ('The Radicalization and End of European Moral Philosophy), in *Problemi*, 1966–7; 'Ontoloski pomen sklopa priozvodmja-potreba v marxovi filozofiji' ('The Ontological Sense of the Production–Need Structure in the Philosophy of Marx'), dissertation, 1971; additional works concerning: *The Main Ideas of Slowenian Philosophy Between Scholasticism and Neo-Scholasticism*, 1971; *Lenin's 'Philosophy' or Imperialism*, 1971; *The Grounds of the Methods of Power. Problem of Philosophical Hermeneutics in Dilthey*, 1976. Numerous articles in Yugoslavian journals, translations of Heidegger and Husserl's *Cartesian Meditations*.

Bernhard Waldenfels: Born 1934 in Essen. Studied philosophy, psychology, classical philology and history in Bonn, Innsbruck, Munich and Paris. Ph.D. 1959 and Habilitation 1967 in Munich. After teaching in Munich, since 1976 professor of philosophy at the Ruhr-University Bochum. From 1970 to 1976 vice-president of the German Society for Phenomenological Research. Publications: *Das sokratische Fragen*, 1961; *Das Zwischenreich des Dialogs*, 1971; individual studies dealing with practical philosophy, social philosophy, philosophy of language and modern French philosophy, many of which are collected in *Der Spielraum des Verhaltens*, 1980. Translated Merleau-Ponty's *The Structure of Behavior* into German. Co-editor of the *Philosophische Rundschau*. Waldenfels is concerned with an opening of phenomenology which would do justice to the transformation of cosmic and social orders, and the conflicts which result from such transformations. This brings phenomenology into a productive tension between Marxism and so-called structuralism.

INDEX